Reflections on Philosophy

■ *INTRODUCTORY ESSAYS*

Reflections on Philosophy

INTRODUCTORY ESSAYS

SECOND EDITION

Edited by

LEEMON McHENRY
California State University, Northridge
Loyola Marymount University

and

TAKASHI YAGISAWA
California State University, Northridge

New York San Francisco Boston
London Toronto Sydney Tokyo Singapore Madrid
Mexico City Munich Paris Cape Town Hong Kong Montreal

Vice President and Publisher: Priscilla McGeehon
Director of Marketing: Tim Stookesberry
Project Coordination, Text Design, and Electronic Page Makeup: Stet, Inc.
Cover Design Manager: Wendy Ann Fredericks
Cover Designer: Nancy Sacks
Cover Art: *Parmigianino*, Self-portrait in a Convex Mirror, photo by Erich Lessing © Art
        Resource, NY
Manufacturing Buyer: Lucy Hebard
Printer and Binder: Courier Corporation—Stoughton
Cover Printer: The Lehigh Press

For permissions to use copyrighted material, grateful acknowledgment is made to the
copyright holders on the chapter opening pages, which are hereby made part of this
copyright page.

Library of Congress Cataloging-in-Publication Data
Reflections on philosophy : introductory essays / edited by Leemon
McHenry and Takashi Yagisawa. — 2nd ed.
        p.   cm.
Includes bibliographical references.
    ISBN 0-321-10057-3
    1. Philosophy—Introductions.   I. McHenry, Leemon B., 1950–   II.
Yagisawa, Takashi.
    BD21   .R44   2002
    100—dc21   2002010340

Please visit our website at http://www.ablongman.com

ISBN 0-321-10057-3

2 3 4 5 6 7 8 9 10—CRS—05 04 03 02

Contents

■ CHAPTER THREE: Metaphysics
Leemon McHenry   37

■ CHAPTER FOUR: Free Will and Determinism
Alfred R. Mele   57

■ CHAPTER FIVE: Epistemology
Frederick Adams   81

■ CHAPTER NINE: Aesthetics
Robert Stecker   171

■ CHAPTER TEN: Philosophy of Religion
Katherin A. Rogers   189

■ CHAPTER ELEVEN: Personal Identity
Gary Fuller   213

PREFACE

The first edition of *Reflections on Philosophy: Introductory Essays* was published in 1993. This is the second edition, published by a new publisher, Longman Publishers. The revisions from the first edition have been substantial. The old chapters on logic, ethics, and philosophy of religion have been replaced with new chapters by new authors. The chapter on cognitive science has been dropped and two new chapters, one on free will and determinism and the other on feminist ethics, have been added. The remainder of the chapters—metaphysics, epistemology, political philosophy, aesthetics, personal identity and philosophy of mind—have been revised and updated. Overall, these revisions strengthen the distinctive feature of this book: *to teach philosophy by actually doing it.* Each chapter presents an opportunity for students to engage themselves actively in the process of philosophical cogitation by navigating through a brief but carefully designed chain of reasoning to reach a specific philosophical thesis, rather than being led through a list of philosophical "-isms" as if part of a hurried museum tour. (The notable exception is the chapter on logic, a subject for which such an approach would be entirely inappropriate for introductory students. The chapter on logic also provides students with basic concepts and tools essential to the methodical reasoning required in the other chapters.)

The second edition is also more uniform in philosophical style; all authors approach philosophy within the analytical tradition. This does not mean that the authors share some substantive philosophical theses. Analytic philosophy is not a specific philosophical claim concerning a specific philosophical issue, or a group of such claims on such issues. Rather, it is a methodological attitude concerning how one should philosophize. It values linguistic and conceptual clarity as well as logical rigor. Linguistic clarity abhors essential reliance on metaphors and other nonliteral uses of language. Conceptual clarity shuns loose talk, rhetoric, and hand waving. Logical rigor demands straightforward application of deductive and inductive argumentative skills. All chapters in this anthology are united in their promotion of philosophizing in the analytic tradition in this sense.

Introductory philosophy can be an exasperating experience for students, because many philosophy texts include selections by philosophers writing *to one another*. Such texts are usually well beyond the comprehension of first-time philosophy students. Students may read and reread the assignment but still have little idea of what it is about and little hope of improving their understanding by sheer effort alone. At the other end of the spectrum, we find textbooks that water down the material to the point that the ideas are banal and arguments are trivialized. Such texts hardly engage students in the real task of philosophical investigation. We seek a middle way by having contemporary philosophers present the subjects of their expertise at the highest level that are still completely accessible to the novice.

The individual chapters of the book can be assigned with any number of primary sources or with readings in an anthology of primary and secondary sources. Although the order of the topics seems most natural to us, some instructors may prefer to begin with later chapters or avoid some altogether. Each chapter is sufficiently self-contained to allow the instructor to skip around the book and take up the issues that best suit the interests of students and the selection of primary sources. While all of the chapters have been written with introductory students in mind, the chapter on free will and determinism and the one on philosophy of mind are somewhat more challenging and may require especially careful guidance from the instructor.

ACKNOWLEDGMENTS

Because this is a collective effort, thanks are due first and foremost to each of the contributors. We are particularly indebted to Priscilla McGeehon of Longman Publishers for her support of this project and helpful suggestions along the way. Her assistant, Frank Morelli, provided sterling assistance with various details in the production process. Thanks are also due to Peg Markow, Editorial Director of Stet Inc., and her staff for expert copyediting. Finally we owe thanks to the following reviewers of the chapters, who provided helpful criticism to the manuscript: Dr. Stewart Kelly of Minot State University and Dr. Barbara Yeager of the University of Charleston (West Virginia).

Leemon McHenry
Takashi Yagisawa
Los Angeles

■ CHAPTER ONE

Introduction

LEEMON McHENRY

■ AIM OF THIS BOOK

For introductory students, philosophy can be bizarre and frustrating because it proceeds in a way unlike that of most other academic subjects and deals with questions that are extremely difficult to answer. This does not mean that mathematics, physics, and other subjects do not have questions that are extremely difficult to answer but that such questions become apparent in these other subjects only at the most advanced levels of study. Although philosophy does require the ability to master central principles and concepts, as well as the ability to remember who said what and in what order, it typically goes further in that it demands that students learn to think for themselves—to do philosophy. In this respect, one must understand that philosophical problems are, by their very nature, controversial and open to a continuous process of argument, rejoinder and reevaluation. Students of philosophy are thus invited to join in the twenty-five-hundred-year-old tradition and grapple with some of the most profound and perplexing questions confronting human existence.

We prepared this collection of essays with the conviction that philosophy is an activity that one learns only by actually doing it, rather than by just memorizing what the great historical figures have said along with the standard objections to these views. These essays, of course, are no substitute for reading the classic texts of philosophy; rather, they are a supplement to such texts and are written to stimulate lively debate and discussion of contemporary philosophical problems. Much of what follows originates with the great philosophers of the past. Instead of a historical or chronological method, however, our approach is problems oriented and aims to encourage the development of a philosophical frame of mind and a reflective attitude of critical analysis.

■ RATIONALE FOR SELECTION OF TOPICS

Each of the eleven chapters that follow introduces a major branch of philosophical inquiry or a special area of philosophical concern and its central problems.

1

The topics of Chapters 2, 3, 5, and 6 cover the main branches of philosophy—logic, metaphysics, epistemology, and ethics—and chapters 4, 7, 8, 9, 10, 11, and 12 address more specialized topics.

We begin with logic as the indispensable tool of analysis necessary for evaluating arguments and further exploring philosophical issues. Chapter 2 also introduces some crucial philosophical terminology used in subsequent chapters. The chapters on metaphysics, free will and determinism, and epistemology address problems concerning the nature of reality, free will, and the conditions by which we can acquire knowledge. The chapters on ethics, feminist ethics, political philosophy, and aesthetics fall under the general area of philosophy known as *axiology*, or value theory. The chapter on ethics is concerned with the standards for judging moral behavior. Feminist ethics, a fairly new and special topic of ethics, raises questions about gender differences in approaches to morality. The chapter on political philosophy addresses the issue of just distribution of wealth by the state, and the chapter on aesthetics focuses attention on the definition of art and problems of judging artistic value.

The chapters on the philosophy of religion, personal identity, and philosophy of mind cover additional issues usually raised in a first philosophy course. The chapter on philosophy of religion takes up the problem of the existence of God. Personal identity raises the question of what makes a person the same person over time. Finally, the chapter on philosophy of mind focuses on the famous mind–body problem. The philosophical questions on free will, the existence of God, the relation of mind and body, and personal identity are all rightly classified as metaphysics, but because they have become so specialized in contemporary philosophy they deserve separate chapters.

The authors of each of the eleven chapters have intentionally simplified the issues discussed to accommodate introductory students. In the interests of clarity, we have omitted some of the more complex topics and disputes that engage philosophers in these fields. Aside from the logic chapter, each contributor takes up one of the central problems in the area of concern and attempts to work through it in a clear and elementary manner. Philosophy is thereby taught in the way that it is actually done—by taking a stand in the controversy and arguing for a solution. We have sought to avoid the method of laying out five or six competing theories and giving the impression that all are equally good and nothing can ever be resolved in philosophy. Our approach encourages students to become acquainted with the ways in which contemporary philosophers formulate and attempt to solve problems, but we also invite students to evaluate critically the solutions offered and to advance their own views.

It should be noted that although we have attempted to give these chapters an overall coherence, each, to some extent, introduces its own method and approach. The approach to aesthetics, therefore, is rather different from the approach to metaphysics or the philosophy of religion. In an effort to keep the topics current, all of the contributors have tried to communicate some of the most recent work in these areas.

■ WHAT IS PHILOSOPHY?

The very attempt to define what philosophy is itself raises a philosophical problem, because the whole enterprise of providing definitions inevitably involves us in the activity of doing philosophy. So, from the start we find ourselves embroiled in controversy. Philosophy is not as easily defined as, say, biology, where "the science of life and life processes" more or less serves as an adequate starting point. That is, biologists are unlikely to see this definition as problematic and would much rather get down to the business of studying function, structure, and evolution of living organisms than trouble over whether the definition of the field precisely captures what the science encompasses. Most philosophers, however, take the very definition of their subject as open to discussion. Let us investigate some of the reasons why philosophy is difficult to define and then, despite the difficulty, offer a working definition.

If we turn to the dictionary for our answer, we are likely to find straightforward etymology from two Greek words, *philein*, "to love," and *sophia*, "wisdom." Thus, philosophy is the "love of wisdom." The ancient Greek mathematician-philosopher, Pythagoras (c. 570–495 B.C.), was the first to use this term and to call himself a "lover of wisdom"; "for no one, said he, *is* wise but God alone."[1] Although this definition stresses the point that philosophy is a kind of attitude or frame of mind, rather than a specific body of knowledge acquired, it remains dreadfully uninformative. Besides, most philosophers today would agree that, perhaps unfortunately, much of what goes on in the philosophical world hardly counts as wisdom. If there is something in this traditional, etymological definition that captures the essence of philosophy, it needs further clarification and explanation beyond mere etymology.

Suppose we now turn to someone who counts himself or herself a philosopher and pose the question. Whether we choose historical figures or living, practicing philosophers, we are likely to find that our definition multiplies with the number of philosophers we consult. Consider, for example, how a Christian, a Marxist, and a feminist will go about answering the question. Each philosopher may define the subject according to some particular manner of doing philosophy or some specific conception of worth in philosophy. So, any single definition advanced will not be satisfactory to all philosophers because the very definition is part of the rivalry between different schools of thought or different traditions of philosophy. We might then, at this point, conclude that philosophy is defined by each individual who engages in the activity. But now we are left with a state of chaos with respect to our original task. Does anything tie this philosophical activity together in such a way as to arrive at a general, all-encompassing definition, that is, a *universal definition*? We may have to be content with some broad characterizations while realizing that the very rivalry among philosophers will create a problem for this approach.

In a certain sense, each of the eleven essays in this book gives an explication of philosophy from the standpoint of some particular area. Philosophy is founded on the problems that essentially drive the philosophical endeavor—problems of how we gain knowledge, how we conceive of the nature of reality and of right and wrong behavior, and how we understand the nature of free will, mind, self, state, religion, or art. I think it is true to say, in addition, at least for this collection of essays, that philosophy is a *rational* discipline that attempts to articulate and solve these problems. This is our first important characteristic of philosophy. Fundamentally, philosophy is an intellectual activity that attempts to arrive at genuine knowledge through the use of reason. What usually passes for knowledge in ordinary social intercourse is often vague, lazy, unfounded, or dogmatic. Philosophers are typically more obstinate about what will serve as a satisfactory account of some claim to know something, and criticism lies at the heart of this quest.

How one *feels* about a philosophical issue or problem, without any further justification, hardly counts at all. Opinions based on purely emotional responses do not score high points in philosophy because feelings are just that—feelings. Reasons, however, can be criticized or praised, judged to be good or bad, plausible or implausible, strong or weak. Indeed it is the job of *reason* to control or keep in check the emotions—to stop the murder by the jealous lover, repudiate the bigot's opinions, or hold back the fanatical zealot.

Hearsay or appeals to authority figures—religious and moral leaders, parents or teachers—do not count for much in philosophy either. The response, "Well, *they* say . . ." is a common appeal to the unknown scientific authority that supposedly settles the issue at hand. Sometimes such appeals are warranted, but all too often they are just poor and lazy substitutes for finding solid evidence. Philosophers will eschew such irrelevant appeals to authority. As noted at the outset of this chapter, we have to learn to think for ourselves about philosophical problems, and this involves the use of sound reasoning; clarifying the meanings of important or controversial terms; drawing out assumptions, presuppositions, and fallacies; and investigating the legitimacy of evidence used to back up knowledge. In this respect, philosophy is much like science, especially the theoretical part of science—both seek truth about the world through the use of reason.

Other important characteristics shape the core of philosophical activity, many of which emerge in the essays in this book. For example, philosophy studies problems of an extreme generality in every area of human inquiry: science, mathematics, religion, politics, morality, law, art, history, medicine. The problems that engage the philosopher's attention, however, are not the same as those of the scientist, mathematician, historian, moralist, or artist. They are, rather, problems of a "higher order." Philosophy is not a specialized form of inquiry that provides particular information about our world. Although some areas of philosophy are indeed technical and detailed, the issues that philosophers discuss arise from broad questions such as, What is knowledge? How do we justify a moral principle? What makes art valuable? What is ultimately real? Thus, the type of knowledge sought is of a very general sort. Philosophy often asks questions of such generality that it inevitably cuts across boundary lines that divide other subjects. So, to discuss the whole question of the nature of mind, the philosopher seeks knowledge of various fields, ranging from neurology to psychology and from biology to computer science. Even knowledge of theology may be required if the discussion involves the notion of the human soul. After all, this is all part of the evidence that is relevant for the evaluation of the theories discussed or the attempt to formulate a new theory. Solutions offered by the philosopher will, in turn, have important implications for each of the separate disciplines.

Finally, although information from the sciences is often relevant to discussing philosophical problems, the problems themselves are of such a general nature that they resist solutions by **empirical** means, that is, by experiment and observation alone. Because philosophical problems are conceptual in nature, they are unlikely to be settled finally by the methods of the empirical sciences such as physics, chemistry, biology, psychology, or sociology. Rather, philosophical problems gain some clarification and find some solution, however tentative, through the use of careful reasoning and critical reflection on the strong and weak points of various theories.

Putting it all together then, our working definition is: *philosophy is the rational, critical investigation of fundamental questions of an extreme generality that resist solutions by the empirical sciences.* Returning to the notion that philosophy is the "love of wisdom," we might find this idea acceptable if we clarify the meaning of *wisdom* such that we understand it to be knowledge of the very broadest sort, knowledge that addresses the most basic concerns of existence, of ourselves and our world. If we love wisdom, we cultivate in ourselves a persistent thirst for this knowledge. In this way, *a lover of wisdom is one who seeks truth in the service of living well.* For having obtained truth about our world and ourselves, we would live a more enlightened and orderly life and happiness would be the ultimate result. This squares with what most of the early philosophers in both the Western and Eastern traditions believed to be the essence of philosophy; our formidable list includes figures such as Pythagoras, Siddharta Gotama (Buddha), LaoTzu, Confucius, Socrates, Plato, Aristotle, Epictetus, Nāgārjuna, Sextus Empiricus, St. Augustine, and many others.

Whether the above definition is satisfactory, I leave for the reader to decide. Undoubtedly I have left out some characteristics of philosophy, and there will always be some school of thought that will reject one or more of the characteristics discussed. Given that the authors of this book's chapters adhere to the contemporary approach to philosophy called **analytical philosophy**, readers can, however, expect to find general conformity with our definition. Analytical philosophy emphasizes the use of logic in the careful analysis and evaluation of philosophical problems and their solutions. Moreover, the problems, although they might have originated with historical figures, are treated in a contemporary rather than a historical manner.

■ *SOME MISCONCEPTIONS ABOUT PHILOSOPHY*

Having said something about what philosophy is, let us now get straight about what philosophy is *not*. Because philosophy is seldom taught outside the college setting, students come to an introductory course with many misconceptions about the subject. This is not to say that the only place one will learn about philosophy is at a college or a university, but because this is where most philosophers happen to congregate, it is where one is more than likely to encounter the subject in a serious context. Popular culture, however, often conveys impressions about philosophy that are caricatures, misleading, or just plain false. We will need to discard these misconceptions before we proceed any further. Hence, we now take up the *via negativa*, or the process of elimination.

1. *Philosophy is what a guru does on a mountaintop.* The picture of an old man with a long beard meditating on some remote, isolated mountaintop captures one popular idea of a philosopher. Perhaps this idea comes from the notion that philosophers are deep thinkers who must escape from the "real world" to arrive at truth.

Certain religious traditions do promote the idea that we must remove ourselves from society to find our true spiritual selves, and there very well might be something in this recommendation that is agreeable to philosophers, in that they generally reject superficial, frivolous, and flashy ideas that surface in contemporary society and clutter the mind. The overall impression, however, is not very accurate. Philosophers generally work in a context in which ideas and theories are advanced and criticized. This means that they learn from one another by vigorously debating one another's ideas. So, for the most part, philosophers aim to work in and with the world to improve our knowledge and our behavior toward one another. Historically, philosophers have made profound contributions to the shape of political and social institutions, public policy, law, science, mathematics, and literature.

2. *Philosophy is one's view on life or other matters.* In popular parlance, the word *philosophy* is used in a loose and misleading way. We find football coaches explaining their "defensive philosophies" before the game, or grandfathers telling grandchildren about their "philosophies of life." And sometimes people explain their "philosophy" as a mere collection of sayings or witty insights about human nature or life in general. This will not do. Philosophical views are often carefully worked out and emerge only after criticism, revision, and years of study. Truth does not come easy, so it is unlikely to be captured in some simplistic or haphazard fashion. We all live in the world and operate with a set of beliefs about it, but the continual quest to challenge those beliefs and improve them requires a particular kind of dedication. As you are likely to discover in what follows, philosophy is anything but an informal "bull session" where anything goes.

3. *Philosophy is psychiatry or psychoanalysis.* Only a little needs to be said to clear up this misunderstanding. Philosophy may, in fact, afford a type of therapy

that one practices on oneself. Indeed if the point of philosophy is to discover truth in the service of living well, it is an edifying experience that one practices for life. Socrates held the view that "the unexamined life is not worth living."[2] For him, philosophy was a type of cure for the soul, because one continually confronts oneself with the truth. But philosophy is not the practice of psychiatry wherein a patient's psychological problems are examined and diagnosed in a clinical setting. The theories of psychoanalysis originated in the writings of philosophers, but this is another matter.

4. *Philosophy is just personal opinion.* This claim is related to the kind of misunderstanding examined in point 2, but the idea here is rather different. After examining some of the controversy that lies at the core of philosophical debate, some students will throw up their hands in frustration and conclude that it is all *just* opinion, and nobody knows any more than anybody else.

To the introductory student, philosophy often *seems* to go around in circles or get nowhere. To the ear untrained in argumentative techniques, philosophy can often give this impression, but this just means that the answers to the problems are very difficult to acquire, and patience is required to make progress. Although there often appears to be little or no agreement on a given philosophical topic, it does not follow that either there is no truth to the matter or any view is just as good as any other. Clearly some opinions are blatantly unacceptable because they are solely based on misinformation, incomplete evidence, or logical fallacies. Consider, for example, Adolf Hitler's opinion that Jews were inferior to Aryans and his actions (based on this opinion) that resulted in the Holocaust. If philosophy is *just* personal opinion, it seems that all are entitled to their opinions, Hitler included. If we are a bit more critical about particular opinions, however, we find that some are seriously flawed. Hitler's view in *Mein Kampf* (*My Struggle*), for example, is based on confusion about superior and inferior races—in this case, that German Aryans are superior and that Jews and other races are inferior. Neither the Aryans nor the Jews, however, are a *race*. Anthropologists typically identify races according to classifications such as Caucasians, Mongolians, and so on, but Aryans and Jews are ethnic groups. And even here, the very concepts of race and ethnicity are subject to question. But let us grant Hitler the issue of race for the moment. We still have to demand a solid answer to the question of criteria for establishing the alleged superiority of the German Aryans. This means that his simplistic notions about blond hair, blue eyes, and military prowess as the basis for superiority are thrown into serious question. In fact, they are ludicrous. In the end, Hitler's definitions turn out not to be, strictly speaking, biological or anthropological. They are rather manipulated for a narrow political purpose, which at the time was largely a matter of economic advantage for the Germans and Hitler's determination to seize *Lebensraum* (living space) for the alleged master race.

Of course, the case of Hitler is an extreme one, and the problem of racism (and other pressing issues of social and moral concern) strike us as having an urgency that is lacking in purely abstract problems of epistemology, philosophy of mind, or metaphysics. The example, however, certainly exposes the naïveté behind the charge that "philosophy is *just* personal opinion." Our task in philosophy is largely a matter of sorting out which opinions are supported by good reasons and which are not. Philosophy is an intellectual challenge. To dismiss it all as "*just* personal opinion" is, in effect, to withdraw from some of the most important questions human beings face.

5. *Philosophy does not make real progress like the sciences.* This is a common charge against philosophy and a much more difficult one to address. One hears, for example, "We are still very much struggling with the same problems that originated with Plato and Aristotle, and today, more than two thousand years later, we still have not definitely answered the questions they raised. But physics, chemistry, and biology have made profound advances in the last two hundred years."

This misconception can be approached by pointing out that philosophy and science have a common historical origin. From the early Greek philosophers to well beyond the time of Sir Isaac Newton, science was simply "natural philosophy," the attempt to discover truth about the physical world. Only fairly recently have we come to see science as detached from the parent discipline of philosophy, largely because of the intense specialization of science in the twentieth century. The great scientists of the past—Aristotle, Galileo, Newton, Maxwell, Einstein, and Bohr, to name a handful—all thought of themselves as philosophers. Science seems to advance much more quickly by the use of scientific method, by observation and experiment, and the immediate result is often of significant practical value, especially when there are technological consequences. But this applies only to its testable content. The theoretical content of science, in contrast, is more difficult to evaluate. Here advance is made in much the same way as it is in philosophy.

Sometimes progress is a simple matter of clarification of a problem or the more precise formulation of the theory that attempts to solve the problem. At other times, progress is measured by subdividing problems and by distinguishing different questions and issues such that we can attempt to analyze them separately and attempt to solve them. Furthermore, progress is sometimes made when some problem or theory is totally abandoned. In this respect, philosophy and science may progress in a curiously negative manner: we abandon that which we believe to be false, inconsistent, contradictory, or simply useless in advancing our understanding of the world.

Progress by elimination, however, does not tell us that we have the truth. It tells us only what is ruled out. Theories are evaluated in terms of their explanatory power, unity, and simplicity as well as their comprehensive ability to account for the facts. One theory may be rejected in favor of another if it is clearly inferior in this way; such a move yields more fruitful results in the long run, and in this respect both philosophy and science are in the same boat.

■ CONCLUSION

We have not arrived at a *universal* definition of philosophy for the reasons articulated above. This does not mean that our project has been fruitless. Having now come to some understanding about what philosophy is and what it is not, we conclude with a few remarks about what our subject attempts to achieve:

1. Philosophy is an intellectual challenge that sharpens the wits through a relentless use of reason.
2. It liberates us from dogmas and forces us to examine beliefs held without good reason.
3. It opens us to diverse views and issues never before contemplated.
4. It develops our capacity for constructive critical thinking.
5. It demands consistency about our various beliefs and encourages us to develop a coherent world view; but, ultimately,
6. Philosophy seeks wisdom as a broad type of knowledge and understanding about issues of fundamental concern.[3]

■ NOTES

1. Diogenes Laertius, *Lives of Eminent Philosophers,* Volume I, translated by R. D. Hicks (Cambridge: Harvard University Press, 1925), p. 13. Also see, John Mansley Robinson, *An Introduction to Early Greek Philosophy* (Boston: Houghton Mifflin Company, 1968), p. 62.

2. Plato, *The Apology,* in *The Dialogues of Plato,* Volume I, translated by Benjamin Jowett (New York: Random House, 1937), p. 420.

3. I wish to thank Frederick Adams and Takashi Yagisawa for helpful comments on an earlier draft of this chapter.

■ QUESTIONS

1. Examine the characteristics of philosophy given in this chapter and compare them with the view of philosophy most often given by the proverbial man on the street. Has your view of philosophy changed after reading this chapter?
2. Why is it difficult to define *philosophy*? What are the different ways in which the author attempts to define *philosophy* in this chapter?
3. Explain one of the five misconceptions of philosophy discussed in this chapter. Can you think of any other misconceptions?
4. What does it mean to develop a "philosophical frame of mind and a reflective attitude of critical analysis"? By contrast, what would it mean to be unphilosophical?
5. Consider the difference between someone you might call "wise" and someone you might call "knowledgeable." What is the difference between knowledge and wisdom? Is wisdom a broad kind of knowledge or something altogether different?
6. Thomas Carlyle: "What is philosophy but a continual battle against custom; an ever-renewed effort to transcend the sphere of blind custom?" Explain what this means and how it characterizes philosophy. Does it address some aspect of philosophy discussed earlier?

■ **FOR FURTHER READING**

■ *General Reference*

Audi, Robert, ed. *The Cambridge Dictionary of Philosophy*. Cambridge: Cambridge University Press, 1999.

Blackburn, Simon. *The Oxford Dictionary of Philosophy*. Oxford: Oxford University Press, 1994.

Craig, Edward, ed. *Routledge Encyclopedia of Philosophy*, 10 vols. London: Routledge, 1998.

Edwards, Paul, ed. *The Encyclopedia of Philosophy*, 8 vols. New York: Collier-Macmillan, 1967.

Honderich, Ted, ed. *The Oxford Companion to Philosophy*. New York: Oxford University Press, 1995.

■ *History of Philosophy*

Copleston, F. C. *A History of Philosophy*. 9 vols. London: Burns, Oates and Washbourne, 1946–1975.

Hamlyn, D. W. *A History of Western Philosophy*. Harmondsworth, Eng.: Penguin, 1987.

Kenny Anthony. *A Brief History of Western Philosophy*. Oxford: Blackwell, 1998.

Matson Wallace. *A New History of Philosophy*. 2 vols. Fort Worth, Te.: Harcourt Brace, 2000.

Russell, Bertrand. *A History of Western Philosophy*. London: Allen and Unwin, 1961.

CHAPTER TWO

Logic

TAKASHI YAGISAWA

■ *INTRODUCTION*

On the first day of your Introduction to Philosophy class, your professor tells you that if you keep perfect attendance, complete every homework assignment satisfactorily, participate in class discussion actively, and score 100% on every examination, you will certainly get an A+ for the course. You work hard, and by the end of the term you think you have accomplished all these things. You are pleased. Why? Because you think: "I have kept perfect attendance, completed every homework assignment satisfactorily, participated in class discussion actively, and scored 100% on every exam. This means I get an A+ for the course because, as the professor said, if I keep perfect attendance, complete every homework assignment satisfactorily, participate in class discussion actively, and score 100% on every exam, I get an A+ for the course."

As you walk to the professor's office to ascertain your course grade, you start wondering about how your classmate Bianca did. So before inquiring about your own grade, you ask the professor, "How did Bianca do in the course?" The professor says, "I am not allowed to discuss any student's grade publicly. All I can tell you is that a majority of mathematics majors got an A– and a majority of philosophy majors got an A+." Hearing this, a smile appears on your face. Why? You are happy for your friend because you think: "Bianca is a mathematics major. This means that she probably got an A–, because, as the professor informs me, a majority of mathematics majors got an A–."

■ *WHAT IS LOGIC?*

Any sustained train of thought on any subject matter is likely to constitute an instance of *reasoning*. Reasoning consists of one or more *arguments*. An argument in the sense relevant here is not a quarrel. An **argument** is a set of statements, one of which is called the **conclusion** and the others are called the **premises**. Intuitively, the premises are supposed to provide rational grounds for accepting

11

the conclusion. Good arguments do in fact provide such grounds, and bad arguments fail to do so. What makes good arguments good and bad arguments bad? **Logic** is the discipline that is charged to answer this question.

There are two types of argument: **deductive** and **inductive**. The argument implicit in the train of thought described in the first paragraph of this chapter is an example of a deductive argument. The argument in the second paragraph is an example of an inductive argument. The difference between deductive and inductive arguments lies in the degree of rational grounding of the conclusion intended to be provided by the premises. The premises of a deductive argument are intended to lead to the truth of the conclusion as a matter of absolute necessity, whereas the premises of an inductive argument are intended to lead to the truth of the conclusion as a matter of high likelihood. Thus, a completely successful deductive argument establishes the truth of the conclusion in a secure manner that is watertight. A completely successful inductive argument, on the other hand, provides overwhelmingly good support for the truth of the conclusion but may not completely exclude the possibility of its falsity.

We acquire knowledge in a variety of ways. One method of knowledge acquisition is logical reasoning, by means of a deductive argument or an inductive argument. Logical reasoning plays an indispensable role in broadening our knowledge significantly. Without logical reasoning, our knowledge would be confined to an extremely limited realm of what is immediately given to us, either in direct sense perception, in introspection, or in some other manner.

We will explore some basic elements of both deductive and inductive arguments. Let us start with deductive arguments.

■ DEDUCTIVE ARGUMENTS

■ *Validity*

The first argument at the beginning of this chapter may be regimented as follows:

The Argument on Your Grade:

1. If I have kept perfect attendance, completed every homework assignment satisfactorily, participated in class discussion actively, and scored 100% on every exam, then I get an A+.
2. I have kept perfect attendance, completed every homework assignment satisfactorily, participated in class discussion actively, and scored 100% on every exam.

So,

3. I get an A+.

The premises in this argument provide a rational grounding of its conclusion that is watertight. This means that it is necessarily the case that if statements 1 and 2 are both true, then statement 3 *must* be true. That is, the truth of both premises would compel the truth of the conclusion as a matter of necessity. In other words, it is absolutely *impossible* for statements 1 and 2 to be both true and statement 3 false at the same time. Thus, we arrive at the definition of our first key term:

An argument is **valid** if, and only if, it is impossible for the premises to be true and the conclusion false.

To determine whether a given argument is valid, first, imagine a world in which all premises of the argument in question are stipulated to be true. Next, try to imagine that the conclusion of the argument is false in that same world. If you succeed in doing so without contradicting yourself, you have successfully imagined a possible world in which the premises are true and the conclusion is false. That is, you have successfully shown that the truth of the premises does not necessarily compel the conclusion to be true, so you say that the argument is invalid. If, on the other hand, you find that you cannot avoid contradicting yourself in imagining such a world, you must say that such a world is impossible and that therefore the argument is valid.

Every successful deductive argument is valid. The Argument on Your Grade is valid. Does validity guarantee the truth of the premises? Does validity guarantee the truth of the conclusion? The answer to both of these questions is no. In fact, validity is compatible with a variety of combinations of truths and falsities in the premises and the conclusion. Some valid arguments have nothing but true premises and a true conclusion.

Example: If you are human, you are mortal.
                   You are human.
    Therefore,   You are mortal.

Some valid arguments have at least one false premise and a true conclusion.

Example: If you are an iguana, you are mortal.
                   You are an iguana.
    Therefore,   You are mortal.

Some valid arguments have at least one false premise and a false conclusion.

Example: If you are human, you are immortal.
                   You are human.
    Therefore,   You are immortal.

[Give an example of a valid argument all of whose premises are false and whose conclusion is false. Give an example of a valid argument all of whose premises are false and whose conclusion is true. Are there valid arguments with no false premise and a false conclusion? Why?]

The notions of "entailment" and "following from" are definable in terms of validity in obvious ways:

Statements $S_1, S_2, \ldots, S_n$ **entail** a statement S_k if, and only if, the argument whose premises are $S_1, S_2, \ldots, S_n$ and whose conclusion is S_k is valid.

A statement S_k **follows from** statements $S_1, S_2, \ldots, S_n$ if, and only if, the argument whose premises are $S_1, S_2, \ldots, S_n$ and whose conclusion is S_k is valid.

For example, "If you are human, you are immortal" and "You are human" entail "You are immortal." "You are immortal" follows from "If you are human, you are immortal" and "You are human." [What do "All walruses swim" and "I am a walrus" entail? What follows from the two statements, "If you are an egg man, you are bald" and "You are not bald"? What follows from the three statements, "No egg man is a walrus," "All of your friends are egg men," and "I am a walrus"?]

A **deductive** argument is one that is purported to be valid. Every invalid deductive argument is a failed argument. [Is the conclusion of every failed argument false? Why?]

■ *Soundness*

Suppose that you are mistaken about your own performance in the final exam and that in fact you scored only 80%. Is the Argument on Your Grade invalid in that case? Of course not. It is still necessarily the case that if statements 1 and 2 were both true, then statement 3 would have to be true. That is, it is still impossible for statements 1 and 2 to be true and statement 3 to be false. Now suppose that scoring 80% on the final exam turns out to be enough for you to get an A. Consider the following argument, which you should have made:

The Better Argument on Your Grade:

1. If I have kept perfect attendance, completed every homework assignment satisfactorily, participated in class discussion actively, and scored 100% on every exam except for scoring 80% on the final exam, then I get an A.
2. I have kept perfect attendance, completed every homework assignment satisfactorily, participated in class discussion actively, and scored 100% on every exam except for scoring 80% on the final exam.

So,

3. I get an A.

This argument is valid. It is also better than the Argument on Your Grade. Why? Because its premises are all true, whereas one of the premises of the Argument on Your Grade is false. [Which one?] Thus, we arrive at the definition of our second key term:

An argument is **sound** if, and only if, it is valid and its premises are all true.

The Better Argument on Your Grade is sound, whereas the Argument on Your Grade is valid but unsound.

We observed that validity does not guarantee the truth of the conclusion. Unlike validity, soundness does guarantee that. In other words, the conclusion of every sound argument is true. Here is a proof: Take any sound argument. By the definition of soundness, it is valid and its premises are all true. So by the definition of validity, it is impossible for its premises to be true and the conclusion false. This means that because its premises are in fact true (from the second half of the definition of soundness), its conclusion must also be true.

A sound argument conclusively establishes the truth of its conclusion.

[Suppose we have an unsound argument. Does this mean that the conclusion of that argument must be false? Why?]

■ ARGUMENTS AND CORRESPONDING CONDITIONALS

It is important to distinguish arguments from *conditional statements*. If Mother says, "Since you eat donuts for breakfast, you care little about your health," she is giving an argument. She is making two statements—viz., that you eat donuts for breakfast and that you care little about your health—in such a way that the first statement is her premise and the second statement is her conclusion. In other words, she is asserting the following: You eat donuts for breakfast, and therefore you care little about your health. In contrast, suppose Father says, "If you eat donuts for breakfast, you care little about your health." Father is making only one statement, a *conditional* statement. He is saying that if something is the case, then something else is the case. This is not an argument. He is not asserting some statement as a conclusion on the basis of another statement. Unlike Mother, Father is asserting only one statement. By definition, an argument must consist of at least two statements, one of which is a premise and the other of which is the conclusion. What Father says is therefore not an argument. Mother is committed to the truth of the statement that you eat donuts for breakfast and the truth of the statement that you care little about your health, whereas Father is committed to the truth of neither statement. Instead, he is committed to the truth of a different, conditional statement, namely, that if you eat donuts for breakfast, then you care little about your health. Thus, what Mother says and what Father says are different.

But is there not some important connection between what Mother says and what Father says? Yes indeed, there is. Mother's utterance has the form "Since P, Q," where P is the premise and Q is the conclusion. So, it can be regimented as "P; therefore, Q." Call this *Mother's Argument*. On the other hand, Father's utterance has the form "If P, (then) Q." Call this *Father's Conditional*. Father's Conditional consists of the premise of Mother's Argument occurring in the **antecedent** position (the "if" part) and the conclusion of Mother's Argument occurring in the **consequent** position (the "then" part). We express this fact by saying that Father's Conditional is the *corresponding conditional* of Mother's Argument. In general:

For any argument "P_1, P_2, . . . , P_n. Therefore C," the **corresponding conditional** of it is the statement "If P_1 and P_2 and . . . and P_n, then C."

■ *TRUTH-FUNCTIONALLY VALID FORMS*

Compare the following two arguments:

> If the dilithium crystal overheats, the warp engine core explodes.
> The dilithium crystal overheats.

Therefore,   The warp engine core explodes.

> If nobody goes to Coney Island, Coney Island is not crowded.
> Nobody goes to Coney Island.

Therefore,   Coney Island is not crowded.

These arguments are valid. Moreover, they are valid for the same reason. In fact, the Argument on Your Grade and the Better Argument on Your Grade are also valid for that same reason. That is, they all share the following *argument form*:

> If *P*, then *Q*.
> *P*.

Therefore,   *Q*.

Any argument of this form is valid. [Really? Try to think of an invalid argument of this form.] This is not the only argument form that guarantees validity. There are many such forms. But some validity-guaranteeing argument forms tend to occur more frequently than others in our reasoning. It is therefore useful to become familiar with those frequently occurring valid forms and be able to recognize them wherever they occur. They are *Modus Ponens*, *Modus Tollens*, Hypothetical Syllogism, Dilemma, Simplified Dilemma, and Disjunctive Syllogism.

■ *Modus Ponens*

> If *P*, then *Q*.
> *P*.

Therefore,   *Q*.

This is the form we have just discussed. *Modus Ponens* is perhaps the most widely used argument form.

■ *Modus Tollens*

> If *P*, then *Q*.
> It is not the case that *Q*.

Therefore,   It is not the case that *P*.

Example: If you are an iguana, then you are a reptile.
> You are not a reptile.

Therefore,   You are not an iguana.

Another Example: If nobody goes to Coney Island, Coney Island is not crowded.
Coney Island is crowded.
Therefore,   Somebody goes to Coney Island.

Notice that both *Modus Ponens* and *Modus Tollens* contain one premise that is a conditional statement. In *Modus Ponens* ("affirming mode") the other premise affirms the antecedent, whereas in *Modus Tollens* ("denying mode") the other premise denies the consequent.

■ *Hypothetical Syllogism*

If P, then Q.
If Q, then R.
Therefore,   If P, then R.

Example: If you watch too much TV, then your brain turns to mush.
If your brain turns to mush, then you get an F in philosophy.
Therefore,   If you watch too much TV, then you get an F in philosophy.

Another Example: If we are not responsible for our actions, morality crumbles.
If our will is not free, we are not responsible for our actions.
Therefore,   If our will is not free, morality crumbles.

Observe that in Hypothetical Syllogism, the two premises and the conclusion are all conditionals. Furthermore, the consequent of one premise is identical with the antecedent of the other premise, and the antecedent of the conclusion is identical with the antecedent of the former premise and the consequent of the conclusion is identical with the consequent of the latter premise. Remember that the premises need not be given in any particular order.

■ *Dilemma*

Either P or Q.
If P, then R.
If Q, then S.
Therefore,   Either R or S.

Example: Either I study or I party.
If I study, I will pass the logic exam.
If I party, I will have a headache.

Therefore,   Either I will pass the logic exam or I will have a
                  headache.

Another Example: Determinism is true or everything happens by chance.
                  If determinism is true, our actions are determined.
                  If everything happens by chance, our actions happen by
                  chance.
Therefore,   Our actions are determined or they happen by chance.

Logicians playfully speak of Dilemma as a kind of beast with two horns. "Either
P or *Q*": Here *P* and *Q* are said to be the two horns of the dilemma. "If *P*, then
R": If we seize one horn, namely *P*, we get *R*. "If *Q*, then *S*": If we seize the other
horn, namely *Q*, we get *S*. Therefore, we get either *R* or *S*.

■ Simplified Dilemma

                  Either *P* or *Q*.
                  If *P*, then *R*.
                  If *Q*, then *R*.
Therefore,   *R*.

Example: You get either rice or potatoes as your side dish.
                  If you get rice as your side dish, you are happy.
                  If you get potatoes as your side dish, you are happy.
Therefore,   You are happy.

Another Example: The universe will oscillate forever or end in a Big
                  Crunch.
                  I am astounded if the universe will oscillate forever.
                  I am astounded if the universe will end in a Big
                  Crunch.
Therefore,   I am astounded.

In Simplified Dilemma, seizing either horn of Dilemma gets us the same thing,
namely *R*.

■ Disjunctive Syllogism

                  Either *P* or *Q*.
                  It is not the case that *P*.
Therefore,   *Q*.

Example: They are smart or they are gorgeous.
                  They are not smart.
Therefore,   They are gorgeous.

Another Example: Something happens by miracle or everything obeys the laws of nature.

Nothing happens by miracle.

Therefore,   Everything obeys the laws of nature.

[Give more example arguments of each of these forms.]

■ *FALLACIES*

Although some argument forms are valid, some other argument forms are invalid. Invalid argument forms are fallacious argument forms, or *fallacies*. This does not mean, however, that all fallacies are invalid argument forms. Among various fallacies, three in particular deserve special mention. The first two are invalid but easily confused with *Modus Ponens* and *Modus Tollens*. The third fallacy is special in that it is valid but is unacceptable for a different reason.

■ *The Fallacy of Affirming the Consequent*

If *P*, then *Q*.

Q.

Therefore,   *P*.

Example: If you are an iguana, then you are mortal.

You are mortal.

Therefore,   You are an iguana.

The invalidity of this argument is not hard to see. The premises are both true, but the conclusion is false. No valid argument can have all of its premises true and its conclusion false. [Why?] So, this argument is invalid.

Another Example: We have a conscience if God created us.

We have a conscience.

Therefore,   God created us.

This argument is invalid, for it has the same logical form as the previous example, which is clearly invalid. Remember it is a matter of logical form whether a given argument is valid or not. Notice that, like *Modus Ponens* and *Modus Tollens*, the Fallacy of Affirming the Consequent has two premises, one of which is a conditional. But unlike *Modus Ponens* or *Modus Tollens*, the other premise of the Fallacy of Affirming the Consequent is the consequent of the conditional, and not the antecedent or the negation of the consequent. Also, the conclusion is the antecedent of the same conditional, and not the consequent or the negation of the antecedent.

■ *The Fallacy of Denying the Antecedent*

	If *P*, then *Q*.
	It is not the case that *P*.
Therefore,	It is not the case that *Q*.

Example:	If you are an iguana, then you are mortal.
	You are not an iguana.
Therefore,	You are immortal.

Another Example:	Our will is not free if we do not have the sense of freedom.
	We have the sense of freedom.
Therefore,	Our will is free.

As before, we can easily see that the first example is invalid because its premises are true and the conclusion false, and the second example is invalid because it shares the logical form with the first example. Again notice that like *Modus Ponens* and *Modus Tollens*, the Fallacy of Denying the Antecedent has two premises, one of which is a conditional. But unlike *Modus Ponens* or *Modus Tollens*, the other premise of the Fallacy of Denying the Antecedent is the negation of the antecedent of the conditional, not the antecedent itself or the negation of the consequent. Also, the conclusion is the negation of the consequent of the same conditional, and not the consequent itself or the negation of the antecedent.

■ *Begging the Question*

	.
	.
	.
	P.
	.
	.
	.
Therefore,	*P*.

Example:	Killing is not good.
	We do not approve of killing.
	To say that something is good is to say that we approve of it.
Therefore,	Killing is not good.

Another Example:	Men box for manly reasons.
	Women should not box.
	If women box, men will feel violated.
Therefore,	Women should not box.

Begging the Question is a fallacy. It is unique among fallacies in that it is valid. In fact, the very reason for its assured validity is also the reason that it is a fallacy. In Begging the Question, the conclusion appears as one of the premises. This obviously makes it a valid argument but also obviously makes it a mistaken argument. The mistake is that what is to be established (the conclusion) is among the statements that are assumed (the premises). Begging the Question assumes what is to be argued for in the conclusion. That is viciously circular. Notice that many people completely misunderstand the verb phrase "to beg the question." They think it means something like "to raise the question." They are wrong. The verb "to beg" here does not mean "to ask for" but instead it means "to steal." Begging the Question "steals" the conclusion and smuggles it in as a premise. It settles the question at hand right from the start by assuming a particular resolution of it as a premise.

■ TRUTH-FUNCTIONAL OPERATORS

The validity of the valid argument forms we have seen so far is the result of the meanings of the expressions "if . . . , then . . ." (*conditional*), "either . . . or . . ." (*disjunction*), and "it is not the case that . . ." (*negation*). These expressions, as well as "both . . . and . . ." (*conjunction*), are known as *truth-functional operators*. This means that the truth or falsity of a statement containing such an expression is completely determined by the truth or falsity of the constituent statement(s). For example, the statement "It is not the case that Los Angeles is evil" is true if the constituent statement "Los Angeles is evil" is false and is false if "Los Angeles is evil" is true. Take another example: "Both Delaware is precious and California is decadent." This statement is true if the two constituent statements "Delaware is precious" and "California is decadent" are both true and is false if at least one of the two constituent statements is false.

■ REDUCTIO AD ABSURDUM

One especially powerful valid deductive argument form is called *reductio ad absurdum* ("reduction to absurdity"). Suppose you want to show that P but do not know how to argue for it directly. You may consider using *reductio ad absurdum*. The first thing you do is to assume that it is not the case that P. Then combine this assumption with a set of statements that are known to be true and derive from them by valid argumentation a statement that is a contradiction. Because no contradiction is validly derivable from true statements, you conclude that the initial assumption, that it is not the case that P, is not true. That is to say, you conclude that it is the case that P. Schematically, we may put this as follows:

"Not-*P* & *A* & *B* & . . . & *M*"
    entails
"Both X and not-X"

Here "*P*" is the conclusion you want to establish, and "*A*," "*B*,". . . , and "*M*" are known to be true. By the definition of entailment, it is impossible for "Not-*P* & *A* & *B* & . . . & *M*" to be true and "Both X and not-X" false. But "Both X and not-X" is a contradiction, that is, it is necessarily false, which means that it is impossible not to be false. So, it must be impossible for "Not-*P* & *A* & *B* & . . . & *M*" to be true. So, it is impossible for all of "Not-*P*," "*A*," "*B*,". . . , and "*M*" to be true. But "*A*," "*B*,". . . , and "*M*" are known to be true. Therefore, "Not-*P*" is not true. That is, "*P*" is true.

Example: Suppose your friend maintains that every opinion is equally correct. You disagree but do not know how to argue against her directly. So you try *reductio ad absurdum*. You say to her, "Let us assume that you are right, that is, that every opinion is equally correct. Now, my opinion that you are wrong is an opinion, so it is correct. That is, it is correct to say that you are wrong. So, you are wrong. Thus, you are right and you are wrong, which is a contradiction. Therefore by *reductio*, the initial assumption that you are right must be rejected. That is, you are wrong."

Another Example: Suppose your friend insists that nothing exists. You try to persuade her out of this unusual opinion by pointing to a tree nearby and saying, "You see, this tree exists. Therefore, something exists." Your friend is not impressed. She says, "I seem to see a tree there but that is an illusion. There is really no tree there at all." You make your friend touch the tree, but she remains unconvinced and states, "The sense of touch is just another sense. All of my five senses are subject to deception." At this point you realize the radical nature of her opinion and switch tactics. You will now employ *reductio ad absurdum* against her opinion. "Assume that there is nothing," you begin. "Is it true that even though there is no tree in front of you, you have a sensory impression of a tree?" Your friend replies, "That's right." You say, "So, there is no tree but there is some sensory impression. Right?" Again she says, "Yes." You continue, "So, there is some sensory impression, obviously?" She concurs, "Obviously." You finish your *reductio* as planned; "So, there is something, namely, a sensory impression. So, there is nothing and there is something, which is a contradiction. Therefore by *reductio*, the initial assumption that there is nothing must be rejected. That is, there is something."

Another Example: Here is yet another *reductio* argument you can make against her: "Assume that there is nothing. That is your opinion. That is, you hold the opinion that there is nothing. So some individual holds that opinion. So, there is something, namely, some individual holder of the opinion. So, there is nothing and there is something; a contradiction. Therefore, there is something."

■ NECESSARY CONDITION / SUFFICIENT CONDITION

Let us say that to get an A+, you need to keep perfect attendance. In that case we say that your keeping perfect attendance is a *necessary condition* for your getting an A+. Can we conclude from this validly that if you keep perfect attendance, you get an A+? No. Why? Because you might need to do something else, like doing well on the exams. To say that keeping perfect attendance is a necessary condition for getting an A+ means nothing more than that if you do not keep perfect attendance, you do not get an A+. It does not mean that if you keep perfect attendance, you get an A+. Suppose, as we assumed earlier, that you need to complete every homework assignment satisfactorily, participate in class discussion actively, and score 100% on every exam to get an A+. Then your completing every homework assignment satisfactorily is another necessary condition for your getting an A+, but you must also participate in class discussion actively and score 100% on every exam. That is, if you do not complete every homework assignment satisfactorily, do not participate in class discussion actively, or do not score 100% on every exam, you do not get an A+. Suppose further that you need to do nothing else to get an A+. Then all these four necessary conditions jointly constitute a *sufficient condition* for your getting an A+. Can we conclude from this validly that if you keep perfect attendance, complete every homework assignment satisfactorily, participate in class discussion actively, and score 100% on every examination, then you get an A+? Yes. Thus we have the following pair of definitions:

"*P* is a **necessary condition** for *Q*" means "If it is not the case that *P*, then it is not the case that *Q*."

"*P* is a **sufficient condition** for *Q*" means "If *P*, then *Q*."

Another way of saying that *P* is a necessary condition for *Q* is to say, "*Q* only if *P*": e.g., "You get an A+ only if you keep perfect attendance." Do not confuse this with "*Q* if *P*," which means the same as "If *P*, then *Q*," which means that *P* is a sufficient condition for *Q*.

If *P* is a necessary condition for *Q* and also a sufficient condition for *Q*, then *P* is a *necessary and sufficient* condition for *Q*. In the above example, your keeping perfect attendance, completing every homework assignment satisfactorily, participating in class discussion actively, and scoring 100% on every examination is a necessary and sufficient condition for your graduation.

"*P* is a **necessary** and **sufficient condition** for *Q*" means "*P* if and only if *Q*."

[Why?] If *P* is a necessary and sufficient condition for *Q*, then *Q* is a necessary and sufficient condition for *P*. [Why?]

■ *QUANTIFICATIONALLY VALID FORMS*

Not all valid argument forms are truth-functional. The validity of some valid argument forms is guaranteed by the meanings of such expressions as "every" (the *universal quantifier*) and "some" (the *existential quantifier*), in addition to the truth-functional operators. Following are two of the standard valid argument forms of that type, Universal Instantiation and Universal Syllogism.

■ *Universal Instantiation*

	Every F is G.
Therefore,	If α is F, then α is G.

Example:	Every whale is a mammal.
Therefore,	If Walt is a whale, Walt is a mammal.

Simplified Example:	Everything is in space and time.
Therefore,	Bianca is in space and time.

Any statement of the form "Every F is G" (or its simplified kin, "Everything is G") is called a *universal quantification*. Here are some more example universal quantifications: "Every philosophy major is a student," "Every mother is a woman," "Everything is blue," "Everything is a number." Because of the validity of Universal Instantiation, any universal quantification is subject to refutation by a *counterexample*. Intuitively, a counterexample is an example that refutes the statement in question.

A *counterexample* to a statement of the form "Every F is G" is an item that is F and not G.
A *counterexample* to a statement of the form "Everything is G" is an item that is not G.

For instance, anything that is a romance novel and is not banal is a counterexample to the statement "Every romance novel is banal." Anything that is not blue is a counterexample to the statement "Everything is blue." [Give a counterexample to the universal quantification "Every act performed with a good intention is morally good." Give a counterexample to the universal quantification "Everything is in space and time."]

Any statement of the form "Some F is G" (or its simplified kin "Something is G") is called an *existential quantification*. Here are some example existential quantifications: "Some mammal is a whale," "Some student is a philosophy major," "Some woman is a mother," "Something is blue," "Something is an abstract entity." Existential quantifications are not subject to refutation by a counterexample. The reason is that existential quantifications yield no entailments concerning any given item. Take "Some philosopher is weird" as an example. We cannot refute this claim by producing a particular philosopher who is not weird, because the claim does not entail that *that* particular philosopher is weird. On the other hand, if we examined all philosophers and concluded that none of them were weird, then we would have refuted the claim. Another way to refute the same claim is to use *reductio* and argue by assuming that some philosopher is weird and deriving a contradiction from this assumption coupled with some known truths. (We are highly unlikely to succeed in this particular case.)

■ *Universal Syllogism*

Every F is G.
α is F
Therefore, α is G.

Example: Every whale is a mammal.
Walt is a whale.
Therefore,   Walt is a mammal.

The validity of Universal Syllogism is assured by the validity of Universal Instantiation and *Modus Ponens*. Here is how: Suppose that (1) every whale is a mammal and (2) Walt is a whale. Then from (1) by Universal Instantiation, it follows that if Walt is a whale, then Walt is a mammal. From this and (2) by *Modus Ponens*, it follows that Walt is a mammal.

■ *Universal Quantification and Negation*

Be careful about sentences of the form "Every F is not G." Take, for example, "Every student is not a woman." This sentence is ambiguous. It could mean either "Every student is a non-woman" or "It is not the case that every student is a woman." The first reading makes the sentence true just in case no student is a woman, whereas the second reading makes it true just in case there is at least one student who is not a woman. The same kind of ambiguity is present in the simplified form "Everything is not G." The sentence "Everything is not blue" may be interpreted as "Everything is non-blue" or as "It is not the case that everything is blue." The first is true just in case nothing is blue, while the second is true just in case there is at least one thing that is not blue.

■ *"Some" and "Not all"*

It is a common mistake to think that "some" entails "not all," that is, to think that the following argument form is a valid argument form:

Some F are G.
Therefore,   Not all F are G.

Example: Some students are philosophy majors.
Therefore,   Not all students are philosophy majors.

The easiest way to see why this is *not* a valid argument form is by *reductio ad absurdum*. Assume for *reductio* that the above is a valid argument form. Then for any argument of that form, it is impossible for the premise to be true and the conclusion false. So, it is impossible for the premise of the following argument to be true and its conclusion false:

> Some students are women.
> Therefore,   Not all students are women.

It is possible, however, for the premise of this argument to be true and the conclusion false. Therefore, by *reductio*, the above argument form is not a valid argument form. Here is why it is possible for the premise of this argument to be true and the conclusion false: Suppose you visit a small college about which you know little. You look around and discover quickly that the few students you see in the quad are women. So you write on page one of your notebook, "Some students are women." You continue to explore the campus and somehow manage to meet every single one of the students. Unexpectedly they all turn out to be women. So you write on page two of your notebook, "All students are women." Does this mean that you now need to deny your previous statement on page one? Of course not. Your statement on page two is true, but your statement on page one is true, too. You just did not know it was a women's college at first. It simply means that you only had a partial picture of the student population and now you have the whole picture.

■ IDENTITY

One particular expression occurring in quantificational logic deserves a special treatment. It is "is identical with," which is customarily abbreviated as "=." The identity relation expressed by "=" holds between x and y just if x and y are one and the same thing. For this reason, philosophers sometimes call this relation *numerical identity* and distinguish it from qualitative similarity. Identical twins are not identical, that is, not numerically identical. In Lewis Carroll's *Through the Looking-Glass*, Tweedledum and Tweedledee are identical twins, but they are not identical. If they were identical, they would be one and the same, hence they would be one, not twins. Your copy of this textbook and my copy of this textbook are not identical. They, like identical twins, are merely extremely similar. Thus, extreme similarity does not entail identity. However, identity entails extreme similarity. In fact, it entails absolute indiscernibility. If $x = y$, then x and y are completely indiscernible, because x and y share all traits. This is a famous principle named after Gottfried Wilhelm Leibniz (1646–1716).

■ *Leibniz's Law of Indiscernibility of the Identical*:

For every x, for every y, if $x = y$, then x and y have exactly the same properties.

If Lewis Carroll = Charles Dodgson, then Carroll and Dodgson share exactly the same properties. But is that really so? Isn't it true to say that Carroll wrote *Through the Looking-Glass* but false to say that Dodgson wrote it? Let us be careful here. If Carroll and Dodgson are one and the same individual, how could Carroll do anything without Dodgson also doing that very thing? He could not. When Carroll was writing *Through the Looking-Glass*, Dodgson was writing the same story at the same time at the same location in the same way. There was only one individual doing that, namely Carroll, viz., Dodgson. That man wrote the story under the name Lewis Carroll. That is, Carroll wrote the story under the name Lewis Carroll, and Dodgson wrote it under the name Lewis Carroll. There is nothing Carroll did that Dodgson did not.

Leibniz's Law of Indiscernibility of the Identical is useful in demonstrating the distinctness of two easily confused things. For example, a certain type of materialists claim that all mental phenomena are identical with some neurophysiological phenomena. Their opponents typically attempt to show that some mental phenomenon has a certain property no neurophysiological phenomenon has. If such an attempt is successful, Leibniz's Law of Indiscernibility of the Identical will entail, through Universal Instantiation and Modus Tollens, that the mental phenomenon in question is not identical with any neurophysiological phenomemon. [How so?]

There is a converse principle, which also bears the name of Leibniz and appears equally plausible.

■ *Leibniz's Law of Identity of the Indiscernible:*

For every x, for every y, if x and y have exactly the same properties, then $x = y$.

This principle may appear to entail that identical twins are identical, but in fact it does not entail that. Identical twins fail to share many properties. One such property is spatial location. No matter how similar they may be, identical twins occupy different spatial locations. Thus, among existing objects, there do not seem to be two of them that have exactly the same properties. But could there possibly be such objects? If there could be, the above principle is not necessarily true. That is, it is not a principle of logic. [Can you imagine a logically possible world in which two distinct objects share exactly the same properties?]

■ INDUCTIVE ARGUMENTS

■ *Strength*

The second argument at the beginning of this chapter may be regimented as follows:

The Argument on Bianca's Grade:

1. A majority of mathematics majors got an A–.
2. Bianca is a mathematics major.
3. So, Bianca got an A–.

In this argument, the rational grounding of the conclusion by the premises is less than watertight. It is not necessarily the case that if statements 1 and 2 are both true, then statement 3 must be true. Even if statements 1 and 2 are both true, it is still possible for statement 3 to be false. Bianca might be among the few mathematics majors who did not get an A–. Such an eventuality is not impossible, even though it may be *improbable* under the circumstances. This means that the Argument on Bianca's Grade is invalid. But this does not mean that it is a bad argument. It is unlikely that the Argument on Bianca's Grade is intended as a deductive argument in the first place. We should judge it as an inductive argument instead. Inductive arguments, unlike deductive arguments, are not expected to meet the high standard of validity but a somewhat lower standard of *strength*, defined as follows:

> An argument is **strong** if, and only if, it is improbable for the premises to be true and the conclusion false.[1]

Unlike validity, strength is a matter of degree, just as improbability is a matter of degree. An argument is weak to the degree to which it is not strong. The Argument on Bianca's Grade is strong, that is, it is strong to a degree greater than it is weak. An **inductive** argument is one that is purported to be strong rather than valid. Thus, not every invalid inductive argument is a failed argument. An inductive argument that is weak to a degree is a failed argument to that degree.

■ *Reliability*

Suppose that you are mistaken about Bianca's major and that in fact she majors in philosophy and not mathematics. Is the Argument on Bianca's Grade weak then? No. It is still the case that if statements 1 and 2 were both true, then statement 3 would probably be true. That is, it is still improbable for statements 1 and 2 to be true and statement 3 false. The argument is exactly as strong as before. Remember what the professor told you about the philosophy majors in the class: "A majority of them got an A+." Now consider the following argument, which you should have made:

> The Better Argument on Bianca's Grade:
>
> 1. A majority of philosophy majors got an A+.
> 2. Bianca is a philosophy major.
> So,
> 3. Bianca got an A+.

This argument is strong. It is also better than the Argument on Bianca's Grade. Why? Because its premises are all true, whereas one of the premises of the Argument on Bianca's Grade is false. [Which one?] Thus we arrive at the second key definition of inductive logic:

> An argument is **reliable** if, and only if, it is strong and its premises are all true.

Notice that reliability is to strength what soundness is to validity. A reliable argument is reliable to the same degree to which it is strong. The Better Argument on Bianca's Grade is reliable, whereas the Argument on Bianca's Grade is strong but unreliable.

■ STRONG FORMS

The four major types of inductive argument are: Enumeration, Statistical Syllogism, Analogical Syllogism, and Inference to the Best Explanation.

■ *Enumeration*

This is the most elementary form of induction.

	A particular F is G.
	Another F is G.
	Yet another F is G.
	.
	.
	.
	Yet another F is G.
Therefore,	Every F is G.
Example:	Raven #1 is black.
	Raven #2 is black.
	Raven #3 is black.
	.
	.
	.
	Raven #k is black.
Therefore,	Every raven is black.

We are said to *generalize* from particular cases (k-many ravens) to obtain the conclusion, which is a universal quantification (about all ravens). It is obvious that the more particular cases we enumerate as constituting the basis of generalization, the stronger the argument is.

■ *Statistical Syllogism*

This is a probabilistic version of Universal Syllogism.

	Most F are G.
	α is F.
Therefore,	α is G.
Example:	Most students are under 40 years old.
	Chad is a student.
Therefore,	Chad is under 40 years old.

Given the truth of the second premise, the more *F*'s (students) we ascertain to be *G* (under 40 years old), the higher the probability is for the conclusion to be true.

■ *Analogical Syllogism*

This is an argument based on a comparison between two items.

	Most of the attributes belonging to α also belong to β.
	α is *F*.
Therefore,	β is *F*.

Example:	Most of the attributes belonging to Ginger also belong to Cinnamon.
	Ginger is good at logic.
Therefore,	Cinnamon is good at logic.

Is it the case that, given the truth of the second premise, the more attributes of α we ascertain to belong to β, the more probable the conclusion is? No. Ascertaining that Ginger and Cinnamon are both blonde will not increase (or decrease) the probability of the truth of the conclusion. The attributes in question must be *relevant* to the conclusion. Being blonde is not relevant in this case but, say, being meticulous is.

■ INFERENCE TO THE BEST EXPLANATION

Inference to the best explanation is an important type of inductive argument. It is hard to classify in relation to the other forms of reasoning, but it is prevalent and powerful.

	P.
	The best explanation for the fact that *P*, entails that *Q*.
Therefore,	*Q*.

Example:	The sun appears to move across the sky.
	The best explanation for the fact that the sun appears to move across the sky entails that the earth rotates.
Therefore,	The earth rotates.

What is necessary and sufficient for an explanation to be the best explanation for a given fact? It is for the explanation to be better than any other explanation for that fact. The size of the set of rival explanations, therefore, determines the strength of the inference to the best explanation. The larger the set, the stronger is the inference.

A particular explanation for a given fact may be the best explanation for that fact at one time but not at another time. Consider:

> The sun appears to move across the sky.
> The best explanation for the fact that the sun appears to move across the sky entails that the sun circles the earth.
>
> Therefore,   The sun circles the earth.

This argument was fairly reliable when uttered in antiquity because the best explanation for the apparent movement of the sun at that time was geocentric. It is, however, unreliable when uttered now because we know the second premise to be false now, so the best explanation now is no longer geocentric.

■ Prediction

Any explanation of a given phenomenon usually gives rise to *predictions* about future phenomena of the same type. If we explain the apparent movement of the sun across the sky by reference to the rotation of the earth, we are in a position to predict that as long as the earth continues to rotate, the sun will likely continue to appear to move across the sky. If we explain the appearance of thin tracks of vapor inside a cloud chamber by postulating the existence of electrons traveling through the chamber, we are in a position to predict that whenever a cloud chamber is placed in the midst of traveling electrons, thin tracks of vapor will likely appear. If we explain the onset of a certain disease by means of a combination of the presence of a particular genetic material and a particular environmental trigger, we are in a position to predict that whenever the genetic material and the environmental trigger are present, the disease will likely be present. Thus, explanation and prediction go *in tandem*. They are really two sides of the same coin. As a general rule, an explanation that gives rise to poor predictions is a poor explanation, and a prediction that is supported only by a poor explanation is not trustworthy.

■ Causal Inference

A particular kind of inference to the best explanation deserves to be singled out. It is *causal inference*. It is an inference from a phenomenon to its cause. If it is successful, it allows us to give a *causal explanation* of the phenomenon. Suppose Jane has a back pain. She wants to eliminate it. She tries everything she can think of: massage, yoga, shiatsu, acupuncture, medication, meditation. Nothing works. Finally in desperation she goes to see a chiropractor who specializes in applied kinesiology and who determines that her left leg is longer than her right leg by half an inch. Jane then theorizes and concludes that the leg-length discrepancy is the cause of her back pain. Jane has just made a causal inference. The reliability of this inference can be tested by checking whether the predictions it gives rise to are confirmed. The crucial prediction says that if Jane corrects the leg-length discrepancy by means of an appropriate shoe insert, her back pain will disappear. Suppose she does this. Suppose further that after a month of wearing the insert, the pain persists as before. This disconfirms the prediction and weakens the causal inference in question. She may then try a different causal inference, for example, that the pain is caused by her wearing high-heels on the job every day. This new inference gives rise to the new prediction that if she stops wearing high heels, the pain will cease. If this prediction is confirmed, then the new causal inference is vindicated and her back pain may finally be causally explained. If not, it is not causally explained. [Is the inference to the best explanation of the apparent motion of the sun across the sky by reference to the rotation of the earth a causal inference? If so, what is the inferred cause and what is the inferred effect? If not, why not?]

■ CONCLUSION

The importance of logic was widely known and appreciated in antiquity, but Aristotle (384–322 B.C.) was the first to study logic systematically. He discovered logical forms, classified arguments according to their logical forms, and investigated the properties of the logical forms and their relationships to one another. Thus, Aristotle is justifiably known as the Father of Logic. His logic is often called Categorical Logic or Syllogistic Logic. Aristotelian logic was as dominant as Euclidian geometry for more than two thousand years. But in the late nineteenth century, Aristotelian logic was beginning to be replaced by a more powerful system known as First-Order Predicate Logic. First-Order Predicate Logic is the logic that philosophers use today and that we have studied in this chapter under Deductive Arguments. Unlike Aristotelian logic, no single person was wholly responsible for the development of this new logic. Two logicians among the non-Aristotelian pioneers deserve to be mentioned, however: Gottlob Frege (1848–1925), who played a major role in creating quantificational logic, and Ludwig Wittgenstein (1889–1951), who proposed the idea of truth-function. The history of the development of inductive arguments is considerably more complicated and overlaps significantly with the history of the development of scientific methods.[2]

■ NOTES

1. For the instructor: I ignore the objection that this definition makes any argument with improbable premises strong. I ignore the distinction between conditional probability and probability of conditional.

2. I thank Leemon McHenry and Ron McIntyre for useful comments on earlier drafts.

■ EXERCISE PROBLEMS

1. Is every sound deductive argument valid?
2. Is the conclusion of every valid deductive argument true?

3. Is every strong inductive argument reliable?
4. Is every valid deductive argument sound?
5. Is it possible to make a valid argument invalid by adding a premise? Why? [Hint: Remember that an argument is valid if, and only if, it is impossible for the premises to be true and the conclusion false. This means that in a valid argument, one can not have true premises and a false conclusion. In view of this, consider the following analogy: Mother tells you, "You can't have ice cream and cookies," to which you respond, "In that case, can I have ice cream, a milkshake, and cookies?" What would Mother say?]
6. Is it always possible to make an invalid argument valid by adding a premise? Why or why not?
7. Is it always possible to make a sound argument unsound by adding a premise? Why or why not?
8. Is it always possible to make an unsound argument sound by adding a premise? Why or why not?
9. Is it always possible to make an unsound argument sound by deleting a premise? Why or why not?
10. Assume the following: (1) If you pass philosophy and physics, you graduate; (2) If you fail literature or chemistry, you do not graduate; (3) If you graduate, that means that you passed philosophy or physics. List all necessary conditions for graduation. List some sufficient condition for graduation.
11. Superman = Clark Kent. So by Leibniz's Law of Indiscernibility of the Identical, Clark Kent has every property Superman has. Lois Lane adores Superman. That is, Superman has the property of being adored by Lois. It then follows that Clark Kent has the property of being adored by Lois. But Lois does not adore Clark Kent. She thinks he is a nerd. Does this refute Leibniz's Law of Indiscernibility of the Identical? Why?
12. For any x, x is x, that is, x has the property of being x. So, anything that has exactly the same properties as x will have the property of being x. But to have the property of being x is to be identical with x. This seems to prove Leibniz's Law of Identity of the Indiscernible. Does it? If it does, does it make the principle uninteresting?
13. Are the following items arguments? If so, should they be considered deductive or inductive? If deductive, are they valid? Can you tell whether they are sound? What argument forms do they instantiate? If inductive, are they strong? Can you tell whether they are reliable? What argument forms do they instantiate?
    a. April will win the race, for she has been undefeated so far this season.
    b. You ate the ice cream. Why did you eat the ice cream? I told you not to eat the ice cream. You are bad. You are really bad.
    c. Every property is possessed by some concrete individual. "Unicornhood" is possessed by some concrete individual, because it is a property.
    d. You will graduate in June if you pass the exam. You don't pass the exam. That means you won't graduate in June.
    e. If God does not exist, life is meaningless. God does not exist. So, life is meaningless.
    f. Children master their first language, whatever it may be, very quickly under normal circumstances irrespective of their intelligence level. So, we conclude that children have innate knowledge of the grammatical rules common to all humanly possible natural languages, for there is no better way to explain it.

g. Nim Chimpsky is smart because most chimpanzees are smart. [Hint: An obvious premise is suppressed.]

h. Get out quickly because there is a fire in the building.

i. Everything I see is my sensation. I see the chair I am sitting on. So, I am sitting on my sensation.

j. I have consciousness. You look and behave like me. So you have consciousness.

k. Either the existentialists are right or the positivists are right. If the existentialists are right, life is absurd. If the positivists are right, metaphysics is nonsensical. It follows that either life is absurd or metaphysics is nonsensical.

l. The difference between a crazy man and Salvador Dali is that a crazy man is not Salvador Dali. (Salvador Dali)

m. Because the soul is devoid of matter, it cannot be divided into smaller bits. Nothing can fall apart unless it can be divided into smaller bits. So, the soul cannot fall apart. But all material beings can fall apart. Therefore, the soul is not a material being.

n. There must be physical objects external to me. Otherwise, how could I have such organized and predictable sensory impressions?

o. If Plato is right, concrete particulars are not ultimately real. The world we perceive through our five senses is an illusion if concrete particulars are not ultimately real. Hence, if Plato is right, the world we perceive by our five senses is an illusion.

p. I know nothing if I am certain of nothing. I do know something. Therefore, I am certain of something.

q. Either there is an objective standard for judging art or it is all a matter of subjective attitude. No objective standard exists for judging art. This means that judging art is purely a matter of subjective attitude.

r. Every student takes logic. Stu is a student. Therefore, Stu takes logic.

s. If every student takes logic and Stu is a student, then Stu takes logic.

t. Santa Claus exists. Here is why: If Santa Claus does not exist, it is false to say that Santa Claus is loved by many, but it is true to say that Santa Claus is loved by many.

u. Exercising regularly is a necessary condition for being healthy. So you must be healthy, because you exercise regularly.

v. Captain Jean-Pierre Lucard of the star ship USSOS Undertaking is a person. Commander Datum behaves very much like Lucard. So Datum is a person.

w. If God exists, evil does not exist. God exists. Therefore, evil does not exist.

x. If God exists, evil does not exist. Evil exists. Therefore, God does not exist.

y. God exists. Evil exists. Therefore, it is false that if God exists, evil does not exist.

z. This apple from the barrel is rotten. That apple from the barrel is rotten. This other one from the barrel is also rotten. So I say all of the apples from the barrel must be rotten.

aa. In 1846, when the farthest known planet was Uranus, Urbain Jean Joseph Leverrier argued as follows: The observed orbit of Uranus deviates from the theoretical orbit predicted by the Newtonian physics. Therefore, there is an unknown planet outside the orbit of Uranus exerting its gravitational influence on Uranus. [Can you name the "unknown planet"?]

bb. In 1845 Leverrier argued as follows: The observed orbit of Mercury deviates from the theoretical orbit predicted by the Newtonian physics. Therefore, an unknown planet inside the orbit of Mercury is exerting its gravitational influence on Mercury. [Can you name the "unknown planet"? Can you offer a better account of the discrepancy between the observed orbit and the predicted orbit of Mercury?]

■   **FOR FURTHER READING**

Aristotle. *Prior Analytics.*

———. *Sophistical Refutations.*

Haack, Susan. *Philosophy of Logics.* Cambridge: Cambridge University Press, 1978.

Hempel, Carl. *Philosophy of Natural Science.* Englewood Cliffs, N.J.: Prentice-Hall, 1966.

Jeffrey, Richard. *Formal Logic: Its Scope and Limits.* 3d ed. New York: McGraw-Hill, 1990.

Quine, W. V. *Philosophy of Logic.* Englewood Cliffs, N.J.: Prentice Hall, 1970.

Salmon, Wesley. *Logic.* 2d ed. Upper Saddle River, N.J.: Prentice Hall, 1983.

CHAPTER THREE

Metaphysics

LEEMON McHENRY

> There is a science . . . that studies Being qua Being, together with those properties which belong to it by reason of its essential nature. This science is quite distinct from what we may call the special sciences, none of which investigates Being in its purely general aspect as Being, but each of which rather cuts off some partial aspect of Being and studies the set of properties belonging to that partial aspect: as do the mathematical sciences. But it is first principles and the highest reasons that we are seeking, and clearly these must constitute a subject-matter with a nature of its own.[1]
>
> —Aristotle

■ INTRODUCTION

It is widely agreed that Western philosophy began with **metaphysics**. Philosophers before Socrates, the "pre-Socratics" (roughly 625–371 B.C.), were essentially concerned with the nature of ultimate reality. Thinkers such as Thales, Anaximander, Pythagoras, Parmenides, and Heraclitus sought what might be called "first principles" of reality, and thus they established metaphysics and natural science in one shot. Perhaps the most important discovery of this period was not so much the *answers* they gave us but rather the *questions* they asked, for the whole context in which they raised their questions presupposed a *naturalistic*—as opposed to a *supernaturalistic*—answer. This is sometimes called the *Mythos to Logos* thesis; philosophy began with the transition from myth to reason.[2] In this respect, the pre-Socratics broke with the strong mythological character of the thought of their predecessors. Instead of giving explanations of humans and the world in terms of the world views of Homer and Hesiod, that is, the struggles between the gods as well as their various dealing with mortals, the pre-Socratics introduced metaphysical concepts such as "substance," "form," "permanence," and "change" into the basic framework of thought about our world. Pre-Socratic metaphysics thus takes as its ultimate conviction the idea that the universe is a natural entity that is comprehensible by rational thought.

Aside from tributes to the ancient Greeks for the origins of metaphysics, and philosophy more generally, anyone who has asked basic questions such as "Who or what am I?" or "What is my place in the scheme of things?" or "What is ultimately real?" has unwittingly taken the plunge into metaphysics. It is at such times of solemn introspection, coupled with profound curiosity about ourselves and the nature of the universe, that we discover *wonder* and its infinite territory. The need to question and the uncertainty or incompleteness of the answers lingers just beyond the veneer of our everyday existence.

In this chapter, we explore the problem of "What is ultimately real?" within the context of the ancient debate between Plato and Aristotle. Each system of thought will be critically evaluated, and a modified version of Plato's metaphysics will be advanced as the solution to our problem. We then examine some criticisms of metaphysics as a whole and end with a defense of metaphysics against such objections.

■ WHAT IS METAPHYSICS?

Before we embark on the main task of this chapter, some attempt at a more precise characterization of metaphysics is essential. This is especially important because misconceptions of the subject are widespread in popular culture. For example, one popular understanding (or misunderstanding) of metaphysics places it wholly within the context of spiritualism or the occult. It may very well be the case that the world's great religions implicitly convey a metaphysical view about the nature of reality as ultimately spiritual, but this is another matter. The type of misuse of the term *metaphysics* I have in mind is current among practitioners of New Age spirituality. This is a poor substitute for the philosophical, critical, and systematic inquiry into the nature and structure of reality.

As the traditional story goes, the word *metaphysics* comes from Aristotle's editor, Andronicus of Rhodes, who in the first century B.C. classified and catalogued Aristotle's works. Andronicus took the writings Aristotle called "first philosophy" and placed them after his treatise on physics.[3] "Metaphysics," from the Greek *ta meta ta physika*, literally means "those things after the physics," but this is purely accidental. Metaphysics is better understood as the systematic investigation of the most general principles of reality, or, as Aristotle himself said, it is "a science that studies Being qua Being." In Aristotle's sense, the metaphysician seeks principles that are prior to or beyond any investigation in the special sciences. A chemist, for example, may explain the particular molecular composition of a substance, but the question, "What is substance in general?" is of no interest to his or her investigations. Similarly, a physicist explains particular causes in material bodies from the effects of magnetism, electricity, light, and so on, but the attempt to understand the very notion of causation falls outside his or her area of concern. Such issues do, however, lie at the center of the metaphysician's quest.

Insofar as metaphysics does not proceed as one of the special sciences, the results of direct observation and experimentation are not the primary means of constructing first principles. The results, however, will have some place within the scheme of principles, given that the metaphysician seeks a system that is consistent with current science. The evidence of sense perception has usually taken a backseat to the attempt to construct first principles of the universe by means of logical investigation, that is, of reasoning *a priori*. In this respect the metaphysician does not need a laboratory or high-tech instruments to do the necessary work. The metaphysician's procedure in attempting to discover the fundamental features of reality is more akin to that of the mathematician or the theoretical physicist. The main tool is logic, but intuition and insight are equally important, if not more so.

The great metaphysicians of the past have always had a vision of the essence of reality, and the picture they paint is always fascinating, if not mind-boggling. I need only mention the likes of Plato, Aristotle, Descartes, Spinoza, Leibniz, Hegel, and Whitehead as typical examples of metaphysical visionaries in the Western tradition. Their views of reality are very different, though, and on many points they directly contradict one another. The attempt to decide whose vision is right is a matter of extreme difficulty, and the criteria for deciding whose vision comes closest to the truth seems to elude our grasp forever. But one thing is sure—a view that is supported by precise and rigorous argumentation can gain the attention and respect of those who are seriously engaged in the pursuit of truth.

Some philosophers see metaphysics as a *superscience* because to do it at all adequately, one must attempt to grasp the essential nature of the universe, not in some fragmentary or piecemeal fashion, but as a whole. The principles put forth therefore have a universal character in the sense that they attempt to give a general account of everything in the universe, including the concrete and abstract, actual and possible. Such principles then serve as foundations from which reasoning in the more special sciences proceeds. Hence, metaphysical principles are the most basic and most general principles of reality.

We can thus provide a characterization of metaphysics, though it is only by examining specific metaphysical problems that we can come to a real understanding of the subject. Let us now proceed to consider the branch of metaphysics called **ontology**. In the course of exploring the issues in this area, we discover some of the most perplexing, yet compelling problems of metaphysics.

■ ONTOLOGY

Questions regarding ontology lie at the heart of metaphysics. Ontology, from the present participle of the Greek verb *on*, "to be," is an attempt to determine what *is*. Thus, philosophers who are concerned with this area are especially interested in questions such as "What sorts of things exist?" "Are existence and being the same?" "What is the status of various types of entities?" and "Do some entities depend on others?"

Let us speculate for the moment about what sorts of things are real, or exist. An initial list might include entities as diverse as people, animals, and material objects such as trees, houses, cars, books, bicycles, computers, and coffee cups. Some might disagree from the start that the list is too narrow and that entities such as minds, ideas, and emotions must be included in a list of things real. Still someone else might find this survey lacking and might wish to include things like numbers, sets, and geometrical figures. And what about God and angels? Indeed for some, God (or gods) is ultimately real. Finally, some consider **possible worlds** and the entities that populate these worlds to be real, such as the world in which your younger sister marries the future King of England or the parallel universe in which time runs backwards.[4]

Now our universe is starting to get *very* populated and, for some, much too cluttered. How shall we decide what to include? An appeal to direct observation will not help us much here, because that would rule out not only God, minds, ideas and, numbers but also the subatomic world of physics and, to complicate matters even more, the past and future, because strictly speaking we observe only the content of the present. Common sense does not fare much better as the final arbiter because it is notoriously defective. What we would like to believe to be common to ourselves is unfortunately uncommon to others. And if we appeal to science, we find that scientists themselves hardly agree about what is really real. Electrons, quarks, cosmic strings, and black holes are all plausible candidates, but none are firmly established beyond doubt.

Perhaps we can clarify things a bit by introducing a few metaphysical concepts and distinguish between particular and universal, concrete and abstract, and real and ideal. Armed with such distinctions, we can move on to classify and categorize some of the entities just mentioned. This prepares us for our real problem, which is to construct a theory that will commit us to what the universe actually contains—no more, no less. This is a formidable task that divides metaphysicians into two schools of thought: **speculative metaphysics**, which is an expansive or liberal approach to determining what is real, and **analytic ontology**, which is a somewhat restrictive or conservative approach. The attempt to construct a full ontological theory is well beyond the scope of this essay, even though some of the entities discussed earlier such as mind and God, are addressed in other chapters. We must therefore be content with addressing one of the most important and perennial problems within ontology. This brings us to the debate between Plato and Aristotle.

■ *Plato's Theory of Forms*

Plato (427–347 B.C.) developed an ontological theory as a means of resolving the disputes of his predecessors. In fact, one way of understanding his hierarchical structure of reality is to see how each of the central metaphysical ideas of his pre-Socratic predecessors—form, substance, permanence, and change—and the inquiries of his teacher, Socrates, are synthesized into one grand theory. His view is sometimes called **dualistic idealism**. The theory is dualistic because Plato believed that two worlds constitute reality—Being and becoming, or abstract Forms and concrete **particulars**—and it is idealistic because he regards the ideal or abstract entities as ultimately real.

The following example will launch us into Plato's way of thinking and provide a basis for understanding Aristotle's subsequent disagreements with his teacher. Consider three different cats—Ginger, Tigre and Minnie. Ginger is an orange and white male, Tigre a tiger-striped male, and Minnie a calico female. These are concrete, particular cats that we are acquainted with in sense experience, but we also know the general term *cat* as that which applies equally to Ginger, Tigre, and Minnie. We perceive particular cats and we form the general concept of "cat" as sameness among particular differences. The general concept "cat" is what Plato calls a **Form**, or perhaps more accurately, our word or concept "cat" corresponds to the Form of Cat. As entities in the world of becoming, Ginger, Tigre, and Minnie are born, grow, mature, and die, but according to Plato, the Form of Cat is an entity in the world of Being. It is an abstract entity because we cannot see it with our eyes; it is discerned only by the mind's eye, so to speak. So, by contrast with concrete particulars, the Form is eternal, unchanging, and outside of space and time. Particular cats become and perish, but the Form of Cat always is and always will be. The Forms are **universals**, as opposed to particulars.

Plato thinks it is the Form of Cat that makes possible the temporary existence of particular cats like Ginger, Tigre, and Minnie, because if there were no Form of Cat, there would be no particular cats. He uses a special, technical term **participation** to describe how the particulars of the world of becoming depend on the Forms in the world of Being. That is, a particular is the kind of thing it is by virtue of its participation in the eternal and universal Forms. This is an asymmetrical relation because particulars participate in Forms, but not vice versa. That is, the particulars depend on the Forms, but the Forms do not depend on the particulars. Plato is quite clear that the Forms do not enter into the world of becoming; rather, what we see with our eyes is merely imperfect copies or shadows of the Forms.

This point is developed in some detail in Plato's "Allegory of the Cave" in his masterpiece *The Republic*.[5] On the one hand, the cave represents the ordinary world of changing material objects, the comfortable, complacent existence of most human beings and their resistance to the truth. On the other hand, the ascent from the cave into the sunlight represents the world of unchanging, ideal Forms known through the activities of reason. Once the released prisoner makes the ascent from the cave, he realizes that the Forms are the true reality and that everything he thought he knew as real in the cave was merely a shadow of something more real. To return to our example of cats, in the cave the prisoners are acquainted with particular cats using sense perception, but once released into the sunlight, the Form of Cat is known through cognition and exists in a reality above and beyond transitory things. Now the odd thing about Plato's theory is that, for him, the particulars are relatively unreal compared with the eternal perfection of the universal Forms. So, Ginger, Tigre, and Minnie are not really real. They are appearances, merely temporary phenomena, of a more fundamental reality.

Plato's teacher, Socrates, sought universal definitions of general concepts such as "piety," "virtue," "love," "justice," "knowledge," and so on. But Socrates was a moral philosopher who wanted a common basis for discussion through clear definitions; he was not engaged in the quest for an ontological theory. Plato, however, was both a moral philosopher and a metaphysician. He extended the inquiries of Socrates so that the pursuit of verbal definitions becomes the quest for knowledge of absolute and universal entities—the Forms existing in a separate, transcendental realm. In this way, using Socrates' dialectic method, Plato thought a definition that would survive the test of rigorous, critical examination would reveal the universal Form in the world of Being. In his dialogue, *The Republic*, for example, a definition of *justice* is arrived at after several unsuccessful attempts of Socrates' interlocutors. Knowledge of justice then consists of grasping the Form of Justice as that which all particular instances of justice have in common. So, when we encounter a just man, a just court case or a just government, we are acquainted with concrete particulars that exemplify, more or less, the one Form of Justice in the world of Being. The Form of Justice provides the standard for evaluating how the concrete particulars either succeed or fail in approximating the universal and absolute.

One argument for Plato's view is as follows. In any significant subject-predicate sentence, we pick out a particular in the subject and then go on to say something about it in the predicate. For example, in asserting "Tigre is a cat," "Socrates is wise," or "This table is round," we are predicating properties to the particular individuals identified in the subjects. What makes these sentences true is that they correspond to the way the world is. But if the words *Tigre, Socrates,* and *this table* refer to concrete particulars, then the words *cat, wise,* and *round* must also refer to something, and the referents of these words are abstract universals, or Forms. So, what makes a subject-predicate sentence true is the fact that the referent of its subject term exemplifies the universal that is the referent of its predicate term. "The way the world is" ontologically must include both particulars and universals.

As for the diversity of Forms in Plato's heaven, literally everything that exists or could possibly exist in the physical world has an eternal Form. Indeed, every word (noun, verb, and adjective) signifies a Form. Throughout Plato's dialogues, he discusses five different types of Forms:

1. Ethical and Aesthetic Forms, such as the Form of the Good, the Form of the Just, the Form of the Beautiful.
2. Very General Notions, such as the Form of Sameness, the Form of Difference.
3. Mathematical Forms, such as the Form of Triangle, the Form of Diameter, the Form of One, Two, Three, and so forth.

4. Natural Kinds, such as the Form of Cat, the Form of Human, the Form of Stone.
5. Artifacts, such as the Form of Table, the Form of Chair, the Form of Chariot.

In the world of Being, there are exemplified Forms such as Table, Cat, and Triangle but also unexemplified Forms. That is, there *is* a Form of Airplane even if there were no airplanes before the Wright brothers produced one in 1903. There *is* a Form of *Tyrannosaurus Rex* even if they disappeared after the Cretaceous period. And there *is* a Form of Hovercraft Skateboard even if that form is not exemplified in 2001. So, for Plato, Being is a much larger ontological category than what exists in the temporal world at any one time. In fact there are mind-boggling infinities of infinities of Forms.

Although Plato does not attempt any precise system of organization of the Forms, in the "Allegory of the Cave" he is clear that the Form of the Good is the supreme Form of value and reality. The philosopher who has knowledge of the Good then would be in a position to understand Justice, Piety, and Virtue as more particular Forms of this supreme Form. Initially, we become acquainted with pale and muddled copies of Forms in our everyday sense experience, but Plato believed that it is only when we recognize the limitations of sense experience and turn within to the activities of pure reason that we begin the journey to true knowledge. This position is called **rationalism**, that is, the view that knowledge is obtained through reason. Plato was greatly impressed by the mathematical knowledge of his Pythagorean predecessors. Indeed the study of mathematics is the key to our release from ignorance and the darkness of the cave. It is the model for Plato's absolute and universal standards realized in his theory of Forms. Consider, for example, the difference between a law of nature believed to be true today but overturned in some future scientific revolution and a law of mathematics such as the Pythagorean theorem, true then, now, and forevermore. The conceptual knowledge gained by mathematical research is the knowledge of a world of permanent and eternal truths.

Plato argued that our knowledge of the Forms is **innate**, that is, present with us at birth. He thought that we knew the Forms in a previous existence, and in this life we merely *recollect* what we already know with the right kind of probing.[6] In other words, we don't really learn about the Forms from scratch, but rather remember what we already know. Sense experience may "trigger" or remind us of this universal knowledge, but this only starts the process of recollection. In itself, sense experience is not sufficient for knowledge of the Forms because it gives us only pale and muddled copies.

■ *Aristotle's Theory of Substance*

Aristotle (384–322 B.C.), while beginning his philosophical career as a disciple of Plato, provided several sharp criticisms of the theory of Forms and developed his own ontology of substance.[7] He had no patience with the otherworldliness of Plato's theory. In fact, he believed that Plato was misled by the model of knowledge provided by Pythagorean mathematics. Aristotle therefore transformed Plato's metaphysics by reversing the dependency of the world of concrete particulars on the world of Forms and ended up with one world instead of two. Dualism is rejected in favor of a complete **naturalism**.

Aristotle's theory can be characterized as **commonsense realism**. This world of individual existing things known to us in sense experience is the real world. There is no other world above and beyond this world that is more ultimately real. As the first biologist, Aristotle's metaphysics was greatly influenced by the notion of organism. Aristotle is also credited with the invention of taxonomy—the classification of plants and animals by genus and species.

Let us return to my cats, Ginger, Tigre, and Minnie, to get clear about Aristotle's disagreement with Plato. First, Aristotle would say that Ginger, Tigre, and Minnie are "individual substances" or "primary substances." Substance is the basic ontological category, because it is concrete, individual things that generate the whole system of classification. So, according to the modern taxonomic system, Ginger, Tigre, and Minnie would be classified in the following way:

Kingdom	*Animalia*
Phylum	*Cordata*
Subphylum	*Vertebrata*
Class	*Mammalia*
Order	*Carnivora*
Family	*Felidae*
Genus	*Felis*
Species	*Domestica*[8]

Aristotle thought that genus and species (and the other classes) were merely abstractions, or what he called "secondary substances." They could not exist without the concrete individuals. So, individual cats like Ginger, Tigre, and Minnie are the things that are real, and what Plato called the "Forms," or in this case the various orders of classes, are dependent on the concrete individuals. In other words, Aristotle thought Plato had this reversed by making the concrete things dependent on the abstract things, but in reality it is the other way around. Aristotle thought it nonsense to believe that the class of domestic cats, *Felis domestica*, exists independently of particular cats. The forms can be entertained in abstraction from particulars in thought but not in reality.

Second, whatever we say about Ginger, Tigre, and Minnie, we do so typically in the predicates of sentences. For example in asserting, "Tigre is a tabby cat," we first introduce the substance by a proper name into the subject of the sentence and then predicate some characteristic of the substance. For Aristotle, the introduction of the concrete particular substance comes first in the grammatical and logical order of understanding, then in the predicate we say something about the substance by using verbs, adjectives and so on. He thought Plato had confused the role of logical subjects and predicates by making predication primary. That is, whatever we say in the predicates typically identifies what Plato called the "Forms," but Aristotle argued that predication is secondary not primary. The adjectives that identify properties or the nouns that identify classes depend on what is identified by a proper name or another noun in the subject that identifies a concrete, individual substance, not vice versa.

Third, Aristotle thought that Plato's theory of Forms failed to explain how things change. Aristotle wanted to know how a tadpole changes into a frog or how a kitten develops into a cat. But the Forms in their eternal perfection are static entities. As completely transcendental and independent, they do not enter into the world of becoming and therefore fail to help us understand the processes that substances undergo.

Aristotle spent considerable time in *The Metaphysics* and *The Categories* working out the precise details of his ontology of substance. As to the question "What is ontologically basic?" Aristotle argued that primary category—substance—is fundamentally real and all other categories are dependent on it. Anything we assert about concrete, individual substances in predication is done so through the categories of quality, quantity, time, place, position, state, relation, action, and affection. So, Tigre (substance), might be a tabby (quality), twenty-two pounds (quantity), at 2:33 P.M. (time), in the garden (place), standing (position), being (state), the offspring of Minnie (relation), running (action), and struck by a ball (affection). Aristotle identified the ten metaphysical categories through the various linguistic forms. Substances are typically identified by proper names or nouns, actions or events by verbs and adverbs, qualities by adjectives, and so on. In this way, he seems to have been working with a basic assumption in his method: *grammar is the guide to ontology*. That is, Aristotle thought that the way we talk about the world in common speech corresponds to the way the world really is.

Aristotle defines *substance* in a variety of ways, but most important, he says that it is characterized as numerically one and the same while being able to receive contraries. That is, substances endure as the self-identical things while undergoing various changes. Tigre the cat is at one time a kitten and then at another time fully grown. He has more fur in the winter and less fur in the summer, but throughout all his changes, he is always the same substance. Aristotle also distinguishes between **essential** and **accidental properties**. Some of the changes that Tigre undergoes do not affect his persistence as the same entity. He might lose an eye in a catfight, but still he will be Tigre. Being one-eyed then would be an accidental property. But there are other properties that Tigre cannot lose and still be Tigre. Essential properties are those without which an individual could not be that individual. Tigre cannot, for example, lose his head in a catfight and still be Tigre. Having a head is essential to the substance *Felis domestica*.

The idea that substances are self-identical centers of change is closely related to another of Aristotle's definitions. Substances are particular combinations of **matter** and **form**. Matter identifies the component stuff of which a substance is made, and form identifies changeable properties. Aristotle thus retained the idea of form in his metaphysics, but unlike Plato, forms exist only insofar as they are components of substances. The component matter remains the same, but the form changes.

Because one of Aristotle's central aims in his metaphysics was to explain how things change, we must introduce his teleological conception of nature. **Teleology** is the branch of metaphysics concerned with goals or purposes in nature. We typically think of ourselves as goal oriented, but Aristotle extended this concept to the whole of nature. His individual substances (and indeed the universe as a whole) are conceived in terms of purposeful activities. This is where the notion of organism comes into play in a particularly impressive way, as all substances are modeled on this notion.

In *The Physics* and *The Metaphysics*, Aristotle analyzes change in terms of the processes that substances undergo when actualizing their potentiality. If we think about any particular substance, we find certain things that are true of it in its present form but also things that can become true of it at a later time. What a substance *is*, Aristotle called its **actuality** and what is *can* become its **potentialities**. So, Tigre at one time was actually a kitten and had the potentiality to become a fully grown cat. Potentiality is the capacity of a substance to undergo a change of some kind, by either its own actions or those of other agents. In Aristotle's teleology, change is explained in terms of what he calls the "four causes." First, to understand some particular substance, we wish to know its material constituents, or the *material cause*. Second, we need to know what type of thing it is, or its *formal cause*. Third, we must know what brought the substance into its present condition, or its *efficient cause*. And finally, to have a full explanation or account of a substance, Aristotle claims we must know its *telos* or its *final cause*, which is the purpose of the substance. The final cause is the fulfillment of the formal cause, because once the substance has actualized its full potentiality it has developed fully its form or essence.

Aristotle rejected the transcendence of Plato's Forms, so it should be clear that he also rejected the mystical doctrine of recollection. As opposed to the view that our ideas of general concepts are innate, he contended that we learn them by sense experience. In fact, Aristotle's whole approach to the acquisition of knowledge is **empirical**. General concepts are abstractions from our experience of particular things.

■ Argument for a Modified Platonism

There is a certain plausibility in Aristotle's commonsense approach to metaphysics. But did he fully succeed in defeating Plato's theory?

One of the major issues of concern to philosophers of the analytic approach is a fear of overpopulation: we end up with more in our philosophy than that which actually exists in heaven and earth. The task of depopulation and the attempt to trim our picture of the world down to just the right size was one of the motivating factors behind Aristotle's critique of Plato's speculative synthesis. As American philosopher W. V. Quine (1908–2000) puts the point, the shaving of

Plato's beard has proven tough and has frequently dulled the edge of Occam's razor.[9] William of Occam (1285–1347) advanced the principle, "Do not multiply entities beyond necessity." In other words, postulate entities only to the extent that we are forced to do so in the course of explanation. Historically the "razor" has always been a logical tool against ontological excess, but as Quine suggests it still proves to be a tough shaving job.

As far as the difficulty of overpopulation is concerned, natural languages, such as English, are often the prime suspects mainly because they allow us to play fast and loose with vocabulary and construction, while at the same time they seem to commit us to the existence of whatever is reflected in our discourse. For example, we say that we do things for the sake of honor or love. But do *sakes* exist in addition to individual acts of honor and love? We speak of them in ordinary language, but perhaps this is just a "manner of speech" and nothing more. The question, however, is: how much more of ordinary language is like this?[10] Plato has been accused of making every noun or adjective signify some entity or Form. But perhaps many of the words are just that, words that help us communicate and nothing more. In other words, not every significant word commits us to the existence of some ontological unit.

Where we can do with less in our ontology, to have more, according to Occam, is superfluous. Consider, for example, how much reduction occurs if, following Aristotle, we think of forms as merely components of primary substances instead of existing in an independent realm. Occam himself, as a follower of Aristotle, argued that everything real is particular and that the universals, or what Plato called the Forms, are merely names that refer to many particular things. This position is called **nominalism**.

Reduction of ontology is important to philosophers who favor theoretical economy. A theory that is simple is preferred to one that is needlessly complex in ontological categories. Other philosophers, however, favor all manner of entities, provided that they serve some important function in theory. Pure mathematicians, for example, are inclined to believe in the existence of an infinite hierarchy of sets for the benefits it yields in terms of theoretical unity. This is where some concession to Plato strikes me as obvious.

A **modified Platonism** of the sort I wish to defend recognizes the existence of both abstract and concrete objects. Concrete objects are broadly construed in terms of what we have called "individuals" or "particulars." They can be physical objects—material bodies like Tigre the cat, scientific objects such as the benzene molecule, or events such as the traffic accident outside my window. Abstract objects are a different sort of entity altogether. They can be properties identified in general terms, such as "whiteness," class terms like "cat" or "animal," or mathematical entities such as numbers, sets, and geometrical figures.[11] Keith Campbell, in his interesting book on metaphysics, suggests that the secret in defining abstract objects "seems to lie in absence of definite spatiotemporal location."[12] The property of whiteness is not itself located at any one place and time. Campbell says: "The distinguishing mark of abstract objects, or at any rate of properties, is that they can be simultaneously completely present in many locations."[13] Another way of understanding the difference between concrete and abstract objects is through the notion of repeatability. Concrete objects are nonrepeatable particulars of space-time. There will never be another Tigre, another sinking of the Titantic, or another apple identical to the one I ate for lunch. Abstract objects, or universals, however, are essentially repeatable. The same shade of white characterizes a car, a surfboard on the car's roof, and the shirt of the man driving the car at the same time or at different times. The number seven characterizes a litter of kittens, the number of tennis balls in my closet, or the number of rings around the planet Saturn.

The admission of abstract objects to an ontology already containing concrete objects involves us in a dualism of the sort advanced by Plato, but there is a major difference. Plato construed the main ontological problem in terms of dependence or what he called "participation." Concrete particulars participate in, or depend on, the Forms, the former being only pale copies of the full reality of the latter. He also believed that the Forms, as ideal or perfect entities, never enter into the world of becoming. The trouble with this view, as Aristotle recognized, is that it denies the full reality of the concrete, physical world. The modified Platonism, however, recognizes the equal reality of the two ontological categories. These two fundamental types do all of the ontological work required of science and mathematics. Concrete particulars instantiate some abstract objects, but there are vast multitudes of abstract objects that are uninstantiated by any particulars. In this way, instantiation is an accidental property of abstract objects. So, we have the independence of the abstract objects from the physical world. Though no concrete particular can exist without instantiating some abstract object, particulars are not merely pale copies of the abstract objects they instantiate. In fact, they are not copies at all.

To further the case for our ontology of abstract objects, let us consider a fairly recent example from mathematics. Andrew Wiles, a British mathematician at Princeton University, worked in secrecy for seven years on a solution to Fermat's Last Theorem. The problem, he said, is very easy to understand but extremely difficult to solve. Fermat's Last Theorem is a problem in pure mathematics. It is intrinsically interesting but widely understood to have no practical value. Pierre de Fermat (1601–1665), working with the famous Pythagorean Theorem, $a^2 + b^2 = c^2$, asked which solutions exist in the equation for the exponents larger than 2 and concluded that there are none. That is, the equation $a^n + b^n = c^n$ cannot be solved for any whole numbers of $n > 2$. For three hundred and fifty years, mathematicians sought a proof for Fermat's claim, but none was successful until Wiles's discovery. In 1994, he published his rigorous proof based on logical deduction — one that mathematicians today recognize as a successful solution to the problem that confirms Fermat's claim. The details of Wiles's proof are extremely complex and well beyond the comprehension of all but a handful of professional mathematicians in the world, but its relevance for our ontology of abstract objects is clear.

What Wiles discovered, provided that his proof is indeed sound, is an eternal truth about abstract reality. Of course, this example (or any other from the history of mathematics) does not show that Plato is right. To claim this would beg the question, because we would be assuming what we are proving. But the example does show us how proofs in mathematics can be interpreted in terms of an ontology of abstract objects. That is, the mathematical statements in the proof are analogous to ordinary subject-predicate statements that refer to states of affairs in the world. What makes mathematical statements true is that they correspond to an objective but abstract reality. Pure mathematics reveals a paradise of form where we fly high in the regions of pure thought and conceptual understanding. Our discoveries of conceptual reasoning correspond to entities in a kind of mathematical heaven. Mathematics and deductive logic provide us with a rigorous concept of objectivity unparalleled in any of our other reasoning processes.

Eternal truths about abstract objects gain further support from the notion that these truths are independent of the physical world. Let us think of the situation before human beings walked on planet Earth or a future state, let us say, a date in the distant future when our sun burns out and destroys all sentient life in the solar system. In both scenarios let us further suppose that there are no other intelligent, thinking beings anywhere else in the universe. Now are the truths of mathematics and logic still true? Is $2 + 2 = 4$ still true? Is the law of the excluded middle—p or not-p—still true? A Platonist would answer in the affirmative because the realm of abstraction is unaffected by whether there are instantiations or whether there are minds contemplating such statements. Mathematical and logical statements are true for all possible worlds because they are ontologically prior and transcendental.

■ METAPHYSICS UNDER ATTACK

As we have seen, philosophy began with metaphysics and it has occupied an esteemed place in the history of philosophy and science. But not all philosophers agree with the assessment of metaphysics as the "queen of the sciences" or the philosophical discipline *par excellence.*

The case against metaphysics gains force from time to time as a result of a turn in philosophical fashion when intense analysis and adherence to method attempt to prune back what is perceived as the excessive speculations of metaphysicians. The antimetaphysicians would, in fact, regard the very attempt to determine the nature of ultimate reality as grandiose, meaningless, or simply useless. The British empiricists of the seventeenth and eighteenth centuries reacted against the metaphysical claims of continental rationalists by concentrating on the epistemological question, "What are we capable of knowing?" In the twentieth century, the attacks against metaphysics have been renewed with increased vigor and have come from many different schools of thought: **logical positivism**, linguistic analysis, **pragmatism**, phenomenology, and deconstruction.

I shall briefly discuss criticisms from logical positivism and from pragmatism and then respond in defense of metaphysics in the conclusion of this chapter.

■ *Logical Positivism*

The logical positivists were notoriously hostile to metaphysics because they believed that any speculative theories claiming knowledge beyond sensory experience should be rejected as nonsense. They argued that metaphysics is a type of misplaced poetry that expresses a kind of romantic vision about the world, but when taken literally, it fails to be meaningful.[14] Moreover, the metaphysician seems to be engaged in a type of propaganda for a given view of the universe, but like all forms of propaganda, the enterprise involves the exaggerated importance of one type of conceptual scheme. The real issue, however, is not the defense of one type of conceptual scheme over another but, rather, the type of **verification** we can get for our statements.

The centerpiece of logical positivism is the **verifiability criterion of meaning**:

A sentence S is meaningful if and only if S (or its negation) is verifiable.

So now the question is, How might we verify a sentence? The positivist contends that two classes of statements are verifiable. The first class is empirical statements, such as "There is a coffee cup in front of me," "Mt. Everest is the highest mountain in the world," or "Earth is the third planet from the sun." These statements are verifiable in the strong sense; that is, they are conclusively verified in experience. But the positivist also recognized a weak sense of empirical verification. In this case a statement is weakly verifiable when experience renders the statement probable. In this way, the positivist was able to claim that scientific laws, such as Newton's laws of motion, are verifiable in the weak sense because no one can observe the infinite number of cases in which the law is meant to apply. Empirical statements are shown by observation to be true. When we deny them, we utter false statements about the way the world is.

The second class of verifiable statements is logically necessary or analytical statements. They can be shown to be true by definition. For example, "All bachelors are unmarried men," or All bodies are extended." Such statements are **tautologies**, that is, necessarily true statements; their truth is merely formal and abstract. When we deny these statements, we utter contradictions or necessarily false statements.

According to this classification of meaningfulness, metaphysical utterances such as "God is the benevolent creator of the universe," "Forms are the ultimate entities of the universe," or "Individual substances are the concrete particulars of reality" fail to be meaningful because they are neither empirically verifiable nor logically true. No experience would prove or disprove these claims, nor are they true or false by definition. Metaphysical utterances are, therefore, neither true nor false. They assert nothing and contain neither knowledge nor error. Positivists contend that once we recognize that metaphysical statements cannot, even in principle, be verified, we can dismiss the whole field of inquiry.

■ *Pragmatism*

Pragmatists typically contend that the metaphysician attempts to view the universe from a Godlike point of view, but because this is quite impossible for finite beings, our persistent attempts suffer from a kind of megalomania. For pragmatists, then, we must give up the attempt to discover absolute truth in metaphysical *foundations* and be content with a concept of truth in terms of usefulness.[15] Truth, according to this view, is good enough when it delivers results and cashes out in practical consequences. In this way pragmatists emphasize the plurality of truths that serve our diverse purposes, but there is no sense to the idea of one system of thought corresponding to the way things really are. Even the very language of appearance and reality can be applied only to some specific context (e.g., apparent direction rather than real direction, dyed hair color rather than natural hair color) but not to the traditional metaphysician's scale as for example in Plato's "Allegory of the Cave." Pragmatists, therefore, discard the attempts of grand systems-building or the attempts to discover the universal and absolute principles of reality, because such systems make no practical difference to our lives. They indict metaphysics for sterility and argue that philosophers should concentrate their efforts on questions and problems that are more fruitful.

■ REPLIES TO OBJECTIONS AND CONCLUSION

Everything in metaphysics is controversial. The fact that an issue is controversial or that a problem is extremely difficult to solve, however, should not force us to see it as "meaningless" or "sterile," because the value of philosophy in many cases lies in the uncertainty of the solutions offered and the never-ending task of criticism and revision. This is what confronts us in much of life's bigger problems anyway, whether we are investigating science, politics, morality, or religion.

One objection to positivism is well known. It involves turning the positivists' procedure on themselves. The verifiability criterion of meaning, at the heart of the positivist doctrine, states, "A sentence S has literal meaning if and only if S (or its negation) is verifiable." This is itself an unverifiable proposition and therefore meaningless. That is, the verifiability criterion is neither true by observation nor true by definition. So it seems that the positivist must be doing metaphysics in the course of demonstrating its meaninglessness, because the verifiability criterion, like metaphysical principles, is theoretical and unverifiable even in principle.

But let us take the positivists' recommendation seriously for the moment and see where it leads. If we are to stick to what is observable, we seem to be restricted to saying things about the present, and the present only. Notice, for example, that we cannot make claims about history because we cannot observe the past. Even if we confine ourselves to the present, our interpretation of experience and our judgments about the world invariably involve us in the use of a language that is fully stocked with metaphysical concepts such as "change," "cause," "substance," "property," "event," "identity," and "individual." Our ordinary language and the logical form of statements already contain a metaphysics dating back all the way to the ancient Greeks, if not before. This involves critical reflection on metaphysics from the very start.

Furthermore, it is extremely difficult to understand what would become of science if we accepted the positivists' recommendation. This is especially troubling since the positivists believed themselves to be providing principles and methods for keeping science honest, that is, rigorously empirical. It is unlikely, however, that we can have any science at all without the essentially unverifiable theories by which we understand the meaning of experimental results or make sense of basic observations. Many of the logical positivists thought that the theoretical terms of scientific theories could be cashed out in observational terms, but this proved to be a very difficult procedure because much of scientific theory involves metaphysical principles—"space," "time," "matter," "motion"—that guide the direction of scientific inquiry. So, in the positivists' attempt to separate metaphysics from science, much of science would be thrown out with metaphysics. The baby goes out with the bathwater. The empirically verifiable and the analytically verifiable statements necessarily exclude or eliminate metaphysical claims from meaningful discourse, but the positivists assume too quickly that the classification is complete and final. Both metaphysics and science seek theories that promise deeper penetration into nature's secrets. Metaphysics is distinguished from science in the sense that it attempts to be a more comprehensive study of reality.

Now, as to the objections of the pragmatist, we might first ask just exactly what is meant by the concept of truth as *useful*. If an idea "works," then presumably there is some sense in which the idea grasps reality or some aspect thereof. Let us take a simple example from astronomy, Kepler's proposal that the planets mark their orbits around the sun in ellipses. This idea works better than Copernicus's idea that the planets travel in perfect circles. But why? The pragmatist would reply that Kepler's idea makes a *practical difference* in our attempts to calculate and predict the motions of the planets, so it is to be preferred to Copernicus's idea. But the metaphysician believes truth is more than just what is useful or practical—in this case, that Kepler's idea "works" because it is more accurate in its grasp of the structure of reality. Besides this, many intellectual pursuits have no immediate practical use but come to be useful only at a later time. Much of the research in pure mathematics or theoretical physics, I take it, falls roughly under this category, as do the type of metaphysical issues I am currently defending. Moreover, clearly many ideas are practical or useful but plainly false. Certain religious or political ideas might indeed be useful in the skillful hands of manipulators, but just because these ideas promote their own advantage or provide some kind of emotional comfort to those who believe them, we don't think them true in the pragmatists' sense of the term.

The metaphysician seeks the ultimate truth of reality, yet the pragmatist contends that this is a hopeless struggle. But *seeking* the truth and claiming to *know* the truth are two entirely different things. On this score we must make concessions to the pragmatist, for human systems are never complete and final. This accounts for the ongoing endeavor of criticism and revision in philosophy. Metaphysics is certainly no exception here, but neither is any other aspect of human inquiry. It very well may be that we never get there—that is, to the end of our search—but this does not mean that the journey is worthless. On this point, perhaps American philosopher George Santayana put it best when he said at the outset of his monumental volumes of *Realms of Being*: "Here is one more system of philosophy. If the reader is tempted to smile, I can assure him that I smile with him. . . ."[16]

Metaphysics is presupposed in much of our thinking about ourselves and our world. The question is not whether we are to do it at all, but whether we are to do it well and in full conscience of its place in the wider context of philosophy.[17]

■ NOTES

1. Aristotle, *The Metaphysics*, trans. by Philip Wheelwright, *Aristotle* (Indianapolis: Bobbs-Merrill, 1977), 77.

2. See Francis Cornford, *From Religion to Philosophy* (New York, Harper and Brothers, 1957), 141 and Werner Jaeger, *The Theology of the Early Greek Philosophers* (Oxford: Clarendon Press, 1947), 18–20.

3. Richard McKeon, *The Basic Works of Aristotle* (New York: Random House, 1941), xviii.

4. See, for example, David Lewis, *On the Plurality of Worlds* (Oxford: Basil Blackwell, 1986).

5. Plato, *The Republic*, Book VII.

6. Plato's dialogue, *Meno*, concerns his theory of recollection and the doctrine of innate ideas.

7. Aristotle's objections to Plato can be found in *The Metaphysics*, Book I, Chapter 6, and in *The Nicomachean Ethics*, Book I, Chapter 6.

8. It should be clear that the modern taxonomic system is a great advance over the rudimentary system of Aristotle.

9. W. V. Quine, *From a Logical Point of View* (Cambridge, Mass.: Harvard University Press, 1953), 2.

10. An excellent discussion of the problem of ontological excess can be found in Keith Campbell, *Metaphysics: An Introduction* (Encino, Calif.: Dickenson, 1979). See especially Chapter 8.

11. On one formulation of this ontology, all abstract entities can be construed in terms of classes, thereby providing a much more refined application of Occam's Razor. See especially, W. V. Quine, *Theories and Things* (Cambridge, Mass.: Harvard University Press, 1980), Chapter 12.

12. Campbell, *Metaphysics: An Introduction*, 111.

13. Ibid.

14. A. J. Ayer, *Language, Truth and Logic* (New York: Dover, 1952), 44.

15. Pragmatism is a twentieth-century American philosophical movement initiated by Charles Peirce and carried on by William James, John Dewey, C. I. Lewis, and more recently, Richard Rorty.

16. George Santayana, *Scepticism and Animal Faith* (New York: Dover, 1955), v.

17. Thanks are due to Frank McGuinness, Alfred Mele, Takashi Yagisawa, Mark Timmons, and Frederick Adams for helpful suggestions to an earlier draft of this essay.

■ QUESTIONS

1. What is metaphysics? How are the investigations of the metaphysician different from those of the scientist? How are they similar?

2. What is the fundamental problem of ontology? What are the two approaches discussed in this chapter? How does the author attempt to solve the problem?

3. Which of the following would satisfy Plato's criteria for being a Form?
   a. Tigre the cat
   b. the concept of love
   c. the square root of twenty-five
   d. a car accident in Los Angeles
   e. the city of Los Angeles
   f. the color purple

4. What is substance? Explain Aristotle's characterization of substance and contrast his view with that of Plato. Which arguments do you think are more persuasive? Explain why.

5. Explain how the following passage from Lewis Carroll's *Alice's Adventures in Wonderland* involves a metaphysical problem discussed in this chapter:

   > "All right," said the Cat; and this time it vanished quite slowly, beginning with the end of the tail, and ending with the grin, which remained some time after the rest of it had gone.

   > "Well! I've often seen a cat without a grin," thought Alice; "but a grin without a cat! It's the most curious thing I ever saw in all my life!"

6. Does our conceptual scheme revealed in our language determine how we see reality, or does reality determine how our conceptual scheme is developed in our language? Which is Aristotle's view? Is he correct?

7. In one of Aristotle's characterizations of substance, he says that substance is what is capable of independent existence. Qualities are incapable of independent existence, whereas substances can exist independently. Explain what is wrong with this characterization. Consider what sort of objects would count as independently existing individuals from the following list: human beings, trees, cars, houses, planets, solar systems, galaxies, clouds, rainbows, rivers, rocks, rays of light, molecules, atoms, electrons.

8. Aristotle distinguished between essential and accidental properties of individual substances. Which of the following are essential and which are accidental for human beings?
   a. having blond hair
   b. being a female
   c. being six foot, four inches tall

    d. being human
    e. being passive
    f. having rational thought
9. What is the problem of overpopulation in ontological construction? What is the guiding principle that attempts to solve this problem?
10. What is the difference between Plato's ontology and the modified Platonic ontology discussed in this chapter? What criticisms of Plato's view does the author accept?
11. Examine each of the following statements, and explain how the statement does or does not commit us to the existence of the entities introduced in the subject of the sentence.
    a. A married bachelor lives next door.
    b. The present King of France is bald.
    c. Quadriplicity eats purple.
    d. Unicorns are horses with horns.
    e. Quarks and leptons are the fundamental atomic particles.
    f. The average man has 2.5 cats.
    g. Ideal sisters never quarrel.
12. The author appeals to the case of Fermat's Last Theorem as an example for interpreting the modified Platonism. Can you think of any alternative interpretations of this example that would not support an ontology of abstract objects? In other words, if mathematics is not about an abstract reality, then how is it correctly interpreted?
13. Which of the following statements would the logical positivist consider meaningful?
    a. God is the omnipotent Creator of the universe.
    b. Grass is green.
    c. Pericles was an Athenian general who lived from 495 to 429 B.C.
    d. All sisters are females.
    e. $[(a + b) + c] = [a + (b + c)]$
    f. Light is composed of electromagnetic waves.
    g. The universe is one substance.
    h. Abortion is morally wrong.
14. Do you find that the defense of metaphysics in this chapter is successful against the antimetaphysicians? Why or why not?

■ FOR FURTHER READING

Aristotle. *The Metaphysics*. Available in various editions.

Burkhardt, H. and B. Smith, eds. *Handbook of Metaphysics and Ontology*. Vols I and II. Munich: Philosophia Verlag, 1991.

Campbell, Keith. *Metaphysics: An Introduction*. Encino, Calif.: Dickenson, 1976.

Carter, W. R. *The Elements of Metaphysics*. New York: McGraw-Hill, 1990.

Craig, Edward. "Metaphysics," *Routledge Encyclopedia of Philosophy*, ed. by Edward Craig. London: Routledge, 1998.

Kim, Jaegwon, and Ernest Sosa, eds. *A Companion to Metaphysics*. Oxford: Blackwell, 1995.

Loux, Michael J. *Metaphysics: A Contemporary Introduction*. London: Routledge, 1998.

Murphy, John P. *Pragmatism: From Peirce to Davidson*. Boulder, Colo.: Westview Press, 1990.

Plato. *The Republic*. Available in various editions.

Pears, D. F., ed. *The Nature of Metaphysics*. London: Macmillan, 1962.
Sprigge, T. L. S. *Theories of Existence*. Harmondsworth, Eng.: Penguin, 1984.
Walsh, W. H. "Metaphysics, Nature of," and Roger Hancock, "Metaphysics, History of,"
    The Encyclopedia of Philosophy, Vol. 5, ed. by Paul Edwards. New York: Macmillan,
    1967.

■ CHAPTER FOUR

Free Will and Determinism

ALFRED R. MELE

■ *INTRODUCTION*

Free will is traditionally associated with determinism. A concise definition of **determinism** is "the thesis that there is at any instant exactly one physically possible future."[1] The basic idea is that if determinism is true, then, relative to any given past moment, the possible futures that are consistent both with the condition of the universe at that moment and the laws of nature are limited to one: there is only one way things can develop—throughout time—consistently with the condition of the universe at that past moment and the laws of nature. If determinism is true and you close this book just after you read this paragraph, the only "physically possible future" you have now—a future that stretches on as long as you continue to exist—includes your closing this book then. If determinism is false, then perhaps there are physically possible futures—futures consistent both with the condition of the universe (including you) as you read this sentence and the laws of nature—in which you close this book very soon and physically possible futures in which you do not.

In light of what has filtered down to philosophy from quantum mechanics, very few philosophers today believe that determinism is true. Even so, much debate continues about whether free will is compatible with determinism. Later, I will say something about why this is so. It is often said that free will is a metaphysical issue, that the topic is bound up with the fundamental nature of reality. This claim raises questions that cannot be tackled until the standard positions on free will are described and discussed. In a way, as you will see, the debate between the two main groups of believers in free will—compatibilist believers and libertarians (see later)—is a debate about how metaphysical a thing free will is.

The primary aim of this chapter is to make salient the main philosophical problems believers in free will face. I will also sketch an approach to a solution. The following section is the first pass at making the problems salient. The second pass focuses on our alleged experience of freedom, and the third features an influential thought experiment that has convinced many philosophers that people can perform an action freely even if they could not have done otherwise at the time than perform that action. I then discuss what a certain kind of believer in free will values in free will and summarize a solution to the free will problem that I have defended elsewhere.[2]

■ *TERMINOLOGY, STANDARD POSITIONS, AND LUCK*

■ *Terminology*

I have already defined *determinism*. Here are definitions of some other standard terms used in this chapter:

> *Indeterminism*: The thesis that determinism is false. (The occurrence of *any* causally undetermined event suffices for determinism's being false. Indeterminism is *not* the thesis that *everything* is causally undetermined.)
>
> *Compatibilism*: The thesis that it is possible for there to be beings with free will in a deterministic universe. More briefly, the thesis that free will is *compatible* with determinism (and hence the name).
>
> *Incompatibilism*: The thesis that it is *not* possible for there to be beings with free will in a deterministic universe. More briefly, the thesis that free will is *incompatible* with determinism.
>
> *Libertarianism*: The combination of incompatibilism and the thesis that at least some human beings have free will.

■ *Standard Positions*

Compatibilists and incompatibilists agree about what determinism is. For example, both sides can accept the definition of determinism as "the thesis that there is at any instant exactly one physically possible future." Their disagreement is about whether determinism leaves room for free will. What bothers incompatibilists about determinism is concisely expressed in what is sometimes called "the consequence argument." Here is a short version from an influential book by Peter van Inwagen:

> If determinism is true, then our acts are the consequences of the laws of nature and events in the remote past. But it is not up to us what went on before we were born, and neither is it up to us what the laws of nature are. Therefore, the consequences of these things (including our present acts) are not up to us.[3]

If your freely doing something requires that your doing it be up to you and determinism entails that nothing is up to you, then determinism is incompatible with your acting freely.

One requirement of free will, incompatibilists claim, is that there not be a continuous deterministic causal sequence that begins before our birth and results in our actions. Libertarians who want to tell us what free will is and how free decisions and other free actions come about should tell us where, in an action-producing process, indeterminism promotes freedom. It is not as though indeterminism in just any location would contribute to freedom. Let me explain.

Imagine that a century ago, extraterrestrial pranksters rigged an indeterministic trigger to a bomb they placed in the ceiling of a certain college dormitory room. The bomb was set to explode on September 15, 1980, if a certain undetermined, physically possible, quantum-mechanical event occurred on that day in that location. Unbeknownst to them, the occupant of that room, Ish, would be out of town that day. Even so, if the bomb had been triggered, it would have blown Ish's room to bits, and his horror when he discovered this would have resulted in his immediately leaving the college, never to return. In that case, Ish would never have met Shaheen, whom he did meet a few months later at that college and subsequently married, and his life would have been very different. So at many instants on and before September 15, 1980, Ish had more than one personally significant, physically possible future.

Does that give Ish some freedom? Given that the bomb does not explode in the thought experiment, is Ish any more free in it than he would be if everything else were the same except that there was no such bomb in his room (and anything entailed by that)? More precisely, is Ish more free in the former scenario than in the latter just by virtue of the presence of the indeterministic bomb in his room in the former? Of course not. Suppose now, in the same thought experiment, that the only thing that ever provided Ish with more than one physically possible future was the presence of the bomb (rigged as I have described) in that dorm room. In that case, did his freedom vanish after September 15 passed with no explosion? That seems preposterous too. How can Ish's freedom hinge, in the case as described, on the physical "openness" of what happens to the bomb on September 15?

Compare a possible deterministic universe $U1$ with a possible indeterministic universe $U2$ that is as much like $U1$ as possible, given that $U2$ has some indeterministic land mines in it—small bombs rigged to be triggered by undetermined quantum-mechanical events. As it happens, none of the mines is ever triggered, because the undetermined triggering events do not occur. Ish has a counterpart in each of these two universes, and some of the land mines are at Ish's counterpart's spatiotemporal vicinity in $U2$. Given that the land mines never explode, their presence makes no difference to Ish's counterpart's life in $U2$, at least in some versions of the story. And in some such versions of the story, I submit, Ish's $U2$ counterpart is no more free than his $U1$ counterpart. One has physically possible futures that the other lacks, and only one has more than one physically possible future, but only because of the presence of certain indeterministic land mines—and the mines never explode. The decisions, other actions, and lives of the two agents might run along parallel lines.

What libertarians want that determinism precludes is not merely that individual agents have, at some instants, more than one physically possible future, but that the future they come to have, among the various ones physically possible for them, is in some sense and to some degree *up to the agents*. They want something that requires that agents themselves be indeterministic in some suitable way.

■ *Luck*

The notion of an agent's not being causally determined to do something he did may be articulated in terms of **possible worlds**. (Here *worlds* means "universes," not "planets.") The following is an illustration from van Inwagen, a prominent libertarian:

> To say that it was not determined that [a certain petty thief] should refrain from stealing is to say this: there is a possible world that (a) is *exactly* like the actual world in every detail up to the moment at which the thief refrained from stealing, and (b) is governed by the same laws of nature as the actual world, and (c) is such that, in it, the thief robbed the poor-box.[4]

Free will is supposed to ground moral responsibility. Given van Inwagen's description of what is required if the thief's refraining is not to be causally determined, one wonders how agents can be morally responsible for what they do when their actions are *not* causally determined. Van Inwagen imagines that "God has thousands of times caused the world to revert to precisely its state at the moment just before the thief decided not to steal" and "on about half these occasions" the thief refrained from robbing the poor-box.[5] But then, one wonders, why isn't the thief's deciding to refrain from stealing in the actual world a matter of dumb luck, in which case he seems not to be morally responsible for deciding as he does and not to decide freely? After all, he might just as easily have decided to steal the money given exactly the same past up to the time of decision and exactly the same laws of nature: in about half of the divine "reruns," that is precisely what he does.

Van Inwagen suggests that in the actual world the thief's "refraining from robbing the poor-box (R) was caused but not necessitated by" a certain desire/belief pair.[6] "R was caused by" this desire/belief pair (DB), and "DB did not have to cause R; it just *did*."[7] He also suggests that in the "reruns" in which the thief steals the money, his stealing was caused by another desire/belief pair.[8] Let's say this is true. Even then, it appears that what the thief does is a matter of luck. It seems to be just a matter of luck that DB causes a refraining, rather than that the other desire/belief pair causes a stealing. If the thief had a little randomizing device in his head—or a natural randomizing part of his brain—that initially gives each of two competing sets of reasons about an even chance of prevailing in his present situation and then randomly issues in the prevailing of one set, the divine "reruns" would show the distribution van Inwagen imagines. (Picture the device as a tiny, genuinely random roulette wheel, half of whose slots are black and half red. The ball's landing on black represents the prevailing of the thief's reasons for refraining from stealing, and its landing on red represents the other reasons' prevailing.) But in that case, if the thief is not morally responsible for what the device does, it is hard to see how he can be morally responsible (or deserve moral credit or blame) for refraining from stealing in the actual world or for stealing in the "reruns" in which he steals. At least, it is hard to see how his moral responsibility for refraining or for stealing can extend beyond his moral responsibility for his having the reasons he has at the time. And if his responsibility for having those reasons is supposed to derive from earlier undetermined actions of his (including decidings) in which a randomizer of the kind described plays a central role, the same problem arises at the relevant earlier times.

Let's look at the problem of dumb luck just a bit more closely. Full-blown, deliberative, intentional action involves the following: (1) a psychological basis for deliberation, including such things as our values, desires, and beliefs, and our deliberative skills, habits, and capacities; (2) an evaluative judgment that is made on the basis of deliberation and recommends a particular course of action; (3) an intention formed or acquired on the basis of that judgment; and (4) an action executing that intention. Starting at the bottom, one finds the following transitions: intention-acquisition to action; judging to intention-acquisition; and a process of reasoning to judgment as output. At the top, one finds input to deliberation along with various deliberative skills, habits, and capacities. Additional input can enter the picture during deliberation.

Consider a particular practical connection, that between forming an intention to write a check to one's favorite charity now and writing the check. Assume that, owing to indeterminism in Al's internal workings, there is some significant non-zero probability that no matter what he intends to do now, even if he continues to judge it best to do it, he does even try to do it. He might intend to write a check to Habitat for Humanity now, but not even make an effort to remove his checkbook and pen from his pocket. This is a problem I imagine you, like me, would prefer not to have. It is difficult to see how such a problem would, in itself, contribute to our being free, but if, in us, the connection between what we intend to do immediately and what we try to do is significantly indeterministic, we have this problem.

A similar point can be made at the level at which judgments are linked to intentions. Significant internal indeterminism here is a problem. If it is causally open that whatever Ann judges it best to do, she does not intend accordingly, even while that judgment is firmly in place, she can go off the rails not only owing to weakness of will but also just because she functions indeterministically at this point in the action-producing process. This is a problem I would prefer not to have, and it is hard to see how my having it would, in itself, contribute to my being free.

These observations leave it open that indeterminism somewhere else in the action-producing process would both contribute to freedom and not be so undesirable. We will return to this issue later. Now, as promised I want to say something about why the question of the compatibility of freedom with determinism still receives a lot of attention even though few people today believe that our universe is deterministic. Part of the answer is *tradition*; another part is that, in light of the problem about luck that I addressed briefly and other apparent problems, compatibilists and other antilibertarians do not see how indeterminism can be useful for freedom. Timothy O'Connor, a libertarian, divides libertarian positions into three kinds.[9] According to some libertarians, the control we have as agents is not a causal matter. Others understand agents' control causally, in a way that features nondeterministic causal connections between things such as reasons or efforts of will and free actions. Yet others, such as O'Connor, are "agent causationists"; they hold that agents themselves are causes of free actions and that "agent causation" is not reducible to causation by events. Each of the three positions is challenged by considerations of luck, and compatibilists are dubious about all three.[10] Roughly speaking, as compatibilist believers in freedom see things, the freedom that we have given the prevailing view that our universe is indeterministic would remain as it is should it turn out that, in fact, our universe is deterministic.

By now you have some sense of important problems that compatibilists and libertarians face. Is compatibilism undermined by the "consequence argument," and is libertarianism undone by the problem of "dumb luck"? Because students feel the worry that determinism precludes freedom more readily than the worry that the kind of indeterminism libertarians want may thwart freedom, I devoted more effect in developing the latter.

■ THE EXPERIENCE OF FREEDOM

Attention to "the experience of freedom" helps highlight some important differences between compatibilism and incompatibilism.[11] John Searle writes:

> Reflect very carefully on the character of the experiences you have as you engage in normal, everyday ordinary human actions. You will sense the possibility of alternative courses of action built into these experiences. Raise your arm or walk across the room to take a drink of water, and you will see that at any point in the experience you have a sense of alternative courses of action open to you. . . . In normal behaviour, each thing we do carries the conviction, valid or invalid, that we could be doing something else right here and now, that is, all other conditions remaining the same. This, I submit, is the source of our own unshakable conviction of our own free will.[12]

The "conviction of freedom," Searle adds, "is built into every normal, conscious intentional action . . . this sense of freedom . . . is part of any action."[13] Even so, he argues, our behavior is never free, in what he takes to be an important sense: "Our conception of physical reality simply does not allow for [libertarian] freedom." And compatibilism, he contends, does not offer "anything like the resolution of the conflict between freedom and determinism that our urge to . . . libertarianism really demands."

Spinoza (1634–1677), in a related vein, imagines a falling stone becoming conscious. "Such a stone," he writes, "being conscious merely of its own endeavour [to move along its path] and not at all indifferent, would believe itself to be completely free, and would think that it continued in motion solely because of its own wish. This is that human freedom, which all boast that they possess, and which consists solely in the fact, that men are conscious of their own desire, but are ignorant of the causes whereby that desire has been determined."[14] The "human freedom" to which Spinoza refers is underdescribed: someone conscious of the desire to close her book, say, and ignorant of its causes will not, other things being equal, take herself to be acting freely, unless she takes herself to be closing her book, or at least "endeavoring" to close it. But that leaves it open to Spinoza to claim that alleged "human freedom" consists solely in consciousness of relatively immediate psychological springs of one's actions and of corresponding endeavors together with ignorance of the sources of those springs. This, one might say, is ersatz freedom; and one might contend that our experience of acting freely in no way supports the claim that human freedom extends beyond ersatz freedom.

Consider in this connection the bearing of experiences of acting *intentionally* on the claim that some people act *intentionally*. That people sometimes act intentionally is difficult to doubt. All readers have had an experience of acting intentionally. (Probably you are having one now.) They can distinguish, in their own cases, between what appear to be clear instances of intentional action and clear instances of unintentional action—for example, reading this line versus typing "toady" when one meant to type "today." The operative sense of "experience of x" here leaves room for experiences of x that are not **veridical** (i.e., experiences that do not match reality). But what would it take to convince *you* to doubt in a serious—hence, not purely academic—way that you have ever intentionally raised your arms, walked across a room, or closed a book? What would convince you that there is a significant chance that all of your experiences of doing such things intentionally are nonveridical? A persuasive argument that you are really just a brain in a vat (or think of the movie *Matrix*, where most people are bodies in vats) should suffice, or a convincing argument that you are only a dreamer or that you do not exist. At any rate, it seems that only drastic hypotheses such as these would turn the trick.

So why is determinism, which used to seem so plausible to so many, and certainly less implausible than the hypotheses just mentioned, thought to be incompatible with free action? Do incompatibilists tend to take our experiences of acting freely to be less robust than our experiences of acting intentionally, or more theory laden, so that one's experiences of acting freely have less evidential merit and are more susceptible to theoretical challenge? Certainly, if any actual mental events count as experiences of acting freely, the occurrence of those (possibly nonveridical) *experiences* is compatible with the truth of determinism. An agent can be causally determined to have such experiences. (An agent can be causally determined to have the experience of acting intentionally also, but that does not threaten the veridicality of that experience.) So the experience of acting freely does not preclude the truth of determinism. Neither, however, does the experience of acting intentionally preclude (at least in any obvious way) the truth of the hypothesis that one is a brain in a vat, and that does not stand in the way of our reasonably taking such experiences to count strongly in favor of the hypothesis that we sometimes intentionally raise our arms or walk across a room.

One might say, correctly, that the experience of acting freely requires more for its veridicality than does the experience of acting intentionally.[15] The "more" that it requires, as some incompatibilists view matters, includes *freedom from deterministic causation* at some juncture or junctures. Is freedom from deterministic causation something that can itself be experienced? Some say yes, alleging that we often have the experience of possessing genuine options—the experience of its being up to us what we do next, in the sense that, given the total state of ourselves and the universe at the time along with the laws of nature, it is open to us to do one thing next, and open to us to do another instead. (Recall Searle's remark that "in normal behaviour, each thing we do carries the conviction, valid or invalid, that we could be doing something else right here and now, that is, *all other conditions remaining the same*" [my italics].) Is that right? Or is our experience of openness better characterized in another way?

Here is an example of my own experience. I am sitting at my desk, rereading this paragraph. I am also a bit thirsty. I now have the experience of entertaining two genuine options: one is to continue to sit here reading, thinking, and revising, for several minutes at least; the other is to walk down the hall to the drinking fountain, in less than several minutes' time. I consciously regard these options as things I can do and as things I may or may not do, as I please. At least in that sense, I have an experience of its being "up to me" which of these I do, or an experience describable in that way. However—and this is just a report on how things seem to me now—I find in myself no experience that the total state of myself and the universe now is compatible with my sitting here thinking for several minutes and compatible, as well, with my instead going to the drinking fountain in less than several minutes. Nor do I find in myself an experience of regarding things this way. Call these last two experiences—experiences that it seems to me I lack—*deep openness* experiences.

How can I have my "up to me" experience without having a deep openness experience? Well, perhaps I just am not a very deep person experientially, just not the sort of person who has experiences that encompass the entire universe at a time. (Are you?) Perhaps my "up to me" experience amounts to nothing more than what I have already described. I need not also have, for example, the experience of its being causally undetermined what I am most inclined to do during the relevant time, or what I intend to do then, or what I do then. Nor need I have an experience of regarding things this way.

As it happened, I stayed here thinking for more than several minutes before I got a drink. While I stayed here, it seemed to me that it was up to me what I was doing, as it also did when I finally walked down the hall for a drink: neither my desire to continue working nor my desire, a bit later, to walk down the hall for a drink was irresistibly powerful, or so it seemed to me. If nothing more is required for an experience of acting freely, then I had an experience of acting freely. If I thought that acting freely required freedom from deterministic causation and that deterministic causation of my behavior is a much less remote possibility than, say, my being a brain in a vat, it would be easy to see how I might not take my experiences of acting freely to count for much, because my having those experiences is compatible with the truth of determinism. So incompatibilists whose experiences of acting freely run no deeper than mine and who take relevant deterministic hypotheses seriously understandably deem those experiences not to count for much as grounds for the belief that they do act freely. In this, experiences of acting freely differ markedly from experiences of acting intentionally—from an incompatibilist view, for a normal agent's experiences of the latter sort collectively do much to ground her belief that she sometimes acts intentionally.

Suppose, with Searle, that the experience of acting freely is very common. Some people also occasionally have the experience of acting *unfreely*—for instance, the experience of being psychologically compelled to do something—just as people occasionally (but more often) have the experience of doing something unintentionally.[16] We can seek insight into how intentional and unintentional actions differ by attending to differences in the relevant *experiences*: the experience of offending someone intentionally, for example, might differ in theoretically instructive ways from the experience of offending someone unintentionally. Similarly, a philosopher might hope to shed light on differences between *free* and *unfree* action by investigating experiential differences in that sphere. For example, the experience of being psychologically compelled to do something presumably is very unlike the experience of acting freely: the experiential difference might point to a deeper one.

A familiar compatibilist distinction between *compulsion* and *causation* merits attention in this connection.[17] Representative instances of compelled action, in this view, include a heroin addict's being moved to use the drug by an irresistible desire for heroin and a kleptomaniac's stealing a trinket owing to an uncontrollable urge. All actions, according to the view at issue, are caused, but most actions are considerably less dramatic than those just adduced. They include, for example, my typing this sentence, and your reading it. Some compatibilists have claimed that their opponents confuse caused with compelled action and that if they were to see the light on this issue they would abandon their incompatibilism. However, incompatibilists can grant the distinction and claim that the compulsion of action and the (deterministic) causation of action are each incompatible with free action—that noncompulsion does not go deep enough and that one acts freely only if it is up to one what one does in a sense of "up to one" that is incompatible not only with compulsion but also with determinism.[18]

Imagine a philosopher, Zed, who starts with the assumption that there is nothing more to acting freely or unfreely than the experience of so acting and eventually constructs an analysis of free action that is faithful to that assumption. Most philosophers would object to Zed's *starting* where he does, although some come to that point as a conclusion. Even so, they can ask how much deeper one would need to delve to construct an analysis that would satisfy them. On this issue, libertarians and compatibilist believers in human freedom are already in disagreement. The former require that a thesis of epic proportions—determinism—be false, whereas the latter can afford to be neutral on the truth of determinism. (Compatibilists can observe, for example, that there is no reason to think that quantum mechanical indeterminacy blocks human freedom, and they can add that, in their opinion, it does nothing to promote freedom either.) For some compatibilists, all that is required for an experience of acting freely to be veridical is that the agent acted intentionally and was not compelled so to act (in a standard sense of *compelled*). Some compatibilists demand more, but what leads them to the metaphysical depths, by and large, are incompatibilists' objections. Except in replying to incompatibilist opponents, compatibilist believers in human freedom generally do not seek metaphysical support for their view. However, a serious libertarian bent on showing that some human beings are free and on explaining what human freedom is would be committed not only to showing that determinism is false but also to explaining how (some of) what falsifies it promotes human freedom.

■ THE CONSEQUENCE ARGUMENT AND FRANKFURT'S STORY

■ The Consequence Argument Revisited

Return to the consequence argument: "If determinism is true, then our acts are the consequences of the laws of nature and events in the remote past. But it is not up to us what went on before we were born, and neither is it up to us what the laws of nature are. Therefore, the consequences of these things (including our present acts) are not up to us."[19] Notice that if the argument is supposed to show that none of our acts is free if determinism is true, it needs another premise, namely, (P) If our acts are not up to us, they are not free.

What does it mean to say that an action of mine was "up to me"? Is an action of mine up to me only if there is a possible world that (a) is *exactly* like the actual world in every detail up to the moment at which I performed that action, and (b) is governed by the same laws of nature as the actual world, and (c) is such that, in it, I perform another action instead. If so, then the fact that an action is up to me brings us face to face with the problem about dumb luck that I described earlier.

■ Frankfurt's Story

Might a person's stealing a car, for example, or his *deciding* to steal a car, be up to him, even though he could not have done otherwise than steal, or decide to steal, the car? Consider the following story, told by Harry Frankfurt:

Black . . . wants Jones to perform a certain action. Black is prepared to go to considerable lengths to get his way, but he prefers to avoid showing his hand unnecessarily. So he waits until Jones is about to make up his mind what to do, and he does nothing unless it is clear to him (Black is an excellent judge of such things) that Jones is going to decide to do something *other* than what he wants him to do. If it does become clear that Jones is going to decide to do something else, Black takes effective steps to ensure that Jones decides to do, and that he does do, what he wants him to do. Whatever Jones's initial preferences and inclinations, then, Black will have his way. . . . [However] Black never has to show his hand because Jones, for reasons of his own, decides to perform and does perform the very action Black wants him to perform.[20]

Suppose that what Jones decides to do in this example is to steal your car. Suppose also that Jones is a relatively normal person: for example, he is not a compulsive thief and is not supporting a bad drug habit. Given that Jones decides, "for reasons of his own," to steal your car, with no intervention on Black's part, you may believe that he is morally responsible for deciding to steal your car and that he freely decided to steal it. If you believe this, while agreeing with Frankfurt that Black's powers are such that Jones could not have done otherwise than decide to steal your car, then you do *not* hold that an agent freely decided to do something only if he could have decided to do something else instead. And you should ask yourself why you might think that determinism is incompatible with free decisions, even though you do not believe that an agent's freely deciding to do something requires that he could have decided to do something else instead. (We return to this question in the following section.)[21]

■ *Philosophical Options*

Now take a step back and consider the premise I added to the consequence argument: (P) If our acts are not up to us, they are not free. If you have the intuitions about Frankfurt's story that he wants you to have, and you want to be guided by them in your thinking, you face a philosophical choice. You can say that P is true and that Jones's decision was free and up to him (after all he decided on his own, with no interference from Black). Alternatively, you can say that P is false, that Jones's decision was not up to him (after all, he could not have decided to do something else instead), and that, despite this, his decision was free.

Considering a modified version of the consequence argument might help you think about your philosophical options:

If determinism is true, then our acts are the consequences of the laws of nature and events in the remote past. But we do not control what went on before we were born, and neither do we control what the laws of nature are. Therefore, we do not control our actions. But actions of ours that we do not control are not free. So, if determinism is true, we do not act freely.

This argument looks invalid. Some people claim that agents do not control anything if determinism is true. That claim is false. When Ann drives her truck (under normal conditions), she controls the turns it makes, even if her universe is deterministic. She obviously controls her truck's motions in a way that pedestrians and her passengers do not. For example, she turns the steering wheel and they do not. The same sort of thing is true of Ann's body. She turns the steering wheel to the left by rotating her hands to the left while holding the wheel. She controls what she is doing with her hands—she controls the action of hers at issue—in a way that her passengers and others do not. Ann does not control what went on before she was born, nor (according to a common view of natural laws) does she control what the laws of nature are. But if what I just said about Ann's behavior while she drives her truck is true, these truths about the past and the laws are consistent with Ann's controlling some of her actions.

Perhaps there is a comparable invalid inference in the consequence argument itself. Perhaps determinism is compatible with our actions being up to us in a way in which the past and the laws are not up to us, just as it is compatible with our controlling actions of ours in a way in which we do not control the past or the laws. What do you think? For a decision you made to have been up to you, is it enough that you made it rationally and were neither compelled to make it nor tricked into making it? Or is it required that, in another possible universe, under exactly the same conditions, you decide to do something else instead?

It can be said, of course, that if Ann's universe is deterministic, she lacks the *kind* of control she needs to act freely, even if she has whatever kind of control it is that is involved in her driving her truck. If that is said, it should be asked what kind of control is needed. To be free agents, do we need a kind of control that entails that we could have acted otherwise than we did? This brings us back to Frankfurt's thought experiment. If Jones freely decided to steal your car and freely stole it, even though he could not have done otherwise than decide to steal it and could not have done otherwise than steal it, then the answer is no.

Thought experiments like Frankfurt's pose a very interesting question for any libertarian who finds them persuasive. Again, libertarians claim that free will (and free action, including free decision) depends on determinism's being false. What traditional libertarians said bothered them about determinism is that it entails that we could never have acted otherwise than we did. But libertarians who are persuaded by a Frankfurt-style story grant, for example, that an agent can freely decide to steal a car even though he could not have done otherwise than decide to steal it. Such libertarians should tell us what bothers them *now* about determinism. They should tell us why determinism is incompatible with free will (and free decision, and free action in general) now that it has been granted that freedom does not require "could have acted otherwise." This is the topic of the following section.

ALTERNATIVE POSSIBILITIES AND ULTIMATE RESPONSIBILITY

Alternative Possibilities

Frankfurt-style stories have what John Fischer has called "flickers of freedom".[22] Incompatibilists maintain that an agent's being deterministically caused to decide to steal your car entails that he did not *freely* decide to steal it. So if Frankfurt-style stories are to persuade incompatibilists that agents can freely decide to steal a car, even though they could not have decided to do something else instead, indeterminism must be a feature of these stories. Even if this indeterminism does not provide such *robust* alternative possibilities as deciding not to steal your car, or deciding to steal my car rather than yours, it does provide alternative physically possible futures. Where there is indeterminism, something or other could have happened otherwise than it did. For example, it could have happened that, rather than Jones deciding *on his own* to steal your car, Black caused him to decide to steal it.

If some Frankfurt-style stories are convincing, libertarians need to tell us why agents who act freely in those stories cannot act freely in any deterministic universe. A salient difference between persuasive Frankfurt-style stories and deterministic scenarios is that the former alone include alternative possibilities, albeit only nonrobust or flickering ones. The libertarian faces the challenge of explaining the bearing of these possibilities on responsibility and freedom.

In principle, a libertarian's incompatibilism might be motivated, not by the thought that determinism precludes our ever having been able to act otherwise than we did, but instead by the thought that in a deterministic universe our actions (including our decisions) are ultimately causally ensured *consequences* of the laws of nature and states that obtained long before we were born. What troubles some incompatibilists about determinism might be what determinism implies about the *causation* of action rather than what it implies about robust alternative possibilities. The incompatibilist's consequence argument expresses this worry. Whatever the merits of this argument may be, the imagined persuasiveness of Frankfurt-style stories does not directly ensure that the argument is unsound. Philosophers who hold that determinism is inconsistent with our actions being up to us in a sense required for freedom might consistently hold on to that belief while granting the moral of Frankfurt-style stories. Their problem with determinism need not be that it precludes robust alternative possibilities. After all, there is a significant difference between characters like Black in Frankfurt's story and deterministic causes, even if both preclude robust alternative possibilities. The former play no role at all in *causing* the agent's choice, but in deterministic universes actions are deterministically caused.

Ultimate Responsibility

If our universe is deterministic, causally sufficient conditions for everything we do are present long before we are born. In a deterministic universe, agents and their actions ultimately are deterministic products of states of the universe in the distant past over which they had no control. These agents lack what Robert Kane calls "ultimate responsibility" for their actions, for they lack *"the power to make choices which can only and finally be explained in terms of their own wills* (i.e., character, motives and efforts of will)," a power that "no one can have . . . in a determined world."[23] In a deterministic universe, the "final" explanation, in Kane's sense, of any action of yours would lie in the distant past and the laws of nature. Persuasive Frankfurt-style stories challenge the libertarian to explain how nonrobust or flickering alternative possibilities contribute to ultimate responsibility and to defend the claim that ultimate responsibility is required for moral responsibility and free will.

What is important about ultimate responsibility? Although I am not an incompatibilist, I have developed a libertarian reply to this question elsewhere.[24] I will sketch part of that reply. Suppose someone were to tell you that she values having a kind of freedom that is not possible in a deterministic universe. She says that her life would have more meaning or importance for her if she were to discover that she has this kind of freedom than if she were to discover that she has only compatibilist freedom. She also reports that she values a certain kind of incompatibilist freedom as an essential ingredient of a life that, by her own standards, would be more meaningful or important than a comparable life in a deterministic universe.[25]

Wanting to hear more, you ask the woman, "Wilma, what bothers you about determinism?" She replies that although she believes the consequence argument to be unsound, her worry about determinism resembles the worry voiced there. Again, you would like to hear more, and Wilma happily obliges.

Wilma says that she is attracted to what I called "soft libertarianism" in an earlier essay.[26] A brief statement of that position is in order. Traditional libertarians are hard-core incompatibilists. They claim that free will (which they believe that at least some human beings have) is incompatible with determinism. I call them *hard* libertarians. A softer line is available to people who have libertarian sympathies. One may leave it open that freedom is compatible with determinism but maintain that the falsity of determinism is required for a *more desirable* kind of freedom. This is a *soft* libertarian line, the line Wilma finds attractive. Soft libertarians would be disappointed to discover that determinism is true, but they would not conclude that no one has free will and that no one has ever freely decided to steal a car or freely stolen one. The version of soft libertarianism that Wilma favors is relativistic: it maintains that at least some human agents have a kind of freedom that is incompatible with determinism and is reasonably preferred *by at least some of these agents* to any kind of freedom that is consistent with determinism.

Wilma reports that the thought of herself and her actions as links in a deterministic causal chain is somewhat deflating and that the truth of determinism is inconsistent with her life's being as important and meaningful as she hopes it is. The thought that she is an *indeterministic initiator* of at least some of her delib-

erative, intentional actions, however, coheres with the importance and significance she hopes her life has.[27] Asked to elaborate, Wilma observes that *independence* is among the things that some people value. Some people value
independence, in some measure, from other people and from institutions. Wilma
values, as well, a measure of independence from the *past*. She values, she says, a
kind of independent agency that includes the power to make a special kind of
explanatory contribution to some of her actions and to her world, contributions
that are not themselves ultimately causally determined products of the state of
the universe in the distant past. She values having an explanatory bearing on
her conduct that she would lack in any deterministic universe. She prizes indeterministic freedom as an essential part of a life that she regards as most desirable
for her. The kind of agency she hopes for, Wilma says, would render her
decisions and actions personally more meaningful from the perspective of her
own system of values than they would otherwise be. Although Wilma emphasizes
that this kind of agency is essential to the kind of meaningful life she prizes, she
reminds us that she is not claiming that it is required for freedom. Wilma is not
a traditional incompatibilist, but she does hold that determinism is incompatible
with the satisfaction of some of her deepest life hopes. Her satisfying those hopes
requires that she have *ultimate* responsibility for some of her actions.

Wilma's concern is with independence as manifested in decisions and other
actions. She acknowledges that she values compatibilist independence, but she
reports that she values indeterministic independence more highly—provided that
it does not place her at the mercy of *luck*. Wilma is trying to understand why
some people might not share her preference for libertarian independence over a
compatibilist counterpart. She is keeping an open mind, and she urges us to do
the same. Wilma hopes that we can understand why, other things being equal,
she would deem her life more important or meaningful if she were to discover
that determinism is false than if she were to discover that it is true.[28]

■ A LIBERTARIAN RESPONSE TO LUCK

I mentioned Wilma's worry that luck might stand in the way of the kind of
freedom she values most. The luck that is problematic in the case of van Inwagen's
thief lies within the thief. He arguably lacks a kind of control over his decisions
that is required for his being morally responsible for the decision he makes and
required for his having the kind of freedom on which moral responsibility
depends. Call the sort of luck featured in this scenario "present luck." Compatibilists appeal to luck of this kind in criticizing libertarianism.

Another kind of luck may also be relevant to moral responsibility and
freedom. Wilma alludes to a kind of luck in attempting to explain why the falsity
of determinism matters to her. Again, if Wilma's universe is deterministic, then
causally sufficient conditions for everything she does are present long before she
is born. Ultimately, she and her actions are deterministic products of states of the
universe in the distant past over which she had no control. One can say that the

sphere of luck (i.e., good or bad luck) for a person is the sphere of things having the following two features: the person lacks complete control over them; even so, they affect his or her life. No human being has any control at all over states of the universe in the distant past, and if Wilma's universe is deterministic, then such states ultimately have the impact on her just mentioned. The luck now at issue may be termed "ultimate luck." Incompatibilists appeal to this sort of luck in criticizing compatibilism. How, incompatibilists want to know, can Wilma be morally responsible for an action of hers, or perform that action freely, if, relative to her own powers of control, it is just a matter of luck that, long before her birth, her universe was such as to ensure that she would perform that action at that time?

Is it possible for there to be a kind of agent whose prospects for freedom are not undermined by either kind of luck, present or ultimate? Can an agent have causally open futures in a way that is conducive to freedom without being a victim of the kind of luck that seems to plague van Inwagen's thief? What might such an agent be like?

Consider the following scenario. On the basis of careful, rational deliberation, Al judges that it would be best to attend a certain meeting, and on the basis of that judgment, he decides to attend that meeting and then acts accordingly. Al has not been subjected to freedom-thwarting mind control or relevant deception, he is sane, and so on. To make a long story short, suppose that Al satisfies an attractive set of sufficient conditions for *compatibilist* freedom regarding his decision and subsequent action.[29] Here is one more detail: while Al was deliberating, it was not causally determined that he would come to the conclusion he did.

In principle, an agent-internal indeterminism may provide for indeterministic agency while blocking or limiting our "nonultimate" control only at junctures at which we have no greater control on the hypothesis that our universe is deterministic.[30] Let me explain. Ordinary people have a great many beliefs, desires, hypotheses, and the like, the great majority of which are not salient in consciousness during any given process of deliberation. When we act on the basis of careful deliberation, what we do is influenced by at least some of the considerations that "come to mind"—that is, become salient in consciousness—during deliberation and by our assessments of considerations. Now, even if determinism is true, it is false that, with respect to *every* consideration—every belief, desire, hypothesis, and so on—that comes to mind during our deliberation, we are in control of its coming to mind, and some considerations that come to mind without our being in control of their so doing may influence the outcome of our deliberation. Furthermore, a kind of internal indeterminism is imaginable that limits our control only in a way that gives us no less nonultimate control than we would have on the assumption that determinism is true, while opening up alternative deliberative outcomes. (Although, in a deterministic universe, it is never a matter of genuine chance that a certain consideration came to mind during deliberation, it may still be a matter of luck relative to the agent's sphere of control.) As

I put it elsewhere, "Where compatibilists have no good reason to insist on determinism in the deliberative process as a requirement for autonomy [or freedom], where internal indeterminism is, for all we know, a reality, and where such indeterminism would not diminish the nonultimate control that real agents exert over their deliberation even on the assumption that real agents are internally deterministic—that is, at the *intersection* of these three locations—libertarians may plump for ultimacy-promoting indeterminism."[31]

The modest indeterminism at issue allows agents ample control over their deliberation. Suppose a belief, hypothesis, or desire that is relevant to a deliberator's present practical question comes to mind during deliberation, but was not deterministically caused to do so (perhaps unlike the great majority of considerations that come to mind during this process of deliberation).[32] Presumably, a normal agent would be able to *assess* this consideration, and upon reflection, she might rationally reject the belief as unwarranted, rationally judge that the hypothesis does not merit investigation, or rationally decide that the desire should be given little or no weight in her deliberation. Alternatively, reflection might rationally lead her to retain the belief, to pursue the hypothesis, or to give the desire significant weight. That a consideration comes to mind indeterministically does not entail that the agent has no control over how she responds to it.

Considerations that indeterministically come to mind (like considerations that are deterministically caused to come to mind) are nothing more than input to deliberation. Their coming to mind has at most an indirect effect on what the agent decides, an effect mediated by the agent's own assessment of them. They do not settle matters. Moreover, not only do agents have the opportunity to assess these considerations, they also have the opportunity to search for additional relevant considerations before they decide, thereby increasing the probability that other relevant considerations will indeterministically come to mind. They have the opportunity to cancel or attenuate the effects of bad luck (e.g., the undetermined coming to mind of a misleading consideration or an undetermined failure to notice a relevant consideration), and given a suitable indeterminism regarding what comes to mind in an assessment process, it is not causally determined what assessment the agent will reach.

Compatibilists who hold that we act freely even when we are not in control of what happens at certain specific junctures in the process leading to action are in no position to hold that an indeterministic agent's lacking control at the same junctures precludes free action. And, again, real human beings are not in control of the coming to mind of everything that comes to mind during typical processes of deliberation. If this lack of perfect nonultimate control does not preclude its being the case that free actions sometimes issue from typical deliberation on the assumption that we are deterministic agents, it also does not preclude this on the assumption that we are *indeterministic* agents.

Is a modest indeterminism of the kind I have described useful to libertarians? Libertarians should feel at least some attraction to agents who suffer from neither of the alleged problems about luck that I have discussed—the problems of ultimate luck and of present luck. I asked what such agents might be like, and perhaps I have succeeded in describing such an agent. Agents of the sort I have imagined have causally open alternative futures the entire time they are deliberating, because, at any point in deliberation, a consideration that has some influence on their reasoning and subsequent judgment may indeterministically come to mind. They are not at the mercy of what I have called ultimate luck. Moreover, these agents are not at the mercy of these undetermined events, because they are able to evaluate the considerations that come to mind and react rationally to them. (Notice that their evaluations themselves may be influenced by considerations that indeterministically come to mind, which further considerations are open to evaluation.)

I have suggested that what at least some libertarians might prize that compatibilist freedom does not offer them is a species of agency that gives them a kind of independence and an associated kind of explanatory bearing on their conduct that they would lack in any deterministic universe. The combination of the satisfaction of an attractive set of sufficient conditions for *compatibilist* freedom, including all the nonultimate control that involves, and a modest agent-internal indeterminism of the sort I have described would give them that. Agents of the imagined sort would make choices and perform actions that lack deterministic causes in the distant past. They would have no less control over these choices and actions than we do over ours, on the supposition that we are deterministic agents. And given that they have at least robust *compatibilist* responsibility for certain of these choices and actions, they would also have *ultimate* responsibility for them. These choices and actions have, in Kane's words, "their ultimate sources" in the agents, in the sense that the collection of agent-internal states and events that explains these choices and actions does not itself admit of a deterministic explanation that stretches back beyond the agent.[33]

Even if compatibilists can be led to see that the problem of luck is surmountable by a libertarian, how are theorists of other kinds likely to respond to the libertarian position that I have been sketching? Some philosophers contend that moral responsibility and freedom are illusions and that these things are absent from our universe whether it is deterministic or indeterministic.[34] Elsewhere, I have argued that the impossible demands this position places on moral responsibility and freedom are unwarranted.[35] But this is a matter about which readers must make up their own minds.

Soft libertarians like Wilma can also anticipate trouble from traditional libertarians, who want more than the modest indeterminism that I have described can offer. It is incumbent on traditional libertarians to show that what they want is coherent. That requires showing that what they want does not entail or presuppose a kind of luck that would itself undermine freedom and moral responsibility. The traditional libertarian wants both indeterminism and significant control at the moment of decision. This is the desire that prompts a serious version of the worry about luck that I sketched early in this chapter.[36]

■ CONCLUSION: AGNOSTIC AUTONOMISM

Must one choose between compatibilism and incompatibilism? No. One can be agnostic about this; one can sit on the fence. In *Autonomous Agents*, I defended "agnostic autonomism," the combination of the agnosticism just identified and the belief that at least some human beings sometimes act freely. This position can draw on the resources both of compatibilism and of libertarianism, since it does not choose between them. Agnostics do not insist that freedom is compatible with determinism, nor do they insist that we are internally indeterministic in a way useful to libertarians. And if it were discovered that we are not suitably indeterministic, they would have compatibilism to fall back on.

I argued in *Autonomous Agents*, and still believe, that agnostic autonomism is more credible than the thesis that no human being acts freely (nonautonomism). Consider the following propositions:

 a. Some human beings act freely, and determinism is compatible with free action (compatibilist belief in free action).
 b. Some human beings act freely, and determinism is incompatible with free action (libertarianism).
 c. Either *a* or *b* (agnostic autonomism).
 d. No human beings act freely (nonautonomism).

Imagine that each proposition has a probability between 0 and 1. Then *c* has a higher probability than *a* and a higher probability than *b*, since *c* is the *disjunction* of *a* and *b* (that is, *c* is "*a or b*").[37] So what about *d*? In *Autonomous Agents* (ch. 13), I argued that nonautonomism, at best, fares no better than *a* and no better than *b*. If that is right, then since *c* has a higher probability than each of *a* and *b*, *c* has a higher probability than *d*: agnostic autonomism beats nonautonomism! That is good news for autonomists of all stripes—compatibilist, hard and soft libertarian, and agnostic. Of course, the news derives from my assessment, in that book, of the merits of *a*, *b*, and *d*, and you might disagree. In any case, the future is likely to bring more powerful arguments for each of those positions and more fully developed compatibilist and libertarian views. As this happens, there will be new material to assess in making a judgment about the relative merits of compatibilist belief in free action and libertarianism, on the one hand, and the view that there is no free will, on the other. This will be exciting philosophical work. Perhaps some of you will contribute to it one day.[38]

■ NOTES

1. Peter van Inwagen, *An Essay on Free Will* (Oxford: Clarendon Press, 1983), 3.
2. Alfred Mele, *Autonomous Agents* (New York: Oxford University Press, 1995).
3. Peter van Inwagen, *An Essay on Free Will*, 16.
4. Peter van Inwagen, *An Essay on Free Will*, 136.
5. Peter van Inwagen, *An Essay on Free Will*, 141.

6. Peter van Inwagen, *An Essay on Free Will*, 140–41.

7. Peter van Inwagen, *An Essay on Free Will*, 141.

8. Peter van Inwagen, *An Essay on Free Will*, 141.

9. Timothy O'Connor, "Indeterminism and Free Agency: Three Recent Views," *Philosophy and Phenomenological Research* (1993) 53: 499–526.

10. Naturally, libertarians find fault with alternative libertarian positions. For example, in *Persons and Causes* (New York: Oxford University Press, 2000), Timothy O'Connor offers detailed criticism of non–agent-causal libertarian views, and in "Free Will Remains a Mystery," *Philosophical Perspectives* (2000) 14: 1–19, Peter van Inwagen argues that "even if agent causation is a coherent concept and a real phenomenon, and we know this, this piece of knowledge will be of no help to the philosopher who is trying to decide what to say about free will" (11).

11. John Searle, *Minds, Brains, and Science* (Cambridge: Harvard University Press, 1984), 96.

12. John Searle, *Minds, Brains, and Science*, 95.

13. John Searle, *Minds, Brains, and Science*, 97.

14. Benedict Spinoza, Letter to G. H. Schaller (1674), in Robert Elwes, trans., *On the Improvement of the Understanding; The Ethics; Correspondence* (New York: Dover, 1955), 390.

15. Correctly, because, for example, a person executing a posthypnotic suggestion to open a window opens the window intentionally but does not open it freely, and a kleptomaniac intentionally steals a trinket but (assuming a common view) does not freely steal it.

16. Searle [*Minds, Brains, and Science*, 96] writes: "If . . . I am instructed to walk across the room at gunpoint, still part of the experience is that I sense that it is literally open to me at any step to do something else. The experience of freedom is thus an essential component of any case of acting with an intention." Supposing that his claim about acting at gunpoint is correct, such cases differ from those in which, say, heroin addicts experience themselves as being *compelled* to use the drug by their craving and as literally having open to them, in the circumstances, no alternative to using the drug. They act with the intention of using the drug in these cases, but they do not have "the experience of freedom," in Searle's sense. This is not to say, of course, that all heroin addicts are like this. Some might "sense," even in the grip of a craving and in the presence of heroin, that it is "literally open" to them to refrain from using the drug.

17. See, e.g., Robert Audi, *Action, Intention, and Reason* (Ithaca, N.Y.: Cornell University Press, 1993), chs. 7 and 10; A. J. Ayer, "Freedom and Necessity," in his *Philosophical Essays* (London: Macmillan, 1954); Adolph Grünbaum, "Free Will and the Laws of Human Behavior," *American Philosophical Quarterly* 8 (1971): 299–317; John Stuart Mill, *An Examination of Sir William Hamilton's Philosophy*, John Robson, ed. (Toronto: Routledge and Kegan Paul, 1979), ch. 26, esp. 464–67; and Moritz Schlick, *Problems of Ethics*, David Rynin, trans. (New York: Dover, 1982), ch. 7. Also see David Hume's (1711–1776) remarks on the liberty of spontaneity versus the liberty of indifference in *A Treatise of Human Nature* (1739), reprinted in Lewis Selby-Bigge, ed., *A Treatise of Human Nature* (Oxford: Clarendon Press, 1975), bk. II, pt. III, sec. 2.

18. Cf. Peter van Inwagen, *An Essay on Free Will*, 17.

19. Peter van Inwagen, *An Essay on Free Will*, 16.

20. Harry Frankfurt, "Alternate Possibilities and Moral Responsibility," *Journal of Philosophy* 66 (1969), 835–36.

21. Whether any Frankfurt-style stories are persuasive is a matter of some controversy. For discussion, see Alfred Mele and David Robb, "Rescuing Frankfurt-Style Cases," *Philosophical Review* 107 (1998): 97–112; and "BBs, Magnets and Seesaws: The Metaphysics of Frankfurt-Style Cases," in M. McKenna and D. Widerker, eds., *Freedom, Responsibility, and Agency* (Burlington, Vt.: Ashgate, N.d.).

22. John Fischer, *The Metaphysics of Free Will* (Cambridge, Mass.: Blackwell, 1994), ch. 7.

23. Robert Kane, "Two Kinds of Incompatibilism," *Philosophy and Phenomenological Research* 50 (1989), 254; Kane's italics.

24. See Alfred Mele, "Soft Libertarianism and Frankfurt-Style Scenarios," *Philosophical Topics* 24 (1996): 123–41, and Alfred Mele, "Ultimate Responsibility and Dumb Luck," *Social Philosophy and Policy* 16 (1999): 274–93. I am officially agnostic about the main metaphysical issue that separates compatibilists from incompatibilists (see *Autonomous Agents*).

25. Cf. Robert Kane, *Free Will and Values* (Albany: State University of New York Press, 1985), 178: "what determinism takes away is a certain sense of the importance of oneself as an individual. If I am ultimately responsible for certain occurrences in the universe, . . . then my choices and my life take on an importance that is missing if I do not have such responsibility." Cf. Robert Nozick, *Philosophical Explanations* (Cambridge: Harvard University Press, 1981), 310–16.

26. Alfred Mele, "Soft Libertarianism and Frankfurt-Style Scenarios."

27. Kane contends that "the desire to be independent sources of activity in the world, which is connected . . . to the sense we have of our uniqueness and importance as individuals," is an "elemental" libertarian desire (Robert Kane, *The Significance of Free Will* (New York: Oxford University Press, 1996), 98; cf. Nozick, *Philosophical Explanations*, 310–16). I am following his lead.

28. To be sure, Wilma may never know whether she has or lacks the agency she prizes, but that does not undermine her preferences. I hope that I will never know how my children's lives turned out (for then their lives would have been cut too short), but I greatly value their turning out well. There is nothing irrational in this, nor need there be anything irrational in Wilma's prizing her having a kind of agency that she can never know she has.

29. I offer sufficient compatibilist conditions for freedom in *Autonomous Agents*, chs. 9 and 10. See 187 and 193 for a summary.

30. For roughly this idea, see Daniel Dennett, *Brainstorms* (Montgomery, Vt. Bradford Books, 1978), 294–99; Laura Ekstrom, *Free Will* (Boulder, Colo.: Westview Press, 2000), 103–29; John Fischer, "Libertarianism and Avoidability: A Reply to Widerker," *Faith and Philosophy* 12 (1995): 119–25; Robert Kane, *Free Will and Values*, 101–10; and Alfred Mele, *Autonomous Agents*, ch. 12.

31. Alfred Mele, *Autonomous Agents*, 235.

32. Regarding the parenthetical clause, bear in mind that not all deterministically caused events need be part of a deterministic chain that stretches back even for several moments, much less close to the Big Bang.

33. Robert Kane, *The Significance of Free Will*, 98.

34. See, e.g., Richard Double, *The Non-Reality of Free Will* (New York: Oxford University Press, 1991), and Galen Strawson, *Freedom and Belief* (Oxford: Clarendon Press, 1986).

35. Alfred Mele, *Autonomous Agents*, chs. 12 and 13.

36. Randolph Clarke recently developed a modest libertarian proposal, the general thrust of which, like that of the modest libertarianism I articulated in *Autonomous Agents* and sketched in this section, may be combined with soft libertarianism. See his "Modest Libertarianism," *Philosophical Perspectives* 14 (2000): 21–45.

37. This is not to say that every disjunction of propositions with probabilities between 0 and 1 has a higher probability than each of the disjuncts. Consider the disjunction "*p* or *p*." My claim is about the propositions at issue here.

38. Parts of this essay derive from my *Autonomous Agents*; "Soft Libertarianism and Frankfurt-Style Scenarios"; "Ultimate Responsibility and Dumb Luck," *Social Philosophy and Policy* 16 (1999): 274–93; and "Autonomy, Self-Control, and Weakness of Will," in Robert Kane, ed., *The Free-Will Handbook* (New York: Oxford University Press, N.d.).

■ QUESTIONS

1. If the indeterministic bomb in Ish's room does not contribute to his having free will, why not?
2. Is the thief's deciding to refrain from stealing in van Inwagen's scenario a matter of dumb luck? Do you think that this thief is morally responsible for his decision?
3. Is libertarianism undone by the problem of "dumb luck"?
4. Is compatibilism undermined by "the consequence argument"?
5. What would convince you that there is a significant chance that all of your experiences of performing ordinary intentional bodily actions are nonveridical?
6. Can freedom from deterministic causation be experienced?
7. Does "each thing we do [carry] the conviction, valid or invalid, that we could be doing something else right here and now, . . . all other conditions remaining the same"?
8. The author says that he is "not a very deep person experientially . . . not the sort of person who has experiences that encompass the entire universe at a time." Do you have "the experience of openness" that he says he lacks?
9. Might a person's deciding to steal a car be up to him, even though he could not have done otherwise than decide to steal it? For a decision you made to have been up to you, is it enough that you made it rationally and were neither compelled to make it nor tricked into making it? Or is it required that, in another possible universe, under exactly the same conditions, you decide to do something else instead? What is the bearing of Frankfurt's story on these questions?
10. Is determinism compatible with our actions being up to us in a way in which the past and the laws are not up to us?
11. What does Robert Kane mean by "ultimate responsibility"?
12. Wilma says that her life would have more meaning for her if she were to discover that she has a certain kind of freedom than if she were to discover that she has only compatibilist freedom. What kind of freedom does she value most? Why is it important to her? Do you share her attitudes about this kind of freedom?
13. What is the difference between "hard" and "soft" libertarianism?
14. Can a person be morally responsible for an action of hers, or perform that action freely, if, relative to her own powers of control, it is just a matter of luck that, long before her birth, her universe was such as to ensure that she would perform that action at that time?

15. What does the author mean by "modest indeterminism"?
16. How, according to the author, does the kind of agent he describes toward the end of the chapter avoid the problems of ultimate and present luck? Is the author right about this?
17. How might someone argue for the view that free will is an illusion?
18. What does the author mean by "agnostic autonomism"?

■ *FOR FURTHER READING*

Dennett, Daniel. 1984. *Elbow Room*. Cambridge, Mass.: MIT Press.

Fischer, John. 1994. *The Metaphysics of Free Will*. Cambridge, Mass.: Blackwell.

Frankfurt, Harry. 1971. "Freedom of the Will and the Concept of a Person." *Journal of Philosophy* 68:5–20.

Kane, Robert. 1996. *The Significance of Free Will*. New York: Oxford University Press.

———. 2002. *The Free-Will Handbook*. New York: Oxford University Press.

O'Connor, Timothy. 2000. *Persons and Causes*. New York: Oxford University Press.

Strawson, Galen. 1986. *Freedom and Belief*. Oxford: Clarendon Press.

Strawson, P. F. 1982. "Freedom and Resentment." *In* Gary Watson, ed., *Free Will*. Oxford: Oxford University Press.

Van Inwagen, Peter. 1983. *An Essay on Free Will*. Oxford: Clarendon Press.

■ CHAPTER FIVE

Epistemology

FREDERICK ADAMS

■ INTRODUCTION

Epistemology derives from the Greek *episteme* (knowledge) and *logos* (account or reason). The study of **epistemology** is the attempt to give an account of the source and nature of knowledge. I would like to tell you about the extent and limits of all human knowledge, but that is a far larger topic than we can approach here. Our discussions are a bit limited in scope. Indeed, we shall only scratch the surface of the study of what knowledge is, and, in particular, we will limit our discussion to what might be called empirical knowledge. Empirical knowledge is the kind that is known by using the senses or scientific instruments or gauges or experimentation. What is the speed of sound? Who was the tenth U.S. president? What songs are sung by the Red-Winged Blackbird? Answers to these questions are the type that can be known empirically. Whereas, why is there no limit to the decimal expansion of *pi*? Why is $12^3 = 1728$? Is it necessarily true that everything is identical with itself? Following a long and established tradition, let's say that these things are known by reason, not by sensory observation. We will call this nonempirical knowledge and will have no more to say here about what grounds our knowledge of mathematical, logical, or other nonempirical knowledge.[1]

In this chapter we will confine our attention not only to empirical knowledge, but to one theory of empirical knowledge known as **reliablism**. This is not because there are not other theories. There are. Rather, it is for the following reasons. First, I happen to think that reliablism has the best chance of being the correct theory of empirical knowledge. Second, this will give us the opportunity to go into significant depth on a single theory so that you will have a very good idea of what the theory says. And third, it is part of the overall aim of this book to present and defend views that authors actually accept. I hope that what we lose in breadth (by not looking at a range of theories) we will gain in depth (by seeing how someone who actually believes that a theory is right goes about trying to defend it against some of the main objections brought against it).

Empirical knowledge is a highly prized commodity. Secret agents around the world kill to get it. Scientists spend billions of dollars trying to find a cure for cancer or to sequence the human genome. If you knew the winning numbers on the next Powerball lottery, you could become rich and maybe famous by purchasing a ticket with those numbers. And we would all like to know many things that we do not now know. Is there life on other planets? Will computers someday actually be able to think?

Of course there are many things that we do know. We know enough physics, engineering, and computer science to send people to the moon and return them safely to Earth. The knowledge that your instructors impart to you in four years at your college or university is but a small fraction of what is known. Indeed, the quantity of knowledge is growing at exponential rates. Science, medicine, and all academic pursuits of knowledge have been paying high levels of return—in many cases faster than we can fully absorb. Pick up any volume of an encyclopedia or professional journal in the library and you will have a partial list of the many things that we now know.

What you won't find in an encyclopedia (except in the *Encyclopedia of Philosophy*) is an answer to the central question of epistemology: "What is it for a person to know something?" The job of answering this question falls to the philosopher. It does not merely ask such things as whether Tom *knows* that Joe uses drugs (or does not use them). More important, it asks *what is required for Tom (or anyone) to know this?* For example, how accurate must a drug test be to give knowledge that someone testing "positive" actually uses drugs—85 percent accurate? 95 percent accurate? The answer can be reached only by examining the very processes and *criteria* of knowing, not merely the kinds of things known. To ask such questions is to turn the pursuit of knowledge inward on itself. What have we said when we say that someone knows something? This is the sort of inquiry that philosophy, the parent discipline of epistemology, is all about—examining the foundations of knowledge. Fundamental epistemology asks what knowledge is, not unlike fundamental chemistry asks what water is. We knew that water was around long before we knew that it was H_2O. Similarly, we have a lot of knowledge long before we know what knowledge is.

■ Uses of the Word Know

A useful beginning to discovering what knowledge is involves distinguishing the kinds of things that a person S may be said to know. (1) S may be said to know *a thing x* (Tiger knows golf, Ken knows Gary, Bill Gates knows computers). (2) S may be said to know *how to do something y* (Colleen knows how to count in German, Howard knows how to fly a plane, Pam knows how to balance the accounts). Or (3) S may be said to know *that p*—that a sentence or statement is true (Paul knows that the human brain has roughly 100 billion neurons, Andrew knows that Fermat's last theorem has now been proved, Albert knows that $E = MC^2$).

Consider knowing things. It is common to say that we know some *place*, such as Chicago; or that we know a *person*, Ken; or even a *language*, Spanish. Consider knowing *how*. We say things, such as *I know how to speak French*, or *Jean knows how to program in BASIC*, or *David knows how to get to John's house*. Consider knowing *that*. Scientists talk about whether (or not) we know *that there is life on other planets*. Students say that they know *that calculus is harder than geography*. In each of these cases, it may seem that because we are using the same word *know*, we must be saying the *same thing* in saying that people know these things. This is not obviously the case, however, as we shall see.

Consider knowing things, once again. A good case can be made that knowing *things* can be resolved into knowing *that* and/or knowing *how*. On the one hand, when we say that Gary knows Chicago, we may mean that he knows how to get around in Chicago when walking or driving. He can find Soldier Field, the Field Museum, the Shedd Aquarium, the Goodman Theatre, and his favorite restaurants. As it may happen, Gary's knowledge of Chicago might be his general *skill* at getting to and around town with very little detailed *propositional* knowledge of the town. For example, Gary may be poor at giving directions in Chicago. On the other hand, Gary's knowledge of Chicago may be propositional; that is, Gary's head may be filled with facts about Chicago. He may know that the best way to get downtown is to approach from Lake Superior Drive to Michigan Avenue. He may know that the Palmer House is on the corner of State and Monroe. He may know that the Memories of China restaurant has excellent food and is located at 1050 North State Street. Furthermore, Gary's knowledge of facts about Chicago may extend on and on. Most likely, Gary's knowledge of Chicago will consist of a little of each, knowing how and knowing that. This tends to show that knowing things is *not* a separate kind or category of knowledge different from the other two. Similar things can be said about resolving knowledge of persons (Ken), or language (Spanish) into knowing how or knowing that, and so on. This leaves us, however, with *two* kinds of knowledge or uses of the word *know*, and it is not clear how they could be further resolved into one.

Having skills (knowing how) seems quite different from knowing propositions to be true (knowing that). Skills are things such as knowing how to ride a bicycle or knowing how to articulate the word *epistemology*. *Knowing that*, however, may involve detailed propositions about the forces exerted on the person riding a bicycle or on the muscles in the face, throat, and mouth that are involved in articulating words. Even when we come to know the detailed propositions about these complex activities, if we were to concentrate too heavily on them, we probably could not ride or talk at all. To ride or talk smoothly, we must concentrate on where we want to go and on what we want to say, not on the theories that explain how we do what we do or the precise details of muscle movement. When you ride a bicycle, you probably cannot say which kind of forces your body is compensating for at any given time. But your body is doing this, if you have not fallen off. When you say *e, pis, te, mol, o, gy* in the act of articulating the title of this essay, you probably have no idea of the position of your tongue. Is it flat, raised, against the teeth, away from the teeth? But you do know how to make these sounds. Thus, knowing how seems irreducibly distinct from knowing that. It is not that there are no propositions that, when known, will explain how we do the things we know how to do (that explain our skills). Rather, it is that in acquiring these skills, we do not have to concentrate on these theories or descriptions of how we are able to do them.

■ THE ANALYSIS OF KNOWING THAT

■ *Knowledge and Truth*

We shall focus primarily on *knowing that*. One reason *knowing that* is highly prized is that it is a kind of knowledge that links us with the world (reality). When we know that something is the case, we know that some proposition (sentence, statement, hypothesis, or theory) is *true*.[2] Because propositions are about reality, if we know that they are true we know something about reality. It seems, therefore, that for a person S to know *that p*, where *p* stands for some proposition, the proposition known must be true. *We cannot know what is false*, but we can know *that proposition p is false*. For example, we can know *that it is false that the Earth is flat*. But if *p* is false, we cannot *know that p*. We cannot know *that the Earth is flat*. We can believe it, but not know it.

We can, I suppose, imagine someone protesting that "I just knew the 76'ers would win that basketball game on Tuesday," when in fact they did not go on to win. This type of statement does not really show that we can know false things. It shows instead that we sometimes *say* things like this when we *mean* only, "I really believed that the 76'ers were going to win the game on Tuesday" or "I was just sure that they would win." The problem, of course, is that the strong belief or high confidence *alone* does not ensure truth or knowledge. We have all had experiences where our memories have played tricks on us. We were just sure that we left our keys somewhere, only to find them somewhere else.

If you are not already convinced that knowing *that p* requires the truth of *p*, imagine the oddity of saying to the ticket taker at the racetrack, "I know that Tag-a-long won in the fifth race," when it is false that Tag-a-long won. You may stand there until the track empties, but the ticket taker will not pay off on your ticket if it is false that Tag-a-long won in the fifth (Gumshoe did). She will insist, rightly, that you may *believe* that Tag-a-long won, but you do not *know* this, because it is *false*.

We have, then, an important ingredient of knowledge—*truth*. Truth seems to be a matter of correspondence with reality.[3] A statement is true if, and only if, it corresponds with reality, with the facts. "Tag-a-long won in the fifth" is true if, and only if, Tag-a-long *did win* in the fifth. It is false if he did not (Gumshoe won). Therefore, S knows that *p* (for some person S and some proposition *p*) only if it is *true that p*. What other conditions (ingredients) go into *knowing that*?

■ *Knowledge and Belief*

A strong case can be made for claiming that *belief* is a necessary condition of knowing *that p*.[4] To begin to see this, consider that knowledge is always *of* or *about* something. If we think of knowledge as a relation between a person and the world—the way marriage is a relation between a person and another person—we can ask what relates a person epistemically to the world? What must happen to bring a person into the knowledge relation with reality (to make the person's knowledge *of* reality)? When one enters into a marital relation with another person, there is usually a member of the clergy and a ceremony that includes the exchanging of vows and rings. Each married person acquires a ring, let us say, and its acquisition symbolizes one's entering into the relation of marriage with one's spouse. What happens to place a person into the relation of knowledge with reality? There are no knowledge vows, or ceremonies, or rings to symbolize that one has knowledge.

Still, something very important *does change* when one acquires knowledge that something is the case. When Sue comes to know *that she is pregnant*, she acquires a *belief* that she did not have previously. In her mind is a representation (*a thought*) of the world and her condition that was not there before. She may have wondered whether she was pregnant before, but she did not actually *think that* she was. Therefore, at least one of the things that is necessary for Sue to enter the knowledge relation with the truth that she is pregnant is for her to have the *thought or belief that* she is pregnant. Thoughts or beliefs are Sue's way of representing the world—her ways of picturing the world or cognitively relating to the world. It is then fairly clear that one could not know that something was true if one had no thoughts at all about that thing. Sue could not know that she was pregnant if she had no thoughts about being pregnant—no beliefs about it one way or the other. It is equally clear that one could not know that something was the case if one believed the opposite. If Tom believes that Nixon *did not* resign from office, Tom certainly does not *know* that Nixon *did* resign. For these reasons, we can add *belief* and *truth* to our list of things necessary for S *to know that p*.

As before, we can find cases where Tom may say, "I don't believe I'm hungry, I *know* I'm hungry!" But this does not show that belief is not required for knowledge. First, when Tom knows that he is hungry, Tom *does* believe that he is hungry. Tom must have some way of representing his hunger to himself, and belief is the usual way. Second, when Tom says "I don't believe that *p*, I know that *p*," this is an elliptical or shorthand way of saying "I don't *merely* believe that I'm hungry, I'm positive that I'm hungry"—or something to that effect. Again, Tom's choice of wording does not show that belief is not necessary for knowledge. It is mainly for emphasis to contrast with cases where we *tend* to believe something is the case, but are not sure or not confident, such as "I'm not sure I'm going to the concert, but I believe that I am going."

■ *Knowledge and Reliable Evidence*

Our list of conditions that must be satisfied for one to know that something is the case now looks like this:

S knows *that p* only if:

1. *p* is true.
2. S believes that *p*.

Is that it? Are we done? We now have good reasons to think that these are necessary conditions for knowing (one could not know that *p* without satisfying these conditions), but are they *sufficient*? That is, if met, are they enough to allow one to know?[5] A **necessary condition** A for something else B is that without A, B would not obtain. Without water (A) there would not be life (B). It is necessary to be admitted to your institution (A) to obtain a degree (B). Admission is not sufficient for the degree, of course. A **sufficient condition** X for something Y is that X can ensure Y by X's occurrence. Thus, receiving a grade of B+ (X) in this course is sufficient for passing the course (Y). Of course, it is not required. Many other grades, A, B−, C+, would do.

It is fairly easy to show that conditions 1 and 2 are *not sufficient* for knowledge. Suppose that I now believe that there is life on planets other than Earth. Suppose further that *there is* life on other planets. Then both of our conditions are satisfied. Let *p* be the proposition that there is life on other planets. Then *p* is true and I believe that *p*. But it can be made pretty clear that I do *not know* that *p*. I have had no contact with extraterrestrial life forms. I have no radio transmissions from outer space that I have decoded. No missions to space have brought back any evidence of life, and so on and so forth. Nor do I have any other evidence to support or justify my belief that *p*. Indeed, I have *no evidence* at all for the truth of *p*. I might just as well have flipped a coin. Heads, I believe that *p*; tails, I believe not *p*. If the coin comes up heads I have a true belief, but it is *just dumb luck*. It could have come up tails—my belief would have been false, and I would have been none the wiser about the truth or falsity of my belief (or about the existence or nonexistence of life). The coin is *no guide to the truth of p*. It does not reliably indicate the presence of life on other planets and therefore cannot give me knowledge, nor can my just guessing.

Consider another example.[6] You are walking in the park one day and see what you take to be fresh deer tracks on the ground. On the basis of this, you come to believe that *p* (*p* = a deer went through here). Suppose that *p* is true—a deer did go through the park—and you now believe that *p*. Do you know that *p*? If you say "yes," let me fill in the rest of the story. Your walk in the park is in November, during deer hunting season. My friend Al is a fanatical animal lover and antihunter who hates for deer to be killed during hunting season. Each November Al trots out his very effective fake deer track maker that he has perfected over the years. Al's device makes fake tracks that are visually indistinguishable from real deer tracks, and Al has made fake deer tracks all through the park in which you are walking. If you were to be looking at one of his fake tracks, you would be unable to tell it apart from a real track right next to it. For all you know, the very track you are looking at could be a fake track made by Al. You would not know the difference. As it turns out, indeed you are looking at a real track, not one Al made, but right next to the real track (and all around you) are fake tracks made by Al. Now, *p* is still true, and you still believe that *p*, because you know nothing about Al or his fake track maker. So, you satisfy conditions 1 and 2, but do you *know* that a deer went through the park?

Remember that it is pure luck that you are looking at a real track, not one of the fakes all around you. Remember also that were you to be in a different park filled only with fakes, and no real tracks, you still would believe that *p*. You would have believed *p*, even if *p* had been false. So your belief is true, but *so accidentally true*, so *luckily true*, that if you had guessed whether or not *p* were true, you would have had as good a chance of being right.

This example and the previous one show that guessing or flipping a coin or receiving equivocal evidence (like the look of the deer track) may bring one to have a true belief, but not knowledge. These sources of belief are not good enough to bring one to know. In the case of the deer track, even something with the distinctive shape of a deer track may not give one knowledge, when something other than deer makes tracks that are indistinguishable from genuine deer tracks. So these examples show that what is missing from our list of conditions for knowing is something that blocks a belief's being true by accident. When Al is around with his fake track maker, something's looking like a deer track is not reliably correlated with the presence of deer.

Contrast the deer tracks which can be faked with, say, fingerprints, which so far as we know cannot be faked. If they cannot be faked, Gary's fingerprints on the gun tell us that he touched the gun, even if he didn't pull the trigger. Gary's fingerprints reliably indicate that he touched the gun. Let us say that the fingerprints are reliable evidence of Gary's presence in a way that the deer tracks in the park are not reliable evidence, when Al is around with his fake track maker.

Let us add to our list of conditions for knowing that in order to know one's belief must be based on reliable evidence.[7] Our revised (and final) list looks like this:

S knows *that p* if and only if:

1. *p* is true.
2. S believes that *p*.
3. S bases his or her belief on *reliable evidence e*.

I will later address what it means for evidence to be reliable, but the fingerprint example gives a useful first start. This type of view is sometimes called a reliability theory of knowledge or sometimes is called a tracking theory of knowledge. I will now say more about this particular version. Although there are many different theories of knowledge, with many different approaches and conditions, this theory has always seemed the most promising to me and the one that I would maintain has the best chance of being true.

■ Why No More Is Required to Have Knowledge

Does that do it? Is that the end of our list of conditions? I claim that it is.[8] Not everyone agrees, however. Many wish to add a fourth condition to the list, saying that a belief must be justified, reasonable, or responsibly formed.[9] Much of contemporary epistemology is devoted to analyzing what is required for a belief to be justified. There are many theories of justified belief (foundationalism, coherentism, reliabilism, and others), and they become very complex very quickly.[10]

As it turns out, some theories of justified belief (reliabilism, for example) identify a belief's being justified with its being based on reliable evidence. These theories may not differ from our theory that identifies *knowing that p* with true belief based on reliable evidence. Other theories do *not* identify a belief's being justified with its being based on reliable evidence alone, or reliable formation by cognitive processes. For example, **coherentism** identified a belief's being justified with its **cohering** (fitting together consistently) with one's other beliefs. These theories of justified belief turn out to be significantly different from ours in that they require that one's belief be justified (or epistemically reasonable or responsibly formed) *in addition* to its being based on reliable evidence.

Why would anyone deny that this is necessary? It surely seems appropriate to require that one try to be reasonable, responsible, and justified in the formation of one's beliefs, if one is to have knowledge. One reason to balk at adding more conditions to our list, especially ones that require cognitive sophistication, is that this would eliminate infants and animals from the class of knowers. It is not clear that animals form their beliefs responsibly, nor infants. It is not even clear what this would mean for my dog, say. It seems clear, however, that my dog knows when I'm home at night and that a newborn can know when it is being held by its mother and not a stranger. If so, they may know these things by only the four conditions of our list.

Here is another example of the type that some find convincing for rejecting the urge to add a fourth condition to our list. Suppose Ken is a clairvoyant, but he does not know this. A clairvoyant, for our purposes, is one who has a direct cognitive connection to the truth about the world by scientifically as yet undiscovered means. So suppose that Ken has this power, but does not know that he has it. And suppose further that when an idea comes to him by his clairvoyant means, his left eye twitches and the idea is so overpowering that Ken cannot help but believe the idea that occurs to him. However, he has no idea why he gets these overwhelming ideas out of the blue, and he has no reason to think that he is a clairvoyant. Indeed, let us suppose that Ken, like any of us, has good reason to think that there are no clairvoyants — to think that they don't exist because there is no such direct way of knowing about the world.

Now, because Ken is a clairvoyant, when an idea pops into his head, seemingly from nowhere, it is reliably true. Ken's reliable mechanism is his clairvoyance. That is, his reliable evidence consists in an idea's popping into his head and seeming true to him (but for no reason he can determine). From Ken's point of view, when this happens, the proposition that *p* seems irresistibly true, but Ken has no clue why. Since, however, Ken does not know he is clairvoyant, he does not know that an idea's coming to him this way is perfectly reliably correlated with the truth. Furthermore, he, like any of us, doesn't believe in clairvoyance and thinks he has very good reasons to think clairvoyants do not exist. So, when an idea pops into Ken's head, he has no more justification for believing it than we would if it happened to us—at least as far as Ken knows. Those who argue for a fourth condition on knowledge want to say that if the idea pops into Ken's head that Mount St. Helens will erupt next Thursday, Ken does not know that it will. They maintain this even though it is true that it will, Ken irresistibly believes it, and he believes it because of his clairvoyance (his left eye is twitching, indicating that Ken's clairvoyance is active). For, they maintain, Ken would be unjustified or irrational to believe something based only on his shoddy, or nonexistent, evidence (the thought's popping into his head from out of nowhere). Having something pop into one's head is usually not good evidence of its truth (for the population at large), and Ken knows this. Let us further suppose that Ken has ideas about things happening at places all over the planet and he never checks to see if his ideas are true (why would he?), so he has no idea of the track record of this ideas that come to him in this way.

Notice that our three conditions alone would suggest that Ken *does know* that Mt. St Helens will erupt on Thursday. We would be forced to admit this because such an idea's popping into the head of a clairvoyant *is reliable evidence* for the truth of the idea (even if the person having the idea does not know his or her ideas are reliable). This is what it *means* to be clairvoyant. As long as Ken *believes* the ideas that clairvoyantly come to him (they are overpowering and he cannot resist believing them), then our three conditions would be satisfied, and we would attribute knowledge to Ken. Proponents of theories of knowledge requiring the fourth condition would be able to deny that Ken has knowledge, for Ken lacks a kind of justification for his belief—something that makes it rational or responsible for him to believe.

In some circles, it may be highly counterintuitive that Ken's clairvoyantly held true beliefs are knowledge. In defense of the view, keep in mind that Ken's beliefs *are nonaccidentally* true. Ken will *never* make mistakes due to error of belief, if he acts on such beliefs. His clairvoyantly held beliefs never fail to be true—they put his beliefs in perfect correlation with reality and they do so through laws of nature that we have not yet discovered. These are qualities we associate with knowledge. True, Ken does not know that he knows, for he does not know that he is clairvoyant, but neither do infants or animals know that they know, despite having knowledge.

It is also true that Ken's belief is not formed in an epistemically responsible sort of way, in having his belief about Mount St. Helens. Still, what would such responsibility add? It may be that Ken would never have the *confidence to act* on the basis of any of his clairvoyantly held beliefs because, from his point of view, they are not responsibly formed. This, however, is not in dispute. We all know many things that we are not now acting on and some things that we might lack confidence to act on in the future. Ken may know, on the basis of his very reliable x-rays from his dentist, that he has no cavities. But if asked to bet $20,000 on his not having a cavity, he may be unwilling to act on his knowledge. He may think he has good justification for his belief, but not enough to risk such a large sum of money. Thus, lack of confidence may influence Ken's actions or nonaction, but this does not imply that Ken lacks knowledge. As long as the x-rays are reliable and Ken believes on the basis of them (not by having the idea pop into his head), Ken will know that he has no cavities—despite his reluctance to wager. Therefore, if the lack of justification or epistemic responsibility does not have a negative effect on the accuracy and reliability of one's beliefs, there is no overwhelming reason to make it a necessary condition for knowledge. For these reasons, we shall move on.

Of course, what makes a belief justified is important in its own right, and the import of existing theories of justification is not diminished, even if justification—supposing that justification is something other than reliability—is not necessary for knowledge. Indeed, Ken's case is hardly the norm. For most of us, gaining knowledge comes with the endeavor to form beliefs in a way that is reasonable and responsible. In endeavoring to do so, we customarily find the evidence that is reliable and able to bring us to know. Ken's case, being the extreme, the non-ordinary, does not diminish the import of having justified beliefs. But if our theory is correct, Ken's example shows that having beliefs that are reasonable or responsibly formed may not be necessary for knowledge to arise (e.g., as in the extreme sort of situation of Ken's clairvoyance or in the cases of infants and animals).

■ RELIABLE EVIDENCE

In this section, we need to say something about what it is for evidence to be reliable. We also need to distinguish its *being* reliable from our *knowing* that it is reliable. As we shall see, the failure to make this distinction can take one down the expressway to scepticism. **Scepticism** is the view that we know nothing or almost nothing. It is a position that one should adopt only as a last resort. No one should start out being a sceptic, nor should one be led to it by bad arguments or by failure to draw important distinctions. We will consider arguments for scepticism in more detail later. For now we will say more about what it is for evidence to be reliable.

■ What Makes Evidence Reliable

Reconsider our example of the fake deer tracks. What would it take for the presence of something that looks like a deer track on the ground near you to *mean* or *reliably indicate* that deer are nearby (or at least that one deer was nearby)? That is, what would it take to screen off or eliminate the fakes? And when I say this, I do not mean that *you* or *anyone* must know that there are fakes and somehow fight to keep them away (deer track police). Instead, I ask what must the environment be like to screen off the fakes? This would require the following: that no local track would look exactly as a deer track does unless it were made by a deer. If there would not be a track that looks *like that* (please either look at a track or recall the look of one) in the park unless it were made by a deer, then the track would be reliable evidence of the presence of at least one deer.

Compare two more examples to help clarify the concept of *reliablility* that we are after. Our fingerprints and our genetic codes are unique to us as individuals. You alone have the fingerprint pattern of your right index finger (or the configuration of your right retina, for that matter). Also, you alone, unless you are an identical twin (or clone), have your genetic code. That is why fingerprints on the gun are reliable evidence that Smith touched the gun, when we find Smith's prints on the murder weapon. Smith may not have killed Jones—he may have been framed. But he *did touch* the gun, if his prints are on it. As you probably know, genetic screening (and retinal imaging) may fast replace fingerprinting in identifying persons and in solving and preventing crimes. These things provide us with nonfakable, reliable evidence. You alone (barring identical twins/clones) have your genetic map, fingerprint, or retinal map.

So a piece of evidence *e* (deer tracks) is reliable evidence that *p* (that a deer was nearby), when the tracks would not be there on the ground unless they were made by a deer. Stated more generally, evidence *e* is *reliable for the truth of p*, when *e* would not exist unless *p* were true.[11] *E*'s presence, under these conditions (no fakes), guarantees the truth of *p*.

We have, then, a definition of reliable evidence. We must now address an important complication. In our earlier example, we used a case where my friend Al made a fake deer track maker. If Al could do that, will it ever be true that a track would not look like that made by a deer unless it were in fact made by a deer? Could it not *always* be the case that something that looks like a deer track might have been made by a fake track maker? If this is always possible in some sense, then, does that not mean that we can never know that there are deer by seeing deer like tracks? Will one ever have reliable evidence for the presence of deer in the park—or reliable evidence of anything for that matter? After all, if Al can fake the *tracks* of a deer, he may be able to fake the *whole deer* (make a computer-activated robot that looks and acts like a deer and is covered in genuine deerskin).

The answer of course is yes. You *will have* the evidence that reliably indicates that certain things are true. We must not confuse knowledge of having such evidence with the having of it. It could be true that we have evidence that is reliable, even if we do not know or cannot prove that we have it. You need not *know* that a piece of evidence is reliable for it *to be* reliable. Just as you need not know that there is life on other planets for there to be life on other planets. All it takes for it to be true that there is life on other planets is for the life to be there. And all it takes for you to have reliable evidence that a deer is nearby is that no one is actually going around with a fake deer track maker (nor that would one).[12] Thus, all it takes for you to know that there are deer nearby is for you to believe that there are because you see a track that is reliable. You do not have to know or be able to tell that the track is reliable. It just has to *be reliable*.

I suppose that one must *believe* that a set of tracks is reliable to *muster up the belief* that there is a deer nearby. For example, if you did not *believe* that your friend was a reliable source of information (she likes to tease), you probably would not believe her when she tells you that your lover has been unfaithful to you. Still, you do not have to *know* that she is reliable to *hear* the distressing news. If somehow you *did* believe her, and if she were reliable, then you would *learn* that your lover was unfaithful—no matter how much you might not want to learn this. For, being reliable, she would not say this to you unless it were true—by definition of *reliable*. You do not have to know that you have knowledge to actually have it, just as you do not have to know that you have a disease to have the disease. We will return to the distinction between knowing that *p* and *knowing that you know*. For now, we simply note that there is such a distinction that we must not lose sight of.

Remember also that my example was fictitious. My friend Al does not (nor does anyone I have ever met) have a fake deer track maker. The mere fact that there *could be* one—that someone could make one—does not meant that *there is* one (nor that there is one anywhere near you, even if there is one). Many things that *could* happen *won't*. Your mother could lie to you when you ask her age. That does not mean that she would lie to you about her age. It does not mean that you cannot trust her or that she is not a reliable informant about her age. In the example, I asked you to imagine that Al actually had a fake track maker and used it. In the world we live in, Al does not have one, nor, let us suppose, does anyone in or near your present location. Let us call the condition of the world that we actually inhabit the NFT condition or region of the world. In this region, deer tracks (things that look like deer tracks) *are reliable evidence* for the presence of deer, even if we cannot prove this. To prove it, for example, we would have to check every house in or near our current location to see if there were fake track makers that may be used or had been used. Surely we could not do this within practical limits. Too many houses, and too little time. Fortunately, we *do not have to prove* that we are in the NFT region of the world for it to be true that we are.

If the world were different or we were in a different region of it (not in the NFT region) where there were practical jokers on the loose with fake track makers, we would all be *robbed of knowledge* of the presence of deer based on *seeing tracks*. We would occasionally have beliefs that were true by luck, but, as we have seen, true belief alone is insufficient for knowledge. Fortunately, our region of the world is not like that, so we *do* get reliable evidence when se see tracks.

■ *Reliability and Vulnerability*

As you no doubt have noticed, our vulnerability and our need for reliability means that we are at the mercy of the world. The world must be in condition NFT (or we must be in this region of the world) to have this particular kind of knowledge. However, we can generalize the lesson of the fake track maker to almost all of our knowledge (as philosophers famously have done through the ages). How do we know we are not brains in vats being stimulated by supercomputers to have the very experiences we are now having? Depending on what we want to know, there must be nothing fake to spoil our evidence. If the world is arranged properly, then we can get reliable evidence for the things that we want to know. If the world does not cooperate, we may think that we have reliable evidence, when we do not.

When you need to check the pressure in your tires, you grab the pressure gauge in your glove compartment. If it is a reliable gauge, it would not read "32 lb./sq. in." unless that much pressure were in your tire. But is it a reliable gauge? On our theory thus far, we can say this much: If the guage is reliable, and you believe what the gauge says, then you know the pressure in your tire. However, the world might not cooperate. The gauge may be defective and you may not be able to tell whether it is just by looking at your tire's inflation at the air pump. Of course, it may be *close enough* that you can tell the tire is sufficiently inflated to drive, even if the gauge is not entirely accurate. That is, you may know that the tire is inflated enough to drive the car safely, but you would not know that the pressure in the tire is *exactly* 32, rather than 30 or 35 lb./sq. in.

We are, then, at the mercy of the world in the sense that we must have a reliable gauge to know the tire pressure. For that matter, we must have reliable instruments to know anything else; how much gas is in the tank, what the oil pressure is, what the engine temperature is, and so on. In addition, *our senses*, the physiologists tell us, are like *instruments or gauges* for processing information coming in from the environment. The eyes detect electromagnetic radiation, the ears detect acoustic wave forms, the tongue and nose detect chemical compounds, and the skin detects physical surfaces or perturbations of the air around us, as well as thermal or kinetic energy of air molecules. So, our senses must reliably function for them to give us knowledge of the world around us.[13] We are at the mercy of our senses and the world to cooperate. If our senses were not conditionally reliable instruments, or if what they detect were not unique to them, we would not be able to gain knowledge via the senses. For example, if sodium chloride (table salt) tastes just like potassium chloride (salt substitute), then *by taste alone* we cannot know that it is salt (NaCl) that we are tasting on an given occasion. Our senses must cooperate (taste buds not on the blink), and the world must cooperate (no joker putting salt substitute in the salt shakers) for our senses to reliably inform us about the world. Radio, television, and newspapers too must be reliable for us to learn anything from them. Our friends and teachers must be reliable sources of information if we are to gain knowledge from them. As long as the world cooperates and makes available to us reliable sources of information, we will acquire knowledge by these means. It should be clear that the worries that arise in regard to the fake deer tracks can be generalized to worries about any of the evidence of the senses. If such sensory evidence can be faked, then the issue of whether our sensory evidence is reliable will arise. We pursue this topic in the next section.

■ KNOWING THAT WE KNOW

Many want *more than knowledge*. They not only want to have knowledge, but also to *know they've got it*. This is understandable. One not only wants to know that the food one is about to eat is edible, one also wants to know that one knows (to be sure). We want to *be confident*, to *feel secure* in acting on the basis of our knowledge. We not only want a reliable instrument to tell us our temperature, we want to know that it is reliable—so that we know whether to trust it, whether to feel confident that our child's fever has come down. We not only want reliable news sources, we also want to know that they are reliable, so that we know whether to believe the news they print.

■ *Second-Order Knowledge Is Not the Same as First-Order Knowledge*

Although, understandably, we want these things, they are not necessary for knowledge. They are something more—not knowing *that p*, but *knowing that we know that p*. As is clear from the structure alone, knowing that we know is a second-order affair. It is knowledge *twice* or at a *second level*. It may seem that knowing that *p* is true and knowing that you know are the same, but they are not; there is an important difference. It may seem that having reliable evidence and knowing that you have it are the same thing, but they too are importantly different. If we confuse these things, we may begin to slide into scepticism without good reason. So we should be very careful to keep these things distinct. Fortunately, we can easily show that they are distinct.

The easiest way to see this distinction is to understand that animals or infants may lack an articulated concept of knowledge. Without a concept of what knowledge is, they cannot know that they know things (or that they don't). Yet a dog may know his master is home, or an infant may know its mother is holding it. Also, as we saw earlier, for S to know that *p*, S must satisfy the three conditions on our list. Let S be *Joyce*. And let *p* be the proposition *that the battery in Joyce's garage is a twelve-volt battery*. Then for Joyce to *know that p* is for the conditions of our list to be satisfied: (1) *p* must be true, (2) Joyce must believe that *p* is true, and (3) Joyce must have reliable evidence that *p* is true. Let us put aside whether Joyce really does know that *p*, for a moment, and consider what it would take for Joyce to know that she knows, because second-order knowledge has importantly different requirements.

■ *Requirements for Second-Order Knowledge*

For one thing, for Joyce to *know that she knows that p* is for her to know, not just the proposition *p*, but a new proposition *q*. Let *q* be the proposition *that Joyce knows that p*. Proposition *q* is clearly *not the same proposition as p*; proposition *q* refers to proposition *p* as part of its content, but proposition *p* alone does not refer to itself. Fully articulated, of course, proposition *q* is as follows: *that Joyce knows that the battery in Joyce's garage is a twelve-volt battery*. Proposition *q* is, at least in part, *about Joyce's knowledge*. Proposition *p* is not about this, it is *only about Joyce's battery*. So we can be assured that *p* and *q* are *different propositions* because they are about different things.

For another thing, as different propositions, knowing that *p* and knowing that *q* require different things. It requires different evidence to know that your checkbook balances than to know it is raining, because these are different propositions. Similarly, to know that *p*, Joyce must have a reliable source of information *about the voltage in her battery*. But to know that *q*, Joyce must have reliable evidence *about her knowledge of p*. So, for example, Joyce must know that her evidence for *p* is indeed reliable. How would she go about finding this out? Suppose that the way Joyce comes to know the battery in her garage is a twelve-volt battery is by using the new voltmeter that she just bought. Then, to know that the battery is a twelve-volt battery requires (in addition to truth and belief) *that the voltmeter is reliable*. But it does not require *that Joyce know the voltmeter is reliable*. If the meter is reliable and reads "12 V," and this is why Joyce believes the battery to be a twelve-volt battery, then she knows that it is one.

Now suppose that Larry, her neighbor, asks Joyce whether she knows that it is a twelve-volt battery. To satisfy Larry, Joyce would have to know *that the new voltmeter is reliable*—that it was checked correctly by the quality-control people at the factory, not damaged on the way home, and so on. In addition to using the reliable meter to gain information about the voltage of the battery, Joyce would need some source of information about the voltmeter itself—reliable information to the effect *that the meter is reliable*. She cannot gain this information just by hooking the voltmeter to the battery. The meter could be broken and still read "12 V." So you can see that to know *q* requires *more and different information than to know p*.

■ *SCEPTICISM*

Finally, we can discuss scepticism. Scepticism is the view that we know almost nothing. Sceptics grant that we believe that we have knowledge and that we may have many merely true beliefs. Obviously we have many true beliefs or we would have all perished by now. But sceptics contend that we lack genuine knowledge. True belief is good enough for survival.

■ Expressway to Scepticism

Here is a specific argument that I like to think of as the expressway to scepticism:

1. To know that *p*, one must know that one knows that *p*.
2. One can never know that one knows that *p*.
3. Therefore, one can never know that *p* (for nearly any *p*).

When we realize that almost any proposition at all can be substituted for *p* in this argument, we see how serious is the challenge the sceptic offers. I shall claim in this section that there is a way out of the sceptic's argument, but first let's see why it is so powerful.

Let us fill in the outline with the example of Joyce. The sceptic would say that Joyce cannot know that her battery is a twelve-volt battery unless she knows that she knows that it is one. As we have seen, to know this she must know that her voltmeter is reliable. But how can she know that? Not by measuring the voltage of her battery itself, for she does not yet know that it is a twelve-volt battery and she does not yet know that her voltmeter is reliable. Not by using some *other* voltmeter, because to use another meter to check this one's reliability, she would have to know that the *new* meter is reliable. But how will she know this? For any new meter she gets, she must know that *it* is reliable. But how? She cannot just go to the store and buy a *new battery* marked "twelve volts" and use it to check to see if the new meter (or old meter) reads "12 V" when connected. For how did the store or battery factory *know* that it was a twelve-volt battery that they produced? Will not someone have to use a *voltmeter* to know that this battery or this type of battery made by the battery factory *is a twelve-volt battery*? And how will *they* know this? Will it not be by using *some* voltmeter? How will *that* voltmeter (the one the factory uses) be known to be reliable? The circle of evidence turns back on itself. You see the problem. If the sceptic's argument is correct, Joyce (or anyone) can never know of any battery that it is a twelve-volt battery.

As you may realize, this would not be such a problem if we were only talking about batteries. For, if you put the battery in Joyce's car and it *runs*, that may satisfy Joyce. The sceptic's challenge is a problem only because, as we noted earlier, *all of our knowledge* of the world relies on *instruments, meters, gauges, or our senses*. The eyes, the ears, the sense of touch, the telephone, the newspaper, the television, the Internet—all these and more—can be seen as sources of information, much like voltmeters. If these sources cannot be known to be reliable sources of information, then, by the argument above, we cannot know anything by consulting them. But, if true, we could know almost nothing (just as the sceptic says). Perhaps we could know that we exist and know what we think about the world, but not much more.

■ Roadblock to Scepticism

Fortunately, the sceptic is wrong to think that the argument is conclusive. As should be clear by now, at the very least we have proved that knowing that *p* is *not the same* as knowing that we know that *p*. So, for the sceptic to be correct, the sceptic must prove that knowing that *p requires* knowing that we know that *p*. And, if these are not the same, why should knowing the one require knowing the other? That is, the sceptic must prove to us that step 1 of the sceptic's argument is true. Any argument is only as good as its weakest link. If one of the steps is false, the conclusion may well be false too. I see no reason to think that step 1 is true. Indeed, I have tried to give good reasons to think that it is *not true*. Because knowing something and knowing that you know it are different things, they require different things to be known and should be kept distinct. If your parents are *reliable sources* of information and they tell you that you were born in the evening, you can know this by believing their testimony. Whereas, to know *that they are reliable* about the circumstances of your birth, you would have to check all claims they have ever made in earnest about your birth or would make in the near future. For unless they would not say something about the circumstances of your birth unless it were true, they are not reliable about those circumstances, and for you to know they are reliable about those circumstances you must know that they have not made or would not make mistakes about those circumstances. Basically, you would have to check all such statements. This you *could not do*, at least I don't think you could (many were made before your cognitive development reached a point where you could begin to investigate their accuracy). But you do not *need* to do this to know that you were born in the evening. To think you must is to confuse the requirements for knowledge with those for knowing that you've got knowledge.

In addition, the sceptic must be able to show that step 2 is true. But to show this, the sceptic must show that there is *no way* of knowing that a reliable source of information is reliable. After all, this is a negative universal claim. How would the sceptic know all possible ways of knowing such a thing had been exhausted? Furthemore, let's go back, for the last time, to the example of Joyce. What if, at the factory, we have reliable ways of knowing that the parts that go into a voltmeter are good ones—excellent quality control? Suppose also that we can tell by a reliable machine that all connections inside the voltmeter are made correctly and are in working order. Then we should be able to deduce, given good parts and good connections and stable laws of electronics, that the voltmeter will be reliable when hooked up to the battery. Wouldn't *that* let us know that we have a reliable meter? And if we know that we have a reliable meter, could we not know, since our meter reads the same as hers, that Joyce's meter is reliable? Consequently, would we not know that Joyce knows that her battery is a twelve-volt battery? And if we can know Joyce knows this, then in principle she can know that she knows this too. So step 2 may be false as well.

Naturally, the sceptic will say that we cannot know that the voltmeter (any voltmeter) is reliable unless we also know that our way of knowing that the parts are good is reliable. We must know that our machine that checks connections is reliable. We must know that the laws of electronics have not changed (the so-called problem of induction), and so on. So, the sceptic will not be impressed, but consider what the sceptic is demanding. We must know all of these *other things* to know that Joyce's battery is a twelve-volt battery. If we *tried* to know all of these other things, we would be led to *more* things and even more in the background that the sceptic would claim that we must know to check the reliability of our knowledge of the parts and connections and laws of electronics. We would have to know *practically everything* about the world just to be able to know something about Joyce's battery. Shouldn't we reply to the sceptic that these demands are *too high* — unrealistically high? Surely we do not need to know everything that can be known just to know that Joyce's battery has twelve-volts!

■ CONCLUSION

We have distinguished ways in which we use the word *know* and have focused our attention on knowing that something is the case. Further, we have given a list of conditions that one must satisfy to know that something is true. If we are right, one of the important ingredients of knowledge is reliable evidence. Reliable evidence is what *guarantees that the truth of one's belief is not an accident*. It is this guarantee that distinguishes merely true belief from genuine knowledge.

Although we have an analysis of propositional knowledge, we have stressed that, in a certain respect, we are at the world's mercy. For if the world does not cooperate in ways that make reliable evidence available to us, then we would not acquire knowledge — not even if we hold true beliefs some or all of the time. The lesson the sceptic wants to draw from this is not that the analysis of knowing that *p* is incorrect. The sceptic can accept our analysis. By accepting it, the sceptic can claim that we know nothing. He or she claims that we can acquire knowledge only if we can eliminate any possible uncertainty. We must, the sceptic claims, knowingly eliminate the respect in which we are at the mercy of the world or we will never know anything. The sceptic's recipe for eliminating this uncertainty is to make knowledge its own prerequisite. That is, to know that *p*, it is claimed that we must know that we know *p*.

Resisting scepticism, I have maintained that either the sceptic confuses having knowledge with knowing that one has it, or the sceptic asks too much of knowers — more than knowledge requires to attain. In either case, the sceptic's arguments are inconclusive, as they stand. It takes far more to show that we do not have knowledge than the sceptic is able to provide.[14]

■ NOTES

1. For accounts of nonempirical knowledge see Bonjour (1997).

2. Strictly speaking, a proposition is not the same thing as a sentence. We know this because "It is raining" and "Il pleut" are not the same sentences — they have different numbers of letters and are in different languages (one English, one French). Yet they express the same meaning or proposition. The distinction between sentences and propositions is important for logic and the philosophy of language. For our purposes, we shall avoid cases where the difference might have an impact on epistemology.

3. The correspondence theory of truth is one of many theories of truth. A full account of knowledge that incorporates this theory of truth would need to justify selecting it, as opposed to one of the others. This can be done, but it would take us on a very long digression. For more on theories of truth see Lehrer (1974).

4. There are dissenters (Radford, 1966), but I maintain that any knower must have a mental representation of the proposition known that would constitute a type of belief (even in Radford's examples).

5. This issue is central to Plato's theory of knowledge in his *Theaetetus*. See For Further Reading.

6. This example is similar in spirit to ones made famous by Edmund Gettier (1963), in which he was able to show that not only isn't true belief sufficient for knowledge, but even true justified belief is not sufficient. The job of figuring out how to give an analysis of what it takes to handle examples like this has been the main task of much of epistemology since Gettier's landmark paper appeared.

7. What it is for a belief to be *based on* a piece of evidence turns out to be a very tricky matter and to be much more complicated than I can go into here. For most of the complexities see Swain (1981).

8. I have defended this account, and a similar version based on information theory, elsewhere in greater detail (Adams, 1986, 1988, forthcoming).

9. For an excellent and representative account of why others wish to add this condition, see Bonjour (1980).

10. For an excellent sources of these theories see Audi (1988, 1998) and Sosa and Kim (2000).

11. Something like this notion of reliability, though he did not call it "reliability," was first proposed by Fred Dretske (1971).

12. Of course, there must not be anything *else* besides the fake deer tack maker that would make a track that looks indistinguishably like a deer track—no strange animals, bugs, falling rocks, and so on. I did dwell on this, but it should be understood to be a necessary condition of reliability.

13. Historically, this is the very problem that led Descartes (the father of modern philosophy) to seek a solution to the problem of knowledge. He worried about whether the senses were reliable instruments for detecting information and, if they were, how we could tell. See Descartes' *Meditations on First Philosophy* (*The Philosophical Works of Descartes*, vol. 1, eds. Elizabeth Haldane and G.R.T. Ross [Cambridge: Cambridge University Press, 1969]). See also the chapter in this book on the philosophy of mind for more on the views of Descartes, especially 236–37.

14. An early version of this essay was written in 1992 for the first version of this book. It was and still is written from the perspective of one who accepts what has come to be known as *reliabilism* (*and externalism*) in the theory of knowledge. Not all epistemologists would agree with this approach. If by "justified" one means more than having a belief based on reliable evidence, I do not agree that more is required for knowledge. Furthermore, in 2001 I have still not seen a convincing argument for adding another condition to the analysis of knowledge, though many reasons have been offered and I cannot go into them here. For more see my (Adams, forthcoming). To fight this battle would take us into territory appropriate for a course devoted solely to the subject of what justifies a belief and the role of justification in knowledge and reason. I have limited my remarks here by not engaging in those disputes. As I pointed out in the beginning of this chapter, I have also limited my remarks to empirical knowledge, avoiding an analysis of knowledge of logical

or mathematical truths. For such matters, see For Further Reading. I would like to thank John Barker, Kevin Possin, and Leemon McHenry for comments on earlier drafts. I would also especially like to thank Robert Audi, John Barker, and Fred Dretske for introducing me to epistemology and making it come alive for me.

■ *QUESTIONS*

1. What are the three different ways in which we use the word *know*? Explain how one of these can be resolved into the other two.
2. What does it mean to say that truth and belief are necessary for knowing that *p*, but are not sufficient?
3. Give some examples of reliable evidence for something and explain what makes the evidence reliable in your examples.
4. Many years ago someone put arsenic in Tylenol Capsules. As a result, Tylenol now makes caplets and tamper-proof bottles. When you take a Tylenol Capsule, do you know that it is safe?
5. In the example of the fake deer-tracks, suppose that while there is no fake track-maker being used anywhere near where you live, there is someone actually making fake deer-tracks in a remote part of the planet. Does the fact that someone remote from you is making fake tracks rob you of knowledge on the basis of seeing deer-like tracks? Does the use of the fake track-maker rob you of knowledge if that use gets closer to your location? How close before it matters?
6. What is the philosophical position called scepticism? Why is it a problem?
7. Show how one could generalize from the problem of the fake deer-tracks to produce an argument for scepticism, generally.
8. Could scepticism turn out to be true? How does the author respond to the challenge of scepticism? Do you tend to agree more with the author or more with the sceptic? Explain.

■ *FOR FURTHER READING*

Adams, F. 1986. "The Function of Epistemic Justification." *Canadian Journal of Philosophy* 16:465–92. [Defends a reliability theory of knowledge. For the serious student.]

Adams, F., and Kline, D. 1987. "Nomic Reliabilism: Weak Reliability Is Not Enough." *Southern Journal of Philosophy* 25:433–43. [For the mature student.]

Adams, F. Forthcoming: "Knowledge." *In*: Floridi, Luciano (ed.), *The Blackwell Guide to the Philosophy of Information and Computing*, Oxford: Basil Blackwell.

Alston, W. 1989. *Epistemic Justification: Essays in the Theory of Knowledge*. Ithaca, N.Y.: Cornell University Press. [For the mature student.]

Audi, R. 1988. *Belief, Justification, and Knowledge*. Belmont, Calif.: Wadsworth. [Very accessible introduction to the subject. For the beginner.]

—— 1998. *Epistemology: A Contemporary Introduction to the Theory of Knowledge*. London: Routledge. [Excellent overview of the field. Accessible.]

Bonjour, L. 1997. *In Defense of Pure Reason: A Rationalist's Account of A Priori Justification*. Cambridge: Cambridge University Press. [For the mature student.]

—— 1980. "Externalist Theories of Empirical Knowledge." *Midwest Studies in Philosophy* 5:53–73. [Very clear, accessible account of perceived shortcomings of the kind of account of knowledge being given in this chapter.]

Chisholm, R. 1966. *Theory of Knowledge*. Englewood Cliffs, N.J.: Prentice-Hall. [A classic for the beginner.]

Descartes, R. 1969. *Meditations on First Philosophy*. In: Haldane, E., and Ross, G. (eds.), *The Philosophical Works of Descartes*. Cambridge: Cambridge University Press. [The first "modern" epistemologist.]

Dretske, F. 1971. "Conclusive Reasons." *Australasian Journal of Philosophy* 49:1–22. [Accessible and influential.]

—— 1981. *Knowledge and the Flow of Information*. Cambridge, Mass.: MIT/Bradford Press. [Not for the beginner.]

Gettier, E. 1963. "Is Justified True Belief Knowledge?" *Analysis* 23:121–23. [A classic to be memorized by all beginning students.]

Hamlyn, D. 1967. "History of Epistemology." *The Encyclopedia of Philosophy*, vol. 3, New York: Macmillan Press. [Accessible to the beginner.]

Lehrer, K. 1974. *Knowledge*. Oxford: Clarendon Press. [Excellent introduction for the beginner.]

Lehrer, K. 1990. *Theory of Knowledge*. Boulder Colo.: Westview Press. [Accessible to the beginner.]

Pappas, G., and Swain, M. (eds.) 1978. *Essays on Knowledge and Justification*. Ithaca, N.Y.: Cornell University Press. [Like Roth and Galis, this is a very classic reader with many of the historically influential articles that have shaped the field of epistemology. Also, still a good introduction to the field and very accessible.]

Plato, 1961. *Theaetetus*. In: Hamilton, E., and Huntington, C. (eds.), *Plato: Collected Dialogues*. Princeton, N.J.: Princeton University Press. [One of the first essays on epistemology.]

Radford, C. 1966. "Knowledge by Examples." *Analysis* 27:1–11. [Very influential and short article that gives several examples purporting to show it is possible to know that *p* without believing that *p*. Accessible to the beginner.]

Roth, M., and Galis, L. 1970. *Knowing: Essays in the Analysis of Knowledge*. New York: Random House. [Classic reader in epistemology with many of the influential, early articles. Very accessible and still a good introduction to the field.]

Sosa, E., and Kim, J. 2000. *Epistemology*. Oxford: Blackwell. [Contains most of the recent formative papers in the field. For the serious student.]

Swain, M. 1981. *Reasons and Knowledge*. Ithaca, N.Y.: Cornell University Press. [This is an important book in the history of the subject. It is intricate in detail and for the serious student.]

■ CHAPTER SIX

Ethics

MARK TIMMONS

■ *INTRODUCTION*

In 1998, Dr. Jack Kervorkian helped Thomas Youk end his life by giving him a lethal injection of drugs—an incident that was videotaped and later broadcast on CBS's "60 Minutes". Youk had been suffering from amyotrophic lateral sclerosis (often called Lou Gehrig's disease), a progressive neurodegenerative disease that attacks nerve cells in the brain and spinal cord and eventually leads to death. In the later stages of the disease, its victims are completely paralyzed, as was Youk at the time of his death.

Kervorkian's killing of Youk was a case of euthanasia, which is defined as the act of killing (or allowing to die) on grounds of mercy for the victim. In this case, because Youk consented to his own death and because Kervorkian brought about Youk's death by an act of lethal injection, Kervorkian's action was an instance of voluntary, active euthanasia.

Kervorkian was eventually tried and convicted of second-degree murder for his active role in bringing about Youk's death. But even if Kervorkian did violate the law, was his action morally wrong? Youk's immediate family and many others saw nothing morally wrong with Youk's decision or with Kerverokian's act. They argued, for example, that proper respect for an individual's freedom of choice means that people in Youk's situation have a moral right to choose to die and that therefore Kervorkian was not acting immorally in helping Youk end his life. Of course, many others disagreed, arguing for example that euthanasia is morally wrong because of its possible bad effects over time on society, including the possibility that the practice of euthanasia could be abused and vulnerable persons might be put to death without their consent. Which side of this moral dispute is correct? Is euthanasia at least sometimes morally right, or is this practice morally wrong?

The moral controversy over euthanasia is but one example of a range of moral issues that are hotly disputed. Most, if not all, readers know something about the contemporary moral disputes over abortion, treatment of animals, the death penalty, preferential treatment, homosexuality, drugs, handgun control, world hunger, and many others. These controversies typically involve both legal and moral issues. In this chapter, however, we are concerned only with questions about morality.

Reflection on these moral controversies often leads thoughtful individuals to ask basic questions about the *nature* of right and wrong, good and bad, and about how we might come to *know* what is right and wrong and what is good and bad. These questions are some of the most central philosophical questions in the field of philosophy known as **ethics**. The primary aim of this chapter is to introduce readers to the study of ethics by surveying some of the most important moral theories that attempt to answer these and related philosophical questions. In doing so, I will argue for a particular type of moral theory that I call limited moral pluralism. Accordingly, I will begin with some introductory remarks about the very idea of a moral theory featured in ethics and then examine some representative moral theories including the one I will defend.

■ WHAT IS A MORAL THEORY?

Before we begin examining various moral theories, let us prepare by going over three main elements of a moral theory: (1) the main concepts featured in such theories, (2) the main aims of such theories, and (3) the role of principles featured in moral theories.

■ *The Main Concepts: The Right and the Good*

In ethics, the terms *right* and *wrong* are used primarily to evaluate the morality of actions. In this chapter we are mainly concerned with moral theories that address the nature of right and wrong action (or right action, for short).

Again, in ethics, the terms *good* and *bad* are used primarily in assessing the value of persons (their character) as well as experiences, things, and states of affairs. Philosophers distinguish between something's having *intrinsic value* (that is, being intrinsically good or bad) and something's having *instrumental value* (that is, being instrumentally good or bad). Something has intrinsic value when its value depends on features that are *inherent* in it, and something is instrumentally good when its goodness is a matter of its being *useful* in bringing about what is intrinsically good. For instance, some philosophers maintain that happiness is intrinsically good—its goodness depends on the inherent nature of happiness—and that things like money and power are instrumentally good (valuable) because they can be used to bring about happiness. Thus, the notion of intrinsic value is the more basic of the two notions and so philosophical accounts of value are concerned with the nature of intrinsic value.

A moral theory, then, is a theory about the nature of the right and the good and about the proper method for making correct or justified moral decisions. Accordingly, here are some of the main questions that a moral theory attempts to answer:

1. What makes an action right or wrong?
2. What makes something good or bad?
3. What is the proper method (supposing there is one) for reasoning our way to correct moral conclusions about the morality (the rightness and goodness) of actions, persons, and other objects of moral evaluation?

To understand more fully what a moral theory is and how it attempts to answer these questions, let us now consider the main aims of a moral theory.

■ Two Main Aims of a Moral Theory

Corresponding to the first two questions about the nature of the right and the good is what we may call the theoretical aim of a moral theory:

> The *theoretical aim* of a moral theory is to discover those underlying features of actions, persons, and other items of moral evaluation that make them right or wrong, good or bad. Features of this sort serve as *moral criteria* of the right and the good.

Our third main question about proper methodology in ethics is the basis for the practical aim of a moral theory:

> The *practical aim* of a moral theory is to discover a *decision procedure* that can be used to guide correct moral reasoning about matters of moral concern and thus a method for making correct moral decisions.

Given these guiding aims, we can evaluate a moral theory by seeing how well it satisfies them. We can gain a clearer understanding of these aims by considering the role that principles typically play in moral theories.

■ The Role of Moral Principles

In attempting to satisfy these main aims, philosophers typically propose moral principles that are very general moral statements that specify conditions under which an action is right or something is good. Principles that state conditions for an action's being right are *principles of right conduct* and those that specify items that have intrinsic value are *principles of value*. Here is an example of a principle of right conduct:

> P   An action is right if, and only if, it would, if performed, bring about at least as much overall happiness as would any available alternative action.

This principle, understood as a moral criterion of right action, purports to reveal the underlying nature of right action—what makes an action right. According to P, it is facts about how much happiness an action would bring about that determines whether it is morally right.

But also, a principle such as P is typically intended to provide the basis of a decision procedure and thus satisfy the practical aim of moral theory. The idea is that if P is a correct moral principle, then we should be able to use it to guide our moral deliberations in coming to decisions about the rightness of actions. P instructs us to consider how much happiness actions would bring about in reasoning our way to moral conclusions about what to do.

To sum up, a moral theory attempts to provide moral principles of right conduct and value that serve to explain what makes an action or other object of evaluation right or wrong, good or bad (thus satisfying the theoretical aim) as well as principles that can be used to guide moral thought in arriving at correct decisions about what to do (thus satisfying the practical aim).[1]

Consequentialism and deontology represent two of the most historically important types of moral theory, so let us address them in order.

■ CONSEQUENTIALISM

Consequentialism is based on the following idea:

> C   Right action is to be understood entirely in terms of the value of the action's consequences.

For the consequentialist, considerations of intrinsic value are most basic and thus can be used to explain the nature of right action. The most prominent version of consequentialism is utilitarianism, to which we now turn.

■ *Utilitarianism*

Utilitarianism was originally developed and defended by Jeremy Bentham (1748–1832) and later refined by John Stuart Mill (1806–1873).[2] There are many varieties of utilitarianism, though my presentation will build on the closely related classic versions of the view that we find in Bentham and Mill. Their basic idea was that human welfare or happiness is intrinsically valuable and that the rightness or wrongness of actions depends entirely on how they affect human welfare or happiness. Let us consider their theory in more detail.

■ A HEDONIST THEORY OF VALUE

Although there are competing philosophical views about the nature of happiness, Bentham and Mill accepted what is called a hedonist account of happiness. Because on their view it is happiness that is intrinsically good, they accepted a hedonist theory of intrinsic value (**hedonism**), which we may express by the following principle of value:

> H   Experiences of pleasure are intrinsically good and experiences of pain are intrinsically bad, and these are the only things having intrinsic value.

There are two points worth noting about the hedonist account of intrinsic value. First, pleasure is to be understood quite broadly to include not only bodily pleasures that result from eating, drinking, getting a massage, and so forth, but also aesthetic and intellectual pleasures of the sort that result from, say, reading a novel or solving a crossword puzzle. Similar remarks apply to the concept of pain.

Second, the classic utilitarians thought that pleasure and pain can, in principle, be compared on a single scale of measure. Their idea was that experiences of pleasure have a certain amount of intrinsic positive value and that experiences of pain have a certain amount of intrinsic negative value. Further, these values can, in principle, be added and subtracted so that we can assign an overall net value to some series of experiences of pleasure and pain. Let us call the overall net value of a set of experiences of pleasure and pain its **hedonic value**. If, for some range of experiences, the total amount of pleasure it contains is greater than is the total amount of pain, then the hedonic value of that range of experiences will be positive, whereas if it is the other way around, the hedonic value will be negative. This hedonist conception of intrinsic value is the basis for the classical utilitarian theory of right conduct.

■ A UTILITARIAN THEORY OF RIGHT CONDUCT

As a consequentialist moral theory, utilitarianism makes the rightness and wrongness of actions depend entirely on the value of their consequences or effects. In this theory, the term *utility* is used to refer to the overall hedonic value of the consequences of an action. Using this term, we can express the basic utilitarian principle of right conduct—the **principle of utility**—as follows:

> U   An action is right if, and only if, its consequences would have as much overall utility (intrinsic value) as would the consequences of any available alternative action.

Utilitarianism, by definition, understands utility or intrinsic value in terms of happiness or well-being. But notice that U does not itself specify how we are to understand happiness. As explained earlier, the classical utilitarians accepted a hedonist theory of utility or happiness that we have expressed by H. So, if the utility of an action is understood in terms of the hedonic value of its consequences, we end up with a version of **hedonistic utilitarianism**.

> HU   An action is right if, and only if, its consequences would have at least as much hedonic value as would the consequences of any alternative action.

There are three points about HU worth making explicit. First, this principle makes the rightness and wrongness of an action depend on how it will affect *all* individuals whose welfare will be affected by the action. Second, this principle is supposed to capture the idea that morality is impartial because in considering the effects of an action on the welfare of individuals, we are not to give special weight to some people because, for example, they happen to be members of our family or our friends. Rather, the welfare of everyone affected by the action is taken into account in an impartial way. Finally, this principle makes the morality of an action a comparative matter: the principle requires that we perform the action that, *from among the various alternative actions we might perform*, would produce at least as much overall utility (hedonic value) as any alternative. In short, we are to maximize good consequences, where goodness is understood in terms of pleasure (and the avoidance of pain). Actions that maximize utility are right; those that do not are wrong.

To understand HU more clearly, let us work with a very simple example. Suppose that I am in charge of inviting a guest philosopher to speak at my university and that I've narrowed the choices to two. On the one hand, I can invite Dr. Brilliant, a very well-known and innovative philosopher but whose manner of presentation is decidedly dull. The philosophy faculty will no doubt take pleasure in his presentation, but others will be bored stiff and get little out of the talk. On the other hand, I can invite Dr. Flash who is not nearly as accomplished as Dr. Brilliant but who I know is an extremely engaging speaker. Suppose that five professional philosophers and forty-five students are expected to attend the lecture no matter which of these two philosophers I invite.

Now if I apply HU to my situation, it would have me invite the speaker whose talk will produce the greatest amount of overall hedonic value. A careful application of HU would require that I consider each person who will be affected by the lecture of Dr. Brilliant and determine how much pleasure that person would experience as a result of this lecture and then determine how much pain that person would experience as a result of this lecture. Once I have done this calculation for each person, I then calculate how much total amount of pleasure the lecture would cause and how much total pain it would cause to arrive at the overall hedonic value associated with Dr. Brilliant's lecture. I do the same for Dr. Flash. The lecture I ought to sponsor and hence the philosopher I ought to invite depends on which talk will result in the greatest amount of hedonic value.

Having explained the main features of classical utilitarianism, let us proceed to evaluate this theory by first considering its attractive features and then turning to various objections.

■ Some Attractive Features of Utilitarianism

Many philosophers are attracted to utilitarianism because it captures certain initially plausible ideas about morality. First, utilitarianism accepts the plausible assumption that the morality of actions depends importantly on how those actions affect the welfare of individuals. Second, as explained earlier, the theory also captures the very common idea that moral considerations are supposed to be impartial. In calculating the morality of actions, we are to consider impartially their effects on everyone who will be affected by those actions. Thus, everyone who will be affected by one's actions is counted equally in determining the overall utility of the action. Nevertheless, despite these attractive features of the view, many critics have argued that it is not a correct moral theory. Let us see why.

■ *Objections to Utilitarianism*

In evaluating a moral theory, we consider how well it satisfies the theoretical and practical aims outlined earlier in the second section. The objections to utilitarianism relate to these aims.

■ AGAINST THE PRINCIPLE OF UTILITY AS A DECISION PROCEDURE

Consider first the practical aim of providing a useful decision procedure for coming to correct moral verdicts about the morality of actions. Can the Principle of Utility possibly serve as a useful decision procedure?[3] Consider, for example, Kervorkian's act of killing Thomas Youk. How many people were affected by this act, which, recall, was broadcast on television? For all those affected, how were they affected, that is, how much utility was brought about by Kervorkian's action? Clearly, it is beyond human capacities to calculate reliably the utility of Kervorkian's action and so U is not useful in this case as a decision procedure. But a great many of our actions have wide-ranging effects on many people and in ways that we cannot reliably calculate. Because U cannot be usefully applied in a great many cases, it cannot function as a decision procedure. Hence, this principle fails to satisfy the practical aim of a moral theory.

In reply to this objection, some utilitarians maintain that even if the principle of utility cannot be used in any rigorous fashion to arrive at correct moral verdicts about specific actions, it can still be used as a rough and ready guide. Making rough estimates of the value of the consequences of actions can still be of use in moral decision making. Indeed, some utilitarians go further and deny that the principles of a moral theory need to function as a decision procedure. Rather, many defenders of this view present the principle of utility as giving us a theoretical account of the underlying nature of morality and thus claim that it is intended only to satisfy the theoretical aim of moral theory. Even so, the utilitarian owes us an account of proper moral thinking and decision making, even if it is not the principle of utility that is supposed to serve this function.

But does utilitarianism satisfy the theoretical aim? There are actually two questions to consider. First, does the theory give us a correct account of the nature of intrinsic value? Second, does it give us a correct account of the nature of right action? Let us take these questions in order.

■ AGAINST HEDONISM

Many philosophers reject hedonism because they think that, even if pleasure and pain are among the items having positive and negative intrinsic value, respectively, other items also possess intrinsic value. One particularly vivid way of making this clear is to consider a thought experiment devised by Robert Nozick:

> Suppose there were an experience machine that would give you any experience you desired. Superduper neuroscientists could stimulate your brain so that you would think and feel you were writing a great novel, or making a friend, or reading an interesting book. All the time you would be floating in a tank, with electrodes attached to your brain. Should you plug into this machine for life, preprogramming your life's experiences?[4]

If the only items of positive intrinsic value are mental states of pleasure, why not plug in? But, of course, most people (except for those who are utterly miserable) wouldn't plug in because we think that there are things we want to *do*, and not just think we are doing, and ways we want to *be*, and not just think we are, that are intrinsically good. Possession of knowledge, virtue, and having close personal relationships are among the things that seem to be intrinsically valuable. If so, then hedonism is incorrect as an account of the nature of value and thus fails to satisfy the theoretical aim of a moral theory. Since a hedonistic theory of value is the basis of the theory of right conduct for classical utilitarianism, we must conclude that this theory of right conduct is mistaken.

In response to this line of criticism, some contemporary utilitarians embrace a nonhedonistic theory of value. Space does not permit us to consider these versions of utilitarianism.[5] However, many critics of utilitarianism claim that all versions of the view—both hedonistic and nonhedonistic—are implausible. Let us see why.

■ AGAINST THE PRINCIPLE OF UTILITY AS A MORAL CRITERION

Many object to utilitarianism by arguing that U cannot possibly provide a correct explanation of the nature of right action because it yields incorrect moral verdicts in a wide range of cases. That is, to be a proper explanation of why an action is right or wrong, a moral principle must at least imply correct moral verdicts about the morality of actions that we are certain about. Utilitarianism fails on this count. Consider the following case.

A physician with a strong utilitarian conscience finds herself in the following situation. A perfectly healthy patient of hers has been admitted to the hospital for alcohol abuse. The physician knows about the personal history of this patient. She knows, for example, that the patient has no family, is homeless, and so forth. Except perhaps for the patient's liver, his other bodily organs are in excellent shape. Now suppose that under the physician's treatment are three individuals who are in need of an organ donor—each needing a different organ. Moreover, time is quickly running out for these patients. You see how the story goes from here. Our physician does some utilitarian calculation and concludes that, because it would be easy and (let us suppose) not at all risky for her to cause the death of the alcohol abuser, she ought to do so since she would then have at her disposal the needed organs for her three needy patients. (We are assuming that the blood types match so that the transplants are medically feasible.) Suppose the chances of successful transplant are very high and that the actual utility of proceeding would in fact yield success. From the utilitarian perspective, our physician ought to kill the one patient to save the other three, but doing so would be murder! The theory clearly leads to obviously incorrect moral conclusions.

It is important to realize that this is not an isolated case. There are many other such examples in which the theory yields incorrect moral verdicts involving cases of breaking promises, knowingly punishing innocent people, and injustice in the way benefits and burdens are distributed in society.

■ DIAGNOSIS: FAILURE TO RESPECT PERSONS

The utilitarian theory is apparently led to mistaken verdicts about, for example, the morality of medical sacrifice because the theory makes the morality of actions depend on good overall consequences *regardless of how those results are brought about*. In short, on this theory, the end (overall good consequences) justifies the means—means that sometimes may allow or even require what we recognize to be immoral actions. In doing so, utilitarianism fails to respect individuals properly, allowing them to be used as means for bringing about the best overall consequences.

Based on these observations about the practical and, in particular, the theoretical implications of utilitarianism, I think we must agree that it is (at least in the version we have considered) implausible. We are in search of moral theory that properly respects persons and does not allow them to be used as means— even for good ends.

■ DEONTOLOGY

Deontology (from the Greek *deon*, "duty") is a type of moral theory that is committed to the following basic claim:

> D The notion of intrinsic value is not more basic than the notion of right action and so right action cannot be explained in terms of considerations of intrinsic value.

If this basic claim of deontology is correct and right action cannot be explained in terms of what has intrinsic value, then all versions of consequentialism, which try to explain right action in terms of the values of consequences, must be mistaken. So consequentialist and deontological moral theories are rivals.

Notice that D represents a negative characterization of deontology, indicating that this kind of moral theory rejects the leading idea of consequentialism. A positive characterization of deontology would be difficult to give because many moral theories, differing significantly from one another, are typically classified as deontological. It is best, then, to work with some examples of this kind of view. The moral philosophy of Immanuel Kant represents an important deontological theory, but before examining Kant's views, let us consider a very familiar moral conception that might be used as the basis for a deontological moral theory.

■ *The Golden Rule*

The so-called **golden rule** directs us to do unto others as we would have them do unto us. If we formulate the golden rule as a moral principle, we have:

> GR   An act is right if, and only if, in performing it, the agent treats others as she would want others to treat her.

The principle represents a version of deontology, because it does not define right action in terms of considerations of value and, in particular, it does not make the rightness of an action depend on the value of its consequences. Rather, according to GR, acts in which you treat others as you would want them to treat you are morally right; acts that treat others in ways you would not want to be treated are wrong.

Notice that GR fairly easily satisfies the practical aim of moral theory. To use it as a decision procedure to arrive at a moral verdict, you simply consider whether you would want to be on the receiving end of that action. In the case of Thomas Youk, the morality of what Kervorkian did depends on whether he was doing something to Youk that he would want others to do to him (were he in Youk's situation).

However, there are two well-known problems with the golden rule when understood as a moral criterion, that is, when it is understood as revealing what makes an action right or wrong. First, it concerns only how you treat *others*. But you can treat yourself in immoral ways as when, for instance, you knowingly take dangerous drugs for fun.

Second (and more important), taken literally, the golden rule has incorrect moral implications. For example, according to GR, it would be right for a masochist to inflict pain on others since he would be willing to have them inflict pain on him. Again, someone who is a staunch individualist may not want others to help him under any circumstances, even if it means he will die. Because he would not have others help him, then, according to the golden rule, it is right for him to refuse to help others. But surely this implication is not correct. The problem here is that the golden rule makes the rightness or wrongness of an action depend entirely on what you would want or not want in the way of treatment by others. There is no limit, however, to what people are capable of wanting as illustrated in the two examples just considered.

These reflections make it clear that what a person might or might not want from others is not a correct moral criterion of right action, and so the golden rule fails to satisfy the theoretical aim of moral theory. Even if the golden rule, taken literally, is not a correct moral principle, there is something about the spirit behind the rule that is attractive. The idea suggested by the golden rule is that morality requires that we not engage in unfair treatment of people, that we respect other persons and not take advantage of them. So what we are looking for is a moral principle that captures the idea of respecting persons while avoiding the problems with the golden rule. This brings us to Kant's moral theory.

■ *Kantian Deontology*

The moral philosophy of the German philosopher Immanuel Kant (1724–1804) represents a deontological moral theory that gives respect for persons a central place in morality and arguably captures the spirit of the golden rule.[6] Let us now consider some of the main elements of Kant's moral theory.

■ KANT'S SUPREME PRINCIPLE OF MORALITY: THE CATEGORICAL IMPERATIVE

Central to Kant's moral theory is the idea that moral requirements can be expressed as commands or imperatives that categorically bid us to perform certain actions—requirements that apply to us regardless of what we might happen to want or desire or how such actions bear on the production of happiness. Kant thought that specific moral requirements could be derived from a fundamental moral principle which he called the **categorical imperative** (CI). Moreover, Kant offered various alternative formulations of his fundamental moral principle. According to what is called the *humanity* formulation, an action is right if, and only if, the action respects persons in that it treats humanity (that is, persons) as an end in itself and not as a mere means. Certain actions are therefore wrong *because* they fail to respect persons, regardless of what we happen to want or how much overall happiness they may produce. But what does it mean to respect persons?

According to Kant, to respect persons properly requires acting only in ways that you could consistently will that everyone act. The idea is that when we act, we act on a general policy that Kant called a maxim. To test the morality of an action, we formulate the general policy of our action and ask whether we could consistently will that everyone act on the same policy, or to put it in Kant's terms, we ask whether we could consistently will that the maxim become a universal law governing everyone's behavior. If so, then the action is right; if not, then the action is wrong. This test of the morality of actions is expressed in the so-called *universal law* formulation of the categorical imperative:

> CI An action is right if, and only if, you can consistently will that everyone act on the general policy (that is, the maxim) of your action.

Notice that CI represents a deontological moral principle because it does not define right action in terms of considerations of intrinsic value and, in particular, it does not make the rightness of an action depend on the value of the action's consequences. To understand Kant's moral principle more clearly, let us see how we are to apply this principle to concrete cases using some of Kant's own examples.

One of his examples involves making a lying promise, that is, a promise that one has no intention of keeping. Consider a case in which I desperately need money right away and the only way I can get it is by getting a loan which I must promise to repay. I know, however, I won't be able to repay the loan. The maxim corresponding to the action I am considering is:

M1   Whenever I need money and can get it only by making a lying promise, I will borrow the money by making a lying promise.

Kant's principle, CI, has us test the morality of making a lying promise by asking whether I could consistently will that everyone act on M1—that everyone who needs money in such circumstances as mine make a lying promise. Is this something I can consistently will that others do?

Kant claims that when you think through what would be involved in everyone acting on M1, you realize that you cannot even consistently conceive of a situation in which everyone in need of money successfully makes lying promises. After all, a situation in which everyone in need of money goes around trying to get the money by making a lying promise is one in which successful promising becomes impossible since, as Kant observes, "no one would believe what was promised him but would laugh at all such expressions as vain pretenses."[7] Thus, trying to imagine a situation in which everyone in need of money acts on M1 involves an inconsistency: it is a situation in which (1) everyone in need gets money by making a lying promise, but because of the breakdown in the institution of promising that would result, it is a situation in which (2) not everyone in need gets money by make a lying promise for the reason Kant gives. If I can't consistently conceive of everyone acting on M1, however, then certainly I can't consistently will that this be the case. And if I can't consistently will that everyone act on M1, this shows me that, in making a lying promise, I am acting on an immoral policy and that my action is wrong.

But why is the fact that I cannot consistently will that everyone act on my maxim an indication that the action in question is wrong? Kant's idea here seems to be that in performing an action whose maxim I cannot consistently will everyone to adopt, I am, in effect, proposing to make an exception of myself, an exception that I cannot justify. In making an exception of myself, I am failing to respect others because I'm taking advantage of the fact that many others do not make lying promises. These reflections lead us to conclude that making a lying promise is morally wrong.

Here is another example Kant uses to illustrate the application of the categorical imperative. Suppose I am in a position to help someone in need but would rather not be bothered. The maxim Kant has us consider is:

M2   Whenever I am able to help others in need, I will refrain from helping them.

Using CI, I am to consider whether I can consistently will that everyone adopt and act on this maxim. On reflection I realize that if I will that everyone adopt and act on M2, I am thereby willing that others refuse to help me when I am in need. But willing that others refuse to help me is inconsistent with the fact that I do will that others help me when I am in need. Thus, I cannot consistently will that everyone adopt and act on M2. Since I cannot consistently will that everyone adopt M2, then according to Kant's test my action of refusing to help others in need is morally wrong.

It is important to notice that in his examples Kant is not arguing that if everyone went around making lying promises the consequences would be bad and therefore making a lying promise is wrong. Again, he does not argue that the consequences of everyone refusing to help others in need would be bad and therefore refusing help to others is wrong. Such ways of arguing are characteristic of consequentialism, but Kant is a deontologist. He has us consider the implications of everyone acting on the general policy behind one's own action because he thinks doing so is a way of revealing any inconsistencies in what one wills, which in turn indicates whether an action fails to respect persons. So the test involved in the categorical imperative is meant to reveal whether one's action shows a proper respect for persons.

Kant thought the categorical imperative could function as a general test and hence an all-purpose moral decision procedure in ethics, and he apparently thought that it expresses a correct moral criterion—indicating what makes an action right or wrong[8]—but his view has been faulted on both counts.

■ OBJECTIONS TO KANT'S THEORY

Consider first whether CI is useful as a decision procedure. To use it in coming to conclusions about the morality of an action, I must first formulate the general policy or maxim behind my action. But how do I do that? For any action I might perform, there are many policies I might be acting on. Take a simple case.

Suppose that I lie to you about your haircut because I want to spare your feelings. What is my maxim? Here are two possibilities:

M3   I will lie whenever I find it useful to do so.
M4   I will avoid causing unnecessary pain to others.

Presumably, M3 would fail Kant's test: I could not consistently will that everyone adopt and act on it for pretty much the same reason that the lying promise maxim fails Kant's test. Kant's test implies that the act mentioned in the maxim—lying, in this circumstance—is wrong. However, presumably I can consistently will that everyone adopt and act on M4, because I can consistently will that everyone avoid causing unnecessary pain to others. If so, then according to CI my act of not hurting your feelings by lying is morally right. So, the moral verdict about lying in this circumstance depends on which general policy I select in applying Kant's categorical imperative. But to be useful, a moral principle should imply only a single verdict about an individual case. Therefore, unless Kant (or a defender of Kant) can specify which general policy or maxim is the correct one to use for purposes of morally evaluating actions, Kant's categorical imperative is not useful as a decision procedure. His theory thus fails to satisfy the practical aim of a moral theory.

Furthermore, there are reasons to doubt that CI represents a correct criterion of right action because there are cases in which, for instance, a maxim corresponding to a morally right action would fail Kant's consistency test and thus be misclassified as wrong. For example, suppose I plan to withdraw all of my money from the bank when the stock market index climbs another fifty points.[9] My maxim is:

> M5   Whenever the stock market index climbs another 50 points, I will withdraw all of my money from the bank.

Clearly, adopting and acting on this maxim is not wrong. One cannot consistently will that everyone adopt and act on my maxim, however, because the situation in which everyone adopts and acts on this maxim contains an inconsistency, that is, it is a situation in which (1) everyone does withdraw their money from the bank under the condition specified in the maxim, but because banks do not have the necessary funds on hand to support massive withdrawals, it is also a situation in which (2) not everyone withdraws all their money from the bank. If I cannot consistently conceive of a situation in which everyone acts on my maxim, then I cannot consistently will that they do so. Thus, the CI implies that adopting and acting on M5 is morally wrong.

This is but one example where Kant's supreme moral principle fails to correctly classify an action. There are many other such examples, which have led critics to conclude that the universal law formulation of the categorical imperative is not a correct moral criterion.

■ *TAKING STOCK*

Before going further, let us briefly pause and take stock of what we have learned. Ideally, at least, we hope to discover moral principles that will be useful as the basis of a moral decision procedure and also serve as a moral criterion by revealing to us the underlying nature of the right and the good. Utilitarianism fails on both counts: its application requires information about alternative actions and the value of their consequences that is often beyond human powers, and although it is plausible to suppose morality does require that we consider the consequences of our actions, right action is not simply a matter of maximizing good consequences.

Kant's moral theory is based on the very plausible, but vague idea that persons are to be respected and, in particular, that they are not to be used as mere means even to bring about good results, that is, part of morality involves there being limits on using people as means even for good ends. But again, Kant's theory involving the universal law formulation of the categorical imperative fails to serve as a useful decision procedure, and we also have reason to doubt that it represents a correct moral criterion.

Still, in developing an adequate moral theory, we should not lose sight of the attractive features of the utilitarian and Kantian approaches. With this in mind, let us now proceed to examine what I consider to be the most plausible type of moral theory, certainly more plausible than the ones we have already addressed.

◼ LIMITED MORAL PLURALISM

Limited moral pluralism is a general type of moral theory that features a pluralist account of the right and of the good (hence, moral pluralism) but is limited in its capacity to resolve moral disputes and uncertainty. To understand this type of theory, let us first explain what is meant by calling a theory "pluralist," and then we will examine the version of moral pluralism defended by W. D. Ross. In presenting Ross's view, we will see how and why the theory is limited.

The idea behind **moral pluralism** is that there is no *one* feature of actions that makes them right or wrong; rather, there is a plurality of such features that underlie and explain the difference between right and wrong. Similarly, for goodness and badness, there is no one feature in virtue of which something is good or bad; rather, there is a plurality of such features. Pluralist moral theories, then, contrast with versions of **moral monism** like utilitarianism and Kant's ethics that attempt to uncover a single underlying feature of actions that makes them right or wrong. For the utilitarian, that feature is the production of good consequences, and for the Kantian it is acting on a policy that you can consistently will that everyone act on. According to the moral pluralist, all such monistic views are mistaken because they attempt to simplify morality by boiling all moral considerations down to some single feature. Morality, according to the pluralist, is too complex to be captured and explained by any monistic moral theory that features a single moral principle such as the principle of utility or the categorical imperative.

One prominent version of this kind of view was developed and defended by the twentieth century philosopher W. D. Ross (1877–1971). His theory of value is the basis for part of his theory of right conduct, which is consequentialist. As we shall see, however, another part of his theory of right conduct is deontological. In this way, his overall view represents a hybrid moral theory that combines elements of the two general types of moral theory we have already examined. Let us begin with his theory of value.

◼ Ross's Theory of Value

According to Ross, the four basic kinds of intrinsic goods are:

1. *Virtue.* The disposition to act from certain desires, including the desire to do what is morally right, is intrinsically good.

2. *Pleasure.* States of experiencing pleasure are intrinsically good.
3. *Pleasure in proportion to virtue.* The state of experiencing pleasure in proportion to one's level of virtue is intrinsically good.
4. *Knowledge.* Having knowledge is intrinsically good.

Ross's main argument for his value pluralism involves reflecting on each of these four items that obviously have value and recognizing that we value them apart from what they might be used to bring about. Furthermore, according to Ross, any other valuable thing or experience you can think of turns out to be an instance of one or combination of these basic four. For instance, aesthetic enjoyment is a combination of pleasure taken in the object of enjoyment together with insight into, and hence a kind of knowledge about, that object. Such enjoyment, therefore, is reducible to a combination of pleasure and knowledge, so there is no need to add it to the list of basic intrinsic goods. As mentioned earlier, Ross's theory of value is a partial basis for his theory of right conduct to which we now turn.

■ Ross's Theory of Right Conduct

A fundamental idea in Ross's theory of right conduct is his concept of a *prima facie duty*. To say that some action is a prima facie duty is to say that it possesses some feature that morally counts in favor of doing the act. For instance, the fact that some action of mine would be the keeping of a promise I've made is a feature of the act that morally counts as a reason for doing that action. To use Ross's terminology, the fact that my action is one of keeping a promise grounds a prima facie duty to do it. Having a prima facie duty to do something, though, is not the same as having an *actual duty* to do it, because there may be some other alternative action that I have a stronger prima facie duty to perform. My actual duty in some context, then, depends on which of my prima facie duties is strongest. An example will help make these ideas clear.

Suppose that I have promised to meet you at a specific time on Saturday to give you a ride to an important job interview. Ross would say that having made this promise means that I have a prima facie duty to show up at the correct time and give you the ride I promised. But my prima facie duty to take you to the interview can be overridden if something that is morally more pressing happens to come up. Suppose that on the way to pick you up I happen to come across the scene of a very serious car accident with victims obviously in need of my help (no one else is around). Ross would say that because there is a prima facie duty of beneficence (to help others in need), I have a prima facie duty to stop and help. So now I'm in a situation where I have a prima facie duty to drive on and pick you up for your interview, and I have a conflicting prima facie duty to stop and help the accident victims. I can't do both. In this case, most reflective people would agree that my prima facie duty to help the accident victims overrides my prima facie duty to keep my promise. My actual, all-things-considered duty, then, is to stop and help—the prima facie duty of beneficence overrides the prima facie duty of promise keeping, *at least in this case*.

With respect to our actual moral duties, Ross's position is that in any circumstance in which there is only one action that I have a prima facie duty to perform, my actual duty is to perform that action. In cases where I have conflicting prima facie duties, however, I must balance and weigh all of my prima facie duties to determine which of them is most important or demanding. In cases of conflict, my actual duty depends on which of the competing prima facie duties is most stringent.

What makes Ross's theory of right conduct pluralist is that he maintains that there is a plurality of basic features of action that, when present, make an action a prima facie duty. As mentioned earlier, one part of Ross's theory of right conduct is based on his theory of value. Let us refer to these as *value-based prima facie duties*. But part of Ross's theory of right conduct involves prima facie duties that are not based on his theory of value. Following Ross, let us call them *prima facie duties of special obligation*. Here, then, is a list of Ross's seven basic prima facie duties together with associated principles.

Basic Value-Based Prima Facie Duties

1. *Justice.* Prima facie, one ought to ensure that pleasure or happiness is distributed according to merit.
2. *Beneficence.* Prima facie, one ought to help those in need and, in general, increase the virtue, pleasure, and knowledge of others.
3. *Self-improvement.* Prima facie, one ought to improve oneself with respect to one's own virtue and knowledge.
4. *Nonmaleficence.* Prima facie, one ought to refrain from harming others.

Basic Prima Facie Duties of Special Obligation

5. *Fidelity.* Prima facie, one ought to keep one's promises (including the implicit promise to be truthful).
6. *Reparation.* Prima facie, one ought to make amends to others for any past wrongs one has done them.
7. *Gratitude.* Prima facie, one ought to show gratitude toward one's benefactors.

The first four basic prima facie duties, then, make reference to what has intrinsic value according to Ross's theory of value. Ross himself points out that the prima facie duties of justice, beneficence, and self-improvement, "come under the general principle that we should produce as much good as possible."[10] This part of Ross's theory fits the characterization of consequentialism.

The duties of special obligation do not make reference to what has intrinsic value; the duties of fidelity, reparation, and gratitude do not depend for their prima facie rightness on the values of the consequences of those actions. This part of Ross's theory is clearly deontological. Overall, then, Ross's theory represents a hybrid: part consequentialist, part deontological.[11]

In defending this list of basic duties, Ross claims that each of them can be seen to be self-evident, that is, that one can, on proper reflection, simply grasp the truth of each of the principles of prima facie duty without needing any additional proof. As for the completeness of his list, Ross claims that, in all probability, any other prima facie duty will be an instance of one or more of the duties on his list. For instance, we recognize a prima facie duty to obey the laws of our country. However, as Ross points out, this duty can be understood in terms of the prima facie duties of gratitude (for the benefits we receive from the government), of beneficence (helping to promote the good of others by obeying the law), and fidelity (since by being members of a country, we implicitly consent to obey its laws), but Ross's theory has its limits.

■ The Limits of Ross's Theory

As we noted before, my prima facie duty of fidelity favors keeping the promise and thus not stopping to help the accident victims, while my prima facie duty of beneficence favors stopping to render aid, thus breaking the promise. What should I do, all things considered?

It is part of Ross's view that in cases where we find ourselves with conflicting prima facie duties, no super moral principle like the principle of utility or the categorical imperative will always yield a correct resolution of the conflict. The principle of utility, for instance, implies that the right act is the one that would produce the greatest amount of value—whatever that happens to be, but Ross denies that right actions are always actions that produce the greatest amount of value. Moreover, Ross denies that we can come up with a fixed rank ordering of the relative importance of prima facie duties so that in cases of conflict the higher ranked duty always outweighs the duty ranked below it. (The prima facie duties on the list I have given are not ranked in order of importance.)

In short, for Ross, when it comes to conflicts among prima facie duties, *there is nothing in the moral theory itself—no super principle or fixed ranking of duties—that determines what we ought to do, all things considered.* In this way, Ross's theory is limited in its implications. Then how can we arrive at correct or at least justified moral verdicts in cases of conflict?

■ The Importance of Moral Judgment

In response to this question, Ross's reply is that we must rely on what he calls *moral judgment* to determine which, from among various conflicting prima facie duties, is the most stringent and represents one's all-things-considered duty. Moral judgment is understood to be a certain kind of capacity for arriving at correct or justified moral verdicts that goes beyond the mere application of moral principles or the use of some ranking system. Sometimes moral judgment is called moral intuition—a capacity for a kind of insight into a situation calling for a moral verdict. The point is that this kind of insight cannot be fully described or summed up in terms of the application of principles. In conflict-of-duty situations, a person with moral judgment can go beyond principles and "see" which of the competing prima facie duties is the most stringent.

The role of moral judgment in Ross's theory reflects the fact that the theory itself—its set of principles of prima facie duty—is limited in what it implies about the morality of concrete actions. Some philosophers find this aspect of Ross's view objectionable, but Ross claims that the complexity of morality requires that we recognize the limits of moral theory and the role of moral judgment in moral thought and practice.

■ IN DEFENSE OF LIMITED MORAL PLURALISM

I wish to defend two claims. First, when it comes to explaining the difference between right and wrong action, pluralist moral theories such as Ross's are superior to rival monist theories like the versions of consequentialism and deontology that we have examined in this chapter. Second, although as a decision procedure Ross's version of moral pluralism is limited, we should *expect* a plausible moral theory to be limited in this way.

My argument that moral pluralism provides the best explanation of the nature of the right and the good is based on the complexity of morality. On reflection, a variety of equally basic moral considerations seem to figure into an account of the right and the good. Focusing on the pluralist account of right action, considerations of good (and bad) consequences of actions represent one important element that contributes to making an action right (or wrong), but also considerations other than good consequences, including considerations of promise keeping, gratitude, and reparation, represent another dimension of moral evaluation. Moreover, it is not plausible to suppose that one of these dimensions can be reduced to the other. After all, the duties of special obligation focus on, and are responses to, actions that have been done in the past. For example, the duty of gratitude is based on past benefits received and not on the value of the consequences of such an action. By contrast, the value-based duties are based on considerations of an action's consequences. Because the two groups of duty differ in their sources, we should not expect the duties of one group to be reducible to, or be special cases of, the duties of the other group. Nor does it seem possible to reduce the duties within one group. (Similar points can be made about Ross's list of basic intrinsic goods.)

The fact that irreducibly basic moral considerations are needed to account for the nature of right and wrong (and good and bad) explains why monist theories are bound to fail and why a theory like Ross's can combine the attractive features of consequentialism and deontology, while avoiding their problems. First, Ross's theory of right conduct captures the idea that, in at least some cases, morality requires that we maximize good consequences. Specifically, in cases where one or more of the value-based prima facie duties concerned with producing what has intrinsic value is concerned (justice, beneficence, self-improvement) and overrides any of the other prima facie duties, one should maximize good consequences. But Ross's theory avoids the unwanted implications of consequentialism because in cases where, for example, I see that keeping my promise is more important than, say, bringing about more overall goodness by acting beneficently, my all-things-considered duty is to keep my promise. Again, the duty of nonmaleficence is generally (though not always) more important than the prima duty of beneficence. So even if one can produce more overall good by sacrificing one innocent person to save three others (as in the case considered earlier), the prima facie duty of nonmaleficence overrides the prima facie duty of beneficence.

Moreover, when one asks why it would be morally wrong, all things considered, to fail to maximize good consequences in this sort of case, one very plausible answer is that in doing so one fails to respect persons properly—one treats that person as a mere means to some end. In other words, Ross's theory can be understood as capturing the idea that morality requires that we respect persons. It is not that Ross's theory accepts a supreme moral principle that directs us to respect persons from which his more specific prima facie duties can be derived. Rather, the idea is that his pluralist system of prima facie duties represents an interpretation of the vague moral ideal of respecting persons. The primary ways in which we can positively respect others is by keeping promises (fidelity), making up for our own past wrongs (reparation), being grateful (gratitude), being just (justice), helping others (beneficence), and not harming others (nonmaleficence), and the primary way of respecting oneself is to develop one's capacities and talents (self-improvement). In cases where one or more of these basic moral considerations conflict, we need sound moral judgment to determine which action, from among the various options, is most important for purposes of maintaining respect for persons. In this way, Ross's theory is able to capture the very attractive idea that morality requires respecting persons, while avoiding problems with the golden rule and with Kant's moral theory.

But what about the role of moral judgment in ethical decision making? Some philosophers think that unless there is some rigorous decision procedure based on moral principles, moral decision making is arbitrary and hence irrational. In response to this worry, I think we should recognize that, because of the complexity of morality, it is unreasonable to suppose that there must be some underlying principle that could function as the basis of a rigorous decision procedure. This does not mean that moral decision making is arbitrary and completely irrational. After all, on a view like Ross's fundamental moral principles of prima facie duty can be applied in contexts of moral decision making to draw attention to morally relevant considerations that should be factored into any reasonable moral decision. Moreover, in cases where moral judgment is needed to resolve conflict among prima facie duties, and where it is clear that one prima facie duty overrides another, we are able to give reasons why, in the case at hand, one type of moral consideration is more important than another, competing one. (Recall the case involving the accident victims in which the prima facie duty of beneficence overrides the conflicting prima facie duty of fidelity. In this case, we can explain why the former duty overrides the latter even though we have no supreme moral principle to fall back on in doing so.) Finally, we should keep in mind that genuine moral dilemmas may arise—that is, cases in which there is no single correct answer to a moral quandary and in which different people using sound moral judgment can reasonably arrive at conflicting moral verdicts about the morality of an action.

■ CONCLUSION

This chapter has focused primarily on philosophical questions about right conduct: What makes an action right or wrong? How is the rightness or wrongness of an action related to what is intrinsically good or bad? What is the proper decision procedure for arriving at correct or at least justified moral verdicts about specific actions calling for moral evaluation? These questions are part of the main subject matter of ethics, and we have considered three types of philosophical theory that attempt to answer such questions. I have argued that some versions of consequentialism and deontology fail to answer these questions satisfactorily. I have also argued that the kind of limited pluralist moral theory of W. D. Ross is arguably superior to its consequentialist and deontology rivals. Even if certain details of Ross's theory are mistaken, I claim that some version of limited moral pluralism is the best form of moral theory there is.[12]

■ NOTES

1. As we shall see in our examination of the utilitarian moral theory, there is some disagreement among philosophers about whether the principles of a moral theory must satisfy both theoretical and practical aims.

2. See Jeremy Bentham, *An Introduction to the Principles of Morals and Legislation* (New York: Hafner Press, 1948, originally published in 1789) and J. S. Mill, *Utilitarianism* (Indianapolis, Ind.: Hackett Publishing, 1979, originally published in 1861).

3. Since the objection under consideration is aimed at all versions of utilitarianism, both hedonistic and nonhedonistic, it is proper to focus on U—what I have labeled as the basic principle of utility.

4. Robert Nozick, *Anarchy, State, and Utopia* (New York: Basic Books, 1974), 42.

5. By definition, a utilitarian is a consequentialist who takes welfare to be intrinsically good and the proper basis for an account of right action. However, some consequentialists who, because they reject the idea that welfare alone is intrinsically valuable and central in explaining right action, count as nonutilitarians. Such views often explain right action in terms of promoting human perfection. Again, space does not allow us to consider this species of consequentialism.

6. Kant published three main works on ethics: *Groundwork of the Metaphysics of Morals* (1785), *Critique of Practical Reason* (1788), and *The Metaphysics of Morals* (1797). All three are translated by Mary Gregor and published in a single volume, *Practical Philosophy* (Cambridge: Cambridge University Press, 1996) as part of the *Cambridge Edition of the Works of Immanuel Kant*, Paul Guyer and Allen Wood, eds.

7. *Practical Philosophy*, 74.

8. Elsewhere, I argue that although the formulation of Kant's supreme principle expressed here by CI does represent a decision procedure, it does not represent a moral criterion. See Mark Timmons, *Moral Theory: An Introduction* (Lanham, Md.: Rowman and Littlefield, 2002), ch. 7.

9. This example is a slightly revised version of the one given by Fred Feldman, *Introductory Ethics* (Prentice-Hall, 1978), 116.

10. W. D. Ross, *The Right and the Good* (Oxford: Oxford University Press, 1930), 27.

11. *Deontology* is sometimes defined very broadly to include any moral theory that does not make the morality of an action *entirely* depend on the values of consequences. On this broad definition, Ross's theory counts as a version of deontology.

12. I wish to thank Josh Glasgow, Leemon McHenry, Linda Sadler, and Takashi Yagisawa for helpful comments on an earlier draft of this chapter.

■ QUESTIONS

1. To be able to add and subtract amounts of pleasure and pain, some *unit* of hedonic value must be established. Is it plausible to suppose that there is some such unit of hedonic value? What might it be?

2. Mill claimed that some pleasures are higher in quality than others and that in calculating the utility of an action we ought to consider both quantity and quality of pleasure (and pain). Are some pleasures of a higher quality than others? If so, what would explain this?

3. Suppose that all of the alternative actions open to you on some occasion would have a negative utility. What does the principle of utility require you to do in that case?

4. Under what conditions, if any, does utilitarianism imply that slavery is morally right?

5. Can the principle associated with the golden rule be reformulated so that it has implications about duties to oneself?

6. Can the principle associated with the golden rule be reformulated to avoid the unwanted implications mentioned in the text?

7. Is there any real difference between the golden rule positively stated (Do unto others as you would have them do unto you) and the golden rule negative stated (Do *not* do unto others what you would *not* have them do unto you)?

8. Kant argued that the categorical imperative could be used to show that we have duties to ourselves including the duty not to commit suicide and the duty to develop our talents. Consider whether and how the categorical imperative might be used to show that we have such duties.

9. In the example of lying to someone about their haircut to avoid causing them unnecessary pain, we considered two very general maxims or policies to be tested by Kant's categorical imperative. Perhaps a better maxim to use in this case would be *I will lie to others to spare them unnecessary pain*. If this maxim is used for purposes of moral evaluation, what does Kant's principle imply about the morality of telling the lie? Should this maxim be used instead of the two mentioned in the text? If so, why?

10. Most people agree that friendship is good. Is a theory of value such as Ross's able to explain the goodness of friendship?

11. Do you agree with the author's claim that appealing to moral judgment does not make morality arbitrary?

12. How would the various moral theories we have examined in this chapter deal with treatment of animals and treatment of the environment? Which of the theories seems most plausible in what it implies about the ethical treatment of animals and the environment?

■ **FOR FURTHER READING**

Feldman, Fred. 1978. *Introductory Ethics*. Englewood Cliffs, N.J.: Prentice-Hall.

Frankena, William. 1973. *Ethics*, 2nd ed. Englewood Cliffs, N.J.: Prentice-Hall.

Nagel, Thomas. 1979. "The Fragmentation of Value." Reprinted in *Mortal Questions*. Cambridge: Cambridge University Press.

Smart, J. J. C., and Williams, Bernard. 1973. *Utilitarianism: For and Against*. Cambridge: Cambridge University Press.

Singer, Marcus. 1967. "Golden Rule." *In:* Paul Edwards, ed. *The Encyclopedia of Philosophy*, vol. 3. New York: Macmillan Publishing.

Singer, Peter, ed. 1993. *A Companion to Ethics*. Oxford: Basil Blackwell.

Timmons, Mark. 2002. *Moral Theory: An Introduction*. Lanham, Md.: Rowman and Littlefield.

■ CHAPTER SEVEN

Feminist Ethics

REBECCA WHISNANT

■ *INTRODUCTION*

Feminist ethics is a relatively new arrival on the philosophical scene. Thinking about the significance of gender in our conduct and institutions is hardly new, but it is only fairly recently that philosophers in large numbers have begun to incorporate such thinking into their investigations of the nature of ethics.

On hearing that such a thing as "feminist ethics" exists, people are often—and understandably—puzzled as to what sort of enterprise it could be. After all, they think, ethics is ethics, and whatever ethical theories and standards turn out to be most rationally defensible, they will presumably be so for everyone alike. Are feminist ethicists suggesting that some different ethical standard or ideal exists for women—or for feminists?

This puzzlement is entirely reasonable and the issue it raises absolutely central. In my view, the core of **feminism** as an ethical and political position is the endorsement of a single standard of human freedom and dignity for every-one, regardless of gender.[1] To make this standard a social reality, however—instead of just a nice idea that we carry around in our heads—we must come to understand what kinds of systems and behaviors undermine it and what theories and assumptions support and underlie those systems and behaviors. We need a substantive standard of human freedom and dignity, a clear view of what stands between it and us, and a conception of what is required to bring us closer to real-izing it. In a world still rigidly structured by gender discrimination, this requires both a feminist analysis of society and an approach to ethical philosophy that takes seriously the influences of gender bias.

This chapter begins with a description of the core tenets of feminism along with some brief support for the most controversial of these. I'll then explain how a male gender bias has pervaded much of philosophical ethics and summarize two different (although related) approaches to remedying that bias: *feminine ethics* and *feminist ethics*. I will argue that feminine ethics alone is inadequate to the task described above, and that feminist ethics incorporates the important insights of feminine ethics while avoiding its sometimes perilous deficiencies.

■ WHAT IS FEMINISM?

Although contemporary feminism is diverse and many faceted, it is nonetheless possible to characterize briefly its core tenets. You may well find one or more of these claims controversial; my aim just now, however, is not so much to defend their truth as to clarify what is being said, which is often, as here, the first concern of philosophers.

■ *Core Tenets of Feminism*

Feminism begins with the claim that:

1. Women and men are *rational and moral equals*.

With respect to the basic rational and moral capacities that define personhood, neither gender is naturally or inherently inferior to the other. To endorse claim 1 does not require denying that there are differences between men and women with respect to their predominant psychological traits and dispositions; as we will see, feminists differ about the existence and extent of such gender-based differences and, perhaps more importantly, about their origins and their meanings. The import of claim 1 is that, however alike or different, men and women are equal in human dignity and worth and as such are entitled to equal concern and respect.

Such equal concern and respect requires granting to both men and women a full and equal complement of rights. To ensure equal social and civil status, these rights must be *effective*, that is, actually respected, rather than merely officially granted. According to the second major tenet of feminism, however, the reality is quite otherwise:

2. Women and men are not currently *social and political equals*. Gender inequality exists, in most if not all societies, and this inequality systematically disadvantages women.

Taken together, tenets 1 and 2 portray a disconnect between an enduring moral reality and a set of prevailing social and political circumstances: a group of people that is in fact equal in human dignity and worth is not being treated as such. Recognizing this disconnect naturally yields the conclusion that:

3. Gender inequality is unjust and should be ended.

■ *Distinguishing Feminists from Nonfeminists*

One virtue of the conception of feminism just outlined is that it helps us distinguish feminists from nonfeminists in ways that are both helpful and intuitively plausible. In particular, it enables us to see that feminism requires the acceptance of *both* claims 1 and 2 and the consequent recognition (as in claim 3) of prevailing conditions as unjust.

It is common to mistake the acceptance of tenet 1 alone for feminism, that is, to think that feminism is simply a matter of believing in the inherent equality of men and women. The belief that women are just as worthy and competent as men, and that they are thus entitled to equality, is certainly important and valuable; however, it does not yet articulate a feminist position. For if one also believes that men and women are *now* socially and politically equal—for instance, that women have fully overcome any disadvantages or obstacles that may have impeded them in the past and now enjoy the equality that they deserve—then one's position is not feminist. Feminism is an oppositional and critical politics, to which the recognition of current injustice is essential. It is for this reason that feminism's aim is to make itself obsolete.

It is also possible (although less easily mistaken for feminism) to accept claim 2 without accepting claim 1. For instance, one might believe that gender inequality exists and that it disadvantages women but that because women *are* naturally inferior to men, that is, are not men's rational and moral equals, the social inequality between men and women is just, fair, and appropriate. Thus proponents of this position will, in light of their rejection of claim 1, also reject claim 3. (It is difficult, these days, to get away with openly articulating this position, at least in mixed company. As a result, we see individuals and organizations publicly defending positions of dubious coherence: the Southern Baptist Conference, for example, recently asserted that women should submit to their husbands' leadership and refrain from preaching in public, while in the same breath declaring that men and women are "equal."[2])

Finally, note that one could accept that systematic and unjust gender inequality currently exists, but hold that it is men rather than women who are disadvantaged by it. This position is advanced by many proponents of the "men's rights" or "masculist" movement.

■ WHY FEMINISM?

Although there are certainly those who reject claim 1, many debates and misunderstandings between feminists and nonfeminists concern the acceptance or rejection of claim 2, that is, of the claim that women now lack social and political equality. Some people deny claim 2 outright; many others contend that, although women in many areas of the world are still seriously disadvantaged, women in the United States and other Western industrial democracies have succeeded in gaining equality.

Although it is not my primary task to defend the truth of the core feminist tenets above, offering some support for tenet 2 will aid further discussion by clarifying some of what is at issue. To this end, let me discuss just two important areas in which women (including U.S. women) are now seriously disadvantaged by gender inequality: the areas of work and of vulnerability to violence.

■ *Women's Work: Separate and Unequal*

You may have heard it said before that women tend to receive less money for doing the same work as men and that women face a form of discrimination in promotion known as the "glass ceiling." These claims are true and important, but far more significant in affecting masses of women is what we might call the "sticky floor"—the fact that in almost any field, women line the bottom. Women face segregation into low-paying and low-prestige "women's work"—largely service occupations such as clerical support, nursing, teaching, home health, day care, and elder care. That there are many exceptions to this rule, and that the segregation is not legally enforced, does not alter its detrimental effects on the lives of most women.

This means that getting less money for the same work is, although important, the least of most women's problems because, in most cases, women are not doing the same work as men, and the work that they do is undervalued and underpaid because they are women. Jobs requiring similar levels of education and training are valued and rewarded differently depending on whether they are performed primarily by men or primarily by women.[3] The issue is not so much whether a female child-care worker or construction worker makes as much as a male child-care worker or construction worker but, instead, why most child-care workers are female and most construction workers male and why construction workers make more money than child-care workers do.

Finally, whether or not women work outside the home for pay, they continue to bear a disproportionate responsibility for domestic labor—the maintenance of households and the care of children, elders, and other dependents. Although recent decades have seen some increase in men's participation in these duties, the increase is substantially less than one might hope, and the time women spend on such labor (again, even when they also work outside the home) still far exceeds that spent by men. This has led some feminists to refer to women's domestic labor as the "second shift."[4] This labor, of course, is not paid at all, and too often is not even recognized as real work, especially when it is done by poor women receiving government assistance. Such unpaid labor by women (or indeed by anyone) is not counted as part of any country's gross domestic product, thus resulting in dangerously skewed portrayals of economic reality.[5]

■ *Violence and Terror in Women's Lives*

Most of us, from time to time, have heard recitals of grim and shocking statistics about the incidence of rape, battering, sexual harassment, and other forms of sexual violence and exploitation in the lives of women and girls. That these statistics vary in their details should not blind us to their underlying *agreement*: that male violence against women is both exceedingly common and dramatically underreported. We know, for instance, that women and girls are raped in all kinds of circumstances—by dates, by husbands and boyfriends, by fathers and step-fathers, by bosses and coworkers, as well as (less frequently) by men who are strangers to them. In a recent survey of 16,000 Americans, jointly sponsored by the National Institute of Justice and the Centers for Disease Control and Prevention, 18 percent of women reported having been victims of rape or attempted rape at some point in their lives.[6] Girls and young women are especially vulnerable to sexual assault: the same study showed that 54 percent of rape victims were under the age of eighteen when they were first raped. Among women who had been raped or physically assaulted after the age of eighteen, 76 percent were attacked by a current or former husband, cohabiting partner, or date. Finally, it is important to remember that many women suffer multiple incidents of sexual violence during their lives: among women who reported having been raped within the twelve months prior to the survey, the average number of rapes per woman during that twelve-month period was 2.9.

Thirty years of feminist critique and activism have brought about important and necessary changes in the law, in prevailing attitudes toward these abuses, and in the services available to their victims. It is important to remember, however, that the primary feminist aim in this area is to reduce the *actual incidence* of these abuses, and ultimately to end them entirely. The goal of feminism is to bring about equality, and equality requires that this damaging and discriminatory burden in the lives of women be removed, not merely that more of its perpetrators be punished or its victims treated better in the aftermath. Unfortunately, no evidence shows that women and girls are being raped, battered, and sexually harassed any less frequently now than ten or thirty years ago; the devastation wrought in women's lives by these abuses continues unabated.

One might reasonably wonder whether these abuses of women are correctly thought of as an element of gender inequality; as terrible as they are (one might say), they do not affect all women, but only those who are their victims. Feminists have argued, however, that this complex amalgam of abuses harms *all* women and girls in our culture. This is so in a number of ways; I'll discuss just one, namely, that women and girls live their daily lives in fear of violence. We are taught that male violence against women is a natural and inevitable feature of the social environment and that women can avoid such violence only by controlling their own behavior in certain rigidly specified ways.[7] The result is that women have less freedom than do men: to walk alone at night, to go on dates without fear of assault, to drink a bit too much at a party, to work late in a deserted office, to dress as they please, to drive across the country alone, and to sleep with the window open, to name just a few. Although no law forbids these actions, our culture teaches that women who do such things put themselves in danger. Too often, the implication is that any subsequent attacks on them are their own fault: "What was she doing there, anyway?"

■ *The Concept of Oppression*

The features of women's lives just described are among many that provide evidence for claim 2 above—that women are not currently the social and political equals of men. Far from being aridly legalistic, claim 2 addresses matters close to the center of our lives as men and as women: what work we do, what burdens we must bear, what dangers we face inside and outside our key relationships, and what resources are available to us to lead the lives that we want to lead. Furthermore, these matters involve some of our most fundamental rights as human beings: the right to bodily safety and integrity, the right to freedom of movement and freedom from terror, the right to work, and the right to the resources necessary to maintain a decent life for oneself and one's dependents.

To aid in understanding of these matters, feminists have employed a concept that has been important in liberation movements of many kinds: the concept of **oppression**. Our claim has been that women are an oppressed group. Although the concept of oppression has been defined in different ways, most theorists agree that oppression is much more than the sum of intentional acts of discrimination by bigoted individuals. According to Marilyn Frye's influential definition, oppression is a "*system* of interrelated barriers and forces which reduce, immobilize, and mold people who belong to a certain group, and effect their subordination to another group."[8]

Because of the complex and systematic nature of women's oppression, its roots and consequences, like those of other forms of oppression, are not always immediately apparent. Instead, elements of gender oppression lie buried in many of our least questioned assumptions about our lives and in many of our most widely accepted practices. According to some feminists, such elements also lie buried, and sometimes not so buried, in the assumptions and practices of philosophical ethics.

■ *ANDROCENTRISM IN PHILOSOPHICAL ETHICS*

The field of academic philosophy, historically male dominated, has in recent decades seen an influx of more women into its ranks. It has become apparent to many such women (and to a number of male philosophers as well) that much of the history of philosophy, including that of philosophical ethics, is male biased, or androcentric. Why this would be so is not difficult to understand. The works constituting that history were written almost entirely by men—mostly privileged and powerful ones, although not without exception—during historical periods when education, freedom of movement, and the production of cultural and intellectual work were largely off-limits for women.

This point, although neither mysterious nor especially complex, is enormously important. It reveals that, however tempting it may be to view the history of philosophy as the continuing effort of human beings to understand themselves and their place in the universe, this history is in fact almost entirely the effort of (again, mostly privileged) *men* to understand themselves and *their* place in the universe. Following are several ways in which this **androcentrism** has expressed itself in the history of philosophical ethics.

■ *Female Invisibility*

Perhaps the most pervasive expression of androcentrism in philosophical ethics has been its tendency to ignore women outright. Whatever the generic uses of the pronoun "he" may or may not be in contemporary discourse, for the authors of most historical works of philosophy "he" meant exactly what it said: the moral agent, the hero, the soldier, the citizen, the man of virtue, are all explicitly and unself-consciously conceived as male. In these texts, for the most part, moral deliberation is something that takes place within the minds or souls of individual males, and communal moral life is the life that men lead in the company of other men. For this reason, female students reading these undeniably important works often find that they have to try to "read themselves into" the texts; given the texts' frequent omission of women's very existence, let alone of women's perspectives or roles in the moral community, this is not always an easy thing to do. This form of androcentrism, while clearly a product of women's oppression, also contributes to that oppression by conveying that the lives, concerns, and choices of women are so unimportant as to be beneath mention.

■ *Overt Misogyny*

Where women have come to the attention of ethical philosophers, that attention has usually been unfavorable: women have often been the objects of overt **misogyny**. (Notable exceptions to this rule include Plato [427–347 B.C.]—at least in *The Republic*—and, centuries later, the strongly feminist John Stuart Mill [1806–1873].) From side comments to extended analyses, what philosophers have had to say on the subject of women—concerning their nature, value, and proper roles—has by and large ranged from mocking to vicious.

Aristotle (384–322 B.C.) and Kant (1724–1804), arguably the two greatest ethical theorists in the history of philosophy, are particularly notorious for their sexism. (I will have more to say about Kant shortly.) Feminist philosopher Cynthia Freeland helpfully summarizes some of Aristotle's views on the subject of women: "Aristotle says that the courage of a man lies in commanding, a woman's lies in obeying; that 'matter yearns for form, as the female for the male and the ugly for the beautiful' . . . that a female is an incomplete male or 'as it were, a deformity', which contributes only matter and not form to the generation of offspring; that in general 'a woman is perhaps an inferior being'; that female characters in a tragedy will be inappropriate if they are too brave or too clever."[9] To Aristotle, the conclusion was clear: "the male is by nature superior, and the female inferior; and the one rules, and the other is ruled; this principle, of necessity, extends to all mankind."[10]

Once we notice invisibility and expressions of misogyny in the history of ethics, it is possible to respond in various ways. One response is to ask whether such authors as Aristotle and Kant can be legitimately *blamed* for their attitudes toward women and for the expression of those attitudes in their philosophical works, that is, whether given their historical and cultural circumstances, they could and should have done better.[11] Although this is a worthwhile line of inquiry, feminist philosophers have typically been more interested in whether and how these authors' misogyny relates to other elements of their own theories and (relatedly) in whether that misogyny has filtered down through the tradition to be picked up and reflected in some of our contemporary moral assumptions, theories, and practices.

An optimistic response to these questions, while acknowledging that it is wrong to exclude or vilify women, would contend that these features of historical texts do not bear on the overall value or truth of the theories they present. That is, one might say that although these authors should have included women in their theories on equal terms with men, their failure to do so does not bear on the fundamental worth of their theories. According to this approach, we should simply ignore these theorists' false beliefs about women, read their theories *as if* they had meant them to apply to women too, and evaluate other elements of their views independently of their misogynist beliefs and assumptions.

There is certainly something to this approach. That a theorist expresses contempt for women does not invalidate his views on a wide range of subjects, and we benefit from studying the works of undeniably great ethical philosophers such as Kant and Aristotle regardless of their opinions about women. The assumption that their misogyny has no bearing on the rest of their theories, however, is open to question. There is at least one important way in which female invisibility and misogyny combine to underwrite some fundamental and continuing assumptions in the history of ethics.

■ *The Male Standard in Ethical Theory*

One central task of ethical theory is to articulate and defend a human ideal, that is, to identify the defining features of an ideally good human life. It is in contrast to this ideal, or standard, that deviations or failures can be recognized as such. As we pursue the task of defining such an ideal, however—as with most tasks of any importance—various forms of bias and blindness tend to infect our perceptions. With this in mind, many feminist philosophers have charged that what passes for a human ideal in much of standard philosophical ethics is in fact a *male* ideal.

Imagine opening a medical textbook and seeing, under the heading "The Human Body," a drawing of the body of an adult male. When you ask where you might find a drawing and explanation of female anatomy, you are told that you need a different book, for this information is to be found in a special subdiscipline of medicine, that of obstetrics/gynecology. Nothing negative has been said about women; the message is simply that the male body "stands in" for the human body unmodified, and the female body is special and different—different, that is, from the *standard* set by the male body.

Something quite similar can occur in ethical theory and, according to feminist ethicists, frequently has. The tendency is to look at men to see how they approach moral life: what they see as ethically relevant decisions, how they make those decisions, and what they think is involved in making those decisions well. (Recall, again, that men have historically been not only the objects of such inquiry but also its subjects—the ones doing the inquiring, often including introspectively inquiring into their own psyches.) What is observed of men, or considered to be ideal for men, is then elevated to be the standard for human beings in general: "man" comes to stand in for "moral agent" and "good man" for "good person," in much the way that the male body stands in for the human body in the earlier example. Men are taken as the paradigm of humanity, and a male point of view is disguised as a universal or objective point of view. As Susan Sherwin puts it, "men have constructed ethics in their own psychological image."[12]

Again, nothing negative has yet been said about women, at least not explicitly. In fact, however, invisibility and misogyny have already made their appearance: when women's experiences, perspectives, and practices are considered irrelevant to the task of defining a human ideal, the assumption that women are inferior and unimportant is already firmly in place. This assumption is then reinforced when, with our "human" (male) standard in hand, we eventually do look at women and find that they *differ* from that standard.

We all know that men and women differ anatomically. However, when a male standard of human anatomy is in place, it is hardly surprising that various aspects of female biology come to be pathologized, that is, treated as deviant, problematic, and indicative of sickness and malfunction. Many health care professionals of both sexes have made valiant efforts to combat this tendency, but the male standard is still influential in our society's medical treatment of women: our medical establishment markets powerful antidepressant drugs to women with premenstrual symptoms, treats childbirth as a dangerous process routinely requiring extensive technological intervention, and pressures postmenopausal women into taking hormones for the rest of their lives.[13]

A male standard in ethical theory has similar implications. Again, to the extent that women are thought to deviate from the standard set by men, women are judged to be defective. We can see this pattern most clearly, again, by looking to a historical example. Kant famously argued that moral duties are "categorical," that is, binding on us irrespective of what we happen to desire. He also argued that one's actions have no true moral worth unless they are performed "from the motive of duty," that is, unless one does the right thing not because one wants to, but because one recognizes that a universally applicable moral principle (the categorical imperative) requires it.[14] In this context, consider Kant's views on the nature and capacities of women: "Women will avoid the wicked not because it is unright, but only because it is ugly . . . nothing of duty, nothing of compulsion, nothing of obligation! . . . They do something only because it pleases them . . . I hardly believe that the fair sex is capable of principles."[15] According to Kant, then, the very form of thought and action that constitutes moral life itself is a form of which women are incapable.

It is important for us to understand what has happened here (and in many structurally similar cases). It could be one of two things. Kant might have determined on independent grounds that a certain form of thought and action is constitutive of moral life and then discovered that, as a matter of empirical fact, women are not capable of that form of thought and action. Alternatively, he might have assumed from the outset that *whatever* it is women do and think is *by definition* not a part of morality proper. According to the second interpretation, the assumption about women comes first, and the conception of morality is built around it; women are locked out of this moral framework not simply empirically but also conceptually and *a priori*.

It is difficult to say which of these interpretations is closer to the truth. Most likely, Kant's beliefs about the nature of women developed as part of a complex interplay with his beliefs about the nature of morality. The central task for feminist ethicists, however, is not so much to discern what went on in Kant's head but, instead, to investigate whether and how some forms of moral theory *may* have shut women out conceptually (instead of, or in addition to, shutting them out empirically) and, if so, how such conceptual error affects these theories' conclusions. We need to take seriously the possibility that male bias can lead us into error not simply *about women* (although such error is important in its own right) but also *about morality itself.*

■ *Implications of the Male Standard*

A theory that adopts a male standard says essentially this: women and men are different, and manhood is the standard or ideal from which women deviate. A frequent corollary of such a theory is that there are in fact separate and distinct ideals, or virtues, appropriate for men and women respectively. Again, Aristotle provides an illustration: he believed that the virtues of free men are those appropriate to full citizenship and political activity, while those of "free" (that is, nonslave) women are those appropriate to servitude, such as silence and obedience. Although few in contemporary U.S. society would openly defend this view, feminists have observed parallels to it in many of our ordinary judgments about what constitutes proper "feminine" versus "masculine" behavior. A "good [properly masculine] man," for instance, is strong, courageous, assertive, rational, and in control, and a "good [properly feminine] woman" is quiet, nurturing, dependent, and compliant.

Such gender-based standards, although clearly in flux and often veiled rather than explicitly expressed, have many important consequences in the lives of women and men. Most obviously, both women and men are often judged harshly and penalized for perceived deviations from the standards deemed appropriate for their sex. A woman may be labeled pushy, aggressive, or "a bitch" for behavior that would be deemed admirably assertive in a man, while a man may be derided as wimpy, weak, or "womanish" when he expresses vulnerability in a way that would be seen as natural or appropriate in a woman. Whenever such double standards are applied, their inherent gender bias must be examined and criticized.

The consequences *for women* of a male-biased standard, however, have an additional and extremely important dimension. Whenever there are different ideals for men and women, and the male ideal is taken to be the paradigm of humanity itself, the result for women is a pervasive and damaging double bind.[16] As mentioned above, to the extent that a woman approximates the male standard, she is defective as a woman: insufficiently feminine, mannish, a freak, a bitch. Granted, she can be judged a "good woman" by conforming fully to the female standard, that is, to norms of femininity. We must remember, however, that on this model, *womanhood itself* is a defective, lesser form of humanity. It thus appears that, whenever a male standard is in place, a woman can be *either* an ideally good woman or an ideally good person—but not both.

■ *The Male Standard, Revised and Updated*

It is worth briefly noting two ways in which one might modify the picture that I've drawn so far. First, one might claim that women really are just like men after all, that is, that women do conform to the male standard and that any suggestion to the contrary is a wholly unfounded stereotype. Alternatively, one might argue that, although women have by and large fallen short of the male standard, this shortfall is owing not to women's nature but to the unjust constraints that have been placed on women's development and activities. For instance, one might say, if attention to abstract principles were as encouraged and rewarded in women as in men, then women would in fact draw closer to this aspect of the human ideal.

These views are certainly improvements, in that neither depicts women as naturally and irredeemably defective. They do, however, leave in place the *sub-stance* of the standard previously deemed male. That is, the qualities previously thought appropriate for men are now thought to be the qualities appropriate for humans in general. It may be, however, that in adopting this standard as the human ideal, we risk losing or disregarding something of great value. Many feminists have argued, in fact, that it is the *substance* of the male standard that is limited and biased, not merely the assumption that only men can or should embody that standard.

■ FEMININE ETHICS: CHALLENGING ANDROCENTRISM

Challenging androcentrism in philosophical ethics requires that we bring women fully into the picture—and that we do so without the inherently misogynist assumption that maleness sets the standard for humanity. That is, ethical theorizing must be undertaken in full recognition of core feminist tenet 1 above: that women and men are moral and rational equals. Incorporating tenet 1 requires that we take women seriously as moral agents: how do *women* understand themselves, perceive the world, and think about moral questions? What do *women* think is important and valuable in human life? Philosophical ethics must embody and express respect for women as human equals by devoting attention to and understanding women's points of view.

The next question, of course, is "What are women's points of view?" And the answer, of course, is that they are many and diverse—there is no single "female" or "feminine" way of thinking (about morality or anything else), let alone any single set of beliefs and values embraced by all women. But it has seemed to many people (feminist, nonfeminist, and antifeminist alike) that there are—at least within particular cultures, if not across them—some very general patterns of divergence between the moral perspectives of men and women. (After all, if no such gendered differences exist, then the male standard in ethical theory will be of little practical consequence.)

The first central claim of "feminine ethics," then, is an empirical one: that the typical or predominant moral perspectives of women and men, respectively, are *different*. (A weaker version of this claim would be that, given the historical tendency to ignore and vilify women, it is at least necessary to *investigate* whether such a difference exists and, if so, what it means.) This empirical claim can be, and has been, assessed in different ways, both through formal research (most often conducted by psychologists) and by the kind of careful and attentive reflection on our own social experience by which we evaluate empirical claims of many kinds.

The second claim central to feminine ethics is a normative one: that women's differences from men in the moral realm—whatever and however extensive these differences may be—should not be assumed to be deficiencies, any more than men's differences from women should be assumed to be deficiencies. Within the historical context that I've outlined, this claim is revolutionary, for it upsets the basic assumption of the male as standard. In recent decades, this conceptual shift away from taking the male as standard has reverberated across many academic fields, not to mention within the personal lives of many women and men.

■ Gilligan's Ethics of Care

Much philosophical work in feminine ethics has been inspired and influenced by the research of Carol Gilligan. Although Gilligan is an educational psychologist, not a philosopher, her observations about patterns of difference between male and female ethical styles (or "voices") have contributed much to philosophers' efforts to begin taking women's moral perception and reasoning seriously.[17]

Gilligan began developing her distinctive research program during the 1970s, largely as an outgrowth of and response to her work with Lawrence Kohlberg, another influential psychological researcher. On the basis of his own studies, Kohlberg had outlined six distinct "stages" of moral development through which people pass in their (often incomplete) journeys to moral maturity.[18] The idea is that, at each successive stage, one has different (and better) sorts of *reasons* for conforming to moral constraints as one understands them. Kohlberg's stages are as follows:

> *Stage 1*: Punishment and Reward. For instance, a child refrains from hitting her little brother to avoid a "time-out" or to get a cookie.
>
> *Stage 2*: Limited Reciprocity. A child shares his own toys in hopes that his playmate will share hers with him.
>
> *Stage 3*: Social Approval. A teenager behaves according to prevailing norms so that others will approve of her. This is sometimes called the "good boy–nice girl" orientation.
>
> *Stage 4*: Law and Order. A person behaves out of a sense of duty to respect authority and maintain the prevailing social order—and out of an accompanying desire to be respected as an upstanding member of society.
>
> *Stage 5*: Social Contract. Here one conforms to society's rules in the belief that those rules regulate people's behavior in ways that allow each to pursue his own interests without undue interference from others, thus benefiting each in the long run.
>
> *Stage 6*: Universal Principles. Here one understands and assesses one's own behavior by reference to universal ethical principles (such as justice, reciprocity, equality, and respect) that are thought of as self-legislated and as independent of the moral codes of one's own (or any) particular society.

Using this scale, Kohlberg set out to assess the level of moral development of his research subjects. In his interviews, Kohlberg asked people to respond to a series of fictional moral dilemmas. One of these dilemmas, later used by Gilligan in one of her studies, is now famously known as the Heinz dilemma. The story goes like this: Heinz's wife is dying, and her life can be saved only by administering a certain very expensive drug, which Heinz cannot afford to buy. The druggist, although aware of the situation's urgency, refuses to lower the price of the drug. Respondents were asked what Heinz should do under the circumstances—for instance, whether he should steal the drug—and why. Their level of moral development was assessed on the basis not of what answer they gave, but of what kinds of reasons and considerations they brought to bear in favor of their answer.

Using his six-stage scale, Kohlberg assessed the moral development of many people from various cultures, nations, races, and walks of life. All of his initial subjects, however, had one characteristic in common: they were all male. Furthermore, when Kohlberg's instrument was eventually administered to females, the results were striking: females tended to score a full level lower on Kohlberg's scale than did their male counterparts. This was partly because female respondents tended to look for solutions to Heinz's dilemma that would preserve *connections* between the various parties. For instance, some suggested that Heinz and the druggist keep negotiating and agree on a payment plan. One young girl pointed out that if Heinz were to steal the drug, then he might go to jail, and then what if his wife needed more of the drug later? In light of this worry, she concluded that Heinz and his wife "should really just talk it out and find some other way to make the money."[19]

Note that this young girl's response resists a simple either-or solution and also avoids a strict priority ranking of the relevant values (for instance, of life over money or of one person's rights over another's). Instead, she emphasizes that this particular event takes place within a network of relationships that extends over time, and she seems to put highest priority on maintaining those relationships and trying to get people's needs met within them. Such a response is difficult to assess using Kohlberg's scale. The temptation, however, is to place answers like this at stage three, that is, to see them as concerned with approval and with being a "good girl." Thus it was that, when Kohlberg's scale was applied, many female respondents appeared to be "stuck" at stage three, while many males ascended to stages four and five.

The gender difference in these results seemed to indicate one of two things: either females are less morally developed than males or there is something skewed about the standards that Kohlberg was using to measure moral development. As we now know, the former is a historically familiar idea. Gilligan, properly wary of its implications, undertook her own research and interviewed both males and females about their responses to ethical dilemmas (both real and imagined). Based on this research, she argued that there are two distinct moral "voices," or ways of thinking about and responding to ethical questions, loosely associated with women and men respectively. Gilligan called these the ethics of care (or responsibility) and the ethics of justice (or rights).

These two moral voices differ in their core themes and values and in the kinds of considerations that they take to be most relevant to reaching good moral decisions. The justice perspective begins with a conception of persons as separate individuals. These separate individuals need common rules to govern their interactions with each other; a primary function of these rules is to safeguard a realm of autonomy within which each individual may operate without undue interference from others. Thus, central to this perspective is the notion of individual rights, which are the same for everyone and must be respected fairly and impartially. Moral decision making is a matter of adjudicating conflicts between rights and of seeing to it that one's actions conform to abstract and universal codes of conduct. According to Gilligan, the justice perspective is more prominent in the moral voices of males than in those of females.

The care perspective, in contrast, begins with a conception of persons as embedded in social relationships, in which they bear different and sometimes conflicting responsibilities to each other. Here, the priority is on creating and preserving such connections between people and on avoiding and ending people's suffering. One's duty is to care about and promote people's well-being, and one's responsibility is to respond to the needs of individuals located in concrete, particular situations—often by strengthening the relationships that support those individuals. Gilligan found that the care perspective is expressed most prominently and most frequently by women and girls.

Many have found Gilligan's picture intuitively plausible, at least in its broad outlines. It seems to describe a difference that we can see operating in our own social experience as (and among) women and men. Moreover, it is not difficult to imagine why there might be substantial differences between men's and women's moral perspectives. For men and women, by and large, lead different kinds of lives.

■ *Gendered Responsibilities*

Whether or not women and men are naturally or inevitably different, what is certain is that women and men encounter the social world differently. This is because that world is structured by a gendered division of labor, in which women and men are assigned different responsibilities. As Marilyn Friedman puts it, "the tasks of governing, regulating social order, and managing other 'public' institutions have been monopolized by men as their privileged domain, and the tasks of sustaining privatized personal relationships have been imposed on, or left to, women."[20] More concretely, women are assigned responsibility for the care of homes, children, and people's intimate emotional and physical needs (such as nurturance, food, cleanliness, clothing, and the like). Even where women work outside the home for pay, as is common in contemporary U.S. culture, we can see the influence of this traditional division of labor: women are overrepresented in fields such as nursing, day care, elementary education, maid service, and food service. Both inside and outside the home, tending to the intimate needs of others tends to be, both in cultural conception and in actual fact, "women's work."

The gendered division of labor is more rigid in some cultures and time periods than in others; furthermore, there is some cross-cultural variance in *what* the gender-specific roles and responsibilities are. Nonetheless, *that* people's assigned activities differ by gender is far less variant. One gender-specific responsibility that has drawn the attention of a number of philosophers interested in women's moral lives is that of *mothering*. Having primary responsibility for the intimate care and nurturing of children seems likely to shape women's moral perspectives in especially deep and pervasive ways.

In any case, it seems plausible to suppose that people's ways of thinking are shaped significantly by what they spend their time doing, with and for whom, governed by what norms and expectations, and so on. Thus, it should not surprise us if men's and women's approaches to many things, including moral reasoning, turn out to be different. Whether or not a particular gendered division of labor is appropriate, necessary, or just, the patterns of moral reasoning and response that emerge from and support women's labor are important and complex. Understanding and evaluating these patterns is crucial to a full understanding of morality and is the primary aim of feminine ethics.

■ THREE CHALLENGES TO FEMININE ETHICS

It is a measure of the importance of Gilligan's work that it has been challenged in a number of ways that can deepen our understanding of the issues it raises. We can imagine feminine ethics being criticized from at least three different perspectives. The first is that of the social scientist, whose primary concern is to describe the social world correctly and to interpret correctly what we observe of that world. The second critical perspective is that of the moral philosopher, whose concerns are (among others) to understand correctly the theoretical tradition of which he or she is a part and to develop theoretical approaches to morality that are reasonable, complete, and useful. The third perspective is that of the feminist, whose aim is to understand a system of gender-based oppression in order to undermine that system and replace it with something better. Although separating these three sets of concerns is useful for organizing our thoughts on the matter, a fully adequate approach to the relevant issues must take into account the insights drawn from all three critical perspectives.

■ *Empirical Complications*

From an empirical point of view, one obvious question is whether Gilligan is correct to associate the justice and care perspectives in any significant way with gender. A number of questions have been raised about Gilligan's empirical attributions of these two moral "voices" to men and women, respectively.

Gilligan herself has repeatedly emphasized that the connections she draws to gender are loose and admit of many exceptions; her position has never been that all women employ only the care perspective and all men only the justice perspective. Many people show some fluency in both "voices." Interestingly, however, Gilligan's research suggests that women are more likely to be ethically bilingual in this way than are men. As Rosemarie Tong points out, "Gilligan stresses that unlike today's women who speak the moral language of justice and rights nearly as fluently as the moral language of care and relationship, today's boys and men remain largely unable to articulate their moral concerns in anything other than the moral language of justice and rights."[21]

Given the complexity and multiple layers of people's moral discourse—let alone of the beliefs, values, and assumptions that underlie that discourse—it is perhaps wise that, in much of her later work, Gilligan has adopted the language of "focus."[22] A person of either gender who is perfectly capable of understanding and discussing moral questions from both perspectives may nevertheless show a preference for, or focus on, one or the other, perhaps somewhat like being right- or left-handed.

Even given these important qualifications, however, some concerns remain about Gilligan's empirical conclusions. I will mention just two such concerns. First, Gilligan's studies were conducted on a relatively small scale, and most of her subjects were people with substantial educational privilege. Thus, it is reasonable to wonder to what extent her results, including the gender distribution of moral "voices" that she observed in her research sample, can be extrapolated to the U.S. population as a whole (let alone to humanity in general). In fairness, Gilligan has never claimed that such extrapolation is justified, and she emphasizes that her main interest is less in the gender distribution of the "voices" than in the relation of these voices to each other and in what each brings to our moral consciousness. Still, it will be important for anyone who is interested in the gender distribution to take seriously the limitations of Gilligan's research sample.

The second empirical concern has to do with the nature of the research rather than the extent of the sample. In short, it is one thing to analyze people's self-reported moral perspectives on (mostly) imaginary situations, and another thing to observe how they actually behave in their lives. Although the former kind of inquiry yields interesting information, the latter kind seems at least equally important to a full understanding of gender differences in morality. We need not criticize Gilligan for pursuing one kind rather than the other, but we can and should seek out other kinds of information about gender differences in moral beliefs and behavior.

Doing so may in turn provide further insight into the nature of the two perspectives Gilligan identified. For instance, many studies have shown a persistent gender gap in people's attitudes toward war, patriotism, and nationalism; in short, men's nationalistic sentiments, and their enthusiasm for particular wars based on those sentiments, tend to be more fervent and pronounced than women's.[23] In one sense, this gender gap bears out Gilligan's view that women tend to adopt more "caring" responses—here, supporting negotiation and reconciliation over armed conflict. This evidence also challenges an aspect of Gilligan's view, however, for in this case the typically feminine position displays a more universal consciousness, whereas the typically masculine position is more parochial in its tendency to valorize and privilege one's own particular nation.

Such issues of interpretation are just as important to evaluating Gilligan's work as are more straightforwardly empirical questions. Jean Grimshaw, for instance, has questioned whether the justice perspective is inherently more focused on principle than is the care perspective.[24] It might be, she says, that persons adopting the care perspective are equally "principled," but their principles simply endorse different priority rankings. For instance, rather than seeing a lack of principle in some of the typically feminine responses to the Heinz dilemma, we might instead see them as implicitly endorsing a principle like this: "Seek the preservation of a relationship over the immediate assertion of your own rights." Carrying out such translations, in both directions, may help assuage the uneasy sense that these two moral perspectives are wholly incommensurable.

■ A Bifurcated Moral System?

The last point raises a question that looms large in philosophical discussions of Gilligan's work and its implications, namely, once we have recognized these two different perspectives on morality (regardless of their gender distribution), what are we to do with them?

One approach is to elevate one perspective, that is, to endorse one as more fundamental, complete, and central to a proper understanding of morality than the other. Another approach is to allow the two perspectives to stand as separate, and perhaps to some degree as competing, emphases in our moral lives. One version of the latter approach resolves the apparent tension between the two perspectives by assigning them to different spheres of moral life: the justice perspective properly governs us in public life (governmental and business inter-actions, for instance), and the care perspective is appropriate for our private and intimate interactions (as with friends, lovers, and families). Such a bifurcation of our moral lives, however, is inadvisable. Public pursuits such as international diplomacy stand to benefit from a focus on mending and maintaining relation-ships, and as feminists have tirelessly pointed out, considerations of justice must be brought to bear even in our most intimate relationships.

A third approach is to try to integrate aspects of both "voices" into one unified moral perspective, that is, into a single analytical framework within which multi-ple goods can be both fully understood and appropriately valued. I believe that this is a worthy goal, but achieving it will require articulating carefully what is being sought. For the best answer to the question "What do women want in a moral theory?" (asked by Annette Baier in the title of her well-known article)[25] is that most women, and most men as well, do not want a moral theory at all. That is to say, most people neither employ nor seek a moral theory, at least if moral theory is understood as a matter of reducing the complexity of moral life to a single ultimate good or to a single principle for the regulation of conduct. Instead, what most of us want is a store of moral *concepts* that clearly articulate what we value and that usefully illuminate the choices we face.

Many of our moral concepts, as we currently understand them, find their natural home in one or the other of the two perspectives that Gilligan observed — autonomy and respect in the justice perspective, for instance, and compassion and empathy in the care perspective. Furthermore, it is difficult to see how those two perspectives, as they stand, can be integrated. Gilligan expresses this difficulty in some of her later work, comparing the shift between the two moral perspec-tives to our perception of ambiguous figures (for instance, the drawing that can be seen either as a vase or as a human face).[26] For our moral concepts to be ideally useful to us, however, they must be able to take their place alongside each other within a single moral perspective — they must be such that we can see them, and the realities they illuminate, fully and clearly with one set of eyes.

The project of developing such a coherent set of concepts must be under-taken in concert with a further analytical step. We cannot ignore the fact that, as they stand, the two moral "voices" and their key concepts are products of an oppressive system, a system that constructs men and women not simply as differ-ent, but as dominant and subordinate. We need to understand more about the location and role of each "voice" (and its associated concepts) within oppressive systems and their ideologies. At this analytical juncture, feminine ethics begins to fall short. To help us revise our moral concepts to fit within a unified moral perspective, feminine ethics must be integrated into a wider frame of analysis—that provided by feminist ethics, and by feminism more generally.

■ *What about Oppression?*

Despite its admirable focus on taking women's moral perspectives seriously, feminine ethics as such has little to say about oppression. It might, of course, point to historical and contemporary gender inequality in explaining the tendency *not* to take women seriously, but once a feminine moral perspective is identified, oppression ceases to play a central role in the analysis.[27] Again, the emphasis of feminine ethics is on core feminist tenet 1—that women and men are rational and moral equals. A feminist approach, in contrast, incorporates both tenets 1 and 2—that is to say, it recognizes that women and men are rational and moral equals whose lives are bound up together within an oppressive system of gender inequality.

Again, gender oppression (like other forms of oppression) is not just an accumulation of hostile or irrational acts; it is a system that perpetuates itself in many ways, including by inculcating gendered ideals of what it means to be a "good woman" or a "good man." Whether or not we like this system, we are its creatures; our perspectives and concepts, moral and otherwise, are formed significantly in conformity with its ideologies and with the roles and responsibilities to which it assigns us—roles and responsibilities that are not only different but unequal. Recognizing this fact, and its implications, is necessary if we are to use the actual moral perspectives of women and men as informative bases either for challenging oppression or for developing a fully coherent set of moral concepts.

■ FROM FEMININE ETHICS TO FEMINIST ETHICS

Within both the justice perspective and the care perspective lie important conceptual resources for challenging oppression of all kinds. Concepts such as justice, equality, autonomy, and respect for individual rights provide a vital basis for feminist and other challenges to entrenched systems of oppression. Such challenges are also motivated and sustained by a desire to alleviate suffering and to promote and preserve valuable human connections. A critical feminist approach, rather than abandoning any of these vital concepts, examines how they become distorted so as to serve rather than undermine an oppressive system.

■ *Toward Integration: Care, Respect, and Autonomy*

Caring labor is vital to sustaining any human society, let alone any worth living in. We all depend on trusting connections with others to meet our emotional, physical, and spiritual needs, and inevitably the most vulnerable members of society, for instance, children and the severely disabled, depend on others' care without being able to offer similar care in return. People who routinely perform such caring labor must become skilled at perceiving people's needs, attentively responding to those needs, and establishing and preserving the relationships within which those needs can continue to be met. These skills are among the most worthy and necessary to which human beings can aspire.

In oppressive systems, however, the caring labor that sustains individuals and communities is not equally or justly distributed. Specifically, the oppressed group is typically charged with tending to others' needs, both those of the oppressor group and those of vulnerable dependents. Certainly this has been the pattern in systems of gender oppression.[28] Women's caring skills, then, are the skills of an oppressed group that has been charged with the responsibility of serving others' needs from a position of little power or authority and whose survival has depended on doing this well.

One conclusion we can draw is that women's facility at caring, although valuable and necessary, risks reinforcing gender oppression by rendering women both very able and very willing to fulfill their assigned function within an oppressive division of labor. Under conditions of oppression, women's tendency to see themselves primarily as responders to others' needs may perpetuate a system that keeps women in positions of service to others. Catharine MacKinnon has put this criticism succinctly, if a bit harshly: "Women's moral reasoning is . . . what male supremacy has attributed to women for its own use. . . . Women are said to value care. Perhaps women value care because men have valued women according to the care they give."[29]

In this context, uncritically embracing "care ethics" can be harmful to women, both individually and collectively, by rendering them dangerously vulnerable to exploitation. Women who fail to rein in their caring may maintain relationships at all costs (including to themselves), avoid legitimate self-assertion to keep the peace, devote their energies to others at the expense of self-development, and protect even those others whose behavior is abusive or exploitative. A number of writers on feminine ethics have addressed these risks; indeed, Gilligan herself argues that the final stage of moral development within the care perspective involves coming to care for oneself *and* others, considered as a relational unit. Although including oneself among those one cares for is valuable as far as it goes, a fully viable ethic of care must go farther. It must reveal modes of life that subject anyone to exploitation as falling short, not only of true justice but also of true caring. By addressing when caring is and is not appropriate—by whom, for whom, when, and why—a feminist analysis moves us toward a different conception of caring itself.

Feminist ethicist Robin Dillon, in her analysis of what she calls "care respect," provides a model of the sort of conceptual revision I am recommending. Although care and respect are typically understood as core concepts of the care and justice perspectives, respectively, Dillon argues that the two concepts are intimately connected, that indeed, "a closer consideration of respect shows that caring for another is a way of respecting her." As Dillon observes, "recognizing the connection between care and respect may provide the basis for a more integrative approach to morality."[30]

To respect something, Dillon argues, is to recognize and respond appropriately to its value. What counts as an appropriate response to something's value depends on what the features of the thing are that make it valuable. Respect for *persons* as such, then, involves recognizing and responding appropriately to the "morally significant features of persons," by which Dillon means "those features that make something a person and make persons things that must morally be taken account of."[31] Our understanding of respect for persons, then, depends on what features of persons we consider to be morally significant.

Dillon contends that the Kantian tradition in moral theory (the influence of which looms large in the justice perspective) has taken an overly limited view of what the morally significant features of persons are, resulting in a correspondingly limited understanding of what respect for persons involves. According to the Kantian tradition, the distinctive value of persons lies in a capacity that all persons have in common—the capacity to act according to principle.[32] As we have seen, the justice perspective emphasizes respecting each person's autonomy, understood as their right to choose and act free from undue interference.

As Dillon points out, however, other voices—both within the mainstream philosophical tradition and especially within the newly emerging ethics of care—have emphasized additional features of persons as morally significant. Among these features are the following: that persons are specific, concrete, and "unrepeatable" individuals; that each person has her own way of perceiving and understanding the world and herself; and that each person has needs and wants that she cannot satisfy on her own. Respecting a person, then, involves more than refraining from interfering with her. It also involves responding to her as the particular individual that she is, attempting to understand and enter into her perspective, perceiving her wants and needs, and trying to address them.

"Care respect" is the sort of respect that emerges from this broadened conception of the morally significant features of persons. Although Dillon's analysis does not foreground relationship and connection in quite the explicit way that Gilligan's care perspective does, it seems clear that care respect for others is best enacted within ongoing relationships of trust and mutuality. Furthermore, the concept of care respect can also help us to understand how true caring precludes exploitation. In short, having care respect for oneself rules out the kind of self-abandonment that is often involved in excessive and unreciprocated service to others.[33]

In redefining caring labor as both respectful and worthy of respect, we challenge both the tendency to devalue caring labor and the closely related tendency to enshrine such labor as culturally feminine. Despite many changes in gender relations in the last few decades, and notwithstanding the existence of notable exceptions, evidence indicates that men as a group are still largely resistant to joining equally in the everyday labor of intimate care for others, that is, in such tasks as changing diapers, caring for elders, sending greeting cards, vacuuming the house, and folding the laundry. Indifference to and incapacity for such caring labor has been a hallmark of male privilege.

Although changing this unfair distribution of labor is not a task for theory alone, feminist ethics can again contribute by redefining a concept that (according to Gilligan) is central to the moral perspectives of many men—that of autonomy. Just as our conceptions of caring may be distorted in the service of oppression, so too can autonomy be misunderstood in ways that obscure and thus perpetuate oppressive gender relations. Again, autonomy within the justice perspective is often understood as a kind of ideal of self-sufficiency and, relatedly, as a right to be "let alone." The ideal of autonomy so understood, however, masks a hidden dependence on (often female) caring labor.[34] Such a conception of autonomy is most available to those who depend on the caring labor of others without having to acknowledge or reciprocate it. Beginning to value properly such caring labor will in turn enable us to redefine autonomy, both as an ideal and as a right, in ways that take full account of human vulnerability and interdependence.

■ CONCLUSION

In my view, feminist ethics subsumes and transforms feminine ethics. Feminist ethics is not an ethics embraced by women, but an ethics embraced by feminists, that is, by persons (female and male) who both value men and women as equals and recognize that gender oppression currently hinders their relating as equals. I have argued that while taking women's moral views seriously is an important first step, we must also take seriously the oppressive context within which both women and men develop their moral perspectives and make their moral decisions. As Rosemarie Tong puts it, "a feminist approach to ethics asks questions about *power*—that is, about domination and subordination—even before it asks questions about good and evil, care and justice, or maternal and paternal thinking."[35]

Analyzing moral concepts within the context of oppression helps us better understand both the oppression and the concepts, so that the latter may be refined and the former undermined. We should recast our moral concepts, where necessary, so that they do not depend for their meaning and force on the mutually exclusive perspectives of justice and care that, at least in their present forms, arise from oppressive gender relations. Our philosophical efforts to develop more fully adequate moral concepts must occur alongside, and as part of, our efforts to understand and challenge oppressive systems that preclude both true justice and true caring. Because we are creatures of the oppressive systems in which we live—and of those systems' ideologies—feminist ethics is, in the end, inseparable from feminist politics.

■ *NOTES*

1. Andrea Dworkin, *Right Wing Women* (New York: Perigee Books, 1983), 216. The account of the nature and task of feminism that I sketch here is deeply influenced by Dworkin's analysis as outlined in the book's final chapter, "Antifeminism."

2. On June 10, 1998, PBS's "NewsHour with Jim Lehrer" featured a segment, entitled "Love, Honor, and Obey?" on the Southern Baptist Conference's resolution concerning men's and women's proper family roles. The transcript is available at http://www.pbs.org/newshour/bb/religion/jan-june98/baptist_6–10.html.

3. For supporting statistics and analysis, see the website of the Committee on Pay Equity: http://www.feminist.com/fairpay/.

4. See Arlie Hochschild, *The Second Shift: Working Parents and the Revolution at Home* (New York: Viking/Penguin, 1989).

5. See Marilyn Waring, *If Women Counted: A New Feminist Economics* (New York: Harper Collins, 1988).

6. See Patricia Tjaden and Nancy Thoennes, "Prevalence, Incidence, and Consequences of Violence Against Women: Findings from the National Violence Against Women Survey," available at http://www.ncjrs.org/pdffiles/172837.pdf.

7. For an insightful analysis of rape as an institution that seriously damages all women's fundamental interests, see Claudia Card, "Rape as a Terrorist Institution" in Morris and Frey, eds., *Violence, Terrorism, and Justice* (Cambridge: Cambridge University Press, 1991).

8. Marilyn Frye, "Oppression," in her *The Politics of Reality: Essays in Feminist Theory* (Freedom, Calif.: Crossing Press, 1984), p. 33.

9. Cynthia Freeland, "Nourishing Speculation: A Feminist Reading of Aristotelian Science" in Bat-Ami Bar On, ed., *Engendering Origins: Critical Feminist Readings in Plato and Aristotle* (Albany: State University of New York Press, 1994), 145–46.

10. Aristotle, *Politics* 1254b 13–14. Jonathan Barnes, ed., *The Complete Works of Aristotle: Revised Oxford Translation* (Princeton: Princeton University Press, 1984).

11. The failure of most philosophers to question their culture's prevailing views of women is especially striking when we recall that these men were able to criticize and challenge prevailing religious and political orthodoxies of many kinds, not to mention questioning such bedrock assumptions as the existence of the external world.

12. Susan Sherwin, *No Longer Patient: Feminist Ethics and Health Care* (Philadelphia: Temple University Press, 1992), 47.

13. For a brief and enlightening account of numerous ways in which the contemporary U.S. medical system treats women's bodies as defective, to the detriment of women's health and well-being, see the early chapters of John Robbins's *Reclaiming Our Health* (Tiburon, Calif.: H. J. Kramer, 1998). Also see Barbara Katz Rothman, *Recreating Motherhood: Ideology and Technology in a Patriarchal Society* (New York: W. W. Norton, 1989).

14. Immanuel Kant, *Groundwork of the Metaphysic of Morals*, trans. H. J. Paton (New York: Harper and Row, 1964).

15. Immanuel Kant, *Observations on the Feeling of the Beautiful and Sublime*, trans. John T. Goldthwait (Berkeley: University of California Press, 1960), 81.

16. For a fuller analysis of double binds and their relation to oppression, see Frye, "Oppression," *op. cit.*

17. See Carol Gilligan, *In a Different Voice: Psychological Theory and Women's Development* (Cambridge: Harvard University Press, 1982).

18. Lawrence Kohlberg, *The Psychology of Moral Development: The Nature and Validity of Moral Stages* (San Francisco: Harper and Row, 1984).

19. Gilligan, *op. cit.*, 28.

20. Marilyn Friedman, "Beyond Caring: The De-Moralization of Gender" in *Justice and Care: Essential Readings in Feminist Ethics* (Boulder, Colo.: Westview Press, 1995), 64.

21. Rosemarie Tong, "Feminist Ethics," in *The Stanford Encyclopedia of Philosophy* (Fall 2001 Edition), ed. Edward N. Zalta: http://plato.stanford.edu/archives/fall2001/entries/feminism-ethics/.

22. See Carol Gilligan, "Moral Orientation and Moral Development" in Virginia Held, ed., *Justice and Care: Essential Readings in Feminist Ethics* (Boulder, Colo.: Westview Press, 1995).

23. See N. W. Gallagher, "The Gender Gap in Popular Attitudes Toward the Use of Force" in Howes and Stevenson, eds., *Women and the Use of Military Force* (Boulder, Colo.: Lynne Reiner Publishers, 1993).

24. Jean Grimshaw, "The Idea of a Female Ethic" in Rachels, ed., *The Right Thing to Do: Basic Readings in Moral Philosophy* (Boston: McGraw-Hill College, 1999), 89.

25. Annette Baier, "What Do Women Want in a Moral Theory?" in her *Moral Prejudices: Essays on Ethics* (Cambridge: Harvard University Press, 1994).

26. See Gilligan, "Moral Orientation and Moral Development," *op. cit.*

27. Many theorists whose work emphasizes feminine ethics, including Gilligan herself, do show some awareness of oppression. Thus the divide between feminine and feminist ethics, although analytically useful, is to some degree artificial. My contention is that *to the extent* that one's analysis "stops at" feminine ethics without integrating it into a broader feminist analysis, one risks undermining two key tasks — the practical task of ending oppression, and the theoretical task of articulating valuable human ideals within an integrated moral theory.

28. Caring labor is also disproportionately assigned to people of subordinated races, as, for instance, when white southerners relied on black house slaves and servants for warmth, compassion, and nurturing, as well as for domestic (and in the case of slave women, often sexual) service. See Patricia Hill Collins, *Black Feminist Thought* (New York: Routledge, Chapman, and Hall, 1991).

29. Catharine MacKinnon, *Toward a Feminist Theory of the State* (Cambridge: Harvard University Press, 1989), 51.

30. Robin Dillon, "Care and Respect" in Cole and Coultrap-McQuinn, eds., *Explorations in Feminist Ethics: Theory and Practice* (Bloomington: Indiana University Press, 1992), 69.

31. *Ibid.*, 72.

32. As we have seen, Kant himself did not believe that this capacity was shared by all humans; contemporary Kantians, however, reject this aspect of his view.

33. A fuller discussion of excessive service to others, and its implications for selfhood and self-respect, can be found in Jean Hampton's "Selflessness and the Loss of Self," *Social Philosophy and Policy* 10:1 (1993).

34. See Allan Johnson's discussion of this phenomenon in his *The Gender Knot: Unraveling Our Patriarchal Legacy* (Philadelphia: Temple University Press, 1994), 142–148.

35. Rosemarie Tong, "Feminist Ethics," *The Stanford Encyclopedia of Philosophy* (Fall 2001 Edition), ed. Edward N. Zalta: http://plato.stanford.edu/archives/fall2001/entries/feminism-ethics/.

■ QUESTIONS

1. In what ways does the author seem to agree with Timmons's view (expressed in Chapter 6) of the aims of moral theory? In what ways does she seem to disagree with his view?
2. Do you agree with the author's characterization of the core tenets of feminism? Why or why not? Given her characterization, are you a feminist? Why or why not?
3. Kohlberg's theory accords the highest level of moral development to those whose moral thinking emphasizes universal ethical principles such as justice, equality, and respect. Does this seem correct to you? Why or why not?
4. In what ways does your experience bear out, or fail to bear out, Gilligan's contention that men tend to employ the "justice" perspective and women the "care" perspective when thinking about ethical questions?
5. Is either of the two moral "voices" described by Gilligan more central to your own moral thinking than the other? If so, is it the voice that Gilligan would say is most typical for people of your gender?
6. Given what you know of Kantian deontology, do you think that Kant's androcentrism and misogyny is fully separable from the rest of his moral theory, or is it plausible to suppose that the theory as a whole incorporates a male bias?
7. Given the three moral theories outlined in Chapter 6—utilitarianism, Kantian deontology, and limited moral pluralism—which, if any, seems most conducive to incorporating the insights of feminine ethics? of feminist ethics?
8. The author contends that many of our cultural norms governing female and male behavior—in the workplace, in the home, as parents, as spouses, as citizens—tend to perpetuate and support oppression. Do you agree? If so, which norms and why? If not, why not?

■ FOR FURTHER READING

Bartky, Sandra. 1991. *Femininity and Domination: Studies in the Phenomenology of Oppression*. New York: Routledge.

Buchwald, Fletcher, and Roth, eds. 1993. *Transforming a Rape Culture*. Minneapolis, Minn.: Milkweed Editions.

Card, Claudia. 1991. "Rape as a Terrorist Institution." R. G. Frey and Christopher Morris, eds. *Violence, Terrorism, and Justice*. Cambridge: Cambridge University Press.

Frye, Marilyn. 1983. *The Politics of Reality: Essays in Feminist Theory*. Freedom, Calif.: Crossing Press.

Gilligan, Carol. 1982. *In a Different Voice: Psychological Theory and Women's Development*. Cambridge: Harvard University Press.

Johnson, Allan G. 1997. *The Gender Knot: Unraveling Our Patriarchal Legacy*. Philadelphia: Temple University Press.

Kittay, Eva Feder. 1999. *Love's Labor: Essays on Women, Equality, and Dependency*. New York: Routledge.

Ruddick, Sara. 1989. *Maternal Thinking: Toward a Politics of Peace*. Boston: Beacon Press.

Sherwin, Susan. 1992. *No Longer Patient: Feminist Ethics and Health Care*. Philadelphia: Temple University Press.

Trebilcot, Joyce, ed. 1984. *Mothering: Essays in Feminist Theory*. Totowa, N.J.: Rowman and Allanheld.

Walker, Margaret Urban. 1998. *Moral Understandings: A Feminist Study in Ethics*. New York: Routledge.

■ CHAPTER EIGHT

Political Philosophy

BRAD HOOKER

■ *INTRODUCTION*

Some people have enough money for palaces, expensive delicacies, conspicuous consumption; others are too poor to afford enough to eat or a warm place to sleep. Governments can do something about the distribution of wealth. They can impose higher taxes on the rich and provide resources for the poor. They can influence unemployment rates, interest rates, and inflation rates. They can try to control wages and prices. But at what distribution of wealth should governments be aiming, if any at all? Presumably, they should aim at a *just* distribution. But what is a just distribution of wealth? Let us refer to this as the question of **distributive justice**.

The just distribution of wealth is but one of many topics that make up **political philosophy**. Much of political philosophy concerns the relation between the individual and the state, the government, and the law.[1] What obligation do individuals have to the state? In particular, do they have a moral obligation to comply with the law? What could justify people's disobeying or revolting against the state? What ought the state to do for its citizens? One thing a state should do is to protect them from other states' aggression. But is this the only defensible reason a state could have for declaring war? And what other protections ought states to provide their citizens?

Most of us agree that states should protect civil and political liberties. To be more specific, most of us accept that the law should accord citizens the rights to vote, to stand for office in free elections, to criticize the government, and to own property as well as the rights to religious freedom, to a fair trial, and to privacy. This consensus about rights, however, stops short of agreement about what justifies these rights. Some people argue that the rights are justified by the fact that, on balance and in the long run, their establishment will promote human well-being. Others argue that they are justified by the fact that each of us would be willing to grant these rights to others in return for having them ourselves. There is also disagreement about how rights apply in certain circumstances. For example, what circumstances warrant the suspension of free speech? Does the right to privacy go so far as to prevent the government from outlawing abortion or the recreational use of dangerous drugs? Should employers be allowed to hire or promote whomever they want, or can the state legitimately require racial diversity at all levels of the workforce?

All these questions are obviously important. But the central issue in contemporary political philosophy is the just distribution of wealth. Therefore, this chapter will focus on the question of distributive justice. I will argue that there is definitely an important place for material incentives to work, which will result in material inequality, but also that some degree of coercive redistribution by the state is morally required.

■ UTILITARIANISM

■ What Is Utilitarianism?

Consider the proposal that wealth should be distributed in whatever way will in the long run result in the greatest aggregate well-being. Aggregate well-being is everyone's well-being added together *impartially*, that is, without regard to race, religion, gender, social class, or the like. So benefits to any one person are to count for just as much as the same size benefits to anyone else.

This proposal that the just distribution of wealth is whatever distribution maximizes aggregate well-being comes from a tradition of moral and political thought called **utilitarianism**. Utilitarians believe that the best distribution is the one that will in the long run maximize utility, and virtually all utilitarians conceive of utility as *well-being*.

But what is well-being? Earlier utilitarians, Jeremy Bentham (1748–1832), John Stuart Mill (1806–1873), and Henry Sidgwick (1838–1900),[2] believed that well-being is purely a matter of happiness. Most present-day utilitarians have moved to the view that, although happiness is a major component of well-being, there are other components as well, that is, other things that can benefit people without increasing their happiness (even indirectly).[3] In any event, most of us share a rough intuitive grasp of what things count as benefits or harms, or (in other words) as increases or decreases to well-being. Let us assume for the sake of argument that we share enough common ground to allow us to talk intelligibly about aggregate well-being.

■ Diminishing Marginal Utility

What particular distribution of goods will result in the greatest aggregate well-being? Some utilitarians think the answer is a socialist economy that produces a *roughly equal* distribution of wealth. Other utilitarians have thought that the answer is a capitalistic economy with a *very unequal* distribution of wealth. Thus, while agreeing on the utilitarian account of distributive justice, utilitarians may disagree about economics in ways that lead them to disagree about what particular distribution utilitarianism endorses. Most contemporary utilitarians, however, acknowledge the fundamental importance of three considerations: the diminishing marginal utility of material goods, the need for individual material (more specifically, economic) incentives, and the corrupting influence of great disparities in wealth.[4]

"Diminishing marginal utility of material goods" is a fancy term for a familiar phenomenon. Examples of material goods are food, houses, clothes, cars, and money. To say that a material good has diminishing marginal utility is to say that the more of that material good I have, the less benefit I derive from a given amount of that good. Suppose I have no winter coat. If I then get a winter coat, my utility goes up dramatically. However, were I to have fifty winter coats, an additional one would benefit me little. Similarly, life was considerably more convenient for me after I got a car; but if I had eighty-six cars already, an additional car would probably not increase my well-being more than a tiny amount. Again, $100 might be the difference between starvation and survival to a desperately poor person; but $100 is unlikely to make much difference to a billionaire's well-being. Of course, in some cases material goods do *not* have diminishing marginal utility (e.g., that eighty-seventh car might have won my collection some prize). But such cases are exceptions. Normally, the more of a material good we have, the less any given amount of it benefits us.

This fact suggests that transferring some goods from the rich to the poor would harm the rich less than it would benefit the poor. So the diminishing marginal utility of material goods gives utilitarians a reason for thinking that equalizing goods (and wealth) will increase aggregate well-being.

■ The Argument for Material Incentives

We can understand the diminishing marginal utility of material goods while thinking about distributions *statically*, that is, while thinking about distributions in the abstract and apart from their connections with past or future behavior. But obviously people's beliefs about how wealth will be distributed can influence their behavior. This influence raises the issue of material incentives.

A number of social institutions influence the distribution of goods and services—the market, taxation policies, public sector spending, and so forth. Let us refer to these as *distributive institutions*. How distributive institutions are configured influences material incentives. Let us refer to any particular configuration of distributive institutions as a *distributive system*. Here, then, is the utilitarian argument for thinking a distributive system should provide material incentives.

Often, one cannot be more productive (that is, produce more of what others value) without working longer or more intensely or both. Now suppose you knew that each person would get an equal share of material goods, no matter how much he or she helped to produce what others valued. With everyone guaranteed an equal share, what incentive do you have for working hard? True, you would benefit greatly if many other people work hard, because then there would be a lot more goods to divide. But this fact is irrelevant when, as is often the case, you know that your working hard would have no significant influence on how hard others work. And what of your own added productivity? Whether or not others work hard, your society may well have a larger stock of goods to divide into equal shares if you yourself work hard. Hence your equal share would amount to more. Still, how hard you work is very unlikely to make more than a small difference in your society's overall productivity. And except in the unlikely event that your work makes an enormous contribution to your society's productivity, the additional amount in your equal share of what is produced will be tiny—probably too small to notice, *certainly* too small to equal the added cost to you of working hard.

Most people will not work hard year in and year out unless doing so brings them greater benefits than costs. So if they believed that goods would be divided equally and independently of how hard people work, then most would not work hard. Now, if there is less hard work than there could be, there will be less productivity than there could be. Thus, a system distributing material goods without regard to how productive individuals are will elicit less productivity than would some different system that rewards individual productivity.

If people produce less than they could, they will have fewer goods and services to share. If they have fewer goods and services to share, there will be less well-being than there could be. Therefore, because a distributive system that divides things equally will result over time in fewer goods and services, such a distributive system will fail to maximize well-being. The need for individual material incentives thus gives utilitarians an argument for accepting an unequal distribution of wealth. Let us refer to this argument as *the argument from the need for material incentives*.

■ Objections to the Argument for Material Incentives

I will now answer five objections to this argument. The first is that *to reward productivity is not necessarily to reward hard work, and vice versa*. Some people are more productive than the rest of us without working harder than the rest of us (they might just be more talented). So, if the distributive system rewards these people's productivity, it will not thereby be rewarding hard work. Some other people work harder than the rest of us and yet produce less of what others value (they might either be particularly *un*talented or decide to work hard at things that others do not value).

All this is true, but none of it counts against the argument from the need for material incentives. The point of the utilitarians' argument from the need for material incentives was not to justify a distributive system that rewards *hard work*. The point was instead that utilitarians have a reason for favoring a distributive system that rewards *productivity* in order to get people to be productive. Reference was made to hard work because productivity often, though not always, requires hard work. Because productivity often requires hard work, there is a need to provide some incentive to get people to be productive.

This brings us to the second objection to the argument from the need for material incentives. This objection is that *the argument ignores the internal, non-material rewards that hard work can bring.* Of course I realize that working hard can make people feel good about themselves, give them a sense of accomplishment, or bring them some other internal reward. For some people in some jobs, the prospect of such rewards is sufficient to elicit hard work year in and year out. But, for very many people and jobs, this is not the case. There must be significant material rewards if these people are to be willing, year in and year out, to do the hard work necessary for productivity.

A third objection to the argument for the need for material incentives is that *the idea that material incentives are needed takes people as they are now (selfish, lazy, materialistic), whereas we should be trying to improve humanity by making people less materialistic, less self-centered, and more concerned about the good of the whole.* Well, could most people's desire to promote aggregate well-being become so strong that it consistently drove them to work hard (even when there was no particular national emergency)?[5] To be sure, the culture in which people grow up can have profound influences on their motivations, habits of mind, and so on. But could cultural changes reshape human nature so that people cared so much about everyone else's well-being that productivity could be maintained without the provision of individual material incentives? Is human nature plastic in the sense that it takes the shape of whatever mould culture imposes on it? And if evolution has left us with genes that limit the extent to which culture can change us, why not use genetic engineering to change the genes themselves? Perhaps scientists could then develop more cooperative and selfless human beings.[6]

For many people, however, the idea of attempting to refashion human nature through genetic engineering conjures up nightmare scenarios (with well-meaning scientists creating monsters by mistake or evil scientists doing so on purpose). I will therefore assume that we do not want to resort to genetic engineering. I will also assume that cultural changes could not make the majority of people care enough about aggregate well-being to ensure that they were consistently willing to work hard even though they garnered no significant additional material goods from doing so. I do not mean that people are entirely selfish. On the contrary, people are willing to make substantial sacrifices for the sake of their family or friends, or, less frequently, their wider community. But I will assume that their concern for people outside their circle of family and friends is not strong enough to eliminate the need for individual material incentives.

A fourth objection is this: *our present, mainly capitalistic system does not actually reward the productive,* but instead rewards those who are underhanded or well connected or rich already. This objection is completely misguided, for I am not defending our present distributive system. My point is only that the need for incentives calls for *some* material incentives. Let us refer to the package of distributive institutions that would result in the greatest sum of well-being over time as the *utility-maximizing distributive system*. Our present distributive system presumably is different in many ways from the one that would maximize utility. But this point in no way conflicts with the conclusion that the utility-maximizing distributive system, whichever it is, would provide some material incentives for productivity.

The fifth objection to the argument from the need for material incentives is that *there is enough production already*, and so there is no need to reward productivity. True, there is a point at which the harm associated with further increases in productivity would be greater than the benefit.[7] Nevertheless, part of the reason there is so much production now is that there have been rewards for it. If there were no material incentives for productivity, productivity would be far lower than it is now. Indeed, productivity would be *too* low. Technological breakthroughs and sustained economic growth, both of which require hard work on the part of many people, can lead to large increases in aggregate well-being. So, while we should not pursue productivity beyond the point at which harms outweigh benefits, likewise we should not ignore the contributions to well-being that productivity can bring.

■ Wealth and the Corruption of Politics

I have discussed two considerations that influence the opinions contemporary utilitarians have about the distribution of wealth. The first was the declining marginal utility of material goods. The second was the need for material incentives. I then replied to five objections to the idea that the need for material incentives provides utilitarians with a reason to favor unequal distributions of wealth. Now let us turn to the third consideration that influences the opinions contemporary utilitarians have about the distribution of wealth.

The third consideration is that great disparities in wealth can have corrupting influences. For example, suppose legislators have before them a bill that would maximize utility overall but would be disadvantageous for the rich. Some of the rich may prevent the passage of the bill by bribing enough legislators (or by contributing to campaign war chests). One way to decrease the chances of this sort of thing happening is to equalize wealth. There might be less radical ways, however, of decreasing the chances that great disparities in wealth will corrupt politics, such as insisting on both public funding for political campaigns and careful public scrutiny of politicians' business relationships.

■ Utilitarian Conclusions about Distributive Justice

Thus, given the diminishing marginal utility of material goods, the need for material incentives, and the corrupting power of great disparities in wealth, what would the utility-maximizing distributive system be? This is a question for economists, who, as you probably know, disagree. If what I have argued is correct, however, we can be confident that the utility-maximizing distributive system would provide material incentives for productivity. In addition, because different people have different levels of talent and ambition, such a system would result in some material inequality.

This is not to say that the utility-maximizing distributive system would be a pure free market system. First, there are overwhelming and relatively uncontroversial arguments for thinking that certain things from which everyone benefits — national defense, police, courts, public parks, protection of the environment — should not be left entirely to the free market but should instead be arranged by the government and paid for by some mechanism intended to ensure that everyone who has more than some threshold of income or wealth helps to pay for these things.[8] Second, some people are too young, too old, or too infirm to earn enough in a competitive market to meet their basic needs. Nothing I have said about incentives militates against the social provision of a safety net to protect the well-being of these people. Almost certainly, the utility-maximizing distributive system would try to secure for these people what they need. Perhaps the most obvious way of providing a safety net would be through public assistance programs funded by taxes on the individuals who are better off. Third, what I have said about incentives does not preclude a form of distributive system in which, although there is a (relatively) free market for labor, there is virtually no private ownership of the means of production.[9]

Let me warn against some possible misunderstandings of a utilitarian conclusion about which distributive system would be just. Suppose the utility-maximizing distributive system would distribute goods much more equally than they are now. Does a utilitarian conclusion about which distributive system would be just require you to rush out and start giving all your time and money to the poor? Maybe not. First of all, your *unilaterally* redistributing wealth might not increase utility. Second, even if utilitarianism is a good approach to the social issue of which distributive system is just, it might not be a good approach to questions of *individual* morality (e.g., the question of what you ought to do with your money and time).[10] So even if you conclude that utilitarianism is right about distributive justice, perhaps all this would require of you is that you support politicians whose policies would bring our system closer to the utility-maximizing one.

Another misunderstanding would be to think that if utilitarians conclude that a different distributive system would produce more utility than the distributive system we now have does, they must favor an overnight change to the different system. A gradual change might cause less economic disruption and social anxiety than an overnight change. Thus the gradual change might have better consequences on the whole.

■ THE DESERT THEORY

Many people reject the utilitarian approach to distributive justice because they believe that what makes a distributive system just is not that it yields the greatest aggregate well-being but that it leaves people with what they *deserve*. Let us refer to this view as the *desert theory*,[11] and let us call its proponents *desert theorists*.

We need to be careful about the locus of the disagreement between desert theorists and utilitarians. Desert theorists may agree *in practice* with utilitarians that the productive should get more than the unproductive. Indeed, desert theorists usually claim that what people deserve depends on what they do, and in particular on how much they produce of what others value. Nevertheless, desert theorists disagree with utilitarians about *fundamental principle*. Desert theorists insist that whether a distributive system is just depends entirely on whether it leaves people with what they deserve; utilitarians insist that what people should get depends entirely on which distributive system would maximize utility.

This disagreement about fundamental principle can be illustrated as follows. Suppose for a moment that the utility-maximizing distributive system would *not* call for the productive to get more than the unproductive. Then, utilitarians would say that the productive should not get more. Desert theorists would say that the productive should get more because they deserve more, whether or not rewarding productivity is part of the distributive system that would maximize utility.

■ RAWLS'S THEORY

■ The Basic Component of Rawls's Theory

In the English-speaking world, John Rawls was the most influential political philosopher of the twentieth century. Rawls allows that justice may call for a different pattern of distribution in a poor country than it would in a reasonably affluent country. I will focus on his view about what justice requires in a reasonably affluent country. He puts forward two principles of justice: the liberty principle, which is about the securing of basic liberties, and the difference principle, which is about how resources should be distributed given that the basic liberties have been secured.

The liberty principle states, "Each person is to have an equal right to the most extensive total system of equal basic liberties compatible with a similar system of liberty for all."[12] By "basic liberties," Rawls means the standard civil and political liberties, such as freedom of thought, freedom of speech, the right to vote and to run for office, freedom of assembly, the right to due process, and so on.[13] He gives these liberties special protection: at least in countries with developed economies, they are never to be restricted for the sake of promoting economic gains.

Rawls likewise contends that, in a reasonably affluent society, fair equality of opportunity should never be sacrificed for the sake of economic benefits, or even for the sake of economic benefits to members of the worst-off class. This contention received some criticism, as has Rawls's contention that in a reasonably affluent society sacrificing equal civil and political liberties for the sake of economic benefits can never be just.[14] Much more attention has been devoted to Rawls's difference principle. Let us also focus on this principle. To make doing so easier, suppose we are talking about societies in which the greatest equal basic liberties and fair equality of opportunity are securely established.

The difference principle states that social and economic inequalities are justified if, and only if, (a) the inequalities are "attached to offices and positions open to all under conditions of fair equality of opportunity"[15] and (b) those who are worst off get more "social primary goods" than those who are worst off under any other distribution would get. Social primary goods are goods that (a) are under society's control and (b) "normally have a use whatever a person's rational plan of life."[16] Think of these as all-purpose means to the pursuit of the good life, whatever it is. Given that the greatest equal basic liberties have been secured and that there is fair equality of opportunity, the main social primary goods are income and wealth and the bases of self-respect.

You might initially think that, because Rawls favors the distributive system with the best worst-off position, he would favor a distributive system that gives everyone an equal amount of goods. Rawls's principle, however, does not necessarily favor the most egalitarian distributive system. Here is an example illustrating the point ("units" in this example refers to amounts of social primary goods):

Distributive System 1		*Distributive System 2*	
gives to		*gives to each member of*	
Everyone	10 units each	Best-off class	25 units
		Middle class	20 units
		Worst-off class	15 units

Given these alternatives, strict egalitarianism favors the first. Rawls's difference principle, however, favors the second.

Why might a system in which everyone gets an equal amount of material goods leave everyone worse off than he or she would be under a system leading to an unequal distribution? A system that distributes goods equally might result in so little productivity that another system, one that distributes goods *unequally* in order to supply material incentives, would produce more goods for everyone — *even for the worst off.*

■ Rawls's Theory Contrasted with Utilitarianism

There are two main respects in which Rawls's difference principle and the utilitarian principle disagree about how resources are to be distributed. First, whereas utilitarians assess distributive systems in terms of how much *well-being* results, Rawls is concerned with *social primary goods.* Second, whereas utilitarians give *equal weight to everyone's interests*, Rawls gives *special weight to the plight of the worst off.* His difference principle calls for the distributive system under which there would be the best worst-off position.

Consider two distributive systems. Under each system, there are only three socioeconomic classes, with 10^n people in each class. (Again, the units refer to amounts of social primary goods.)

Distributive System 1		Distributive System 2	
gives to each member of		*gives to each member of*	
Best-off class	60 units	Best-off class	35 units
Middle class	30 units	Middle class	20 units
Worst-off class	10 units	Worst-off class[17]	15 units
Total	100×10^n units	Total	70×10^n units

Because the units are amounts of social primary goods, not amounts of well-being, utilitarians would say that they do not yet have the information they need in order to choose between these systems. For the sake of argument, though, assume that the first distributive system would indeed produce more total well-being than the second. Therefore, utilitarians would favor the first system. In contrast, Rawls would say that the second is more just, because its worst-off class is better off than the worst-off class under the first distributive system would be. After all, why should anyone be left with as little as the members of the worst-off class under the first system when there is an alternative system that would leave no one so badly off?

Which particular distributive system would Rawls's principle favor for our society? This again is a question for economists. The answer might be a system under which there is a large gap between rich and poor. The answer might instead be a system under which there is little gap between rich and poor. Actually, Rawls himself explicitly leaves open the question of whether his theory supports market socialism or a system in which natural resources and the means of production are privately owned.[18] He suggests, however, as have others who have written about his theory, that his principle mandates more redistribution from the rich to the poor than occurs now.[19] If we accept Rawls's principle about the just distribution of wealth, and if we believe it calls for increased redistribution from the rich to the poor, then we should support politicians who will push for this increase.

■ THE DESERT THEORY REVISITED

■ *The Objection That Rawls Ignores Desert*

Rawls put forward powerful arguments for his principle, arguments over which scores of books have been written. I will not survey that literature. Instead, I will focus on one of the most common objections to Rawls's principle—the objection made by those I am calling desert theorists.

Just as desert theorists reject utilitarianism because they think people should get what they deserve whether or not this accords with the utility-maximizing distributive system, desert theorists reject Rawls's principle because they think people should get what they deserve whether or not this accords with the system that produces the least bad worst-off position. Suppose for the sake of illustration that the least bad worst-off position would come from a distributive system giving only a tiny amount more to those who work very hard and produce much more than to those who are lazy and produce much less. Rawls would say that in this case the productive should get only that tiny amount more. Desert theorists would object that, where the difference in what people do is large, the difference in what they get should be more than tiny. They would object that to give only a tiny amount more to people who work much harder and produce much more is to give them less than they deserve.

■ Rawls's Reply to the Objection about Desert

Rawls's reply to the desert theorists is as follows.[20] Suppose you end up with a much more comfortable life than I do because you inherit more from your parents than I do from mine. It is difficult to believe that you therefore *deserve* these advantages more than I do. Desert, according to the common view, has to do with what you *do*, and to get that wealth you did not *do* anything that I failed to do. A system that allows people to pass on their wealth to their offspring is justified, if at all, by something other than the *desert* of the offspring.

Now suppose, for the sake of argument, that passing along wealth to offspring is made impossible. You may nevertheless end up with a much more rewarding job than I do because of other things your parents did for you that my parents were unable to do for me. Perhaps your mother introduced you to important professional contacts, or your father taught you how to be exceptionally charming. You did not deserve these advantages any more than I did, so how could you deserve the better job they helped you to get?

Desert theorists might say that *at least* if two people start out from the same position and one then outperforms the other, the one with the better performance deserves greater rewards. But what counts as the same starting position? Suppose that your parents were neither wealthier nor better connected than mine. It might nevertheless be the case that, because of the genes you inherited, you are much better looking than I am and you therefore make more as a model than I can make. Or your reflexes may be quicker than mine because of your genetic inheritance, and this may enable you to make much more money as a professional athlete than I can make. Or you may have inherited a steady, easy-going temperament, which helps you become popular and professionally successful, while I suffer from a mercurial temperament, which alienates people and limits my career advancement. But the beauty or quick reflexes or easy-going temperament would not have been advantages you deserved; you would have been merely lucky to inherit them. So why would you *deserve* the advantages they help you obtain? This is Rawls's reply to the desert theorists (and utilitarians would agree with it). As Rawls writes, "once we are troubled by the influence of either social contingencies or natural chance on the determination of distributive shares, we are bound, on reflection, to be bothered by the influence of the other. From a moral standpoint the two seem equally arbitrary."[21]

Many people would acknowledge that if you end up with more wealth than I do because you inherited more money, or because your parents provided you with better contacts, or because you inherited more brains, brawn, or beauty than I did, then you do not deserve to have more wealth than I. They would go on to insist, however, that if the cause of your ending up with more was that you were more *ambitious* than I was and thus worked harder, then you do deserve your additional wealth. The idea seems to be that things beyond your control (such as how much you inherit) cannot provide a basis for desert, but things within your control (such as your level of ambition and industriousness) can.[22]

This line of thinking is questionable. Our ambitions and dispositions to work were largely shaped by what environment we were born into, how we were raised, what alternatives we were encouraged to consider, what talents we found in ourselves. Thus, our ambitions and appetite for work were largely shaped by facts about us that were beyond our control. If facts about us that were beyond our control cannot provide a basis for desert, and if our ambitions were largely shaped by facts beyond our control, then so much the worse for ambition as a basis for desert.

If we are persuaded to reject the desert theory, there remains the question of whether Rawls or the utilitarians have the better theory of distributive justice.

■ GOOD SAMARITANISM AND REDISTRIBUTION

Actually, utilitarianism and Rawls's theory are far from the only theories of distributive justice that contrast with the desert theory. There is a wide variety of competing theories to choose among, including some that mix utilitarianism with priority for the worst off.[23] Which of these theories of distributive justice is most plausible? I will not try to answer this question here.[24] Instead, I will put forward my own justification for redistributive taxation—a justification that does not require rejection of the desert theory.

We should eschew, as much as possible, political justifications that appeal to controversial philosophical views.[25] Views about desert are certainly controversial. Indeed, most people believe—and probably will continue to believe—what we have called the desert theory, the view that, necessarily, people who are more productive deserve more than no people who are less productive. So, even if the desert theory is in fact wrong, any argument for redistribution that involves rejecting it is unlikely to gain general acceptance.

I will now argue for redistribution in a way that does not require rejection of the desert theory. Furthermore, I think that all of the premises on which I shall rely are more likely to gain wide acceptance, at least after due reflection, than is the rejection of the desert theory.

■ *The Good Samaritan Duty*

My first premise is that the rest of us have a duty to help, if we can, those who cannot on their own obtain the food, shelter, medicine, or basic education they need. Now add the premise that the rest of us *can* help these people by making available to them the goods they need. The conjunction of these two premises entails the conclusion that the rest of us have a duty to help these people. Refer to this as the *Good Samaritan duty*.

■ *Compelling Compliance with the Good Samaritan Duty*

What does this have to do with the state, you might be wondering. Consider this: if there is not an institution for *compelling* compliance with the Good Samaritan duty, many people will not comply. When some do not comply, others will no doubt make up *only some* of the difference. It follows that the badly off will not get some of the help that others have a duty to provide unless there is an institution that compels compliance with this duty. We might now add the premise that we should ensure that people get all the help that others have a duty to provide. This would generate the conclusion that we should have an institution that compels compliance (e.g., redistributive taxation funding public assistance programs).

The premise that we should ensure that people get all the help others have a duty to provide is controversial, so consider a different argument. This argument starts from the premise that, if some well-off people do not comply with the Good Samaritan duty, the Good Samaritan principle requires more of the conscientious compliers, that is, it requires them to make up at least some of difference. This premise is easy to defend. Suppose you and I see ten innocent people drowning and each of us is able to throw life vests to all of them. Suppose you throw life vests to five of them and then notice that I am doing nothing to help save the remaining five. Clearly, morality requires you to throw life vests to the other five — or, in other words, to make up for my noncompliance with the Good Samaritan duty.

Admittedly, there may be limits on the extent to which compliers are required to make up for the noncompliance of others. This acknowledgment, however, is perfectly compatible with the modest claim that compliers are required to make up at least *some of* the difference created by the noncompliance of others, and this modest claim is enough for the purposes of my argument. Even making up only some of the difference created by others' noncompliance with the Good Samaritan duty is burdensome. Thus, if some people do not comply with the Good Samaritan duty, the burden on those who do comply will be greater.

As we concluded earlier, if no institution compels compliance with the Good Samaritan duty, many people will not comply. As we have now concluded, if some people do not comply with the Good Samaritan duty, the burden on those who do comply will be greater. The conjunction of these two conclusions entails that, if there is not an institution compelling compliance with the Good Samaritan duty, the burden on the well off who comply will be greater.

Now consider the following argument. We should do what will protect compliers from the extra burden placed on them by noncompliers, if we can do this in a way that is not morally objectionable. Having an institution compelling compliance with the Good Samaritan duty is not morally objectionable.[26] Thus, we should have an institution compelling compliance with the Good Samaritan duty.

■ Objections to the Argument for Compelling Compliance

Some would object to this argument by insisting that compelling people to do their duty *is* morally objectionable. Even if compelling people to comply with their duty is morally objectionable, I cannot see that it is so objectionable as to be more important than protecting the compliers from the extra burden put on them by the noncompliers.

Some think that the moral value of people's complying with the duty to help others depends on its coming *from their own free will*, not from external coercion. But, again, I cannot see that the loss (if such it is) of the value of people's free compliance would be greater than the gain in preventing the increased burdens on them.[27]

Here is another argument against the premise that an institution compelling compliance with the Good Samaritan duty (such as redistributive taxation funding public assistance programs) is not morally objectionable. We have a duty to oppose injustice. Consider people who either are not actually needy or are needy because they refuse to help themselves. For any of these people to get benefits paid for by the hard work of fellow citizens is unjust. Public assistance programs funded by redistributive taxation do distribute benefits to at least some such people. We thus have a duty to oppose such programs.

Here is how we should reply to this argument. Of course, a distributive system should not give people an incentive to free ride on the productivity of others. On the contrary, the system needs to give to those who can work incentives to produce goods and services that benefit others. But the system also morally ought to provide for those who cannot provide for themselves. With this in mind, many systems use forms of "means-testing" to channel aid to those who really cannot earn enough in a free market to meet their basic needs.

Admittedly, there may be *some* "leakage" of benefits to those who could provide for themselves but decide instead to "exploit the system." Systems should be designed to minimize leakage, unless the cost of minimizing it is greater than the overall gain. Even if every known system of public assistance contains at least some leakage, however, is the leakage so morally terrible that it must be eliminated even if this means eliminating public assistance programs? On the contrary, having public assistance programs, even with some leakage, is morally better than having no public assistance programs at all.

■ YOUR COUNTRY AND BEYOND

Governments normally have more control over what happens within their own country than over what happens in others. But governments can influence what happens to the poor in other countries.[28] Here are some examples of the many ways they can do this. Rich countries can push down interest rates, thereby leaving poor debtor countries with more money after servicing their debts to spend on their poor. Rich countries can open their markets to agricultural products or textiles or other things that low-income countries can supply at low cost. This can increase the employment opportunities for the poor in those countries. Governments of rich countries can pressure the governments of poor countries to pursue policies that will reduce poverty.[29] One obvious way of applying such pressure is to provide aid on the condition that those policies are pursued.

Many millions of people in Africa and Asia are starving. Why focus on distribution *within* a country and ignore distribution *across national boundaries?* Of course, questions about helping the poor in foreign countries can be more complex than questions about helping the poor in your own country. Yet, despite the added complexity, questions about helping the poor in other countries can be more urgent, because the poor in those countries might be facing far worse threats than the poor in your own country.[30]

■ CONCLUSION

This chapter has surveyed some of the most prominent approaches to the question of what a just distribution of wealth would be.

The utilitarian approach may initially seem to favor equality of wealth, because of the diminishing marginal utility of material resources. However, utilitarians can and typically do acknowledge that people's beliefs about how wealth will be distributed can influence their willingness to work hard. Utilitarians also nowadays typically acknowledge that dividing material resources equally, even if some people work hard anyway, would not elicit hard work from *enough* people. Thus, for utilitarians, distributive justice is a matter of balancing the equalitarian pull that comes from the diminishing marginal utility of material resources with the antiequalitarian push that comes from the need for material incentives to elicit hard work.

Utilitarianism contrasts with what we might call the desert theory, which holds that whether a distributive system is just depends entirely on whether it leaves people with what they deserve, not on whether distributive arrangements will maximize utility. Both utilitarianism and the desert theory contrast with John Rawls's idea that (once equal liberties and opportunities have been established) justice favors the economic system that would result in the best position for the worst off.

Rather than try to adjudicate the debate among utilitarians, desert theorists, and advocates of Rawls's principle, I put forward an argument based on a Good

Samaritan duty. I also argued for the need to compel compliance with this duty. If my arguments are sound, they support redistributive taxation to help the needy. Admittedly, any system of public assistance to the needy will be open to some degree of exploitation. But, at least within limits, this can be a cost worth bearing.

Finally, I suggested that the question of distributive justice should not be construed as limited to distribution only within any one country.

■ *NOTES*

1. As Joseph Raz says, "the state . . . is the political organization of a society, its government, the agent through which it acts, and the law, the vehicle through which much of its power is exercised." Raz, *The Morality of Freedom* (Oxford: Clarendon Press, 1986), 70.

2. Bentham, *Introduction to the Principles of Morals and Legislation*, 1789, many editions since; Mill, *Utilitarianism*, 1863, many editions since; Sidgwick, *The Methods of Ethics* (London: Macmillan, 1874 and 1907).

3. See Derek Parfit, *Reasons and Persons* (Oxford: Clarendon Press, 1984), 493–502; and James Griffin, *Well-Being: Its Meaning, Measurement and Moral Importance* (Oxford: Clarendon Press, 1986), Part 1.

4. I do not mean to suggest that these are the *only* considerations utilitarians can think relevant and important.

5. This is but one of many places where a question about human nature is relevant to political philosophy.

6. Jonathan Glover's *What Sort of People Should There Be?* (Hamondsworth: Penguin Books, 1984) is a fascinating meditation on philosophical questions raised by the possibility of improving humanity through genetic engineering.

7. Why might increasing productivity beyond a certain point produce greater harms than benefits? There are any number of possible reasons. One is that beyond a certain point increases in productivity might be obtainable only by means of cutting back on public assistance programs for the needy, and the harm to the needy might be greater than the benefit to others of the increased productivity.

8. Look in an economics textbook for discussions of "externalities" and "public goods".

9. For a discussion of this sort of view, which is called "market socialism", see ch. 4 of Allen Buchanan's *Ethics, Efficiency, and the Market* (Totowa, N.J.: Rowman and Littlefield, 1985).

10. Why? Perhaps utilitarianism requires a kind of impartiality that is appropriate when we are assessing social goals but not appropriate when we are making decisions as private individuals about what to do with our own resources. (Incidentally, it is also possible to think that utilitarianism is a good approach to private moral decisions but not to questions of justice. This thought might appeal to those of us who believe that our conception of justice, though not our private morality, needs to be founded on beliefs others share and that others do not share some of the beliefs on which utilitarianism is founded.)

11. Arguably, it is the most common view of justice. "Popular morality continues obstinately in its belief that distribution ought always in justice to be according to desert." (J. R. Lucas, *On Justice* (Oxford: Clarendon Press, 1980), 170.) For an excellent anthol-

ogy on desert, see Louis P. Pojman and Owen McLeod (eds.), *What Do We Deserve? A Reader on Justice and Desert* (New York: Oxford University Press, 1999).

12. Rawls, *A Theory of Justice* (Cambridge, Mass.: Harvard University Press, 1971), 302; Revised edition 1999, 266.

13. Rawls, 1971 edition, 61; 1999 edition, 53.

14. Imagine a case in which giving up a small amount of liberty or equality of opportunity is necessary to bring about enormous economic gains. For an influential discussion of Rawls's giving liberty overriding importance, see H. L. A. Hart, "Rawls on Liberty and its Priority," in N. Daniels (ed.), *Reading Rawls* (New York: Basic Books, 1975).

15. Rawls, 1971 edition, 302; 1999 edition, 266.

16. Rawls, 1971 edition, 62; 1999 edition, 54.

17. Do not assume that the particular people who would end up in the worst-off class under this system must also be the people who would end up in the worst-off class under the other one.

18. Rawls, § 42.

19. See, for example, Thomas Pogge, *Realizing Rawls* (Ithaca, N.Y.: Cornell University Press, 1989).

20. Rawls, § 12.

21. Rawls, 1971 edition, 74–5; 1999 edition, 64.

22. Ronald Dworkin, "What is Equality? Part II: Equality of Resources." *Philosophy and Public Affairs*, 10 (1981), 283–345.

23. Derek Parfit, "Equality and Priority." *Ratio* 10 (1997), 202–21.

24. See my *Ideal Code, Real World: A Rule-Consequentialist Theory of Morality* (Oxford: Oxford University Press, 2000), 43–65.

25. See Rawls's "Justice as Fairness: Political not Metaphysical." *Philosophy and Public Affairs* 14 (Summer 1985), 223–51; and "The Idea of an Overlapping Consensus." *Oxford Journal of Legal Studies* 7 (Spring 1987), 1–25. Both of these papers are reprinted in Rawls's *Collected Papers* (Cambridge, Mass.: Harvard University Press, 1999).

26. J. S. Mill seems to concur—see his *On Liberty* (Indianapolis, IN: Library of Liberal Arts, 1956), 15, 95.

27. Contrast the last section of Baruch Brody's article "The Role of Private Philanthropy in a Free and Democratic State." *Social Philosophy and Policy* 4 (1987).

28. See the World Bank's annual *World Development Report* (New York: Oxford University Press).

29. See Jean Drèze and Amartya Sen, *Hunger and Public Action* (Oxford: Clarendon Press, 1989).

30. For very helpful comments on an earlier draft of this chapter, I am grateful to Fred Adams, Roger Crisp, Will Kymlicka, Leemon McHenry, Guy Marsh, and Peter Vallentyne.

■ QUESTIONS

1. Which do you think matters more from the point of view of justice—the size of the gap between the richest and the poorest, or how badly off in absolute terms the poorest are?
2. Could an economic system depending on slave labor ever accord with utilitarianism?
3. Do you agree with the author that the best defense of redistributive taxation will be one that does not depend on rejecting the desert theory?

4. The author concluded that we should have an institution compelling compliance with the Good Samaritan principle. Which premise in his argument for that conclusion do you think is weakest?
5. We can calculate aggregate well-being only if we can compare amounts of benefit and harm to different people. Can we really do this in anything but an arbitrary way?
6. What importance should national boundaries have to the distribution of wealth?

■ *FOR FURTHER READING*

Aristotle. *Nicomachean Ethics*. Available in many editions, bk. 5.

——— *Politics*. Available in many editions.

Arthur, John and William Shaw. 1991. *Justice and Economic Distribution*, 2nd edition Englewood Cliffs, N.J.: Prentice-Hall.

Dworkin, Ronald. 1985. *A Matter of Principle*. Boston: Harvard University Press.

von Hayek, F. A. 1976. *Law, Legislation and Liberty*, vol. II: *The Mirage of Social Justice*. London: Routledge Kegan Paul.

Knowles, Dudley. 2001. *Political Philosophy*. London: Routledge.

Marx, Karl. 1977. *Karl Marx: Selected Writings*. D. McLellan (ed.). Oxford: Oxford University Press.

Nagel, Thomas. 1991. *Equality and Partiality*. New York: Oxford University Press.

Pettit, Philip (ed.). 1991. *Contemporary Political Philosophy*. New York: Macmillan.

Plato, *The Republic*, many editions, and *The Laws*, many editions.

Rakowski, Eric. 1991. *Equal Justice*. Oxford: Clarendon Press.

Rosen, Michael, and Jonathan Wolff (eds.). 1999. *Political Thought*. Oxford: Oxford University Press.

Wolff, Jonathan. 1996. *An Introduction to Political Philosophy*. Oxford: Oxford University Press.

Social Philosophy and Policy 1 (1983).

■ CHAPTER NINE

Aesthetics

ROBERT STECKER

■ *INTRODUCTION*

Art is always considered among the most important products of a culture. A book about almost any great civilization would discuss at considerable length its artistic achievements. Thus, a survey of the great achievements of ancient Greek civilization would include the invention of democratic forms of government, the discovery of philosophy and science, and, inevitably, its great artistic creations: its painted vases, its sculpture, its architecture, and its poetry. Artistic forms, like forms of government, religion, and philosophy, are commonly perceived (at least in retrospect) as central to the life of a civilization and are perhaps the only items that are always mentioned when we specify which of its products are to be most highly valued. It appears, then, that art is something very valuable. Why, then, can it seem that this value plays little or no role in the lives of most people? How many of us are art lovers? It may seem that the obvious answer is, not all that many of us.

The philosophy of art, or **aesthetics**, asks many questions, but among its central questions are several about the value of art: What makes art seem so valuable to some people? Are other people, perhaps the majority, indifferent to these values? Is art really as valuable as it is sometimes said to be? Are different works of art, or different art forms—such as painting and music—valuable in the same way? Most generally, what is valuable about art? In this chapter, I shall try to answer these questions. I shall indicate what is valuable about art and argue that few of us are, and no one ought to be, indifferent to these values.

These questions, however, cannot be answered without having a clear conception of our subject matter. The most straightforward way to do this is to answer the question, What is art? We will have to spend a good deal of time on this question before we can return to questions about value. In this chapter, I will argue that there is a definition of art that answers this question by identifying the historically shifting functions of art. For this reason, the definition is called the historical functionalist definition of art.

■ WHAT IS ART?

Consider the following list:

Literature	Architecture
Painting	Pottery
Sculpture	Furniture
Music	Carpets
Opera	Jewelry
Musical Comedy	Wine
Cinema	Cigars

Which items on this list are arts? If only to avoid confusion, we should note that there is a sense of art according to which all of these items are arts. Art in this sense simply means (something like) a product of human skill. When people write books with titles like *The Art of Cooking* or *The Art of Renovating Old Houses*, they are using art in this sense. This is not the sense of art we are interested in defining. If art in the sense we are interested in could simply be defined as any product of human skill, there would be no explanation why items at the top of our list are so much more readily thought of as art than are items at the bottom.

In the relevant sense of art, few of us would classify a fine cigar or a fine wine as art. We may be less certain about furniture, carpets, jewelry, or musical comedies. The other items on the list, however, are definitely to be counted. Yet, it is not clear that they have more in common with one another than with the more questionable items. A fine wine or a fine cigar can be appreciated for the way it accents and harmonizes the various sensuous qualities a wine or cigar is capable of possessing—its bouquet of flavors, its odor, its visual appearance. It is sometimes claimed that this is the sort of thing we appreciate in painting, although with paintings, of course, our appreciation is confined to visual appearance.

If there is something peculiarly valuable about art, it is plausible to hope that we can define art precisely in terms of these valuable properties. Many traditional definitions of art seem to be based on this hope. Let us examine three of the most important attempted definitions: (1) art as representation, (2) art as expression, and (3) art as **aesthetic experience**.

■ *Traditional Attempts to Define Art*
■ ART AS REPRESENTATION

For centuries, some of the most central art forms were devoted to the representation of reality. Ancient Greek sculpture, in its representation of gods and heroes, aimed to capture (and sometimes idealize) the human form. This aim dominated well into the nineteenth century (as can be seen in the sculpture of the French artist Rodin). Paintings commonly represented the human figure and human scenes: scenes from myths, from the Bible, from great historical events. Eventually, painters became interested in representing scenes from common life, things such as food, artifacts, and landscapes. Drama and poetry represent human beings acting in various ways. Until the seventeenth century, even music was seen as an exclusively representational art (one view was that it represented the human voice in the act of expressing various emotions). It seemed plausible, then, that art could be defined in terms of its representational function: art is the representation of reality (perhaps in certain specific media).[1]

We obviously value art for its representational capacities. For example, many people value certain novels for their ability to represent vividly the way of life of a time or place or of a particular class of people. Paintings are valued because they represent things in beautiful or surprising ways or simply because they capture and preserve a bit of transient reality. For similar reasons, we value photographs, including the snapshots most of us take. We want to capture a certain moment. We are pleased when we find represented in the photograph an aspect that typifies what we valued in that moment. Sometimes, however, the photographs we most value reveal something surprising, something we did not expect to find.

Despite the fact that we value the representational aspects of art, the definition of art in terms of representation is no longer viable. Not only are we all familiar with nonrepresentational painting and sculpture, it also seems so obvious now that there are many nonrepresentational art forms. Many now think of music, pottery, and architecture as such art forms. Furthermore, the mere fact that something is a representation gives it no claim to being art. Last year, I threw away an extremely ugly carpet that represented a hunting scene. It never occurred to me that I threw away a work of art. Furthermore, I just represented myself by describing myself as throwing away a carpet last year. I didn't, however, just create a work of art. Hence, there can be art that is not representational, and there can be representations that are not art.

■ ART AS EXPRESSION

Many artworks that do not represent an outward reality, nevertheless, are expressive. And, of course, representational art can also be expressive. Instrumental music that represents nothing can be expressive of sadness or joy, grief or anger (at least, many would claim this is so). Buildings can express power or stability or upward aspiration of one kind or another. Painting and poetry can express these things as well. Not only does art possess expressive qualities, art also is valued for possessing these qualities. We enjoy sad music, tragic dramas, scary movies. The fact that the finest Gothic cathedrals are expressive of the arduousness and ardor of religious aspirations seems to make them better buildings—both more functional and more beautiful. A poem that represents someone's grief that was neither sad nor ironic would not be a good poem.

Because the expressive function of art is both highly valued and seemingly pervasive, it is not surprising that people have attempted to define art in terms of this function. What might such a definition look like?

There are several ways of thinking of artistic expression. Because it is usually people who express things, it is plausible to think of artistic expression as a case of the artist expressing thoughts and feelings. During the nineteenth and early twentieth centuries, many attempts were made to define art in terms of the artist's expression. Two of the most famous expression theorists, Benedetto Croce and Charles Collingwood, thought of expression as taking place wholly within the mind of the artist.[2] Collingwood liked to distinguish between betraying an emotion and expressing one. I might betray my anger with you by my face turning very red and my shouting at you. To express my anger, in Collingwood's sense, I must articulate the thoughts and perceptions and the likes and dislikes that underlie it. Compare one's face turning red with these lines from William Blake's poem "London."

> I wander thro' each charter'd street,
> Near where the charter'd Thames does flow,
> And mark in every face I meet
> Marks of weakness, marks of woe.
> In every cry of every Man,
> In every infant's cry of fear,
> In every voice, in every ban,
> The mind-forg'd manacles I hear.

Here the speaker of Blake's poem is expressing the thoughts and informing us of the perceptions that cause (or constitute) his anger. One does not just hear the expression of thoughts in these lines, however. One hears a particular sort of anger with its indignant quality and its peculiar subject matter. Art, for Collingwood and Croce, is expression as articulation. Because such expression takes place within the artist's mind, that is where works of art primarily exist; it is at best in a derivative way, for them, that works of art exist on pieces of canvas, in pieces of bronze, or on the pages of a book.

Many people object to the idea that art is the expression of an artist. For an artist to express an emotion, he or she must actually have had that emotion. The Gothic cathedrals mentioned earlier, however, would express religious emotions whether or not their designers and builders experienced, much less personally expressed, those emotions. If we discovered that the designers and builders lacked the requisite emotions, we would not thereby discover that the buildings were not works of art. The same is true of poems expressing grief and for music expressive of sadness. Look, for example, at these lines from an untitled poem by Alfred, Lord Tennyson:

> Break, break, break,
> At the foot of thy crags, O Sea!
> But the tender grace of a day that is dead
> Will never come back to me.

We don't have to know what Tennyson was feeling to know that what we are reading is an expression of grief. This is not to say that artists never express their thoughts and emotions in artworks or that we are never interested in an artist's expression when we are enjoying artworks. It is simply to say that the artist's expression is neither what defines an object as art nor even a necessary condition for an art object being expressive.

Some people, by contrast, think the value of art consists in the evocation of emotion. For example, a proponent of this view might say that a work expresses anger if it evokes anger in us. The following consideration might seem to make this view plausible. As we have seen, the Gothic cathedrals could express religious aspiration even if their designers and builders neither had nor personally expressed such aspirations. What might seem to matter, however, is that the building gives us these feelings. Without them, why would we even think that religious aspirations were being expressed?

As an account of the expressiveness of art, the evocation view strikes me as implausible. When I express my depression, I might make you depressed, but my expressing depression is one thing and my evoking it in you is another. Likewise, when art evokes emotions in us (as I suppose it often does), that may be a symptom of its expressiveness (as spots are a symptom of measles), but it seems just wrong to say that it is what its expressiveness consists in (as it is wrong to say measles consists in having spots). It also seems wrong to say that I can only know that a work expresses something by feeling it myself. I can hear the sadness in music without feeling sad. I don't myself have to have religious aspirations to perceive them in the Gothic cathedral.

Even if we cannot define expression in terms of evocation, one might wonder if art can be defined in terms of an object's capacity to evoke such things as emotions in us. As I said earlier, artworks are often highly evocative. Unfortunately, so are many other things. Even if we confine ourselves to standard artistic media such as paint, photography, the written word, and so on, many highly evocative items are produced in these media that are not works of art. Advertisements are just one type of such evocative items.

I said earlier that it is usually people who express things. It is not typically people who are expressive of things, however. A person expresses sadness, but a person's face or behavior is expressive of sadness. Furthermore, some faces are expressive of sadness even when the person whose face it is is not sad. It is just a sad face. The property of being expressive of a feeling is not confined to human faces. It is obvious how the weeping willow tree got its name; it has that sad look that makes it expressive of sadness. Until now, I have not carefully distinguished expressing and being expressive. Many contemporary philosophers think that this distinction is crucial for understanding expression in art. Art is essentially expressive of such things as emotions and moods. As with the sadness of the weeping willow tree, such expressiveness is a perceptual property, something we see or hear. It is not necessarily indicative of anyone's state of mind, either the artist's or the spectator's.

This conception of expression brings us no closer to defining art. Our discussion should make it obvious that many things other than artworks are expressive in the sense just specified. Nevertheless, some people would claim that expression is at least a necessary condition of art. This is a hard claim to refute partly because there are, as we have seen, many senses in which works of art are expressive and partly because whether a work is expressive and what, in particular, it is expressive of, is so much a matter of disputable interpretation. Still, it is not clear that artworks must possess expressive properties. Some artists just don't seem interested in expression in any of its varieties. Some painters want to capture the appearance of a landscape without making it expressive of anything (such as impressionists like Monet). Expression is one, but only one, of the many things an artist can try to achieve, and some artists may wholly exclude it in favor of other things.

■ ART AS AESTHETIC EXPERIENCE

Sometimes we enjoy works of art because we perceive in them expressive qualities; for example, we might enjoy a piece of music because of the sadness we hear in it. Sometimes we enjoy works of art because they represent things in fascinating ways. Although in one case we are enjoying works of art for their expressive properties and in another we are enjoying them for their representational properties, in both cases our perceiving these properties gives us enjoyable experiences. These experiences have a lot in common: they typically result from closely attending to the sensuous qualities of the work. Having such experiences also requires, commonly, the exercise of the imagination. The people and scenes we see in pictures, after all, are not literally there. Similarly, music isn't literally sad. Hearing sadness in music might require perceiving analogies between patterns of sound and patterns of sad human behavior. Finally, the experiences this attentive, imaginative perception gives us are enjoyed for their own sake, whatever further benefits they might bring.

Furthermore, we have other enjoyable experiences in perceiving artworks that seem to follow the same formula. We sometimes enjoy patterns we perceive in the organization of a piece of music or a painting. Thus, we enjoy following the development of a theme in a musical work, and we can take pleasure in the way different parts of a painting form a balanced whole or stand in tension with each other. Though such properties are neither representational nor expressive, their perception requires close attention and imagination. The experience of these properties is enjoyed for its own sake.

Such reflections have encouraged many philosophers to suppose that what is peculiarly valuable about artworks is a certain experience they are capable of giving in terms of which they might be defined. This experience has been dubbed aesthetic experience. Unlike the terms *art*, *expression*, and *representation*, the term *aesthetic* is a technical one—a term coined by philosophers for a special purpose—so one would expect it to have a precise meaning. Unfortunately, such expectations are unfulfilled. When the word **aesthetic** was first used, in the eighteenth century, to characterize a new discipline that would study the human experience of art and beauty (as well as the sublime, the gorgeous, the awe inspiring, and so on), the seeds were sown that grew into a concept covering a diversity of experiences. Beauty can be found almost anywhere—certainly in nature, in art, and in mathematics and science.

There are many different attempts to define the aesthetic and, hence, little agreement about the boundaries of aesthetic experience. From the remarks just made, one might think that an aesthetic experience is any experience that is enjoyed for its own sake resulting from close and imaginative attention to the sensuous features of an object. Well, that is a possible definition, but it excludes things that many, including myself, would regard as aesthetic experiences. Imaginative attention is not always required to enjoy natural beauty. Our enjoyment of a pretty flower, a gorgeous sunset, or an awe-inspiring snowstorm is aesthetic pleasure, but the element of imagination often does not seem required. The fact that imagination is much more commonly required in the enjoyment of works of art might suggest that we are dealing with two quite different types of experience and that we should give the enjoyment of natural beauty a different name. Unfortunately, this will not work because we often enough experience pleasure from the sights and sounds of artworks, the appreciation of which also requires little imagination: the shape and color of a ceramic bowl, the beautiful colors of a painting. If we deny that these enjoyable experiences are aesthetic, we risk making aesthetic experience a rather specialized experience that we have in connection with art (and perhaps other things), rather than the pervasive and dominant feature of our intercourse with art that it is often said to be.

So far I have spoken of aesthetic experience as a kind of perceptual experience, in particular, a kind of visual or **aural experience**. This raises the question of whether, on the one hand, it extends to other senses, and, on the other, whether it extends beyond perception. A connoisseur of cigars is able to discriminate among and enjoy the tastes and smells (as well as the color and shape) of fine cigars. Is the sort of experience the connoisseur enjoys an aesthetic experience? Although aestheticians are by no means unanimous, the majority answer has been no, for reasons I shall let readers try to determine for themselves. On the other hand, there is considerable pressure to extend aesthetic experience beyond perceptual experience, primarily because there is at least one extensive and important art form the enjoyment of which is primarily not perceptual, namely, literature. When we read a novel or a poem, the sound of the words, and even their visual appearance on the page, can be important, but what is more important is the meaning these words convey. What is typically conveyed is a world we contemplate in our imagination rather than with our senses. Because, however, as we have already seen, even perceptual aesthetic experience often requires a good deal of imagination, it seems natural to extend the concept of aesthetic experience to those pleasurable experiences we have when attending to the imaginary worlds found in literature. Once we allow this extension, the problem of the cutoff point once again arises. Are the pleasurable experiences we get when attending to an elegant mathematical demonstration or an ingenious scientific experiment also aesthetic experiences? The word aesthetic often enough crops up in characterizing these experiences.

For the purposes of defining art, this would not matter if there were a special variety of aesthetic experience peculiar to the enjoyment of artworks or at least particularly intended by artists. This does not seem to be the case, however. Furthermore, in the twentieth century whole artistic movements as well as individual works have attempted to separate art and the aesthetic. Probably the most famous example of these are Marcel Duchamp's ready-mades: mass-produced objects that Duchamp simply chose, sometimes scribbled on, mounted, and exhibited.[3] One of Duchamp's criteria in choosing these objects was a complete lack of aesthetic interest. It could be argued that insofar as Duchamp succeeded in "making" artworks with his ready-mades, he necessarily failed in his intention to present unaesthetic objects. The fact is that some of the ready-mades are rather beautiful, his bicycle wheel being one of these. The consensus, however, is that many of the ready-mades are aesthetically boring and that they are art for other reasons. For example, they suggest certain compelling questions: What does an artist have to do to make an artwork? Can unaesthetic artworks exist? What does it mean for an artwork to be original? How do artworks differ from functional artifacts? To not only raise but make compelling such questions by embodying them in a striking object also seems to be a function of art. So, artworks cannot be defined as those objects that give, or are primarily intended to give, aesthetic experience.

■ *Some Recent Attempts to Define Art*

The failure of definitions of art in terms of representation, expression, and aesthetic experience has led many philosophers to suspect that there is something fundamentally mistaken in these attempts. For one thing, no fixed set of valuable properties or functions seems to characterize all works of art. What counts as a valuable artistic property or function is subject to continuous evolution.

This realization has suggested at least three quite different views about the definition of art: (1) the **open concept view**, (2) the **institutional theory**, and (3) the attempt to define art historically.

■ THE OPEN CONCEPT VIEW

The first view claims that art cannot be defined. Proponents of this view claim that art is an open-ended concept, meaning by this that it has no necessary or sufficient conditions. The concept of a game is often given as an example of an open-ended concept. It is claimed that there is nothing that all games have in common. Many games are competitive but some (solitaire) are not. Most games involve winning and losing, but some do not. Something is a game if it resembles one of the standard examples of a game. This results in different things being games for different reasons. Similarly, we classify particular items as art in terms of a "family resemblance" they share with one or another of the works that are, at a given time and place, considered standard examples of art. Different works have different strands of similarity to these acknowledged standard examples.[4]

One point that early proponents of the open-concept theory failed to make clear is how classification by family resemblance works. The problem is that, if we think of the resemblance of two objects as their sharing some properties, then everything resembles everything, and we have no reason for picking one object over another as a work of art. Thus, consider the office chair on which I am now sitting. Why isn't it a work of art? (Believe me, it's not.) It resembles works of art in many ways. It resembles some Henry Moore sculptures in, among other things, being a material object, being partly composed of objects with rounded shapes, having legs, having lots of green in it. Take any work of art at all. There will be some property or other it shares with my chair. What family-resemblance theorists failed to give us was a rationale for taking certain properties as relevant and others as irrelevant for classification.

Once we realize that we make *no* headway in understanding what art is by reference to family resemblance, unless we specify what counts as a relevant similarity, we are back on the track of a definition. For if we can specify such relevant resemblances, we can perhaps define art in those terms. Further, the fact that so impressed the open concept theorists, viz. that the properties for which we value art change over time, is perfectly consistent with the possibility of defining art, as long as we don't cast our definition in terms of one or several such valuable properties.

■ *THE INSTITUTIONAL THEORY*

The second view is that art can be defined but that traditional attempts to do so look for a definition in the wrong place. It should not be sought in the properties that traditional definitions focused on, such as representation, expression, or the capacity to give aesthetic experience. The best known version of this view is the institutional theory of art. According to this view, arthood is a matter of social fact, in particular, that of an object standing in the appropriate relation to something called "the art world" or "the institution of art." Some understand this as the possession of status—art status. Others claim that objects are art when they are treated in certain ways by people occupying certain roles or following certain rules. Thus, George Dickie, a contemporary philosopher, has proposed that an artwork is an artifact of a kind created to be presented to an art world public.[5]

Some people remain dissatisfied with this definition. One reason for this dissatisfaction is that it seems to tell us too little. What is an art world public? Obviously it consists of people, but is it a special group of them? If so, what places someone in this group? If it is not a special group of people, it is everyone. But art can hardly be defined by the fact that it is a kind created to be presented to everyone. So is Coca Cola. This suggests a second reason to be dissatisfied with this theory. As we have seen, there are two ways of thinking of an art world public. Either it consists of a special group, or it consists of everyone. If we take the second option, we won't be able to define art in terms of the art world public. However, if we take the first option, we seem to exclude many works of art, because it is not clear they belong to the relevant kind. Consider for example African masks, which many regard as works of art and which are often displayed in art museums. Do they belong to a kind created to be presented to special art world group? It is far from clear that they do. Finally many objects are directed at such a group, but are not artworks. For example, I often receive requests to give money to a particular art institution such as the Metropolitan Opera in New York. These appeals are *clearly* made to be presented to an art world public. They are based on lists of people who have attended performances or shows in the relevant category or have otherwise shown themselves to be interested in the arts. So the requests must belong to the kind of thing created to be presented to a public interested in art, and yet *clearly* are not works of art.

Despite these reasons for dissatisfaction, Dickie's proposed definition has provided an invaluable example, because it demonstrates that one can attempt to define art without mentioning a particular function or valuable property of art, such as its being a source of aesthetic experience.

■ HISTORICAL APPROACHES

The underlying idea of historical theories of art is that what makes something art at a given time is not its standing in a relation to an institution but its standing in the right historical relation to earlier artworks until we arrive at the very first artworks that need to be defined in a different way. One of the best known historical definitions of art claims that an item is an artwork just in case it is intended for regard in a way preexisting artworks are or were correctly regarded.[6] Notice how this view exploits, but also improves on, one of the claims of the open concept view: that objects are correctly classified as art in virtue of many different strands of similarity to other artworks. Unlike the earlier view, the historical approach specifies how we determine whether a similarity is relevant.

Call this particular version of the historical approach the **intentional-historical definition** because of its emphasis on an *intention* regarding preexisting artworks. This view too has its problems, three of which will now be pointed out. First, it not clear the intention that works be regarded as preexisting ones are correctly regarded is enough (is a sufficient condition) to make something art. In 1915, French artist Marcel Duchamp attempted to make the Woolworth Building in New York into a ready-made as he did with the bicycle wheel we mentioned earlier in this chapter. All agree that in the instance of the Woolworth Building he failed, though he had the intention mentioned in the definition we are now considering. Or consider a forger of paintings. He too seems to have such intentions, but his forgeries are not necessarily works of art. Second, it is not clear that it is necessary to have such intentions to bring an artwork into existence. Perhaps one can create art from an intention derived from a *misunderstanding* of earlier artworks[7] or from utilitarian intentions that happen to result in an object with artistically valuable properties. For example, one might set out to make a vessel to hold water and end up with a remarkably beautiful pot. Finally, even if the intentional-historical definition can meet these challenges, it is incomplete without an independent account of the earliest artworks. The art status of so-called first art cannot be defined in terms of a relation to earlier art, because it is the earliest art of all.

One way to get around these problems with the intentional-historical definition but maintain something of its spirit is to articulate a theory that refers not only to the intentions of artists, but also to the evolving functions or valuable properties of art (so that we can account for things like the beautiful pot mentioned above) and that is explicitly *disjunctive* in character. A disjunctive definition of art tells us that something is art if it satisfies condition A *or* if it satisfies conditions B *or* for some finite number of conditions. The intentional-historical definition is implicitly disjunctive because it has to define first art one way and the rest of art in another way. The proposal now is to look for a definition that is explicitly disjunctive in form.

What are art functions? Some theorists claim that art is distinguished from other artifacts like chairs, knives, and automobiles in not being functional. However, this does not appear to be true. Traditional definitions of art, even if they are problematic as definitions, are quite good at picking out some of the most important, and most enduring, art functions. Representational properties of art function to present the appearance of things, to portray probable ways humans will behave, to present ideals, and so on. The expressive properties of art explore the intentional and dynamic structure of the emotions, evoke emotional reactions from its audience, and join people together in a common bond of similar feelings, among other things. The provision of aesthetic experience satisfies a human need for the stimulation of the senses and the imagination, as well as expanding our powers of discrimination. These are by no means the only art functions. Some are specific to an art subform, such as the function of horror movies to be scary. Just which functions representational, expressive, and aesthetic properties of artworks possess changes over time.

Here is a proposal. At any given time, art has a finite set of functions (though these may be different at different times). These functions range from genre-specific ones like being scary in the case of horror movies to those longstanding and widespread representational, expressive, and aesthetic values enshrined in some of the definitions considered earlier. The functions of art at a given time are to be identified through an understanding of the art forms central to that time. At any given time, certain forms or media are the standard ones in which art is produced. Thus, a writer with literary aspirations is now most likely to write poetry, novels, short stories, or drama. These standard ways of producing art are what I am calling the central art forms. (A form can lose its centrality, while new central forms are constantly coming into existence. In the eighteenth century, the essay was a central literary form, while the novel was just emerging as such a form.) However, this does not mean that items that don't belong to central art forms are never art. A work of philosophy, such as a dialogue by Plato, may be correctly considered a work of art. Almost anything can be art, but artifacts outside the central art forms have to meet a higher standard. We can gather these ideas together in the following disjunctive definition: Something is a work of art at a time t (where t is time no earlier than the time the item is created) just in case either (A) it is in a central art form at t and is made with the intention of fulfilling a value art has at t, or (B) it is an artifact that achieves excellence in fulfilling such a function. Call this view **historical functionalism**.[8]

This theory accepts the idea that motivated traditional definitions, namely, that art is to be understood in terms of the valuable functions it fulfills. It also, however, accepts the insight of the more recent theories discussed in this section that the whole of art—the art of the past, present, and future—cannot be characterized in terms of a single function or even in terms of several functions. It accepts from the open concept view the idea that these functions evolve in an open-ended fashion so that there will be resemblance rather than identity between the valuable functions of art at one period and those at another. From the institutional theory, it accepts the idea that, for an object to be art, it does not necessarily have to fulfill one of these functions. For works produced in the central art forms—such as poetry, painting, and music (but not philosophy or furniture)—the intention to fulfill is enough.

Whether or not historical functionalism turns out to be a satisfactory definition of art, it points to a partial, emerging consensus about what a definition of art should look like.[9] All of the more promising recent definitions are implicitly or explicitly disjunctive in form. (This is true even of some of the more recent institutional approaches.[10]) This suggests that the attempt to say what art is has abandoned the traditional goal of identifying an essence of art, since essences are necessary features of a kind, and the disjunctive character of art implies a lack of individually necessary features. However, if this traditional goal has been abandoned, what are we doing instead? Are we attempting to describe our actual concept of art or refine various beliefs people have about art into a more ideal concept? Should we even continue to assume that we are looking for a single correct definition? Should we now accept the possibility that there can be several equally useful definitions of art: several equally good solutions to the same problem or, perhaps, several problems calling for different solutions?

■ CONCLUSION: THE VALUE OF ART

In the previous sections, in discussing what art is, I mentioned many features of works of art that people value. Let us now, by way of concluding this chapter, bring together some of these thoughts by focusing on the questions about value raised at the beginning of this essay.

■ *What Makes Art Valuable?*

Although there is no completely satisfying simple answer to this question, a good partial answer can be given by mentioning some of the functions that art fulfills especially well, though they can be fulfilled by other things too.

Earlier in this chapter, I introduced the notion of an aesthetic experience—a pleasurable (sometimes intensely pleasurable) experience we have when we closely and imaginatively attend to the sights and sounds of things or when we vividly imagine certain represented states of affairs. Such experiences are by no means confined to art, but many works of art are the richest sources of these experiences. This is one reason why art is found in all cultures. To be a human being with eyes and ears and an imagination is to be a seeker of aesthetic experience. Aesthetic experience is not simply a pleasure human beings are capable of having; it is a human need, although we can be conditioned or can condition ourselves to ignore this need, unlike certain physical needs. Many of the formal, representational, and expressive features that formed the basis of various definitions of art are valued because they contribute to aesthetic value.

In addition to fulfilling the function of giving aesthetic experience, many works of art are especially good at helping us understand ourselves, the world around us, and the possibilities open to us. (Let us call this art's cognitive value.) The key word is "possibilities." Works of art present to us possible ways of experiencing things, of conceiving things, and of valuing things. They exhibit surprising ways of seeing the world around us. They suggest ways of thinking about ourselves and our actions. They explore what may be of value or disvalue in experiences, relationships, and ways of living. It would be wrong to say that art gives us knowledge of any of these things because, as I have been saying, a work of art can only present us with a possibility. Knowledge requires something more—that the possibility be realized in the world we live in, not just in the imaginary world of the artwork. But to find out anything, we have to have possible ways of seeing, thinking, and valuing. Many works of art are better than anything else at enabling us to make these explorations.

In our own century, a third function has been assigned to works of art that is as highly valued as the first two (and is not entirely independent of them). This is the function of being an object for interpretation—an object to be construed in accordance with aims we bring to it, rather than in accordance with the intentions with which it was made.[11] The sort of interpretation that has fascinated many contemporary critics is a kind of revisionary, creative interpretation that attempts to blur the distinction between artist and critic. This sort of criticism has shocked more conservative practitioners, but it seems to me that it is simply an extended pursuit of the artistic values already mentioned. A creative critic does not aim to discover something but to "collaborate" with the work to create something new—a new work with its own aesthetic and cognitive properties. Such criticism is simply the attempt to create more aesthetic and cognitive value. The only question such critics need to ask themselves is whether they create enough new aesthetic and cognitive value for their efforts to be worthwhile.

■ *Are All Art Forms Valuable for the Same Reason?*

I have been speaking of the value of art, but this requires qualification. Not all the broad categories of value apply equally well to all art forms. Aesthetic value does apply, but this is not surprising because we can try to appreciate almost anything aesthetically. The cognitive value just discussed is a different story. It applies preeminently to representational arts such as literature, painting, and dance, and much more dubiously elsewhere in the art world. So, largely for reasons of space, the above account of artistic value is somewhat biased in favor of the representational arts. To counterbalance this approach, let us very briefly examine what sort of value (other than aesthetic value) might be attributed to two largely non-representational artforms: instrumental music and architecture.

Music possesses something that is at least analogous to the cognitive value discussed earlier. Many writers about music have observed that we perceive music as movement. We hear it moving slowly or quickly, as moving up or down, as moving with a certain rhythm. We hear parts performed by different instruments moving together or in different directions. In addition to hearing movement, we hear many other dynamic qualities. Music can sound languid or bouncy, aggressive or peaceful. It would be wrong to say music represents these qualities, for if it did, we could say that a piece of music is about languor or bounciness, and that is hardly necessary for the music to be languid or bouncy. Furthermore, very often it would be wrong to say that a work of music represents anything as having these qualities. The music is simply perceived as having them. Nevertheless, many things besides music literally or metaphorically have these qualities too. Bodies move through space. We walk, run, work, play with a certain pace and rhythm. Breathing and heartbeat are movements within our body. Our thoughts and feelings have dynamic qualities as well and impart dynamic qualities to our bodies. (Think of your body when you are sad and when you are filled with joy.) I believe that music helps us conceptualize the qualities of movement and other dynamic qualities that permeate our lives. When we talk about sad music, we are thinking of sadness as a certain kind of dynamic quality. Because such conceptualization is not easily accomplished with words (at least in English and many other languages), this is one reason we value music.

Architecture intervenes in our environment much more aggressively than most other arts. Once a building is put up, we may have little choice whether to look at it, move through it, and move around it. When an architect or planner is considering what building to build, he or she is choosing among possibilities, but once the building exists, we are not being presented with a possible way of thinking or experiencing things beyond the artwork. Rather, we are being presented with a new set of actual experiences. It is in these terms that we have to evaluate a work of architecture. If we like, we can confine this evaluation to the aesthetic experience such works give us, which, in the case of architecture, means evaluating our visual experiences of buildings and their surroundings. Because this is only one aspect of the way we experience buildings, however, there is no reason why we must confine our evaluation to this aspect. Our evaluation can include all the ways buildings shape the environment and affect our lives.

The best approach to understanding the value of art would begin by considering the value of individual art forms and work from there to sets of generalizations. Limitations of space make that approach impossible here. I hope that the alternative I have adopted is not wholly unenlightening or off-base.

■ *Who Cares about Artistic Value?*

Everyone cares about the values I have been describing. Everyone seeks aesthetic experience; everyone seeks new, fruitful ways of thinking about themselves and the world. Everyone would like an enhanced rather than an impoverished environment. Of course, great works of art are not the only place to find these valuable things, and not everyone seeks them there. There are many reasons for this, but one is that many, though not all, great works of art can be daunting, either because they are difficult and demanding or because they come from a distant era. Such works cannot be appreciated effortlessly and without preparation. But if you become prepared and make the effort, the rewards will be surprising.

■ NOTES

1. The classical sources of the representational definition of art are Plato's *Republic*, Book 10, and Aristotle's *Poetics*.

2. R. C. Collingwood, *The Principles of Art* (Oxford: Oxford Univ. Press, 1938); B. Croce, *Aesthetic*, trans. D. Ainslie (London: Macmillan, 1929).

3. Duchamp was a member of the movement known as Dada, which sometimes claimed to create "antiart" rather than art. However, antiart seems to have been used ambiguously to denote either something other than art or art stripped of its usual presuppositions. I think Duchamp's ready-mades are best understood as antiart in the latter sense. The most famous ready-made is a urinal known as *Fountain*.

4. The best known statement of this view is found in Morris Weitz, "The Role of Theory in Aesthetics," *Journal of Aesthetics and Art Criticism* 15, no. 1 (1956). The notion of family resemblance is borrowed from Ludwig Wittgenstein, *Philosophical Investigations*, trans. G. E. M. Anscombe (New York: Macmillan, 1953), 67.

5. George Dickie, *The Art Circle* (New York: Haven, 1984). Though very influential, this view has received a barrage of criticism. See Richard Wollheim, *Art and Its Objects*, 2nd ed. (Cambridge: Cambridge University Press, 1980) and Robert Stecker, "The End of an Institutional Definition of Art," *British Journal of Aesthetics* 26, no. 2 (1986) Dickie replies to me in "Reply to Stecker," G. Dickie, et al., *Aesthetics: A Critical Anthology*, 2nd ed. (New York: St. Martin's, 1989), 214–17.

6. The chief proponent of this view is Jerrold Levinson, *Music, Art, and Metaphysics* (Ithaca, N.Y.: Cornell University Press, 1990).

7. That such misunderstanding provides the basis for many artworks is famously argued by Harold Bloom in *A Map of Misreading* (New York: Oxford University Press, 1975).

8. For a more detailed presentation of this view, see Robert Stecker, *Artworks: Definition, Meaning, Value* (University Park: Pennsylvania State University Press, 1997) 48–65.

9. For a more elaborate explanation of this convergence, see Robert Stecker, "Is it Reasonable to Attempt to Define Art," in Noel Carroll (ed.), *Theories of Art Today* (Madison: University of Wisconsin Press, 2000) 45–64. The convergence is only partial because there are still proponents of aesthetic definitions of art and there are those who are skeptical of the whole enterprise.

10. See Stephen Davies, "First Art and Art's Definition," *Southern Journal of Philosophy*, 35, 1997, 19–34.

11. The expression "object for interpretation" was coined by R. A. Sharpe, "Interpreting Art," *Proceedings of the Aristotelian Society*, supp. vol. 55 (1981). This function of art has been incorporated into many schools of contemporary literary theory, for example, reader-response theory, pragmatism, and deconstruction. Comparable ideas are to be found in the criticism of other arts.

■ QUESTIONS

1. Which items from the list at the beginning of the chapter are arts or works of art? Can you explain why you chose those items and rejected the others?

2. How would you answer the question, What is art? Among the definitions discussed in this chapter, to which one does your view most closely correspond?

3. What do traditional definitions of art have in common? Is this a common failing?

4. The Dutch artist Van Meegeran took the art world by storm by claiming to have discovered several unknown works by his great predecessor Vermeer. These works attracted intense interest until it was discovered that Van Meegeran himself painted them. Are Van Meegeran's "Vermeers" works of art? Are these works less valuable, or of no value, because Van Meegeran rather than Vermeer painted them? How would the various definitions of art discussed in this chapter answer this question?

5. What is the historical functional view the author defends? Does it constitute an advance over traditional views? Is it a complete and final definition of art?

6. An objection to the intentional-historical definition is that it cannot explain how Duchamp could fail in making the Woolworth building a "ready-made". Can historical functionalism do a better job of explaining this?

7. Can enjoying a good meal be an aesthetic experience? Can a good meal be a work of art? Why, or why not?

8. Do you think that art is a source of insight or understanding? For example, do you think that people who read a good deal of "serious" literature have a better understanding of other people, are more sensitive to ethical issues, or are more in touch with their emotions? Does the way we answer this question provide a good test of the cognitive value of art?

9. Is it true that not many people today are art lovers? If so, do you think those people who are not art lovers are missing something important?

■   *FOR FURTHER READING*

Beardsley, M. C. 1958. *Aesthetics: Problems in the Philosophy of Criticism*. New York: Harcourt, Brace.

Carroll, Noel. 2000. *Theories of Art Today*. Madison: University of Wisconsin Press.

Davies, Stephen. 1991. *Definitions of Art*. Ithaca, N.Y.: Cornell University Press.

Dickie, G. 1984. *The Art Circle*. New York: Haven Press.

Kivy, Peter. 1980. *The Corded Shell: Reflections on Musical Expression*. Princeton, N.J.: Princeton University Press.

Levinson, Jerrold. 1990. *Music, Art and Metaphysics*. Ithaca, N.Y.: Cornell University Press.

Stecker, Robert. 1997. *Artworks: Definition, Meaning, Value*. University Park: Pennsylvania State University Press.

Tolstoy, Leo. 1960. *What Is Art?* Indianapolis, Ind.: Bobbs-Merrill.

CHAPTER TEN

Philosophy of Religion

KATHERIN A. ROGERS

■ *INTRODUCTION*

Philosophy asks terribly practical questions, and one of the most pressing is this: Should you believe in God? This huge and multifaceted question is central to the area of philosophy known as philosophy of religion. Religion, the system of beliefs and practices associated with the supernatural or divine, is an almost universal human phenomenon. The study of religion can take many different forms. Anthropologists, for example, may record and compare the religious beliefs and practices of different cultures, and so are concerned with what people *actually* believe and do. Philosophers, operating on the assumption that our beliefs and behavior ought to conform to logic and reason, are concerned with what people *should* believe and do. The philosopher of religion thus asks what beliefs about the supernatural it is reasonable to hold and what behavior might suitably follow from those beliefs. Philosophy of religion is not limited to discussion of the question "Is there a God?" but this is a fundamental question and a good place to start.

In this chapter we will sketch briefly some of the reasons for believing in God, and then we will focus on a closely related, narrower question: Can you prove that there is *not* a God? If you could demonstrate that God does not exist, then, at least for those who prefer to hold rationally respectable beliefs, the question about whether or not to believe in God would be answered in the negative. Our conclusion will be that you can*not* prove the nonexistence of God. It will lie beyond the scope of this chapter to address adequately the vaster question of whether or not you can prove, or at least ought to believe, that God does exist. However, our discussion will lay the groundwork for that question in two ways. First, it will spell out what we mean by "God." If you are asking whether or not something exists, it is helpful to know *what* it is that you are talking about. Second, our discussion will address what has traditionally been a major stumbling block for belief in God: How could an all-good and all-powerful God possibly allow all the evil we see in the world? The reader can then take this chapter as a necessary first step toward answering the larger question of the rationality of belief in God.

As philosophy developed in ancient Greece, two basic views emerged on the overall nature of the universe, and it is safe to say (though volumes of qualification could be added) that most Western philosophers have aligned themselves with one side or the other. One camp held that our universe is the product of a divine cause, a supernatural source, which explains why things are as they are and which imbues the whole with a meaning, purpose, and value that are objective and absolute; that is, the value is really *there* in the world and is not a matter of the mere opinions of particular individuals or cultures. As the transcendent source of all and the ultimate standard of value, this cause must not be subject to the limitations that circumscribe natural objects. It would in fact be perfect. So, for example, Plato (c.428–c.348 B.C.) in *The Republic* held that the ultimate source of everything is "The Good," a being that is unlimited goodness itself and that all things somehow share in and reflect in order to be what they are. And Aristotle (384–322 B.C.), noting that things in the world change in an ordered way that involves striving for fulfillment, hypothesized an "Unmoved Mover" as the perfect standard that everything in some way imitates. We can call the adherents of this basic world view **theists**, from the Greek word for *god*.

In the Middle Ages Jews, Christians and Muslims used the resources offered by Greek philosophy to reason about the God of "The Book," the God whom they took to be revealed in the Bible, Hebrew or Christian, or in the Koran, which includes much of the same material. (The capital "G" will be used to distinguish this God from other candidates for "divine source of all." The scriptures in question refer to God as "He" rather than as "She" or "It," so the masculine pronoun is used in this chapter.[1]) The great medieval philosophers believed in a God who was at once the personal and providential agent of biblical revelation and the perfect being of Greek philosophy. When modern or contemporary philosophers ask, "Should I believe in God?" it is usually some variant on this God that they have in mind.

Contemporary philosophers differ on exactly how to understand the nature of this God, but most allow that a being fitting the description must be worthy of worship and, in the famous words of St. Anselm of Canterbury (1033–1109 A.D.), "That than which a greater cannot be conceived." Such a being, it is generally agreed, would be at least **omnipotent**, **omniscient**, and perfectly good. (Philosophers disagree on the list of essential divine perfections, but most will grant that these three properties are on it.[2]) I will argue throughout that the most adequate understanding of the nature of God and the relationship of God to the universe is that offered by the great medieval philosophers, especially St. Augustine of Hippo (354–430 A.D.), St. Anselm of Canterbury, and St. Thomas Aquinas (1225–1274 A.D.). I will call their view **classical theism**. It lies beyond the scope of this chapter to attempt a general description of classical theism or a systematic comparison with other types of theism, but some of the basic outlines of the view should emerge in the course of discussing the selected topics at issue here.

The other basic philosophical camp, which we can call the "atheist" side, denies the existence of a god and holds that the natural universe is all there is and does not require an explanation beyond itself. Things are as they are because of the behavior of material particles obeying natural laws. A common corollary is the view that there is no meaning, purpose, or value to things beyond what particular individuals or societies bestow upon them. Democritus (c.460–360 B.C.), a contemporary of Socrates (c.470–399 B.C.), held that everything could be explained by hypothesizing minute, everlasting particles, "atoms," whose random motions in the "void" (empty space) resulted in clusters arranged and rearranged to constitute the objects of the universe, including human beings and even human thought processes. A somewhat earlier pre-Socratic philosopher, Empedocles (c.490–430 B.C.), explained the existence of present species of animal as wholly the result of random mutation and survival of the fittest. Most Western atheists today accept the contemporary versions of these views, which are radically more detailed and sophisticated than their ancient Greek counterparts but which, in their barest essentials, boil down to the same idea; everything ultimately comes from and is made of the purposeless behavior of "atoms in the void."

In addition to theism and **atheism**, there is a third possible opinion. One might simply withhold judgment. Someone who remains undecided is an agnostic. It is safe to say that the philosophers who have earned a place in the history of Western philosophy have almost all chosen either theism or atheism. Perhaps philosophical greatness is ill at ease with fence-sitting. In any case the consensus has been that the rational person can and should answer the question "Is there a God?" one way or the other.

■ REASONS TO BELIEVE IN GOD

■ Without Proof

Is it reasonable to believe in God? A number of past and present philosophers have held that, even in the absence of proof for the existence of God, one can justifiably make a commitment of faith or take belief in God to be a properly basic belief that cannot and need not be proven. Blaise Pascal (1623–1662 A.D.), for example, offered his famous Wager as an argument for the reasonableness of believing in God when you judge the universe to supply equal amounts of evidence pointing to theism on the one hand and to atheism on the other.[3] Pascal held that the choice you made had a profound practical impact on how you lived, so that in practice **agnosticism**, failing to make a choice, is not really possible. But reason leaves you poised between the two viable options. Because you are forced to gamble, the safe bet is to commit yourself to belief in God and the theist lifestyle that entails. If you're right and God does exist, you win everlasting happiness. If you're wrong and it's all atoms and the void, you haven't really lost anything. In Pascal's view the only apparent advantage of atheism is that the universe of atoms and the void does not offer an objective moral order, so you are free to indulge your selfish desires with impunity as you would not be were there a God. (Obviously there are plenty of virtuous atheists and nasty theists. Pascal holds that these folks haven't thought through their beliefs properly.) In fact, though, Pascal holds that the theist lifestyle will result in a happier life in the here and now than the atheist lifestyle. If you bet against God and you're right, you don't win anything because the atheist universe offers no rewards. But if you're wrong, you've lost the chance for everlasting happiness. So it's reasonable to believe in God even in the absence of proof.

■ *Causal Proofs*

Of course, many great philosophers have held that it is indeed possible to prove the existence of God. St. Thomas Aquinas, in his famous thirteenth century textbook on God, argues that only God can explain how our world is as we observe it to be.[4] For example, Aquinas offers a version of what is called the **cosmological argument** to show that there must be a divine cause for the universe. We recognize that all of the objects in our spatiotemporal universe are contingent, that is, they are the sorts of things that might conceivably *not* exist. Aquinas takes this point to entail that for anything you can point to in our universe, from the galactic cluster to the subatomic particle, the question "Why is it here?" is appropriate. Whatever the object in question, the assumption is that there is some sufficient explanation for its existence. And, at least on Aquinas's understanding of what it means to be contingent, this sufficient explanation must take the form of pointing to the cause on which the contingent object depends for its existence.

But if absolutely everything depended on something else to exist, there wouldn't be anything. Why? Because if each thing could cause the existence of something else only once it had been caused itself, and if each thing could pass existence along only once it had it, there'd be no source of existence. Imagine a series of mirrors. Each mirror can pass the light along once it's received it, but even an infinite series of mirrors couldn't generate any light to begin with. You need a different kind of thing, a light source. It's the same with existence. You need something that is the uncaused cause of the caused objects we observe in the world around us. You need something quite different from the contingent objects of the spatiotemporal universe. You need a **necessary being**. By a necessary being we mean something whose very nature it is to exist, that is, something that cannot possibly fail to exist. You need something for which the sufficient explanation cannot be given in terms of some further being on which it depends but that is, by nature, its own sufficient explanation. No inhabitant of the spatiotemporal universe can satisfy this criterion, nor can the spatiotemporal universe taken as a single, collective whole.[5] There must be something above and beyond it to serve as its ultimate cause, God.

It is important to note that Aquinas does not take the above argument to prove that there had to be a temporal beginning to our world. Reason cannot show that the universe had a first day. Whether past time is finite or infinite, the point about contingency remains. Aquinas, in fact, holds that the chain of contingent causes ending in a necessary cause is most adequately seen as a chain that exists right now, in which the links of causal dependency are all simultaneously present. Your existence is caused right now by the existence of other things. If those other things are contingent, then their existence depends on the existence of still other things. The chain ends in a necessary being who is causing the existence of all contingent beings right now. Classical theism holds that everything that exists is being sustained in being from moment to moment by God.

This is quite different from "deism," the view that a divine creator designed the universe and set it going "in the beginning," but does not sustain it or interfere with its further progress. It should also be noted that, though classical theism insists that God constantly sustains everything in being, this does not entail that created things do not have causal powers. Classical theism holds that although God is the primary cause of things, created things can produce effects as "secondary" causes. There is a view, "occasionalism," which holds that God produces all objects and events immediately such that created things do *not* have causal powers. It might have looked like it was the match flame that burned the cotton, but that is not what happened. God, and God *alone*, caused the flame and He caused the burnt cotton. The difference between classical theism and occasionalism will prove very important when we get to the problem of evil.

Aquinas also offers a version of the argument from design or the **teleological argument** (from the Greek word for "end" or "purpose"). We see that things in our world that do not themselves possess reason, nonetheless seem capable of acting toward future goals. There are, for example, ants that built suspension bridges long before people figured out how to do it. Because they lack the intellectual capacity to conceptualize that future goal and connect it with their present behavior, it must be the case that a rational creator designed them so that they could act to achieve their purposes. There must be a God. The contemporary reader may hold, and rightly so, that accepting the theory of evolution dilutes the force of this argument somewhat. It should be noted, though, that there is no contradiction between evolution of species and divine creation. The Book of Genesis records that God made man from inanimate matter. It does not address the question of whether or not He made man from dirt via protozoa and apes. The theist can view the processes of evolution as constantly sustained and guided by God, while the atheist will see them as just more purposeless motion. The question is: Is it more likely that the world as we see it is the product of a designing mind or of "atoms and the void"? (Some philosophers reserve the term *proof* for a demonstration that will convince any reasonable, sufficiently attentive person. I shall use the term more loosely so that it is acceptable to talk about a proof that is plausible, even if it is not universally convincing. Thus one might take a proof as offering good reason to believe something, without requiring that it be conclusive.)

And then there is the issue of value. We observe, says Aquinas, that some things are objectively better than others. It is not a matter of personal opinion or social custom that feeding a hungry five-year-old child is better than sexually abusing her. There is much in these claims to dispute. Many philosophers hold that values are not objective, but this is a difficult position since it seems to entail that there is nothing really wrong with sexually abusing a five-year-old child if personal opinion or social custom should incline in that direction. Even if values are objective, can we "observe" them? Aquinas himself holds that we do indeed "observe" values in the world. The rational mind is able to operate on the data it receives from the senses to go beyond bare sense information (colors, smells, tastes, etc.) and recognize more abstract truths, including truths about values. For the purposes of the proof for God from objective value, it is not necessary to agree on the very difficult question of how we might come to recognize the truth about values. Different philosophers offer different hypotheses. All that needs to be granted is that there is an objective truth to value and we can (somehow) recognize it.

The atheist universe, ultimately constituted by the purposeless motions of atoms in the void, is badly suited to explaining an order of value that transcends the changeable and conflicting opinions of individual humans and cultures. Evolution is no use because its one rule is that the fittest survive. But there is in this no objective value that anyone need care about. Perhaps obeying some sort of moral rules will enhance the longevity of my genetic line or the human species, but if I'm not interested in these goals then there's no reason for me not to do whatever I please. Perhaps in my own self-interest I should obey the rules and encourage others to do so as well, because an orderly society will prove a more comfortable place for me to live. This advice may hold for most ordinary human beings, but those uniquely talented at seizing and keeping power, people such as Hitler and Stalin, have no reason to toe the line. A moral order binding on everyone, whatever their personal tastes and interests, cannot be generated by the subjective attitudes and desires of individual people and cultures. Only by taking God as the standard of value can we explain the objectivity of value that we observe in the world around us.

■ *The Ontological Argument*

In addition to arguing for God as the cause of observable phenomena, there is quite a different sort of proof, first offered by St. Anselm of Canterbury in his *Proslogion*, and known to modern and contemporary philosophers as the **ontological argument**.[6] (Ontology is the study of being itself, and the argument rests on a comparison of two sorts of being.) Anselm held that, given the definition of God, with the addition of a key metaphysical principle, one could prove that God *has* to exist. His nonexistence is as unthinkable as a round square. Anselm begins his proof by defining God. We understand God to be "that than which a greater cannot be conceived." Now, whether or not such a being has extramental existence, that is, is there in the world outside of the mind of the human knower, it certainly does exist in the mind, since we can understand what the definition means. Given time and patience we can unpack the definition into a well-developed and coherent view of what such a being must be (and that is how Anselm spends the next twenty-five chapters of the *Proslogion*).

The key metaphysical principle on which the argument rests is this: extramental existence is greater than fictive existence. Something that exists only as an object of thought has a very limited kind of existence. The unicorn in your mind is utterly dependent on you and has only those limited properties that you are thinking it to have. Suppose now that a real, extramental unicorn comes wandering in. It has a better, fuller, and more robust sort of existence than that fictional unicorn of which you are thinking. It is not dependent on your mind, it has a fuller set of properties, it has a life history. There is just more *to* it than there is to the fictive unicorn. The real unicorn is greater than the unicorn that exists only in the mind. And this comparison holds true for anything that can have both fictive and extramental existence.

Contemporary philosophers will find much to dispute in this metaphysical principle. Does a fictive object really have any sort of existence at all? Is it coherent to think that the fictive unicorn and the extramental unicorn are both really unicorns such that comparing their mode of being is possible? Are there really different sorts of existence, and is extramental being really greater than fictive being? Anselm believed that you could answer all these questions in the affirmative, but it would take us too far afield to attempt to address them here. (If at this point the reader begins to feel that to answer one question in philosophy you need to answer an underlying question, and then one underlying that, so that what looked like a relatively simple issue turns out to be an iceberg of deeper questions, I can only respond that nobody said philosophy would be easy.)

Given the key metaphysical principle, we can now prove the existence of God using the method of *reductio ad absurdum*.[7] We assume the negation of what we are trying to prove, show that the negation is false, and thus prove the affirmative. So suppose God exists only in the mind, and not extramentally in reality. Then we could conceive of a greater being, one who existed both in the mind and in reality. But then, by definition, God would not be God, and that is absurd. Therefore God must exist both in the mind and extramentally. God really exists!

■ DISPROVING GOD

There are many variations on these reasons for believing in God and proofs for God and many other reasons and proofs besides. These brief sketches are intended to give the reader an idea of how one might go about defending the reasonableness of belief in God, and they will also serve as examples to illustrate the point that our central question—Can you prove that there is *not* a God?—is a vital first step. So for example, Pascal's Wager is dependent on the idea that the theist and the atheist world views are equally reasonable given the observable evidence. This initial premise is called into doubt if there is good reason not to believe in God.

In that case reason might give the edge to atheism and there is no need to "wager" at all. And even if Aquinas is right that there must be some being that does not depend on others for its existence, if we could show that there is no God, we know that whatever this being may be, it is not God. Even if we find it unlikely that the purposeless movements of particles (including evolution of species) could have produced the world we see around us, if we know that there is no God, we may have to accept atheism as the best explanation that fits all the facts. And suppose it is impossible to reconcile the existence of evil with the existence of God. The point here is that an all-powerful and perfectly good God would not permit the evil that we know exists. But in that case attempting to prove that God must exist as the source of all value appears especially wrong-headed, since it is precisely God's goodness that seems irreconcilable with evil. Or suppose that our very concept of God is self-contradictory. In that case Anselm's argument is dead in the water because it depends on our being able to have a coherent concept of God, God "in the mind." Even if the proofs for the nonexistence of God are merely plausible and not conclusive, might they not cast serious doubt on reasons for believing in God and supply good reason to opt for atheism? I hope to show that the attempts to prove God's nonexistence are not even plausible. So let us turn to our main question: Can you prove that God does *not* exist?

It is rather difficult to prove that something does not exist. Absence of evidence cannot always be taken as evidence of absence. Sometimes it can. If you wonder whether or not there is a rabbit in your bathtub, and you go and look and don't see one, you ought to conclude that one is not there. The test becomes more difficult when the object in question is not to be expected at a particular time or place. It becomes extremely difficult when the object in question is not something physical and so you cannot expect to observe it directly at all.[8] That is the case with God. There are basically two ways to prove the nonexistence of something like this. One way is to show that the very concept of such a being is incoherent or contradictory. By way of analogy, suppose the question is: Do round squares exist? You know that the answer is no without searching the world and turning over every rock. A round square cannot possibly exist. It is a logical impossibility because to be round means to be not square.

Some philosophers have argued that God cannot exist because the essential properties He is supposed to have entail logical contradictions. An essential property is a characteristic that makes a thing to be what it is. For example, most philosophers of religion agree that God is essentially all-powerful, all-knowing, and all-good. Something that lacked any one of these properties just would not be God. (It might be Aristotle's Unmoved Mover, it might be Zeus or Odin, but it would not be the God in whom Western philosophers now take an interest.) The argument for God's nonexistence can focus on one property and insist that it is intrinsically contradictory, or it can argue that ascribing one property to God means denying another. Either way, if it can be shown that the essential properties ascribed to God cannot really be possessed by something, then God does not exist.

The other way to prove that something does not exist is to show that its nonexistence follows from some fact that is generally accepted. The atheist uses this form of argument in disproving God through the "problem of evil." A perfectly good and powerful being would not permit the evil we recognize in the world. The evil obviously exists, so God does not. We will look first at the coherence of the divine attributes and then at the problem of evil.

■ *The Concept of "God" Is Incoherent*

■ OMNIPOTENCE

At first glance one might suppose that to say that God is omnipotent is to say that He can do anything, but this understanding immediately generates paradox. The old question "Can God make a rock too heavy for Him to lift?" may sound frivolous, but it has a terribly serious point. If God cannot make such a rock, then there is something He cannot do. And if He *can* make such a rock, there is *still* something He cannot do, lift the rock. Necessarily these are the only two options, and since either entails that there is something God cannot do, God cannot be omnipotent. But to be perfect and unlimited, He must be omnipotent. A less than omnipotent being is not God. Therefore there is no God.

Classical theism, the approach to God taken by the great medieval philosophers like Thomas Aquinas offers a standard response. It is incorrect to define omnipotence as the ability to do everything. The word actually means "all-powerful," and that is a preferable understanding of the divine attribute. There are all sorts of things God cannot do. First and foremost is the logically impossible.[9] God, for example, cannot make a round square. But this is not an instance of divine weakness. In fact the *round square* is just two words stuck together and not really a possible thing to be made at all. The classical theist is quite comfortable with saying that God cannot make a rock too heavy for Him to lift. Why? Something is "heavy" only relative to the limited strength of a physical lifter. According to classical theism, God is the absolute source of all, bringing all things with their properties into being and sustaining them from moment to moment by the sheer power of His thought. Nothing could possibly be heavy for God, and a "rock too heavy for God" is in the same class as the round square.

As so often happens in philosophy, however, doesn't this solution to the paradox entail a larger and even more difficult problem? If God cannot do the logically impossible, then apparently the laws of logic govern His options and He is not unlimited and perfect. Some philosophers, moved by this point, have decided that God is above the laws of logic as their inventor. Logic as we know it applies only because God *decided* that it should.[10] Classical theists did not make this move, and for very good reason. If God is the creator of logic, two wildly unpalatable conclusions follow. First, the laws of logic are arbitrary and might have been other than they are. In fact, God may decide to rescind them and then they will not apply. That is to say, for example, that the principle of noncontradiction—you can't have A and not-A in the same way at the same time—might not have been or might cease to be the case. Had God chosen other laws or no laws, your book might be both a book and a horse in the same way at the same time . . . and may yet be. But that is literally unthinkable. When your argument leads you to a conclusion that is absurd, it is time to think again. One might suggest that God's nature and actions are simply beyond human comprehension and that God can be and do the unthinkable. But this move basically denies the possibility of doing philosophy of religion, for in order to *philosophize* about the nature and behavior of God one must play by the rules of rational thought. Worse, this move is similar to the position that God is above logic and falls prey to the second problem with that view.

The second problem with the idea that God is the inventor of the laws of logic is that on this analysis His nature would transcend logic. But then the principle of noncontradiction, for example, would not apply to the nature of God. If that is the case then, though God is omnipotent, He might simultaneously be weak. Though He is omniscient, He might simultaneously be ignorant. Though He is good, He might be bad. The term *God* ceases to have any coherent meaning, and we have arrived at what is in effect a version of atheism by a curious route that began with an effort to defend divine perfection.

Are we then just stuck saying that God must conform to the laws of logic and hence that He is limited by them? No. The classical theist held that the laws of logic are not a set of rules external to God. There is absolutely nothing in the universe except for God and what He creates. God is the perfect being and source of all other beings. The laws of logic, the rules that govern how we have to think and how things have to be, flow from and reflect His *nature*. He neither chooses His nature, nor is He confined by it. This is a difficult concept that may perhaps be clearer when we come to a similar conclusion on the question of the relationship of God to the laws of morality. For now, suffice it to say that God cannot do the logically impossible, and this is no weakness.

There are other sorts of things that God cannot do, according to classical theism. He cannot stub His own toe or forget your telephone number or cease to exist. *You* could do all these things. Is God then not omnipotent because He lacks these talents you possess? But the "ability" to do these things is not really strength. These actions require and flow from being weak and limited. They represent a lack of power. Any activity that requires being essentially imperfect will be impossible for a perfect being, but that brings us back to logic again, and we know God does not violate the laws of logic.

A further apparent limitation on God is that He is necessarily good. He can do good things, but no bad ones. Whereas you or I might deliberate between two choices, one good and one bad, and choose either way, God can choose only one way. But the ability to make a choice seems to be a power, not like stubbing your toe or forgetting your phone number. If He has the power to choose one way but not the other, surely we must say that He is limited. Classical theism offers a well-developed answer to this problem: God's very nature is the absolute standard of all value in the universe. He does not *choose* the good. *Good* just means what is like God. For God to be bad is for God not to be God. We will discuss this point at greater length in the section on the problem of evil.

■ OMNISCIENCE

God knows everything about everything. Traditionally this has been held to mean that He knows not only the past and the present but also the future. If God does not know the future, then He is not "That than which no greater can be conceived." We can think of a greater, more perfect, less limited being, one who *does* know the future. Moreover, if God does not know the future, then He cannot really be providential, that is, He cannot make sure that things turn out as He plans. This is extremely important for most religious believers, and so a being that doesn't know the future is not really God.

But again a paradox arises. This one is generated by what many people take to be an evident fact about human existence. We have free will, which means that, when we are debating between options, it is really true that we could choose one or the other. Having chosen one option it is still literally true to say, "I could have done otherwise." Perhaps most important, it is really up to us what we choose. We are the ultimate causes of our choices. This view of freedom, often called libertarian, is a much-debated position in the history of philosophy. Many philosophers, including theists, past and present, reject it, believing instead that every event, including every human choice, is the determined product of preceding causes. If I choose this over that, it is because of a chain of causes that extends back in time to before I ever came on the scene. I would argue that the theist ought to accept libertarian freedom, though. The classical theist holds that, with the possible exception of human free choice, God causes everything. He keeps every object with all its properties in existence from moment to moment. True, it is the fire that burns the cotton ball, but it does so because God is causing the fire and the cotton and all that they are and do. If human choices do not originate with their human agents, but are determined by preceding causes, then God ultimately causes them. I take it as evident that sometimes people chose things that are wrong—things they ought not to choose. But if the choice originates with God, then it's really God who's responsible for the evil. Impossible! So the theist ought to be a libertarian.

But now the paradox: Suppose God knows today what I will choose tomorrow. Then it is true today that I will choose as God knows I will. I cannot change the past. When, tomorrow, I deliberate between options, I must choose as God foreknows I will choose. But then I don't really have open options and I am not free. But, as I argued above, libertarian freedom seems a vital part of the theist picture. So it cannot be the case that God knows the future, but that is another way of saying that there is no God.

Classical theism offers a standard response to this puzzle about freedom and foreknowledge. God is eternal in the sense of being "outside of time." All of time, past, present, and future, is equally and immediately "present" to Him, while His existence is not circumscribed by any time but "encompasses" it all. This does entail the four-dimensional view of time, which is difficult to conceptualize. All of time exists. Past and future are *there* as much as is the present, and there is nothing special about the present. What we timebound beings call past, present, and future is relative to the temporal perceiver. This position is difficult to grasp, but it is apparently as standard in contemporary relativity physics as it was in classical theism. An analogy between space and time may help. "Here" and "there" are relative to a particular spatial being, but in fact both exist equally. Even if we can only perceive what's "here," "there" exists just as much. And for a nonspatial being like God, it's all "here." So on the four-dimensional view of time, from God's perspective, it's all "now."[11]

Thus God does not really *fore*know what is future to us. He just knows it all, seeing all of time as immediately present. (*Present* is a temporal and spatial term, but it is probably the best we can do in expressing the mode of God's knowledge. As we perceive what is present to us temporally and spatially, God perceives all time and space and all they contain as immediately "here and now."[12]) Thus it is open to the classical theist to say today that God knows what I will choose tomorrow *because* I choose it and God sees me choosing it. On the libertarian understanding, my choice is the cause of God's knowledge. It may be that the present truth of the proposition "God knows what I will choose tomorrow" makes my choice "necessary," but this is not the necessity of *compulsion*, of a cause inevitably producing an effect. It is not that God's knowledge *determines* that the choice will occur, or that God knows some present causes that will determine that the choice will occur in the future. The "necessity" in question is what the classical theists called conditional or subsequent necessity. It is necessarily the case that if I know that you are sitting now, then (at least by the operant definition of *know*), you are sitting now. But my knowledge didn't cause your sitting and does not in any way interfere with you sitting freely and having the option to stand. The necessity in question here is not the necessity of compulsion, but rather the necessity entailed by, "If x is known, then x is true." If God's knowledge is the product of my choice which He observes as present, then divine foreknowledge and libertarian freedom are reconciled.[13]

But at this point some contemporary philosophers have raised a new paradox regarding omniscience. If, to preserve both freedom and divine foreknowledge, we need to hold that God sees all of time as equally present, then God cannot really know everything, because He cannot know what time it actually is *now*.[14] This one can be resolved relatively easily, so long as you are willing to allow that the universe is a pretty bizarre place. The paradox is generated by a misunderstanding of the four-dimensional view of time. There is no such thing as what time it *really* is. What time it is *now* is relative to temporal perceivers, and God knows all the temporal perceivers and what it means to them when they say, "now." He knows that "now" to William the Conqueror is 1066, and that "now" to us is the twenty-first century and that "now" to the perceiver in 2199 is

2199. From the God's eye point of view, which is, after all, the most correct point of view, there really is nothing special about what we call "present." God knows what time it is "now" relative to the different perceivers; He doesn't know what time it *really* is, because *all* of time is equally real. That the past and future exist as much as the present does seem a very odd way of looking at things, but surely classical theism is no worse than contemporary relativity physics on this score. When you really start to dig, it turns out that the universe is very strange indeed.

■ GOODNESS

Most theists have held that, in addition to being omnipotent and omniscient, God is essentially good. He always loves, chooses, and does what's right and good. This introduces a puzzle that goes back at least to Plato's dialogue *The Euthyphro* and so is sometimes called the Euthyphro dilemma. The question is this: Does God choose what is good *because* it is good or is something good *because* God chooses it? The first horn of the dilemma suggests that God is not the source of value but, rather, simply recognizes the good and conforms to it. But then the source of value exists independently of God and He is limited since He must conform to it to be what He is, essentially good.

The other horn of the dilemma suggests that God just decides to make something good. He is the creator or inventor of value. A corollary of this position is the **divine command theory** in ethics; the right action is the one commanded by God, just because it is commanded by God. This divine command theory has a certain following among contemporary theists, but classical theism rejected it and its parent idea that God simply chooses what should be of value, for two reasons. The astute reader will notice that these reasons are analogous to problems raised against the suggestion that God is the inventor of the laws of logic. Suppose there is no objective value to anything apart from God's bestowing value on it by divine *fiat*. God cannot violate the laws of logic, but short of a choice that is somehow self-contradictory, God is free to make absolutely anything good or bad, any action right or wrong. (This, at least, was the position of the late medieval "founding fathers" of divine command theory, who were motivated by a desire to ensure the perfect freedom and sovereignty of God.) But then values and morals are arbitrary. God happens to have made murder, rape, and pillage wrong. He could have made them right. He could (in His eternal present) decide that on the stroke of midnight in the year 2050 the rules of the Ten Coammandments will be reversed and one *ought* to murder and steal and covet . . . and perhaps even worship other gods.[15] Some theists apparently accept this unappealing conclusion, but many find it almost impossible that "You ought to torture small children for fun" could at some place and time be true. Some hold that intuitively this is almost as difficult to believe as that "This is a round square" could ever be true. Most theists are committed to the idea that morality and value are objective and thus will reject the view that at their core they are arbitrary.

There is a second, perhaps even more serious, problem with saying that God is the inventor of values. If God transcends good and bad and simply decides what they will be, then He Himself cannot be called "good" in any meaningful sense. Suppose that all *good* means is "loved/chosen/commanded by God." And suppose that God might have chosen that what we call "good" is in fact not-good, or that He might actually choose that what is good up until some point in time will thereafter be not-good. In that case the term *good* means only loved/chosen/commanded by God and, when we say that "God is good," we are not really saying anything *about* Him beyond that He is loved or chosen or commanded by Himself. But theism has traditionally held that the goodness of God must be related to the goodness we recognize in the myriad things we call "good" in creation. Otherwise the term *good* as applied to God is meaningless for us.[16] If what is good might equally well have been not-good, and vice versa, then the term *good* is empty of positive value content, and we have in effect denied one of the essential attributes of God. In that case, though, we are talking about someone other than God. The attempt to safeguard God's limitlessness by making Him the inventor of morals and values has brought us to a denial of classical theism. Whatever this proposed creator of values might be, He is not God.

But if God does not invent value and if He is not bound by some standard external to Himself, what *is* His relationship to the order of value and morals? The classical theist answer was that God Himself is the standard. His nature is the perfect good that all other things imitate to be good.[17] He does not invent His nature. It is just there. Nor is He limited by it, because it is identical to what He is. Moreover, in the tradition of classical theism, perfect goodness means the unlimited possession of all absolutely positive properties. (These are the properties, like knowledge and power, which, all other things being equal, it is better to have, and possession of which does not require limitation. Being muscular might be a positive property for a human being, but it is only a good within the context of being a limited corporeal being.) Evil or badness is the lack of or the falling away from goodness. Evil is essentially just a failure of the good. It is true to say that "by nature" God cannot do evil, but this is just to say that He cannot fail to possess all the positive properties perfectly. So, when the classical theist says that "God is good," what he means is that God is the absolute standard for all value, and everything else that is good is good as somehow sharing in and reflecting the divine nature.

■ The Problem of Evil

At this point the theist may have painted himself into a very difficult corner. He has insisted that God is omnipotent, sustaining all being in existence from moment to moment, and able to do everything that is logically possible and consistent with His perfection. Moreover, he has argued that God is necessarily good, not just as someone who adheres to an external moral order, but rather as being Himself the absolute standard for all good. If this is how we view the source of all, how can we possibly explain the existence of evil? The first question is this: If absolutely everything is made by God, then God must be the cause of evil. Absurd!

St. Augustine of Hippo offered a solution to this difficulty that became the standard view for classical theism and that remains the accepted position among many theists today. God did indeed make everything, and everything God made is good. Evil is nothing. This is not a fatuous optimism. The idea is that evil is a destruction, a corruption, a falling away from the good. It is an absence of the good that ought to be present. Blindness, for example, is no problem for a stone. It is not made to see in the first place. For the human being, blindness is a source of pain and suffering. Yet blindness is not a *thing* but merely the absence of a faculty that ought to be there. Murder does not produce some new thing; rather, it simply destroys an existent good. (The "new" corpse is the original body, but in an inferior condition since it is now bereft of life.)[18] On the classical view, evil is parasitic upon good, and not a thing made by God at all.[19]

This is only the first step in answering the question, since it is clear that even if God does not cause evil He *permits* it, and that still poses a terrible problem. Epicurus (341–271 b.c.) made the point forcefully in ancient times: An omnipotent God would be able to get rid of evil. A perfectly good God would *want* to get rid of evil, and yet there is evil. Therefore there can be no God of classical theism. David Hume (1711–1776 a.d.) elaborates this argument very powerfully.[20] Contemporary philosophers of religion, too, have found it telling. Some have seen it as an actual proof for the nonexistence of God, claiming that it is logically contradictory to assert both that there is evil (which seems undeniable) *and* that there is an all-good, omnipotent God. Others have defended the more moderate claim that the existence of evil is at least good reason not to believe in God.[21]

The task for the theist, then, is to show that the existence of evil can be reconciled with the existence of God. Different theists have taken different approaches. One move is to grant that, at least possibly, the evil serves some good divine purpose, and then note that our human knowledge of the universe is so limited that we really have no basis for judging whether or not the amount of evil we perceive is evidence against the existence of God.[22] This argument from ignorance is plausible, given that it is driven by the indisputable fact that, in comparison with all there is to know, human beings know almost nothing. Classical theism, though, ever optimistic about the capabilities of human reason, held that we could do a bit better. In a rough and general way, we can explain why it is that God permits evil, thus showing that the existence of evil does not prove, or even provide good evidence to believe, that there is no God.

First it is important to distinguish between two kinds of evil, which we can call **moral evil** and **natural evil**. They are very different phenomena, but they are connected in that both are seriously in need of explanation in a God-governed universe. By "moral" evil we will understand bad or wicked choices on the part of human beings (and other rational, created agents if such there be) and any pain and suffering that results from those choices. The murderer's choice to murder and the harm that choice produces will be considered moral evils. The pain and suffering that are not moral evil, but rather are simply the result of natural phenomena like earthquakes, fires, floods, and so forth will be called "natural" evils.[23]

First, why does God permit moral evil? The standard response of classical theism, suggested by St. Augustine and given its first really clear and systematic treatment by St. Anselm of Canterbury, is a version of what is today known as the **free will defense**.[24] As perfect being, God chooses, through love, to make a universe full of different kinds of very valuable things, each good because it reflects the nature of the Creator, and all differing in value in that some are a closer reflection than others. The best sort of creature will be the one that provides the closet mirror of the Creator, a metaphysical point that classical theists took to be expressed in Genesis where God is said to "make man in His own image." In creating human beings, God wanted something better than lower animals and better than robots. He wanted creatures who could actually contribute to their own creation, in a way, by making themselves better *on their own*. For this to be possible, however, the human being had to have the option to *choose* to love and obey God. Were the creature simply *made* or *caused* to love and obey God, it might be a very nice lesser sort of being, but it would not have the value and stature of a free being who chooses God on its own. St. Anselm accords to the human being the godlike ability of genuine causal agency and the independence of self-determination regarding its moral place in the universe. Of course all goods come from God, but human dignity requires that it be up to the human being to accept or reject them *on his own*. Human dignity requires libertarian freedom.

The dark side of the equation is that the possibility of choosing the good on one's own entails the possibility of rejecting the good on one's own, that is, it entails the possibility that free beings will in fact choose evil. And of course that is exactly what we have done. The theist can grant that all of the wickedness and ensuing suffering that we see in the world is a terrible price to pay for human dignity and still hold that it is not *too* high a price and that it has to be paid.

If God is omnipotent couldn't He simply prevent the evil choices? Yes, but only by negating the creature's freedom in that instance. As we have seen, even an omnipotent being cannot do the logically impossible, and, on the libertarian analysis of freedom, it is logically impossible that a choice that is freely made by the creature should be caused by God. Perhaps God does now and again step in and miraculously switch off someone's freedom. Assuming that human dignity is really as valuable as classical theism took it to be, He will not do so often.

But God is omniscient. Since He foreknows what everyone is going to do, couldn't He simply decide to create only those human beings who would freely choose the good? Can't He thwart those whom He foreknows will freely choose evil by simply failing to create them? This suggestion fails to take into account the nature of divine omniscience. As explained above, God foreknows our choices and actions because He is eternal. He is outside of time, and all of time is present to Him. If we are free in the libertarian sense, then it is true today that He knows what we will do tomorrow only because He sees us doing it. For God to foreknow what a creature will choose, He must create it and it must choose.[25]

This view entails the consequence, which the theist may well find somewhat uncomfortable, that God learns from us and is not in absolute control of everything. This is the inevitable result of ascribing libertarian freedom to human beings. It is not a real weakening of the divine omnipotence if God, because of His goodness in wanting to create man in His image, chooses to impose a sort of limitation *on Himself*. The alternative is to hold that God *is* in control of everything. In that case evil is His fault and the problem of evil becomes insoluble. One could still opt for the argument from ignorance; God causes Auschwitz and all the rest for some good reason and only heaven knows why. But that seems to be another way of saying that the problem is insoluble.

Could God leave people free to make their choices but then step in after the choice is made and miraculously prevent any harm from resulting? He could and perhaps He has. He could not, however, do it very often without diluting the creature's freedom. That is, if you know that should you choose evil you are unlikely to be able to carry through with the chosen action and its consequences, then that option becomes less viable for you. But if you choose the good only because you recognize that chances are you won't be able to pursue the bad, your choice of the good is less valuable. We do not know to what extent God may have acted to water down the harmful consequences of moral evil, but genuine freedom requires that by and large He must stand back and let the results of human choices run their course.

Moral evil, then, can be justified as the price paid so that human beings can be real causal agents, genuinely good on their own, and hence made in the image of God. But what are we to say of natural evil? The first thing to note is that much of what appears to be natural evil is actually the result, one way or another, of moral choices, at least some of which are bad. It is not the drought, per se, that causes the thousands to starve in Africa. There are droughts in North America and nobody starves. It is the drought coupled with war and the behavior of national and international governments, groups, and institutions that produces the fatal situation. Imagine, if you can, that human history had been radically different. Instead of the cruelty, ignorance, violence, selfishness, and lust for power that make up most of the fabric of the human story, imagine that people had in general behaved well, devoting their time and energy to working together to make the world a better place to live in. It is at least possible that the amount of apparently natural evil could have been greatly reduced. The cure for cancer might have been discovered millennia ago. The hurricane might do no damage since our advanced meteorology could predict it weeks in advance and whisk everyone to safety or perhaps we could simply build hurricane-proof houses. It is not unreasonable to think that without moral evil, natural phenomena would not have caused nearly so much pain and suffering.

This point can supply only part of an answer, though. Even if we grant that much apparently natural evil is traceable to or would not have existed without moral evil, we cannot explain it all this way. Human beings might have suffered much less from natural phenomena had there been no moral evil, but surely they would not have escaped entirely.[26] Even if the cure for cancer had been discovered two thousand years ago, what of those who died in pain before that? Wouldn't a good God have prevented *all* natural evil? A standard theist response is, "No. Natural pain and suffering serve an indispensable purpose in the divine plan." If the whole point of human existence were earthly pleasure and comfort then, indeed, the presence of any natural evil would be puzzling. But if, as claimed above, the point of human existence is to develop the image of God in ourselves, then a perfectly comfortable world might not do the job at all. A world with hard edges may be far superior if the goal is soul-building.[27] For us to become all we can be, it might be best for us to contend with an environment that confronts us with problems. For us to build our moral muscles, develop virtues like perseverance, patience, and courage, a world that offers some resistance may be necessary. In the final analysis, it may be a good thing for us that there is natural evil.

Moreover, the natural evil in question is an inevitable result of the ordered causal system that is our universe. We human beings, too, are the result of that system. To say that the natural evil should not exist is to say that the causal system should have been different than it is. But since it is *this* system that produced us, were it not to exist we would not exist. And surely it would have been a bad trade for us if God had abolished human suffering by opting for a universe in which we do not exist. This point may seem to conflict with divine omnipotence. Couldn't God just wish us into being without going through the rigmarole of causation—the Big Bang, evolution, and so on? Classical theism held that although God *could* produce any logically possible creature without the benefit of "secondary" causes, He prefers to maintain an ordered system in which creatures produce causal effects. For any creature or event (with the possible exception of free choice), God is the primary cause that keeps it in being with its properties, but among these properties will be the power to produce an effect. The fire really is the cause of the cotton burning, while God keeps the whole process in existence.

Some theists have held that **secondary causation** is an illusion. Everything is immediately caused by God and only by God. It is not really the fire that burns the cotton at all. This position, **occasionalism**, was rejected by classical theists on the grounds that a thing that has causal power is a much better kind of thing than a thing that merely appears to have it. Fire that can burn cotton, cook dinner, and warm the house is better than fire that cannot do anything.[28] (In fact, as will be seen below, there's good reason to believe that an object with no causal power at all is an impossibility.) If God *cannot* create things with causal powers, then He is not omnipotent. If He could, but chooses instead to create an illusory world in which things *seem* to have causal power but don't, then He's not perfectly good. Not only is He a deceiver, but He's made a poor excuse for a world. The classical theist held that a universe of secondary causes is really good,[29] but then the argument for the necessity of natural evil stands. Assuming that a fixed system of cause and effect is a great good, if we wish away natural evil, the inevitable effect of the causal system of our actual universe, then we are really wishing that the universe had been such that *we* could not exist, since we are the product of the actual causes at work.

Granted that some natural evil may be necessary and valuable for human beings, what about the rest of the sentient universe? Lower animals suffer. What about them? Some animal suffering might be justified as necessary for human beings. Here we could include not just the animals that we use, but also those involved in the struggle to survive that led to the evolution of the human species. But without question there is animal pain that is unrelated to any benefits for human beings. Animals are not moral agents, so there can be no issue of soul-building. The rabbit eaten by the fox or the fawn burned slowly to death in the forest fire surely suffer. How could a good God permit it?[30]

The standard response of the classical theist was this: rabbits and foxes and fawns and fire are all good things. To be what they are they must possess the properties they actually do possess and play their actual roles in the ordered system of causes that makes up our world.[31] It is the nature of foxes to chase and eat living prey. A "fox" that ate only herbs is not really a fox at all, but something else. What a thing *does* is part of what constitutes what it *is*. This is why occasionalism is even more problematic than the earlier discussion made clear. Something worthy of the title "thing" that literally doesn't do anything, does not interact with other things in any way at all, is inconceivable and couldn't exist. One who wishes that the suffering that the fox causes the rabbit not occur is in effect wishing the fox out of existence. But (again given the value of secondary causation) when we wish the fox out of being, we do away with the rabbit as well. Rabbits have evolved as they have in response to the behavior of predators. Remove the predators from the causal system and you remove the prey as well. If you really wish to spare the rabbit and his ilk any suffering you will have to wish them out of existence altogether. I do not think they will thank you. The same point holds with the fire and the fawn. A "fire" that does not burn is not fire. A "fawn" that feels no pain on contact with fire is not a fawn. True, God could step in and work a miracle from time to time. He could whisk this particular rabbit out of harm's way or coat that particular fawn with a layer of asbestos produced *ex nihilo* (out of nothing). But if He steps in too often, then the fabric of interconnected secondary causes begins to unravel. If the actual causal system that we have is valuable, He will as a rule not interfere with its natural operations. Though God is omnipotent and *could* prevent moral and natural evil, human dignity is so important and the actual universe with its causal system is so good, that His goodness requires that He permit the evil that these valuable things entail.

Some philosophers claim to be able to conceive a world that God could have made that would have been better than our actual world. Perhaps in this alternate world there are no rabbits, foxes, fawns, fires, or human beings as we know them, but there could be other, better, and happier creatures produced by other, better means. Were there a good, omnipotent God, He would have made that world. So there is no God. However, when one tries to put flesh on the bare skeletal outline of the "superior" world imagined by this or that philosopher, one always seems to find that it is not really a conceivable world, not really a better world, or both. (The fact that no one *has* been able to conceive a better possible world than ours does not entail that such a world is absolutely *inconceivable*, but given the apparent failure of all attempts to date, the burden of proof is on the one who claims to be able to conceive of a better world than ours.) With all its pain and suffering, ours is a very good world, perhaps even the best world God could make.[32] Evil can be justified as necessary, given the purposes for which the universe and we exist. So the existence of evil cannot be presented as evidence that there is no God.

■ CONCLUSION

I have tried to suggest, albeit briefly, that the God of classical theism can be coherently conceptualized. The idea of a being who is at once omnipotent, omniscient, and perfectly good does not entail contradictions or insurmountable paradoxes. Nor does the fact of evil count as evidence against the existence of God. If anything, the existence of *moral* evil, if it is taken to be an objective phenomenon, suggests that there is an objectivity to values which, as discussed in the section on the **argument from morality**, is hard to account for on the atheist view of reality. Perhaps the existence of evil serves as reason *for* belief in God rather than against.

In the absence of good reason *not* to believe in God, should one commit oneself to theism? We are confronted with a universe full of contingent things behaving in a beautifully ordered way. (It is popular now to talk about "chaos," but the supposed chaos seems in fact to be a more elusive and deeper order.) This universe apparently contains objective value, a moral order, which human beings can recognize. Could our world really be nothing more than "atoms and the void"? Or is it the creation of a divine designer? Suppose, with Pascal, that reason leaves the scales evenly balanced; which belief is likely to allow you to lead a happier life? We have taken the first step of showing that reason does not require us to be atheists. Next comes the harder task of assessing whether or not reason permits or even requires belief in God. But that discussion lies beyond the scope of this chapter.

■ NOTES

1. Some philosophers, past and present, argue that to use gender language of God is to anthropomorphize and hence to limit Him. Others, however, hold that such language tells us something important about the nature of a perfect being.

2. St. Anselm of Canterbury offers a sustained and careful analysis of which attributes are entailed by perfection in his *Proslogion*. (For a recent English translation, see

Anselm of Canterbury: The Major Works, Brian Davies and G. R. Evans eds. (Oxford: Oxford University Press, 1998).

3. Pascal, *Pensees*, trans. Honor Levi (Oxford: Oxford University Press, 1995), especially 153–56.

4. Thomas Aquinas, *Summa Theologiae*, Part I, Question 2, Article 3. (A nice compendium of Aquinas's thought can be found in the two-volume set, *Basic Writings of Saint Thomas Aquinas*, Anton C. Pegis, ed. [New York: Random House, 1945]). The reader will notice that Aquinas's premises depend on underlying assumptions that can be and have been questioned by philosophers, past and present. It would take us too far afield to spell out and try to defend all the assumptions at work here. Suffice it to say that a case can be made for them.

5. On Aquinas's analysis of contingency, if the universe is constituted entirely of contingent beings it must itself be contingent. The analogy with the mirrors makes this clear. If each mirror is such that it is merely reflective, but not light-producing, then the entire collection of mirrors will be merely reflective. Putting them together or thinking of them as a single object will not bestow upon them the power to produce light. They aren't that kind of thing. It will not help to suggest that though the individual objects that constitute the universe are contingent, the universe which they constitute might not be.

6. Anselm of Canterbury, *Proslogion* 2.

7. See "Logic" chap. 2, 21–22.

8. For much of the mid-twentieth century, a dominant philosophical position, logical positivism, held that talking about something that could not be observed through the senses was just meaningless. Thus even asking whether or not God existed was nonsense. By about the mid-1970s this position had been abandoned as indefensible dogma, and now a more open-minded attitude toward religion prevails among philosophers.

9. Thomas Aquinas, *Summa Theologiae*, Part I, Question 25, Article 3; Anselm of Canterbury, *Proslogion* 7.

10. For example, Rene Descartes, *The Philosophical Works of Descartes*, trans Elizabeth S. Haldane and G. R. T. Ross, vol. 2 (New York: Dover Publication, 1955) 250.

11. Boethius, *Consolation of Philosophy* V, 6. (Available in a Penguin Classics edition, translated with an introduction by Victor Watts [London: Penguin Books, 1999]).

12. *Perceive*, too, is a word that can be applied only analogously to God, since His mode of cognition is undoubtedly radically different from our own. In fact, the question of how we can apply *any* term correctly to God is a difficult and perennial one in philosophy of religion.

13. Anselm of Canterbury, *On the Compatibility of God's Foreknowledge, Predestination, and Grace with Human Freedom* I, Chaps. 1–4. (Included in *Anselm of Canterbury: The Major Works* [1998].)

14. A. N. Prior, "The Formalities of Omniscience," *Philosophy* 37, (1962) 114–29.

15. William of Ockham (fourteenth century) is perhaps the most famous and most radical divine command theorist. He holds that if God should will that you hate Him, you would be morally obligated to do so. For an overview of the subject see Janine Idziak's introduction to Andrew of Neufchateau, OFM, *Questions on an Ethics of Divine Commands*, xxv–xxxii.

16. One analysis of this relationship of terms used for creatures and for God is Aquinas's famous doctrine of analogy. See *Summa Theologiae*, Part I, Question 13.

17. Thomas Aquinas, *Summa Theologiae*, Part I, Question 6.

18. One might argue that in killing an evil person, Hitler, for example, one destroys an evil. Of course, the *justified* killing of an evil person would not fit the description of "murder," but Augustine's point is different. A morally wicked person can and does possess what is sometimes called "metaphysical" value. Everything that exists has some value, and human beings, just in virtue of being human, have great importance and worth. A bad man, Augustine insists, is still a better kind of thing than a good dog. (See his *On Free Will*, Book III, section 15, *The Works of St. Augustine*, I.3, ed. J. E. Rotelle [New York: New City Press, 1990–].) Presumably it is this position that underlies the insistence in our own society on the rights and human dignity of even the most depraved criminal.

19. Augustine of Hippo, *Confessions* VII, 12. (Available in a Penguin Classics edition translated with an introduction by R. S. Pine-Coffin (London: Penguin Books, 1961).

20. David Hume, *Dialogues Concerning Natural Religion*, Part X (Indianapolis, Ind.: Hackett, 1980).

21. For discussion of the problem of evil as a logical proof of the nonexistence of God, see J. L. Mackie, "Evil and Omnipotence" *Mind* 64 (1955) 200–12. For an influential recent statement of the view that evil provides very good evidence for there being no God, see William Rowe, "The Problem of Evil and Some Varieties of Atheism," *American Philosophical Quarterly* 16 (1979) 335–41.

22. See for example, William Alston, "The Inductive Argument from Evil and the Human Cognitive Condition," in *Philosophical Perspectives* 5, ed. James E. Tomberlin (Atascadero, Calif.: Ridgeview Publishing, 1991) 29–67.

23. A third category might be the pain and suffering resulting from good choices. For example, if I have cancer, chemotherapy might be the right choice for me to make, though it will cause me pain and suffering that the cancer might not have. I do not address this third category because we do not need to explain why God permits *good* choices. In this case what we need to explain is the cancer, a natural evil, which introduces the situation in which my good choice will result in pain and suffering.

24. Augustine emphasizes the view that free will is necessary if we are to be able to choose the good in a way that will deserve praise (*On Free Will* III, 1–3). It is Anselm who introduces the view that God wanted the rational creature to be able to make itself better on its own (*On the Fall of the Devil* 18 (included in *Anselm of Canterbury: The Major Works*, 1998).

25. An alternative to the eternalist answer to the problem of freedom and divine foreknowledge is Molinism, a view that holds that God can indeed know what free choices any possible person (including those that He will never create) will make in any possible situation. This position is subject to a number of difficulties, including a severe problem with evil, since it entails that God does indeed know what choices a creature will make without that creature being created, and hence He could create only those whom He foreknows will choose only the good.

26. The "surely" here is perhaps a bit too strong. The believer in Christian revelation who accepts the doctrine of original sin may hold that human suffering is *all* traceable to moral evil in that had the first human beings not sinned, the race would have been properly related to God in such a way that suffering could be avoided.

27. One recent defender of this view is John Hick, *Evil and the God of Love* (Glasgow: Collins, 1966).

28. Thomas Aquinas, *Summa Theologiae*, Part I, Question 105, article 5. I discuss the various problems with occasionalism in "What's Wrong with Occasionalism?" *American Catholic Philosophical Quarterly* 75 (2001) 345–369.

29. A contemporary argument for the value of a fixed causal system similar to the soul-building argument is offered by Richard Swinburne (*Providence and the Problem of Evil* [Oxford: Clarendon Press, 1998] 177). God could just pour learning into our heads. He chooses not to because it is ultimately to our benefit that we develop in knowledge, including science, on our own. But to do this we must work to study the world around us. A world in which God simply caused things willy-nilly by divine fiat, could not ground the discipline of science. Thus secondary causation is valuable in that it enables us to grow on our own as knowers.

30. The example of the fawn in the fire comes from Rowe (1979).

31. Augustine of Hippo, *City of God* XII, 4–5 (Available in a Pelican Classics edition, translated by Henry Bettenson with an introduction by David Knowles [Hammondsworth, Middlesex, England: Penguin Books, 1972]); Thomas Aquinas, *Summa Theologiae*, Part 1, Question 96, Article 1.

32. I argue that the actual world is the best world God could actualize in "Anselm on Praising a Necessarily Perfect Being," *International Journal for Philosophy of Religion* 34, (1993) 41–52.

■ QUESTIONS

1. Pascal thinks that if you believe in God you are likely to lead a happier life in the here and now than if you do not. Do you think this is true?
2. If, when we say that an object is contingent, all we mean is that it might or it might not exist, is Aquinas right, do you think, in insisting that all contingent objects must have some external cause?
3. Why might the theist who believes in evolution still hold that one needs God to explain the nature of things?
4. Is it true that an objective moral law requires a divine lawgiver? What might be some other options for the source of objective morality?
5. Did Anselm prove the existence of God in his ontological argument? State the argument. Is it a sound deductive argument?
6. Apparently there are all sorts of things the God of classical theism cannot do. Give some examples. Does this mean that God is less powerful than He might be? Would it be better to say that God can do absolutely anything?
7. Classical theism's solution to the problem of reconciling free will with divine foreknowledge depended on the idea that God is eternal. Explain. Is it really possible to imagine an eternal person?
8. Explain the free will defense as a response to the problem of moral evil. Might it not have been better if God had made people so that they would always choose the good?
9. What is occasionalism? Why does the classical theist reject it?
10. Can you conceive of a possible world that serves all the purposes the classical theist takes to be important (e.g., it allows for the existence of free human beings, it offers the opportunity for "soul-building") but that contains less suffering? Try.

■ FOR FURTHER READING

St. Anselm of Canterbury. 1998. *Proslogion.* Available in many editions including *Anselm of Canterbury: The Major Works*, Brian Davies and G. R. Evans eds. (Oxford: Oxford University Press, 1998).

——— 1998. *On the Compatibility of God's Foreknowledge, Predestination, and Grace with Human Freedom.* Available in many editions including *Anselm of Canterbury: The Major Works.*

St. Augustine of Hippo. 1961. *Confessions.* Available in many editions including Penguin Classics (London: Penguin Books).

——— 1990–. *On Free Will.* Available in many editions including *The Works of St. Augustine*, I.3, ed. J. E. Rotelle. (New York: New City Press, [series is in process of being published]).

Boethius. 1990. *The Consolation of Philosophy.* Available in many editions including Penguin Classics (London: Penguin books).

Hume, David. 1980. *Dialogues Concerning Natural Religion.* Indianapolis, Ind.: Hackett.

Pascal, Blaise. 1995. *Pensees,* trans. Honor Levi. Oxford University Press.

Rogers, Katherin A. 2000. *Perfect Being Theology.* Edinburgh: Edinburgh University Press.

St. Thomas Aquinas. 1945. *Summa Theologiae.* Available in many editions including in *The Basic Writings of Saint Thomas Aquinas* ed. by Anton C. Pegis (New York: Random House).

CHAPTER ELEVEN

Personal Identity

GARY FULLER

■ *INTRODUCTION*

You and I are persons. We persist, or survive, over time. The problem of personal identity is mainly the problem of saying what it is for a person to persist, or survive. This is a problem of **identity** because it is natural to think that one and the same person is crucially involved in persistence, or survival. The boy who (supposedly) cut down the cherry tree was one and the same person as (was identical to) the first American president. The boy George Washington did not die young: he survived and became President Washington. For a person to survive is for there to be a person at a later time with whom he or she is identical. I used to fear flying. During turbulent flights, I would fear that the plane would crash and that I would not survive. My fear can be expressed in terms of personal identity: it was the fear that the next day there would be no person who was identical to me. Some of you may have hopes about life after death. Your hopes involve the notion of personal identity: you hope that after your death there will be a person, perhaps in a pleasant, heavenlike setting, who will be identical to you.

The problem of **personal identity** is to explain what personal identity involves. An adequate account, or theory, of personal identity will tell us, among other things, what is required, or necessary, for personal identity. It will tell us what is necessary for a person to survive over time. For me to survive, must my body survive? An account of personal identity will also tell us what is enough, or sufficient, for identity. Suppose that President Washington remembered cutting down the cherry tree as well as many other experiences connected to the cherry-tree incident. A good theory should be able to tell us whether Washington's having such memories is enough to guarantee that he was identical to the boy who chopped down the tree.

In this chapter I will defend a modified version of the psychological continuity theory as the most aequate account of personal identity. Before we try to come up with an adequate account of personal identity, though, we need to make a few preliminary clarifications. We need to distinguish between identity and similarity, to say something about the important role personal identity plays in our lives, and, finally, to make a few remarks about constructing and testing theories of personal identity.

First, it is important to stress that a difference exists between personal identity and personal similarity. To say that a person X is identical to a person Y is quite different from saying that X and Y are qualitatively similar, even to a very high degree. Washington the boy was identical to Washington the president—they were one and the same person—although they were dissimilar in many respects. The boy was shorter than, and much less worldly than, the man. Conversely, two *identical* twins can be qualitatively very similar, although they are not identical in our sense. If X is identical to Y, then there is just one person: if they are not identical, then there are two. The identity that we are interested in is, then, *numerical* identity and not similarity, or even exact similarity.

Consider the remark that you might make on running into an acquaintance after a number of years and being shocked by the changes in her physical appearance and personality: "Greta is not the same person that she was." Here, of course, you do not mean, paradoxically, that Greta is not identical to Greta, or, perhaps less paradoxically, that the person whom you knew, namely Greta, has died and that the person you just met is a numerically different person. Rather, what you mean is that Greta has survived but is now very dissimilar in many respects from what she was when you knew her. The person you knew is one and the same person as the person you just ran into, but she has undergone great changes in personality.

Second, the problem of personal identity is not merely an academic problem. Personal identity plays an important role in our lives. There is, to begin with, an obvious connection between personal identity and that special concern that we have about *our* future. You have good reason to believe that a terrorist group is going to kidnap and torture an innocent person in the near future. You feel sympathy and some pity for the victim. Suddenly, you discover that the victim is going to be you! Your whole attitude changes drastically.[1] True, you may be an altruistic person, so your initial concern, sympathy, and even identification with the supposed victim may have been deep and genuine. Still, there seems to be a big difference between even the most altruistic concern for others and your own special concern for yourself.

Personal identity is connected to our special concern about our future and, hence, to our hopes and fears about an afterlife. It is also deeply connected to our moral attitudes regarding punishment, commitment, fairness, and so on. Think of our attitudes about punishing a person for a crime. Suppose that yesterday a person stole Bob's valued 1973 Buick. Should Leemon be punished today for the crime? Only if Leemon is identical to the real thief. Or, again, think of our attitudes about fairness. It may be morally permissible to make a certain person suffer now for that very person's own future benefit (for the benefit of a future person identical to him), but it is unfair and wrong to make a person suffer solely for *another* person's future benefit.[2]

Third, we need to say something about constructing and testing a theory of personal identity. A theory of personal identity can be more or less ambitious. It can try to provide only necessary conditions, or only sufficient conditions, or, ideally, conditions that are both necessary and sufficient. A theory of personal identity that attempts to provide **necessary conditions**, for example, will have the following form:

X = (is identical to) Y only if X ____ Y.

X is a person picked out at an earlier time, Y is a person picked out at a later time, and the blank space is to be filled in with an appropriate relational term, for example, *has the same body as*. A theory that attempts to provide **sufficient conditions** will have the form:

X = Y if X ____ Y.

Finally, a theory that attempts to provide both **necessary and sufficient conditions** will have the form:

X = Y if, and only if, X ____ Y.

When we talk about conditions for personal identity, we mean conditions that hold not simply in all actual cases but in all possible cases. Suppose that you hold that having the same body is a necessary condition for personal identity. Now, it may well be that there never has been a case of body switching, for example, your waking up one morning and finding that you have a completely different body. Your theory, however, makes a much stronger claim than that.

It claims that there never *could* be such a case. If I can show that there could be such a case, then I will have shown that your theory is false.

How do we think up a good theory, or even a tentative theory, of personal identity? In other words, how do we discover what to put in the blank in "X ____ Y"? Here a certain amount of creativity is needed, but a good way to start is by looking at typical cases. Among other things, in typical cases of personal identity there is bodily identity as well as brain identity, and even though many physical and psychological changes take place, they happen gradually.

In thinking up a theory, two dangers need to be avoided: obscurity and circularity. The terms in our theory must be clear and must be defined without appealing back (around in a circle) to the idea of personal identity. Later in this chapter, we shall explore the soul theory of personal identity. If such a theory is even to get off the ground, however, it must avoid our two dangers: the terms *soul* and *soul identity* must be made clear and must not just be synonyms for *person* and *personal identity*.

Of course, it is not enough for a theory of personal identity to be well formulated, clear, and noncircular: We want it to be true. How do we find out whether it is true, or at least reasonable to believe? We do so by submitting it to various tests. An especially important kind of test is that of hunting for counterexamples. If we find no counterexamples, this provides some reason for thinking that the theory is true; if we do find a counterexample, then this shows that the theory is false and needs either to be revised in such a way that it can accommodate the counterexample or, in extreme cases, be abandoned altogether.

We are now in a position to examine and think through various theories of personal identity. In the following section, we shall look at three theories: the body theory, the psychological continuity theory, and the brain theory. In the third section, we shall consider the soul theory. Finally, in the last section, we shall relate the issue of personal identity to other issues about persons.

■ BODY, PSYCHOLOGICAL CONTINUITY, AND BRAIN THEORIES

■ The Body Theory

An initially plausible theory of personal identity is the **body theory**. According to this theory, personal identity is explained in terms of the identity of the person's body as follows:

X = Y if, and only if, X's body = Y's body.

What makes Tiger Woods identical to the teenage golfer who won the 1991 U.S. Junior Amateur Championship is that the teenager's body is identical to Tiger Woods'.

Let us try to make the body theory somewhat clearer. Two points need to be made. First, the body theory does not restrict itself to human bodies. Of course, according to the body theory the identities of you, me, and Tiger Woods will be explained in terms of persisting human bodies; but E.T.'s identity will be explained in terms of his extraterrestrial body, and, if there could be robots that are persons, their identities would be explained in terms of the persistence of their inorganic bodies. Second, bodily identity can tolerate many changes, including loss or replacement of at least some parts. If I lose an arm or leg, or have a heart transplant, my body does not go out of existence; similarly, if my brain is replaced by the brain of someone else, my body also remains in existence—it has simply acquired a new brain.

Does the body theory give us a true account of personal identity? It certainly seems initially plausible, for in just about every actual case body identity and personal identity go together. Remember, however, that the theory is supposed to apply to all possible, as well as actual, cases. Can we think up any possible cases that are counterexamples to the body theory? Unfortunately, at least for the body theory, we can. One example will show that bodily identity is neither necessary nor sufficient for personal identity. Here is the example. I go to bed tonight and wake up tomorrow morning, not with my body, but with the body of Tiger Woods. I am amazed. I get up and look in the mirror: What is reflected is not my old familiar face, but Tiger's face. I weigh myself: the scale registers not my old weight, but Tiger's weight.

Surely, this example is possible. I can easily imagine such a thing occurring. And if it is possible, then the body theory fails. Bodily identity is not necessary for personal identity, because in the example I survive, although my body is replaced by that of Tiger Woods. Nor is bodily identity sufficient, because Tiger's body was formerly associated with Tiger, but now it is associated with me.

Someone might question whether the imagined example really is possible. Sometimes what initially seems possible turns out to be impossible when we try to fill in details. Can we fill in the details in a consistent way in the example? Is the body that I end up with really the body of the famous golfer? If so, how did I end up with it? For that matter, what happened to my original body and what happened to Tiger Woods himself? Luckily, there is a consistent story that we can tell to answer these questions. What has happened is that during the night my brain and Tiger Woods' brain have been switched, Tiger's brain ending up in my body, my brain in Tiger's body.[3] (We can imagine that the doctors who performed the operation used incredibly advanced surgical and postsurgical procedures.) Because it is the brain of a person that supports the person's mental life—his or her beliefs, memories, personality, and so on—it seems plausible to think that persons go where their brains go, and that I end up in Tiger's original body and he in my old body. What has happened, then, is best described as two persons switching bodies rather than brains. The original example of my waking up with Tiger Woods' body is thus quite possible, and, consequently, the body theory really does fail.

The body theory of personal identity has failed.[4] The brain-switching example used to refute the body theory, however, suggests an alternative theory—the brain theory. According to this theory, a person survives if, and only if, his or her brain survives.

The brain theory looks promising, but we need to ask why it seems promising. Surely, this is because there is (or at least it is widely assumed that there is) an especially close association between a person's mental, or psychological, life and what goes on in his or her brain. Before turning to the brain theory, then, it will be worthwhile to consider a theory that brings in a person's psychological life in a more explicit way: the psychological continuity theory.

■ *The Psychological Continuity Theory*

According to the **psychological continuity theory**, personal identity is explained in terms of psychological continuity as follows:

X = Y if, and only if, X and Y are psychologically continuous.

The idea of psychological continuity requires some elucidation. We can proceed in two stages. First, we introduce the idea of psychological *connectedness*, and then we explain psychological *continuity* between X and Y in terms of a chain of appropriate psychological connections between them.

Consider what was going on in my life yesterday. I was in a number of psychological states and had many psychological characteristics: I had various beliefs, desires, emotions, memories,[5] mental skills, and capacities. States and characteristics of these types tend to persist or evolve over time in familiar ways. Yesterday, I was listening to Mozart's Piano Concerto in D Minor; today, I remember listening to the concerto. Yesterday, I believed that no human has lived past the age of 150; today I will continue to believe it unless I am presented with strong evidence to the contrary. Yesterday, I could do arithmetic, understand and speak English, and play the piano; today, I am also able to do these things. Notice that there is a causal connection between my states and abilities of yesterday and those of today. If yesterday I had not been listening to the concerto, I would not have remembered doing so today. If I had not had the ability to play the piano yesterday, then I would not have that ability today.

The person I was yesterday and the person of today are psychologically connected. More generally, X and Y are psychologically connected if, and only if, one or more of Y's psychological states (abilities and so on) have evolved out of X's psychological states in the familiar way illustrated above. Further, we can talk about degrees of psychological connectedness. The degree of psychological connectedness will be determined by the number of psychological connections and perhaps by their type as well—experiential memory may count as more important than the retention of certain skills. I am psychologically connected to the person I was yesterday to a very high degree: I have retained most of the beliefs, memories, and skills that I had yesterday. I am also psychologically connected to the six-year-old me, but to a much lesser degree: Among other things, I remember very few of my experiences back then, and my emotional patterns have changed greatly. There might have been no psychological connectedness at all between the nine-hundred-year-old Methuselah and his six-year-old self!

We are now in a position to explain psychological continuity: X and Y are psychologically continuous if, and only if, there is a chain of psychological connections of a suitably high degree between them (included here as a chain will be the simplest chain, namely, that of one link). Here there are two new ideas. First, there is the idea of a suitably high degree of psychological connectedness—of enough connectedness. The degree of psychological connectedness of me today with the person I was yesterday is easily high enough; indeed, it is far over the threshold. That of me today with my six-year-old self is probably too low. To be sure, the idea of a suitably high degree of psychological connectedness is somewhat vague, and there will be cases in which it is unclear whether or not there is enough connectedness. Second, there is the idea of a chain of suitable psychological connections. The old Methuselah may have had no psychological connection with his younger self, but there probably was a chain of suitable psychological connections linking them: The 900-year-old was suitably linked to the 899-year-old, the 899-year-old to the 898-year-old, and so on.

The psychological continuity theory of personal identity, to repeat, is that:

X = Y if, and only if, X and Y are psychologically continuous.

We are now in a position to evaluate the theory. Is the theory a good one? What are its strengths and weaknesses?

One of its strengths is that it gives the right answer about what happens in the brain-switching—or, much better, body-switching—example. That example was the downfall of the body theory. The psychological continuity theory implies that the person who ends up in Tiger Woods' body is identical to me, because he is psychologically continuous—because he is psychologically connected to a high degree with me. This implication squares well with our intuitive judgments.

Are there weaknesses with the psychological continuity theory? Amnesia seems to present a problem. It seems to provide a counterexample to the theory's claim that psychological continuity is necessary for personal identity.

The American philosopher William James describes the case of the Reverend Ansel Bourne, a preacher living in Rhode Island, who in 1887 suddenly moved all the way to Pennsylvania where he set up a shop under the name of Brown.[6] For two months, he could not remember anything about his earlier life as a preacher. Then, again suddenly, he recovered his "identity" as Bourne the clergyman, only to become amnesiac with respect to Brown's life. This example seems to present a counterexample to the claim that psychological continuity is necessary for personal identity, for although there was a sharp break in psychological continuity, most of us would agree that Bourne did not cease to exist: We would agree that he became Brown, that Brown was numerically identical to him.

Further reflection shows that this example is not a genuine counterexample. Psychological continuity requires that Bourne just before the attack of amnesia and Brown just afterwards should be psychologically connected to a suitably high degree. It is true that the two were connected to a lesser degree than normal: Brown, for example, did not have experiential memories of Bourne—of living in Rhode Island, of preaching on such and such a day, and so on. Nevertheless, we can assume that he retained a great number of other psychological features of Bourne, for example, psychological abilities, such as the abilities to speak English, do arithmetic, read a map, and start a business; and general knowledge of various sorts, for example, knowledge about politics or geography.[7] The psychological connectedness between the two was lower than normal, but still high enough to be counted as psychological continuity.

The Bourne case, as well as many other examples of actual amnesia, then, presents little threat to the psychological continuity theory. What about cases that do not occur, but are at least possible? Can we find counterexamples among them? Philosophers have concocted cases of total amnesia in which, perhaps as a result of extreme shock treatment, what are obliterated are not only all of a person's memories in the ordinary sense, but also all psychological features that are the result of learning and experience over the years. We can assume that what remains is an individual with the mentality of something like that of an infant, although, of course, the brain would be more developed.[8]

Is total amnesia a genuine counterexample to the psychological continuity theory? There are three possible reactions to such cases. First, one could hold that the original person does not survive and that this is precisely because all, or at least most, psychological continuity is indeed broken. Second, one could hold that the original person does survive, but, again, that this is because there really is much more psychological continuity than meets the eye. Such a person might be impressed that the individual after the shock treatment does have, just as an infant has, many innate psychological capacities—capacities for consciousness, for learning language, for primitive reasoning of various sorts—and that these capacities are continuous with the innate capacities of the original person. Finally, one might hold that there is no psychological continuity, but that the original person still does survive. Total amnesia would be a counterexample to the psychological continuity theory only if this third reaction were plausible. It does not seem plausible. If there really is no psychological continuity at all, not even some minimal continuity of basic psychological capacities, would we not feel strongly that there is no survival? The other two reactions, or perhaps a hesitation between the two, seem much more plausible.

Total amnesia, then, does not undermine the psychological continuity theory. It does show, however, that our idea of personal identity is somewhat vague—total amnesia seems to be a borderline case—and, hence, that the idea of psychological continuity needed to explain it may also be somewhat vague.

Psychological continuity seems plausible as a necessary condition of personal identity. Is it also plausible as a sufficient condition? In other words, does the existence of psychological continuity guarantee personal identity? Here the theory has to confront examples of teleportation. (In what follows, remember that a theory of personal identity aims at providing conditions that hold in possible, and not merely in actual, circumstances and that therefore looking at possible examples, including examples from science fiction, is quite appropriate.)

Mr. Spock is beamed down from the spaceship *Enterprise* to the nearby planet. What happens, we can suppose, is this. Spock enters the teleportation machine, which takes a detailed blueprint of the precise states and configurations of all of his molecules and at the same time completely vaporizes his brain and body. The blueprint is then beamed by radio to a replicator machine down on the planet. The replicator makes use of the blueprint to construct out of new molecules (similar but nonidentical molecules) a body and brain just like Spock's.[9] The new Spock is of course psychologically similar to the old. Moreover, the new Spock is psychologically continuous with the old Spock: the old Spock's psychological features cause the new Spock to have similar features. (Notice that psychological continuity does not require temporal continuity. There may well be a temporal gap between the old Spock and the new Spock—a time during which no person exists—but psychological continuity can pass over such a gap, as it does here.)

Is the new Spock numerically identical to the old, or just an exactly similar, but nonidentical, replica of the old? If you were confident that the teleporter always functioned perfectly, would you be willing to be beamed down? Or, do you think that teleportation is tantamount to death? If it were clear to everyone, at least on reflection, that Spock does not survive—that identity is not preserved—then this example would be a counterexample to the psychological continuity theory as giving a sufficient condition for personal identity. Unfortunately, most people probably do not feel confident about what to say about Spock here. (The assumption common to the creators of and characters in "Star Trek" that Spock does survive may complicate our reactions here and make it difficult to come up with a confident verdict.)

Altering a number of nonessential features of the Spock example, however, does enable us to come up with a more decisive counterexample. This time it is you who is going to be "transported" from the spaceship to the planet below. As before, a complete blueprint is taken just before you are "destroyed," but this time destruction involves not the vaporization of brain and body but simply your being shot through the head ("death" will be instantaneous, so you will not feel a thing). Another difference is that this time the transportation process is somewhat slower. The blueprint is not beamed down to the planet; rather it is stored on disk, which in turn is filed away in the *Enterprise*. After a few weeks, the *Enterprise* lands on the planet, the disk is carried over to and inserted in the replicator, and the new you is created. Here, surely, our reactions are much more confident: You do not survive. This second example, then, shows that the psychological continuity theory, as it stands, fails as a sufficient condition of personal identity. Further, because it is relevantly similar to the Spock example, it provides support for a verdict of no survival there as well.

We need not, however, abandon the psychological continuity theory. We can try to modify it in such a way that it will rule out teleportation cases (and variations of such cases). Psychological continuity requires causation, or chains of causation, between earlier and later psychological states. The trouble is that it requires nothing more specific than that. There is causation between my listening to the concerto yesterday and my remembering listening to it today. There is also a causal connection between old Spock's experiences on the *Enterprise* and new Spock's "memories" of these experiences (these "memories" are of course not genuine memories, for that would require that new Spock is identical to old Spock—which we have decided he is not). Our modified psychological continuity theory needs to restrict causation in such a way as to rule out teleportation.

How should we restrict it? In normal cases, psychological continuity occurs when causation stays within the body, indeed the brain, of the person. My experience of listening to the concerto yesterday caused my remembering the experience today by way of a causal process that probably involved a memory trace, a persisting neural structure, within the brain. On the other hand, the psychological continuity in teleportation proceeds outside of the body and brain via the blueprint.

A modified psychological continuity theory is going to have to involve within-brain causation, and not merely causation within the body. Psychological continuity with causation within the body is not sufficient for personal identity. An extreme variation on the "Star Trek" process shows that. This time a device is inserted in my body, say in my arm, which performs three tasks: It takes a detailed blueprint of my brain; at the same time, it vaporizes my brain, without harming the rest of my body; and finally, after a certain time, it uses the blueprint to construct out of spare cells in my head and neck a new brain relevantly similar to the original one. The whole process occurs within my body. Surely, however, if I do not survive the original process, then I do not survive this inside-the-body process. Our modified account, then, will bring in the brain and will look like this:

> $X = Y$ if, and only if, X and Y are psychologically continuous via within-brain causation.

This looks like a pretty good theory. It gives the right answer to the examples we have discussed so far. Another good consequence of the theory involves examples of memory, or better, memory transfer. Philosophers and science-fiction writers have imagined cases in which your and my memories are somehow peeled off our respective brains and switched: Your memories are stuck on my brain in the appropriate places, and vice versa. The details of the transfer are usually obscure, but what is clear is that the process involves a causal story that goes outside of the brain, indeed outside of either brain. Our modified theory, then, will rule out saying that I end with your brain and body and vice versa. This consequence seems intuitively satisfying.

There is one last hurdle that our theory must surmount. This is the problem of splitting.[10] Suppose that person A divides into persons B and C. We can actually imagine such a case without being too unrealistic. Apparently, a person can survive quite well with only one of the hemispheres of his or her brain, and so the following seems possible: A's brain is removed from her body and divided into two, and each hemisphere is rehoused in a new (brainless) body. We start with A, then, and end up with B and C, each functioning perfectly well with just one hemisphere. To make things easier, let us suppose that the two hemispheres are very similar to each other, so that B and C each end up with all the "memories," psychological abilities, character traits, and so on, of A.

In this example, B will be psychologically continuous via brain causation with A and so will C. Indeed, B will be confident that she is A and so will C. The modified psychological continuity theory will imply that this is so: $A = B$ and that $A = C$. But that *cannot* be so! If Fred is identical to Colleen's father and also identical to that red-haired man in front of me, then Colleen's father is identical to the red-haired man. Similarly, if $A = B$ and $A = C$ then it must be that $B = C$. It is clear, however, that it is false that $B = C$: B and C are two different persons—if a bee stings B, C will not feel any pain, and if someone kills B, C will still survive. Our theory, then, implies something false and will have to be modified one more time.

The way to modify the theory is simply to insert a clause that prohibits the branching of paths of psychological continuity. Our final psychological continuity theory, then, looks like this:

> X = Y if, and only if, X and Y are psychologically continuous via within-brain causation, and there is no branching—(roughly) there is no person Z who is psychologically continuous with X but not with Y.[11]

■ The Brain Theory

Let us at long last go back to the **brain theory**. The brain theory asserts that

> X = Y if, and only if, X's brain = Y's brain.

Here, as in the body theory, what counts as a brain will include not only human brains but human-brain analogues, like E.T.'s brain and robot "brains."

The brain theory appears much simpler than the psychological continuity theory (in its final version), and so we need to know why we should not prefer it to the psychological continuity theory.

The brain theory and the psychological continuity theory are really very close to each other. Indeed, both theories require brain persistence as a necessary condition of personal identity. It would be nice if we could just accept the brain theory outright. Unfortunately, it has one drawback that the psychological continuity theory does not have: it seems to permit survival in the case of brain scrambling.

Suppose that as a result of a powerful electric field, the insides of your brain are completely scrambled—all the connections between neurons are broken, and all persistence of neural structures is disrupted. As a result, all psychological capacities are lost, including even the capacity for some kind of minimal consciousness. Suppose also that later, this time perhaps as the result of another completely coincidental electrical field, the neurons are reconnected completely differently, but still in such a way as to support psychological life.[12] Notice that this case is much more extreme than even the case of total amnesia: Here, all psychological continuity is broken.

It seems clear on reflection that you would not survive such a brain scrambling. Even if the reconnected individual turned out to have many psychological similarities to you, he or she still would not be you—even less so than in teleportation cases—for here there is no causation at all between your psychological states before the scramble and those of the reconnected individual.

Your brain, however, does survive the scrambling: It stays alive throughout the whole process. According to the brain theory, then, you do survive. The brain theory gives the wrong verdict here, and so comes off worse than the psychological continuity theory.

■ THE SOUL THEORY

We have ignored one of the most widely believed theories of personal identity—the **soul theory**. According to this theory, each person has, indeed must have, a **soul**, and personal identity is explained in terms of soul identity as follows:

X = Y if, and only if, X's soul = Y's soul.

If we are going to continue to hold the psychological continuity theory, then we need to show that the soul theory is not a serious competitor.

Persons, unlike unicorns, really do exist and persist over time. This is an assumption that we have been making, and will not question, in this chapter. It follows that if the soul theory is correct, there really are such things as souls that exist and persist over time. Rather than ask directly whether the theory is true or whether there are counterexamples to it, we shall ask the easier question of whether there are such things as souls. If it turns out that souls do not exist, or at least that there is no good reason for thinking that they do, that will of course mean that we should reject the soul theory.

To find out whether or not there are souls, we need to understand what souls are supposed to be. We need to clarify the idea of a soul, which admittedly is pretty unclear. Not surprisingly, the soul is generally associated with the soul theory of personal identity. Think of the role that the soul plays in many religions. According to some versions of Christianity, it is the soul that survives death and, after a period of disembodiment, goes to heaven where it acquires a glorified, or transformed, body. In some Eastern religions, the soul is reincarnated in a series of different human (and perhaps nonhuman) bodies. In all of these cases, survival of the soul means survival of the person.[13]

In addition, most people would agree on the following two general features of souls. First, souls must have psychological features—they must have beliefs, desires, intentions, and so on. Second, they must be nonphysical: they can exist separately from body and brain and, hence, are not identical to either. A third feature, more closely associated with philosophical than with popular conceptions, is that of simplicity. Souls are simple: They cannot be divided into parts, and so cannot be split into two souls in the way that an amoeba can divide into two amoebas.

Let us look at the last two features in more detail. Souls are supposed to be nonphysical, but what exactly does this mean? An extreme view, often associated with the French philosopher René Descartes,[14] is that this means that souls have no spatial features at all. Not only do they lack solidity, like ghosts, and size and shape, like the North Pole, but they also fail to have spatial *position*; strictly speaking, it makes no sense to ask where a particular soul is located. The trouble with this conception of the soul as something nonphysical is that we can hardly understand what is meant by it. Suppose you are told that there is a heaven populated by souls, but that this heaven and its inhabitants are completely nonspatial. Can you really understand what you are being told? Do you not have to think of this heaven as a spatially extended area and of its souls as occupying positions within the area?

A more intelligible conception of the soul as nonphysical is that souls do have spatial features—position as well as size and shape—but they are made up of stuff that physicists have not as yet discovered. The picture here is that of the soul as a kind of second brain in our heads, made out of mysterious, but still very spatial, "soul" stuff.[15]

Souls are also supposed to be simple: they cannot be divided into further parts. This means that one soul cannot divide, or be divided, into two souls like an amoeba or, say, a long garden hose. This has consequences for the splitting example introduced earlier. Remember that we started off with A and ended up with B and C, each with half of A's brain. According to the psychological continuity theory, identity cannot be preserved here. There is a branching of psychological continuity that had to be ruled out by the final version of that theory. On the soul theory, however, identity can be preserved. It can turn out that A is identical to just one of the offshoots, say to B: for A to be identical to B, rather than C, is for A's unsplittable soul to be transferred to B.

The simplicity of souls can also mean that souls and soul identity have no borderline cases. Either there is a soul here or there is not; either this soul is identical to that soul or it is not. Contrast souls with tables. Someone has decided to use your favorite antique table for firewood. What is left is a badly burned chunk of it. Is what is left a table or not? There may be no definite answer. Later, using the chunk plus a lot of new lumber, you build a "new" table that looks quite similar to the old. Is the new table identical to the old? Again, there may be no definite answer. In the case of souls, there is always a definite answer.

The picture of the soul that is emerging is that of a kind of second brain that has or supports psychological states, is made of spatial soul stuff, and is somehow unsplittable into parts. Notice that an important consequence of this picture is that the scientific view of the brain (the actual brain) as the sole supporter of psychological states and psychological continuity must be wrong. According to the soul theory, much of my mental life, indeed the essential features of my mental life, are explained by appeal to my soul; my brain, on this account, plays a secondary role.

Are there good reasons for believing that there are souls? There could be.[16] Suppose that we found that many persons seemed to remember in detail experiences of persons who existed centuries ago, and that later on historians came across completely new evidence that confirmed that there were such persons and that they had such experiences. Further, suppose that we could find no physical explanation for all these "memories." Then we would have some reason for postulating something nonphysical, like a soul, to explain them. Again, suppose that we found that psychological changes in people occurred in such a way that there were never any borderline cases of personal identity. For example, suppose that no amnesia cases were ever like Bourne's—where there was a moderate amount of psychological continuity—but all involved either just a very small psychological change, a small memory loss for example, or a radical psychological change involving all psychological states and characteristics. If that were so, then it would give us some reason for postulating something simple, again like a soul. Finally, discovering that large areas of a person's brain could be damaged with little effect on his or her mental life would certainly provide further reason in favor of the existence of the soul.

Unfortunately, at least for those who would like to believe in souls, we have no such evidence, or at least no good evidence of any of these kinds. There have of course been widely publicized accounts of alleged recollections of past lives of hypnotized subjects, as well as lesser-known reports of children's spontaneous memories of previous lives. Psychologists and other scientific investigators of such cases generally agree, however, that there are alternative and more familiar explanations of these cases. For example, many of the cases of hypnotic recollection have been successfully shown to be cases of source amnesia, in which the subjects are remembering in an ordinary way but have forgotten the source of their memories.[17]

Surely, however, there must be reasons in favor of souls, for otherwise why would anyone believe in them? Indeed, there are reasons, but they are not good reasons. Some people believe in souls because this provides them with hope for an afterlife. Unlike most of the theories we have mentioned or discussed, the soul theory does make an afterlife possible; many people would like there to be an afterlife, and so they would like the soul theory to be true. Merely wanting something to be true, however, does not provide a good reason for its being true.

Philosophers have suggested, and often been seduced by, nonempirical reasons for souls and the soul theory. These arguments rely on such things as the special features of the word *I*, imaginings of situations from the first-person point of view, and our supposedly special knowledge about ourselves and our identity. These arguments are often intriguing, but it is questionable whether any of them are sound.

Here is one example of such an argument. I can know certain facts about myself and my identity—for example, that I now exist and that I was experiencing anxiety a few moments ago (and, hence, that I am identical to the anxious person)—without knowing anything about my body, brain, or any other physical thing. This premise seems true. If I had been knocked out in a bad car accident and was just recovering consciousness, I might well wonder whether I still had a body or brain but know that I existed and that I was feeling anxious a short moment before. The conclusion of the argument is that my existence and my identity do not depend on any facts about my brain or my body (or any other physical object), and so I must be a soul.

The argument is seductive but invalid. It depends on the general claim that if one can know that p without knowing that q then the fact that p is not dependent on the fact that q. It is easy to think of a clear counterexample to this general claim. A child can know that there is water in front of her without knowing that there is H_2O in front of her (she will not know about H_2O until she studies some science), but the two facts are clearly dependent.

■ FURTHER QUESTIONS

We have been concentrating on personal identity, on what it is for a person to persist over time. There are, however, other questions about persons that are related to a greater or lesser extent to that of personal identity. Becoming aware of these questions, and of possible answers to them, should help deepen our understanding of personal identity. In this concluding section, then, we shall list and briefly discuss some of these questions.

Here is a list of questions that philosophers ask about persons:

1. What is it to be a person?
2. What is it for a person to persist over time?
3. What is it for there to be one, rather than two (or more), person at a certain place at a certain time?
4. Where are persons located?
5. Are there different concepts, or ideas, of personhood?

What follows are brief discussions of each of these questions.

1. *What is it to be a person?* You and I are persons, but can the same be said about the insane or the mentally impaired, or even about normal infants? Could computers ever be persons? What about families, business corporations, or nations? We want to know what are the features, or conditions, that are central to being a person (to personhood).

Compare persons with nonhuman animals. Many people think that dogs, cats, and even apes are not persons. What is the difference between them and us? Animals, like us, have desires, beliefs, and intentions, and so have, or are, *minds*; but something more is needed. One plausible suggestion is that persons must have, or be capable of having, **higher-order psychological states**—states *about* psychological states.[18] My cat, K.K., can want to eat her food, but she cannot want to want, or to want to stop wanting, to eat her food. I can. I want to lose weight and therefore want to stop having my present strong desire to eat the sundae in front of me. Higher-order states are connected to the ability to choose and act *morally*, to being a moral agent. To make a moral decision, I must be able to think about and evaluate the desires of others as well as my own.

2. *What is it for a person to persist over time?* This, of course, is just our main question about personal identity, and we answered it by appealing to psychological continuity.

What is important to notice here is that there is a connection between questions 1 and 2. Question 1 is about the essential conditions for personhood. Question 2 is about the persistence conditions for persons. What counts as persistence for persons, however, may depend on what one takes to be the essential features of personhood. Suppose that you reject the suggestion above that persons must have higher-order states; for you, persons are just *minds*. Then you will certainly hold that continuity of higher-order states or capacities is *not* necessary for personal identity. On the other hand, if you sympathize with the suggestion, you will probably hold that such continuity *is* necessary. Suppose that Al is in a horrible accident, as a result of which he loses all higher-order capacities: he now has the condition of an impaired individual. Then, if you think that higher-order capacities are necessary for being a person, you may claim that the *person* Al ceased to exist as a result of the accident. On the other hand, if you think that persons are just *minds*, then you will hold that Al survives.

3. *What is it for there to be one, rather than two (or more), person at a certain place at a certain time?* This usually becomes the question of how many persons inhabit a single body at a certain time. This time we do not have to turn to fiction, or science fiction, for an illustration; science gives us the example of brain bisection.

The two hemispheres of the brain divide their labor with respect to many functions. For the most part, the functions of each hemisphere are associated with the opposite side of the body. For example, the left hemisphere receives visual input from the right side of the visual field and controls the right arm. One of the most important "communicative" channels between the hemispheres is the band of fibers known as the *corpus callosum*. In brain-bisected subjects, these fibers are severed. In normal everyday circumstances, these subjects show little behavioral change; under special experimental conditions, however, they exhibit somewhat odd behavior.[19]

Here is an example of such behavior. The subject is placed in front of a screen. The words *key ring* are flashed on the screen quickly enough so that the subject's left hemisphere receives *ring* alone and the right hemisphere receives *key*. The subject is then asked to search through a group of objects that are hidden from view, and to pick out with both hands what he or she saw. The left hand will select a key, the right hand a ring![20]

It seems plausible to say that someone saw *key* and that someone saw *ring*, but that no one saw *key ring*.[21] Does this mean that we should say that there are really two persons existing in the subject's body, or would it be more reasonable to say that there is just one person there, but with a divided consciousness?

4. *Where are persons located?* This looks easy: Persons are located where their brains and bodies are located. My brain and body are here in this room, so I am in this room. Suppose, however, that we pry apart my brain from my body. We put my brainless body in the Swiss Alps and hook it up to my brain (in a vat) here in Michigan via radio transmission. If you ask me where I am, and to do so you will have to travel to Switzerland (where my ears and mouth are), I, of course, will say that I am in Switzerland. On the other hand, if you try to kill me and successfully push me off a mountain precipice, I will almost instantaneously travel back to Michigan where I will survive indefinitely in my vat.[22]

5. *Are there different concepts, or ideas, of personhood and of personal identity (or persistence)?* This question opens up fascinating territory about which we can make only a few brief comments and raise yet further questions.

There are concepts more or less similar to our concepts of a person and of personal identity. We have already suggested that there might be a distinction between *person* and *mind*. Others have argued that we can pry apart and distinguish *personal identity* from *personal survival*.[23] According to this view, there is a sense of survival that does not require identity. Consider again the example in which person A divides into B and C. If we describe this example in terms of identity, then we must say that A ceases to exist. A can be identical to neither B nor C, because identity does not tolerate branching. If, however, we describe the example in terms of *survival* (in the new sense), then A survives as both B and C. Personal survival here is simply psychological continuity (via within-brain causation, of course) minus the stricture against branching. Personal survival is important, it is also argued, because it is reasonable to extend our special concern about the future to our *survivors* (again in the new sense). According to this view, if A knows that either B or C, or both of them, is going to be tortured after the division, then A should indeed worry about being tortured rather than treat the splitting operation as tantamount to death.

Social scientists have employed the somewhat vague notions of self-concept, of social role, and indeed of "*identity*."[24] These concepts, however, are different from our concepts of personhood and of personal identity. When a psychologist, for example, tries to characterize a person's "identity," he or she will most likely mention significant beliefs of the person about what he or she is and what he or she ought to do and be. An opera singer's identity in this sense might be closely connected to his or her beliefs that he or she has great musical and vocal talent, and that music, and especially opera, is a very valuable human activity that ought to be seriously pursued. It is clearly possible, however, for the opera singer to cease to hold these beliefs, and thereby to lose or change his or her "identity," without ceasing to be a person or to exist.

Our concepts of a person and of personal identity are different from the social scientist's concepts of social role, identity, and so on. Perhaps things could be different. Perhaps they are different in some cultures. It has been suggested, for example, that the people of the Indonesian island of Bali have a concept of personhood that is much more closely connected to *social role* than is ours.[25] This suggestion is intriguing, but there is a problem. The problem is that it is not very clear what the suggestion means. Perhaps it means that the Balinese think of change in social role as the death of one person and the birth of a new one. If that is right, then, at least at first glance, the Balinese way of thinking may seem extraordinary. However, perhaps we are being, and have been, too quick. On further reflection we may find analogies in our own culture from which we might extrapolate. In our society people do cease to occupy a position, role, or office. A politician ceases to be president. A person loses his or her job. A husband gets divorced and ceases to be a married man. We do not treat these changes as actual death. In some cases, however, there is enough loss—loss of many rights and privileges, loss of status and self esteem, loss of a stable structure—that at least the persons themselves are willing to describe the changes as "a kind of death"; they certainly experience the change as a radical break with the past.

Finally, our concepts of a person and of personal identity are closely tied to our commonsensical notions of desire, belief, intention, and so on. Perhaps psychologists and other cognitive scientists will refine these folk-psychological notions into more scientific ones. This may lead to the development of a more scientific concept of personhood and of personal identity.[26]

As we saw early on, our concepts of personhood and of personal identity—and this means our ordinary concepts—play an important role in our lives. They are bound up with our attitudes and concerns about our own future, about punishment, and about fair treatment. If there really are many different concepts of personhood and of personal identity, then this raises the question of whether one of them, or some of them, are better in some sense, or for some purposes, than others.[27] It raises the question of whether, and if so on what grounds, we should revise or change our ordinary concepts of a person and of personal identity.

■ CONCLUSION

The problem of personal identity over time is the problem of giving an adequate account of what it is for a person to persist, or survive. The problem is not merely an academic problem; it is one that concerns us all. This is because of the close connection between personal identity and many of our concerns about morality as well as our hopes and fears about an afterlife. There are a number of theories of personal identity over time, including the body theory, the psychological continuity theory, the brain theory, and the familiar soul theory. In this chapter we have examined the strengths and weaknesses of these theories of personal identity and concluded that the best theory is a modified psychological continuity theory: personal identity over time requires nonbranching psychological continuity via within-brain causation. There are other philosophical questions about persons, and in a final section we discussed them briefly and distinguished them from the question of personal identity over time.[28]

■ NOTES

1. See John Perry, "The Importance of Being Identical," *The Identities of Persons*, ed. Amélie Rorty (Berkeley: University of California Press, 1976), 67.

2. See Derek Parfit, *Reasons and Persons* (Oxford: Clarendon Press, 1984), 333.

3. Sydney Shoemaker introduced this type of example to contemporary philosophers in *Self-Knowledge and Self-Identity* (Ithaca, N.Y.: Cornell University Press, 1963), 22–25.

4. For an important recent attempt to defend the body theory, however, see Eric Olson's *The Human Animal* (New York: Oxford University Press, 1997). For Olson, we are essentially living human animals, and what is necessary, as well as sufficient, for us to persist

over time is the "continuity of life-sustaining, vegetative functions." Psychological continuity, however, is "completely irrelevant . . . to our persistence" (20).

5. Historically, the psychological continuity theory is an ancestor of John Locke's
memory theory. See John Locke, *An Essay Concerning Human Understanding* (Oxford:
Clarendon Press, 1975), 328–48. In recent times, psychological continuity theories have
been articulated by a number of philosophers, including: Paul Grice, "Personal Identity,"
Personal Identity, ed. John Perry (Berkeley: California University Press, 1975); John Perry
"The Problem of Personal Identity," *Personal Identity*; David Lewis, "Survival and Identity," *The Identities of Persons*, ed. Amélie Rorty (Berkeley: University of California Press,
1976); and Sydney Shoemaker, "Personal Identity: A Materialist's Account," *Personal Identity*, eds. Sydney Shoemaker and Richard Swinburne (Oxford: Basil Blackwell, 1984).

6. See William James, *Principles of Psychology*, vol. I (London: Macmillan, 1891),
391–93. I owe this citation, as well as much of my discussion of the Bourne example,
to Kathleen Wilkes, who deals with the example in some detail in *Real People* (Oxford:
Clarendon Press, 1988), 103–106.

7. See Wilkes, *Real People*, 104–105.

8. The case of total amnesia is taken from Sydney Shoemaker, "Personal Identity,"
86–88.

9. This description of teleportation is essentially from Parfit, *Reasons and Persons*,
199. See also 199–306 and 474–77 for detailed discussion of teleportation and related
cases. Parfit should not be held responsible for any views about how the beaming-down
process is supposed to work in "Star Trek" (he does not mention the well-known science-
fiction series); indeed, "Star Trek" fans will probably claim that Spock's atoms, and not
simply his blueprint, are beamed down. I shall stick to the "mere blueprint" version,
however, because it provides a better example for philosophical purposes. Richard Hanley
has provided more knowledgeable account of various beaming-down mechanisms in his
popular *The Metaphysics of Star Trek* (New York: Basic Books, 1997), Part II, starting on
121.

10. David Wiggins was one of the first of recent philosophers to discuss splitting cases.
See David Wiggins, *Identity and Spatio-Temporal Continuity* (Oxford: Basil Blackwell,
1967), 50.

11. Some philosophers think that the prohibition on splitting here is too ad hoc. See,
for example, John Perry, *A Dialogue on Personal Identity and Immortality* (Indianapolis,
Ind.: Hackett, 1979).

12. This example is due to Michael Lockwood. See his discussion remarks in Arthur
Peacocke and Grant Gillett, eds. *Persons and Personalities* (Oxford: Basil Blackwell, 1987),
94–96.

13. See Martin Gardner, "Immortality: Why I Do Not Think It Impossible," *The
WHYS of a Philosophical Scrivener* (New York: Quill, 1983), 307–308. A biblical chapter
often cited in connection with the immortality of the soul is I Corinthians 15. Interestingly enough, although in that chapter St. Paul does describes a transformation from a
"natural" and "corrupt" body to a incorruptible "spiritual body," he does not make it clear
either what a spiritual body is supposed to be or how the transformation is supposed to
occur.

14. See René Descartes, *Meditations on First Philosophy*, esp. 2 and 6 (London: Cambridge University Press, 1931).

15. See Paul Churchland's discussion of this account of the soul in his *Matter and
Consciousness* (Cambridge, Mass.: MIT Press, 1984), 9–10.

16. The paragraph that follows is heavily indebted to Derek Parfit, *Reasons and Persons*, 227–28.

17. See Paul Edwards, ed. *Immortality* (New York: Prometheus Books, 1997), esp. his discussion of reincarnation, 5–19. For a balanced discussion of whether near-death experiences provide good evidence in favor of the existence of the soul, see Susan Blackmore, *Dying to Live* (London: HarperCollins, 1993).

18. See Harry Frankfurt, "Freedom of the Will and the Concept of a Person," *Journal of Philosophy* 68 (1971); and Daniel Dennett, "Conditions of Personhood," *Brainstorms* (Cambridge, Mass.: MIT Press, 1981), 267–85.

19. Kathleen Wilkes has an excellent discussion of brain bisection in *Real People*, 132–67.

20. This account of the key ring example is taken from Charles Marks, *Commissuratomy, Consciousness, and Unity of Mind* (Cambridge, Mass.: MIT Press, 1981), 4–6.

21. See Marks, *Commissuratomy*, 5.

22. For an amusing discussion of this question see Daniel Dennett, "Where Am I," in Dennett, *Brainstorms*, 310–23.

23. See Derek Parfit, "Personal Identity," *Philosophical Review* 80 (1971) 3–27. The summary below of Parfit's views is greatly oversimplified.

24. Eric Erikson is a well-known example of such a social scientist. See *Identity, Youth and Crisis* (New York: Norton, 1968), 15–44.

25. See Clifford Geertz, "Person, Time, and Conduct in Bali," *The Interpretation of Cultures* (New York: Basic Books, 1973), 360–411, esp. 386.

26. Some philosophers hold that scientific advances will force us to eliminate altogether from science the notions of desire, belief, and so on, and with them those of personhood and of personal identity. See, for example, Paul Churchland, *Matter and Consciousness*, 43–49.

27. Is there a concept of person and of personal identity that in some sense we *have* to have if we are to do any thinking at all? This question, associated with the philosopher Immanuel Kant, has been recently discussed in depth by Fred Doepke in *The Kinds of Things* (Peru, Ill.: Open Court, 1996).

28. Thanks to Frederick Adams, Ann Bardens, Chuck Hastings, Leemon McHenry, and Andy Naylor.

■   QUESTIONS

1. Dora is going through an identity crisis and is consulting a psychotherapist. Would it be helpful for her to read this chapter on personal identity?

2. How is the topic of personal identity related to real-life concerns?

3. What is the difference between giving a *necessary* condition and giving a *sufficient* condition of personal identity?

4. Consider the stuff theory of personal identity:

   X = Y if, and only if, X is made of the same stuff as Y. (We can define the stuff of X as the collection of physical atoms that make up X, and same stuff to mean *numerically* the same.) Is the stuff theory a good theory?

5. Suppose that you are caught in an arctic blizzard and literally frozen solid. A hundred years from now, your frozen brain-body is discovered, unthawed, and brought to life.

Does the original you survive here, or is what is brought to life a mere replica? Compare this case to the teleportation case in which Spock is beamed down to the nearby planet.

6. The psychological continuity theory (in its final version) prohibits splitting. According to this theory, if A splits into B and C, then A does not survive; on the other hand, the theory gives a verdict of survival in the case where during the splitting operation half of A's brain (say the half that would have become C) is destroyed and the only resultant person is B. According to the theory, then, whether or not A continues to exist depends on something other than A's relations to B: It depends on the fate of C. But this seems counterintuitive. Division just does not seem as bad as death. What do you think? If you were split, would that be as bad as death? If it is not, what does this mean for the psychological continuity theory?

7. The soul theory allows for the possibility of an afterlife. Do any of the other theories that we have considered allow for that possibility?

8. There have been many reports of people who have had out-of-body experiences (OBEs), in which they seem to be floating above and looking down at their bodies and the surrounding scene, and there is no reason to disbelieve these reports. These experiences are often linked to "near-death" situations, in which the person's life is seriously threatened, for example, by a heart attack, a car accident, or a mountain fall. Moreover, many of their descriptions of what they saw during the OBE, for example the color of the dress of a newly arrived visitor to the operating theater, have been surprisingly accurate (Blackmore, op. cit., Chap. 6). Do these OBEs provide good evidence in favor of the existence of the soul?

9. Suppose that there really are souls that are distinct from brains and bodies. Would this mean that the soul theory of personal identity is correct? The philosopher John Locke thought not. He thought that if you had vivid enough memories of, say, Julius Caesar's experiences—of crossing the Rubicon, of being stabbed by Brutus, and so on—then you would be one and the same person as Julius Caesar, and this would hold even if your soul was numerically different from Caesar's! (See Locke, op. cit. Book II, Chap. xxvii, Sections 12–17.) What do you think about this?

10. What is it to be a person? How is that question relevant to the question of what is it for a person to persist over time?

■ **FOR FURTHER READING**

Baker, Lynne Rudder. 2000. *Persons and Bodies*. Cambridge: Cambridge University Press.

Doepke, Frederick C. 1996. *The Kinds of Things*. Peru, Ill.: Open Court.

Fuller, Gary, Robert Stecker, and John P. Wright (eds.). 2000. Introduction (esp. 28–37), John Locke, *An Essay Concerning Human Understanding* in focus. London: Routledge.

Gardner, Martin. 1983. Essays 17, 18, and 19. *The WHYS of a Philosophical Scrivener*. New York: Quill.

Hanley, Richard. 1997. *The Metaphysics of Star Trek*. New York: Basic Books.

Kolak, Daniel, and Raymond Martin (eds.). 1991. *Self and Identity*. New York: Macmillan.

Marks, Charles. 1981. *Commissuratomy, Consciousness, and Unity of Mind*. Cambridge, Mass.: MIT Press.

Olson, Eric. 1997. *The Human Animal*. New York: Oxford University Press.

Parfit, Derek. 1971. "Personal Identity." *Philosophical Review* 80: 3–27.

Perry, John. 1978. *A Dialogue on Personal Identity and Immortality*. Indianapolis, Ind.: Hackett.

—— (ed.). 1975. *Personal Identity*. Berkeley: University of California Press.

Sachs, Oliver. 1987. *The Man Who Mistook His Wife for a Hat and Other Clinical Tales*. New York: Harper and Row.

Shoemaker, Sydney, and Richard Swinburne. 1984. *Personal Identity*. Oxford: Basil Blackwell.

Wilkes, Kathleen. 1988. *Real People*. Oxford: Oxford University Press.

■ CHAPTER TWELVE

Philosophy of Mind

JOHN HEIL

■ *INTRODUCTION*

If you are capable of reading and understanding these words, then you possess a mind. That is not to say that *only* creatures capable of reading and understanding words have minds. Nevertheless, an investigation of the character of mind is bound to begin with one's own case. Were we clear about that, we might come to appreciate what it is in general to possess a mind, and thus to gauge the breadth of the concept. People evidently have minds. What about nonhuman creatures? Does Koko, the Stanford-educated gorilla, have a mind? Koko certainly *behaves* intelligently, and it seems natural to describe Koko as having thoughts and feelings. If evidence of thoughts and feelings is evidence enough for the possession of mind, however, then Spot, the neighbor's dog, would seem to qualify. And what of the squirrel that Spot chases? Or the flea on Spot's ear?

Perhaps, by the end of this chapter we shall be in a position to evaluate these and related questions sensibly. Before pushing ahead, however, a word is due concerning the relation of the **philosophy of mind** and the discipline of psychology. After all, someone might think, if we want to discover whether squirrels or fleas have minds, we should consult those who profess competence in the science of mentality. The suggestion is off-base. Philosophy of mind, though certainly related to empirical psychology, differs both in approach and in subject matter. Psychologists engage in experimental research. This research presupposes some conception of what is under investigation. Philosophers, in contrast, focus on conceptions of mind. We might wonder whether minds are thinking and feeling *things*, for instance, or whether possessing a mind is merely a way of being organized (or "programmed").

This way of characterizing the distinction is somewhat artificial. In practice, there is no sharp division of labor. Conceptual investigations reflect empirical discoveries at the same time that they serve to direct those studies. The aim of this chapter is, among other things, to illuminate such matters and to provide a basis for more serious consideration of the mind and its place in the universe.

I shall begin by looking at some traditional conceptions of mind; turn to a discussion of issues that exercise contemporary philosophers of mind; and conclude with a sketch of my own preferred view according to which minds are firmly grounded in natural, wholly physical phenomena.

■ MIND–BODY DUALISM

It is in many ways natural to regard the mind and body as distinct kinds of *entity*. Minds and bodies are no doubt intimately related, but, in death, the body persists, at least for a time, without any sort of obvious mental accompaniment. Perhaps minds are forms of energy—analogous to heat energy. On death, bodies cease to produce heat. Perhaps they cease also to generate minds. This thought may be dispelled, however, by another: it is at least imaginable that minds exist *independently* of bodies. Many religions envision the soul departing the body and traveling elsewhere. The apparent ease with which we can imagine minds persisting apart from bodies suggests that our everyday conception of mind is consistent with **dualism**: minds and bodies are separate, though intimately related, entities.

■ *Interactionism*

A dualist view of **interactionism** is associated with René Descartes (1596–1650). Descartes was struck by three things. First, the mental and the physical seem, on the face of it, utterly different categories of entity. Physical bodies are inevitably spatial: they are located in a definite region of space relative to other physical bodies, they exclude other bodies from the region they occupy, and they possess measurable dimensions. Mental entities and states seem different. It is hard to make sense of the idea that thoughts or ideas have a precise location, and even harder to suppose that they could have some definite size or shape. True, we do locate thoughts in the head, emotions in the breast, and pains in teeth and toes. But this may be largely metaphorical. An idea may be in your head, but not in the way that a neuron is. Neurons are in particular locations. Neurons, like physical objects generally, exclude one another from the space they occupy. It makes little or no sense to speak of thoughts excluding one another in this way, or being next to or on top of one another. And, although pains are straightforwardly locatable, the sense in which they have a location seems special. If you have a pain in your right index finger and clutch that finger in your left hand, you do not then have a pain in your left palm. The phenomenon of *referred pain* suggests that pains may be *felt* to be at locations other than their sources. An extreme case of referred pain—so-called phantom pain—occurs when pain is felt to be in an amputated limb.

The second thing that Descartes noticed was that, despite apparent differences, minds and bodies continuously *interact*. Goings-on in the mind affect the body (as when your decision to eat a Whopper, a mental act, leads you to order a Whopper), and bodily occurrences are reflected in the mind (you delight in the Whopper's heft and aroma). Interaction of this sort seems obviously *causal*. Mental events cause bodily events, perhaps by affecting processes in the brain that lead to the stimulation of output—*efferent*—nerves, and bodily events induce mental counterparts via input—*afferent*—nervous stimulation.

Third, Descartes noted that we employ different patterns of explanation for mental and physical events. Whereas ordinary physical occurrences are explained *mechanically*, that is, by reference to material causes, the behavior of people, insofar as it was influenced by thought, requires explanation in terms of *reasons*. This suggested to Descartes that mental systems and physical systems are governed by very different principles: physical systems by mechanical, natural laws, mental systems by the laws of reason, or logic. This, in turn, suggests that mental and physical things belong to very different *realms*.

Descartes's idea was that mental events (your forming the intention to order a Whopper, for instance) made contact with the physical world (and so could have physical effects) in the pineal gland, a small bean-shaped structure in the middle of the brain. The pineal gland also served as a channel from the physical world to the mind. The steaming Whopper excites nerves in your nose that send messages into the brain, through the pineal gland, and thus into the mind. The result is your experience of that distinctive Whopper aroma.

The implications of such a view are momentous. If minds and bodies are distinct sorts of entity (Descartes, following tradition, called them **substances**), governed by distinct sorts of law and yet causally interact, then the physical universe is not, as we should like to think, *causally closed*. That is, the occurrence of some physical events—certain events in the brain, for instance—would be *physically* inexplicable: their causes would include nonphysical, mental occurrences. But if physical events are influenced by nonphysical happenings, then the principle of the conservation of energy does not hold. Energy would be introduced into the physical universe every time a mental cause had a physical effect. And perhaps physical energy would be lost whenever a physical cause induced a mental event.

Anyone with strong scientific leanings would find this prospect repellant. Interactionism, if it requires us to abandon such fundamental principles as the conservation of energy, perhaps requires too much. Even if it did not, however, interactionism gives rise to other, related worries identified by Descartes's contemporaries. If we regard bodies and minds as distinct substances, the former spatial, the latter nonspatial, how can we make sense of the notion that mental and physical things interact causally in the first place? Indeed, how are we to understand mental causation at all? In the material world causal interactions occur when one thing bumps into, or pushes or pulls, another thing; at the microlevel, causation involves spatially distributed fields. Our concept of causality, at least as it concerns the physical realm, incorporates a strong spatial component. If minds are nonspatial, however, it is not easy to see how they might affect or be affected by spatial objects.

■ *Parallelism*

Although such objections to interactionism are scarcely decisive, they have encouraged philosophers to look elsewhere for an understanding of the mind. Some, attracted to Descartes's dualism but not to his picture of causal interaction, have advanced a view, called **parallelism**, according to which minds and bodies operate independently, yet *in parallel*. Minds function in accord with their own principles. Bodies function in accord with principles governing physical systems. The world is organized, however, in such a way that the two systems are perfectly coordinated—just as two clocks may keep the same time, not because they are causally connected, but because their own internal workings are synchronized. (The metaphor is due to the philosopher, Gottfried Wilhelm Leibniz [1646–1716], a prominent advocate of a version of parallelism.) To an observer, of course, it will appear that the mental and the physical interact causally. Every time you stub your toe you feel a throbbing pain. But the stubbing is not the cause of the pain. The stubbing and the pain belong to isolated systems operating in harmony.

Parallelism's "solution" to the problem of causal interaction makes the relation of mental and physical things more, rather than less, mysterious. If it is difficult to grasp causal relations between mental and physical events, it is surely no easier to grasp the notion that the mental and physical realms, though entirely self-contained, are miraculously coordinated. What could account for such coordination? Leibniz's solution depended on the postulation of a benevolent, all-powerful God. Even if we grant that such a being might exist and might so arrange the world, however, it is far from clear that we have any very good reason to suspect that the world *is* so arranged. Parallelism, while fitting our evidence, is an extravagant hypothesis, one it would be unwise to endorse so long as simpler explanations are at hand. (The hypothesis that my watch keeps time because it houses tiny, punctual leprechauns is *consistent* with the facts, but there is a simpler explanation available, one framed in terms of springs, gear wheels, and familiar physical laws.) The question is whether there *are* simpler accounts of minds available.

■ *Epiphenomenalism*

Concerns over the plausibility of parallelism and interactionism have pushed some theorists to **epiphenomenalism**, the view that mental occurrences are fleeting by-products of physical happenings, but that physical occurrences themselves constitute a self-contained system. Consider conscious human beings. We have evolved as finely tuned biological mechanisms. Our bodies are monitored and controlled by a complex and highly organized nervous system. One by-product of this nervous system is, according to epiphenomenalists, a capacity for conscious thought. Mental states and processes *arise from* physical—biological states and processes. But these mental by-products themselves have no causal oomph: they have neither physical nor mental effects. In this regard they resemble smoke given off by a steam locomotive, or the shadows cast by a farmer pumping water. Puffs of smoke and shadows result from ongoing physical processes. Neither contributes to the production of those processes, however. Nor do puffs of smoke and the motions of shadows contribute to the production of further puffs of smoke and shadow movements. One puff of smoke follows another, but successive puffs do not make up a causally connected system. A shadow moves now this way, now that way, but its so moving is due exclusively to motions of the physical system casting the shadow.

As in the case of parallelism, it may *seem* to us that our conscious states have bodily effects. This, say epiphenomenalists, is an illusion arising from the fact that physical events responsible for those bodily effects are also responsible for certain mental accompaniments. When you decide to eat a Whopper, your body moves appropriately. This is not a result of your *decision*, however, but the product of a particular neurological occurrence. As in the case of a steam locomotive, one occurrence gives rise *both* to a certain conscious state (or a puff of smoke) *and* to your subsequent bodily motions (the locomotive's moving forward). Because conscious states of the one sort inevitably precede bodily motions of the other sort, you mistakenly infer the presence of a causal connection—just in the way a child might imagine that the puffs of smoke emitted by the locomotive push it along the tracks.

Interactionism and parallelism divide the world into mental and physical *substances*. Epiphenomenalism, in contrast, envisages only a single sort of substance, material substance. According to the epiphenomenalist, complex material systems give rise to *immaterial*, mental events and states. The epiphenomenalist conception of our world, then, although dualistic, is in this respect *simpler* than those advanced by substance dualists. There is a single world: the physical world. That world includes events that have, in addition to their physical effects, nonphysical, mental effects. Mental events (like your feeling a sudden pain) are effects of physical causes, but do not themselves cause anything. The world is a self-contained system of physical causes that, when the conditions are right, can have purely mental side effects.

Epiphenomenalism renders mysterious the status of mental occurrences. Thoughts, for instance, are depicted as causal by-products of complex neural events. But this requires that we countenance causal relations between events within the physical world and events in some sense *outside* the physical world. Such causal relations are as difficult to understand in their own way as are the mental-physical causal relations envisaged by Descartes. Certainly, the notion that physical occurrences might have effects that fall outside the purview of the physical sciences will be hard to swallow if you suppose that the physical universe is, in respect to its causal relations, self-contained or *closed*. These are matters that would take us far afield. Rather than pursuing them, then, let us turn to non-dualist theories of mind. Such theories hold out the promise of a solution to the sorts of difficulty associated with dualism.

■ *IDEALISM*

Dualistic conceptions of mind, although capturing certain ordinary beliefs about mental and physical occurrences, give rise to puzzles about the relation between the mental and the physical. Interactionism and epiphenomenalism tolerate odd sorts of causal relation; parallelism requires a miraculous correlation between causally isolated domains. This suggests that we might improve matters by giving up dualistic conceptions and developing a picture of mind that does not require the postulation of distinct realms. If there is but a single realm, perhaps both mental things and physical things could be understood as belonging to it.

Some philosophers, following George Berkeley (1685–1753), have argued for **idealism**: all that exists are minds and their contents. This contention may be understood either as calling for the *elimination* of physical entities or as a claim that physical things are really nothing more than combinations of mental things. Idealists might simply deny that there are any physical things at all. More likely, an idealist will argue that physical bodies and events are, at bottom, mental *constructs*. The book you hold in your hands, for instance, is indisputably a physical object. That is merely to say, however, that it *looks* and *feels* a certain way. Looks and feels, like sounds, smells, and tastes, are *sense perceptions*, and sense perceptions are mental states. We naturally suppose that the *actual book* lies behind these sense perceptions, that the *actual book* is causally responsible for them. As idealists are quick to point out, however, we never encounter any such "actual" book. We encounter only more and varied sense perceptions. If the physical book is something that we perceive, we should say that it is nothing more than a pattern of actual or possible sense perceptions. In saying that the book exists as a physical object, I say only that I am now perceiving the book or that anyone *would* perceive it under the right conditions. Physical objects, in John Stuart Mill's (1806–1873) phrase, are nothing but "permanent possibilities of sensation."

An idealism of this sort appears wrong on the face of it. Our awareness of physical objects seems obviously an awareness of bodies at a distance, objects outside us, in space, and independent of our minds. But is this so clear? We sometimes *dream* that we are perceiving familiar objects in the world, yet these experiences are wholly mental. John Locke (1632–1704), although not an idealist, argued that our awareness of objects as being at a distance from us is merely a learned correlation among sensory experiences. You seem to be visually aware of a three-dimensional sphere resting on a table across the room, for instance. But, according to Locke, what is actually before your mind is a two-dimensional visual disk shaded in a distinctive way. (Think of a drawing or photograph of a sphere reproduced on a two-dimensional surface, like the page of a book.) You have *learned* there is a correlation between such visual images and sensations of motion and touch. Before you can feel the sphere, you must move across the room (that is, you must sense your body moving in a certain way, and simultaneously experience a visual expansion of the sphere and table on which it rests). Once you acquire these correlations (presumably at an early age), the visual image alone can serve as a "sign" of a distant body. Your subjective impression is *as of* objects at a distance, but their *being* at a distance is not a part of your perceptions. This, at any rate, is Locke's conclusion.

It might be thought that none of this establishes that physical things are only patterns of sense experiences. Why not allow that physical objects *cause* experiences in us? Thus, although we are only ever aware of the effects of physical objects on us, and never the objects themselves, we can still reasonably suppose that physical objects exist outside our minds.

Idealists are after bigger game. We have, they insist, no way of knowing whether physical objects persist independently of our sense perceptions in the way just described. Claims that they do, then, are absolutely *unverifiable*. An unverifiable claim, however, is one we could never have reason to accept. There is, then, *no reason* to suppose that physical objects are anything more than "permanent possibilities of sensation." In fact, as the example of the desk illustrates, our concepts of physical objects are so closely tied to actual and possible sensory experiences that the thought of physical objects existing independently of those sensory experiences, is, at bottom, literally *unthinkable*! A world of mind-independent objects and events is, Berkeley contends, not merely beyond the reach of human knowledge, but flatly *inconceivable*.

Idealism sidesteps many of the difficulties associated with dualism. There is only one kind of substance, mind, and no commitment to puzzling causal relations between physical things and mental things. Physical things turn out just to be mental constructs. At least one significant puzzle remains, however. What accounts for the orderly pattern of ideas and perceptions that we associate with the material world? The world you perceive and negotiate differs from worlds you dream up in your imagination. It is natural to suppose that this is because there is an independent physical world that impinges itself on your senses. You perceive this book every time you enter the room because the book persists in the room even when you are not about. But if the book is merely "the permanent possibility of sensation," what accounts for the orderly character of your experiences of it? One possibility is that your mind contains resources of which you are unaware. As a result, you unconsciously produce for yourself the pattern of ideas you associate with the material world. A view of this sort flirts with **solipsism**, the notion that all that exists is oneself and one's own thoughts. Another possibility, that advocated by Berkeley, is that God (a *super* mind) sees to it that perceptions are planted in our minds in a regular and orderly way.

Although both of these possible explanations fit our evidence, neither has very much else to be said for it. Rejection of the material world carries with it rejection of an important source of explanation for the occurrence of mental states. Surely the simplest, most plausible explanation of our having the perceptions we have of books, mountains, and other people is that there *are* books, mountains, and other people, that these things are, on the whole as we perceive them to be, and that they are in some way causally responsible for our perceptions of them. This may seem to push us back in the direction of interactionism or epiphenomenalism. Perhaps not. Idealism is not the only sort of monism.

■ MATERIALISM

Perhaps, then, there is only one sort of substance, *material* substance. Minds are material—if you like, physical—entities. To distinguish **materialism** from epiphenomenalism, we should add that every event and state is a material event or state. The trick now is to account for our mental lives. Consider a simple example. A flashbulb goes off in front of you and, as a result, you experience a round greenish afterimage. The afterimage is not an item in your physical environment, but neither would it turn up were a neuroscientist to examine your visual system or brain. Nowhere in your physical constitution is there anything greenish, yet you are indisputably *aware* of a greenish something. Of course, things are happening in your visual system and in your brain. These happenings are no doubt in some sense *responsible* for your experiencing the greenish image. None of those happenings *is* the greenish image, however; indeed nothing inside you (or anywhere else in your vicinity) need be either round or greenish.

Considerations of this sort might seem to mandate dualism—though perhaps not. Perhaps materialists could accommodate the phenomena. Before looking over the possibilities, it will be useful to distinguish, as we did in discussing idealism, between *eliminative* and *reductive* materialism. An eliminative materialist holds that there are no minds, no mental states or processes. A reductive materialist, in contrast, contends that, although there are mental states and processes, these are in fact nothing more than complex physical states and processes. According to an eliminative materialist, then, you never really experience an afterimage because you never really experience anything at all. Reductive materialists are more cautious. Your experiencing an afterimage is just your undergoing a certain kind of brain process, perhaps, or your being disposed to say "I'm aware of a greenish afterimage" when prompted. We shall return to eliminativism presently. For the moment, however, let us focus on non-eliminative versions of materialism.

■ The Identity Theory

Proponents of the **identity theory**, identify mental goings-on with physical (typically neurological) goings-on. The concept of identity here is one familiar to students of logic. If you discover that Mark Twain *is* Samuel Clemens, you thereby discover that Mark Twain and Samuel Clemens are one and the same person. In the same way, you may learn that water *is* H_2O or that lightning *is* an electrical discharge. The *is* in these cases is the *is* of identity. And it is in this sense that identity theorists hold that mental events or states and physical events or states are identical: mental things *are* in fact nothing but physical things.

Does this mean that your round, greenish afterimage is really a state of your brain? That seems unlikely. The afterimage, after all, is round and greenish, but no part of your brain is round and greenish. An identity theorist can concede the point but argue that the identity in question holds between mental states (or processes) and physical states (or processes). The distinction is a subtle one. When you experience a round, greenish afterimage, the relevant mental state is your *experience*. That experience is not *itself* round or greenish, hence there is nothing to prevent *its* being identified with — that is, its turning out to *be* — a state of your brain. What of the afterimage? An identity theorist may simply deny that there is any such entity. Rather, when you experience a round, greenish afterimage something is going on in your nervous system very like what goes on in your nervous system when you visually apprehend a round, green physical object. In neither case is the roundness or greenness *in you*. In the latter case, of course, there is *something* round and green, namely, a particular physical object. The world, then, contains round, green things. It contains as well experiences of round, green physical things. Some of these experiences are **veridical**: these are induced by the presence of round, green things. Some, however, are in one way or another illusory. When that is so, you could experience something round and green even though nothing physical — hence nothing at all — in your immediate vicinity is either round or green.

This dismissal of afterimages and their ilk may seem excessively cavalier. Perhaps it is. In any case, the identity theory provides a straightforward way of understanding how causal interaction between mental and physical events is possible. If mental events are at bottom physical events, mental-physical interaction is just a species of physical-physical interaction.

Other problems remain, however. The identity required by the identity theory holds between *kinds* or *types* of mental and physical state or process. If water *is* (in the sense of *is identical with*) H_2O, every instance of water is an instance of H_2O. Similarly, if experiencing a round, greenish afterimage is a matter of being in a certain brain state, every instance of the experience of a round, greenish afterimage is an instance of being in a brain state of *that kind*. But how plausible is it to suppose that this is so? We know, for instance, that other terrestrial creatures have nervous systems importantly different from ours. Such creatures may never be in neurological states of the sort we are in when we have visual experiences. If the identity theory is right, however, it seems to follow that such creatures could not have visual experiences like ours: the having of visual experiences like ours is just a matter of being in certain sorts of neural condition; but these creatures, owing to differences in their nervous systems, are never in *those* kinds of neural condition; consequently these creatures never have visual experiences like ours! Further, it seems possible to imagine alien creatures very different from us biologically, yet similar psychologically. Perhaps the aliens possess a silicon-based nervous system. If these aliens talked about the world as we do, claimed to have experiences of afterimages and the like that they described just as we do, it would seem unreasonable on our part to deny that this was possible solely on the grounds that they differed from us biologically. Yet this, apparently, is what the identity theory requires.

■ *Behaviorism*

Other species of materialism may be more promising. Behaviorists, have argued that talk of mental states and processes is really nothing more than an oblique way of talking about behavior or dispositions to behave in certain ways depending on how you are stimulated. Suppose, for instance, you become angry. You turn red, clench your fists, and, were I to enter the room, you would shout at me. Behaviorists argue that your anger is not some state hidden *behind* your behavior; it is that behavior itself (or this, together with its associated dispositions). Your anger, then, just is your turning red, clenching your fists, and being disposed to shout should you encounter anyone. Anger, of course, might be manifested differently by different people (or by you) at different times. The concept of anger, however, covers familiar patterns of behavior and behavioral disposition. And so it is for all mental concepts. To be in pain is to wince, moan, and be disposed to seek relief. To believe that it is raining is to carry an umbrella, to be disposed to answer "Yes," to the question, "Is it raining?" and so on.

Philosophical behaviorists differ in a number of respects from behaviorist psychologists. **Psychological behaviorism** is a mish-mash of methodological precepts ("Do not appeal to unobservable mental states in explaining behavior"), and empirical theory ("The mechanisms responsible for behavior are, in the final analysis, simple stimulus-response mechanisms"). In fact psychological behaviorists often disagree about these and other matters, so that it is difficult to characterize the doctrine in any simple way. What is important for our purposes is to distinguish psychological behaviorists of whatever stripe from philosophical behaviorists. The latter are notable for defining mental states and processes in terms of behavior. In what follows, I shall mean by *behaviorism*, **philosophical behaviorism**.

Behaviorism, unlike the identity theory, is compatible with the possibility that creatures with utterly different biological makeups could be in the same mental states. Behavioral dispositions, presumably, are realized in a creature's biological structure, but, because dispositions are defined only by their causal inputs and outputs, the very same disposition might be realized in a wide range of physical structures. To see why this is so, consider a simple, nonmental disposition: *being fragile*. To say that an object is fragile, is to say (roughly) that it would break if it struck or were struck by a solid object. A vase's being fragile, then, is a matter of its possessing a certain causal propensity. Perhaps the vase possesses this propensity in virtue of its possession of a particular molecular structure. Now some other object, say an egg, might possess the same propensity, yet do so in virtue of possessing a very different molecular structure. A range of molecular structures, perhaps an open-ended range, could give rise to the same causal propensity. In describing an object as fragile, then, we ascribe to it a causal propensity. This propensity will be realized in some particular, though perhaps unknown, structure. In describing the object as fragile, we abstract from this structure, we describe it at a "higher level."

Behaviorists, in taking mental states to be propensities to respond to stimuli in familiar ways, allow that such states might be *biologically realized* in many different ways. Suppose that your perceiving a round, greenish blob, is solely a matter of your being in a state of a sort typically produced by round, greenish blobs, a state that disposes you to behave in certain ways—to say, for instance, that you are now perceiving a round, greenish blob, when prompted. There is nothing to prevent a creature with an utterly different biology, even an alien with a silicon-based nervous system, from being in the same dispositional state, that is, a state with similar causal propensities. Every *instance* of a mental state or process would then be identifiable with an *instance* of a physical state or process. But the *kind* of physical state or process might differ from case to case. What makes objects fragile is something about their physical constitution, but that something could differ from one case of fragility to another. Similarly, what gives rise in you to the sorts of behavior and behavioral dispositions we associate with anger might be very different from what gives rise to these in an octopus or a Martian.

This aspect of behaviorism may seem attractive. It enables us to see how, on the one hand, mental descriptions of intelligent creatures depend on those creatures' physical constitution, while, on the other hand, mental descriptions are not reducible to purely physical descriptions of those creatures. If this sounds strange, think of the parallel case of fragility. That this vase is fragile depends on its physical constitution. But in describing the vase as fragile, you are not thereby providing a detailed description of its physical constitution. You are rather ascribing a causal propensity to it, one it apparently shares with countless physically dissimilar objects.

The trouble with behaviorism is that it is extremely difficult to come up with plausible behaviorist accounts of particular states of mind. What are you disposed to do when you have just spotted a round, greenish blob? There is no general answer. You might be disposed to say "There's a tennis ball," but not if you do not know what a tennis ball is or you want, for some reason, to keep this information to yourself. You might say or do *anything or nothing* depending on *what else* you think and want at the time. There is, it seems, no generally specifiable causal propensity to be identified with your perceiving a round, greenish blob. And a moment's reflection will reveal that the same could be said about any other state of mind. What do you do or say if you believe that the gun is loaded? That will depend in obvious ways on what else you believe and what you happen to want at the time.

■ Functionalism

One attraction of behaviorism is that it enables us to associate mental states and processes with physical states and processes identified at a "higher level of abstraction." We imagine that mental states resemble fragility in being causal propensities that might be *realized in* and manifested by many different sorts of physical structure. A resourceful spin-off of behaviorism, **functionalism**, endorses this point but extends the notion of a causal propensity to include, in addition to inputs (stimuli) and outputs (responses), connections with other mental states and processes. Your perceiving a round, greenish blob is a matter of your being in a certain state defined by its typical causes (a nearby round, greenish blob in clear view) and by its effects, not on your behavior, but on other mental states and processes. Your perceiving a round, greenish blob, then, typically causes you to *form the belief* that there is a round, greenish blob nearby. Your subsequent behavior, if any, is determined by your *overall* psychological state at the time.

Functionalists are called functionalists because they take states of mind to be *functional* states of creatures possessing those states of mind. A functional state, like a simple disposition, is a state characterizable in terms of its causal propensities. Functional states, like dispositions, are usually taken to be realized by some physical condition or other. A given functional state need not always and everywhere have the same physical realization. Such a view differs from that of behaviorism chiefly in regarding causal relations of *other* mental states (all of which are themselves functional states) as being relevant to the character of every mental state. A creature with a mind—a human being, for instance—is a creature incorporating a *system* of functional states in virtue of which the creature responds intelligently to its surroundings.

Functional states, unlike behaviorist dispositions, then, cannot be characterized independently of the system of functional states to which they belong. An object is fragile if it will break when struck, not if it won't. Behaviorists apply this model to states of mind. In contrast, if you become aware of a round, greenish blob, there is, functionalists insist, no end to the ways you might be disposed to react. How you do react will depend on your overall state at the time. Functionalists take minds to comprise hierarchically organized systems. Particular mental states are what they are in virtue of their *role* in such an organized system. You and I are in the same mental state provided that we are each in a state that figures in a similar system of states. That state is one an alien might be in, as well, despite vast differences in biology. To return to an earlier example, your being angry is a matter of your being in a state that has certain typical causes and effects. So far this sounds like behaviorism. But functionalists suppose that many, or perhaps all, of those causes and effects are other mental states. Anger, then, is caused by, among other things, your *believing* you have been wronged in some way. Your being angry might, for instance, cause you to form the *intention* to insult me. Beliefs and intentions themselves are characterized partly by patterns of relations they might to other mental states. The result is a picture of the mind as a complex causal web or network.

Functionalism won favor with those who find analogies between minds and computing machines illuminating. If the mind is a complex functional system, then it would seem that a suitably programmed computing machine might itself count as a mind. This would be so if we could provide the device with a functional architecture similar to ours. If functionalism is correct, then our accomplishing this feat is at least in the cards. In any case, so far as functionalists are concerned, the fact that a computer is made of plastic, metal, and silicon need be no barrier at all to its possessing a mind—unless devices made of plastic, metal, and silicon could not, for some engineering reason, come to have a functional structure resembling ours. On such a view, the possession of a mind amounts to the possession of a highly abstract set of abilities. This accounts for the remarkable idea, endorsed by many "cognitive scientists," that minds can be studied by studying computer programs that simulate human cognitive processes.

Functionalism is sometimes attacked on the grounds that it is implausible to suppose that the nature of every state of mind is exhausted by its functional role. Imagine experiencing a throbbing pain in your toe. Is this simply a matter of your being in a certain functional state (one that results from my treading on your toe, produces a belief that you have a pain in your toe, and disposes you to rub the toe and think ill of me)? If that were so, it would seem a simple matter to program a computing machine to be in a very similar functional state. Yet it is at least odd to imagine that such a device might, solely because of the way we have programmed it, *feel pain*. What appears to be missing from the functionalist account is the *feeling* of pain. Thus (it might be argued) your being in pain may be *partly* a matter of your being in a certain functional state. But it is also, and essentially, a matter of your experiencing a certain feeling. And feelings, whatever they are, seem not to be functionally characterizable.

■ *Kinds of Mental State*

Mental categories encompass two broad classes, and these may have less in common than is implied by a long tradition of lumping them together under a single designation. One category of mental state, *sensations*, includes feelings of pain, twinges, tickles; feelings of uneasiness, emptiness, or nausea; and perhaps sensations obtained by way of the operation of the senses (visual sensations and sensations produced by hearing, touching, smelling, and tasting). As noted earlier, it might be best to suppose that it is the *experiencing* or *having* of sensations, not sensations themselves, that should count as mental states.

A second, very different category of mental state includes the so-called **propositional attitudes**. A propositional attitude is characterizable by reference to two factors, a particular *content* or *proposition*, and a particular *attitude* toward that proposition. Consider the proposition that it's raining. You could have many different attitudes toward this proposition: you might *believe* that it's raining, *hope* that it's raining, *doubt* that it's raining, *fear* that it's raining, *want* it to be the case that it's raining, and so on. In each case you are in a distinct state of mind identifiable by reference to a proposition (roughly, what is included in the *that*-clauses above) and an attitude you take up toward that proposition.

Philosophical tradition lumps sensations and propositional attitudes together under the rubric, *states of mind*. This is unfortunate. It might easily turn out that accounts of sensation are, of necessity, very different from accounts of the propositional attitudes. Sensations, for instance, seem to possess—essentially—distinctive introspectable qualities. Pains *hurt*, tastes are *sweet* or *salty*, sounds are *loud* or *soft*. Such qualities raise difficulties for materialist conceptions of mind generally, and for functionalism in particular. Propositional attitudes, in contrast, seem not to possess—at least not essentially—introspectable qualities. Your belief that it is raining exhibits no special "feel" (although, of course, your coming to have the belief may engender a variety of feelings: anxiety, disappointment, happiness).

It may be too much to ask of a particular theory of mind that it provide a single, unified account of sensations and propositional attitudes. And, in fact, in recent years philosophers have concentrated on elaborating theories of mind that can cope with propositional attitudes. The strategy is one of divide and conquer. For surely if you could come up with a really satisfactory explanation of one class of mental state, such an explanation need have nothing much in common with proposed explications of another class.

■ *Qualia*

Many philosophers who regard functionalism as providing a plausible account of propositional states of mind—beliefs, desires, intentions—doubt that the theory could accommodate sensational states. Thus challenged, a functionalist could retreat to the claim that some, but not necessarily all, mental states are functional states. Beliefs, for instance, might be functionally specifiable, pains not. The worry here is sometimes expressed by noting that there is *something it is like* to be in particular states of mind. What it is like to stub your toe eludes a purely functionalist characterization. You might know all there is to know about the physical makeup and functional organization of a person experiencing a painful sensation without thereby knowing what it is like to experience that sensation. To know that, you must undergo a similar experience yourself. Some philosophers contend that cases of this kind show that functionalism fails to capture a—or perhaps *the*—central feature of our mental lives: *qualities of conscious experiences*, the so-called **qualia**.

One response to worries about qualia involves extending a strategy we have encountered already. Identity theorists insist on distinguishing qualities of experiences from qualities of objects experienced. A tomato is red and round, but your visual experience of a tomato is not red and round. Might it turn out that what we regard as qualities of conscious experiences are in fact not qualities of the experiences themselves but qualities we represent objects or events as having? The distinctive qualitative "feel" of your visual experience of a tomato might be exhausted by the roundness, redness, and other such qualities you represent the tomato as having. On this view, qualities of experiences—*qualia*—are qualities we represent experienced objects as possessing, not mysterious intrinsic characteristics of the experiences themselves. If experiences possess qualities, these are just boring qualities of their neurological "realizers." These qualities (sponginess, say, or a particular grayish color) fall outside the purview of accounts of consciousness. Qualities that matter to us in our conscious lives are those we take experienced objects to possess, or so a functionalist might argue.

An advantage of such a view is that it offers a way of reconciling functionalism and the qualitative dimension of consciousness. Functionalists hold that the intrinsic qualities of systems that possess minds are irrelevant. You and a functionally similar computing machine are vastly different qualitatively. Could you possibly undergo qualitatively similar conscious experiences? If conscious qualities are just those we represent objects as having, these very same qualities could be shared by systems that differed utterly in their material composition, provided only that those systems possessed a capacity to represent those qualities.

Imagine describing a tomato to a friend, committing your description to paper, and typing it into a word-processing program on a desktop computer. In each case representational *medium* (spoken words, pencil and paper, deflections on a magnetic disk) differs, but the *content* of the representation—what is represented—remains the same. You and a functionally similar computing machine could have qualitatively identical experiences so long as the content of what you and the computing machine represented were the same.

■ *Eliminativism*

Most of us are *realists* about the mind. We suppose that beliefs, desires, intentions, hopes, and fears are genuine, causally significant states of intelligent, conscious agents. An *instrumentalist*, in contrast, imagines that talk about states of mind serves an important explanatory function, one with vast practical significance, but one that stops short of the assumption that there really are beliefs, desires, and intentions. We speak of centers of gravity, the average American, the Asian economy as though these were entities, but we recognize, in our more reflective moments, that these ways of speaking are merely a convenient shorthand way of referring to more complex phenomena. A view of this kind applied to states of mind leads naturally to more radical *eliminativist* thoughts. Eliminative materialism—**eliminativism**—begins with the reflection that talk about mental states and processes constitutes a somewhat primitive *folk theory* of human behavior, a theory we absorb at an early age. According to this folk theory—**folk psychology**—human beings are animated by beliefs, desires, and intentions. If I know what you want and what you believe, I can, in many cases, anticipate what you will do. If I grasp your intentions, I can, as often as not, infer what you believe and want. Folk psychology, eliminativists admit, is remarkably successful. Novelists and playwrights rely on its subtlety and power. Experimental psychology represents an ongoing attempt to refine and systematize its categories.

Despite this admirable track record, folk psychology, eliminativists contend, is utterly false. Consider a parallel, *folk medicine*. Folk medicine can have endless useful applications. But that is not because the theoretical vocabulary of folk medicine—talk of *humors*, for instance, or of *yin and yang*—refer to actual features of living bodies. To the extent that folk medicine works, it does so not because it correctly comprehends the underlying mechanisms of disease and infection. Its aptness lies exclusively in its instrumental capacity for prediction and control. It can be successful on this dimension without incorporating a correct account of the relevant mechanisms. Folk medicine might tell you that you can cure a rash by applying a certain herb. The treatment might work even though folk medicine's *explanation* for its working—the herb restores your yin-yang balance—is wildly off-base. The *real* explanation of the herb's efficacy is a pharmacological one utterly foreign to the categories of folk medicine.

The phenomenon of elimination on which eliminativists focus is perfectly general. As science evolves, theories replace theories. When this happens, entities postulated by the replaced theory may be eliminated in favor of entities postulated by the new theory. At one time chemists explained combustion by reference to *phlogiston*, a fluid said to be driven out of objects when they were heated. When it was noticed that heated bodies in fact *gained* weight, this was accommodated by the supposition that phlogiston had *negative* weight: the addition of phlogiston to a body resulted in that body's becoming lighter. The oxygen theory of combustion eventually replaced the phlogiston theory. As a result, talk of phlogiston was eliminated from chemistry, and chemists no longer regarded beliefs that phlogiston existed as reasonable. Chemists gave up **realism** about phlogiston.

Eliminativists envisage a similar fate for the propositional attitudes. Beliefs, desires, and intentions, like phlogiston, are *theoretical entities* postulated to explain the observable behavior of certain objects: intelligent agents. It is reasonable to suppose that such things exist only so long as it is reasonable to accept the theory in which they have a place. Advances in the neurosciences, however, suggest to eliminativists that folk theories of behavior are on the verge of being replaced by neurobiological theories that purport to explain intelligent behavior without reference to beliefs, desires, intentions, or anything comparable. There is, they insist, or soon will be, good reason to doubt that beliefs and the rest exist. We should abandon realism about states of mind.

We can, of course, continue to *use* folk psychology—and folk medicine—while at the same time doubting that the theoretical vocabularies of either refer to anything at all in the world. For folk medicine, pharmacology plays an eliminative role analogous to the role played by neurobiology in the case of folk psychology. As strange as it sounds, if eliminativists are right, there are no beliefs, desires, or intentions. There are only neurobiological states and processes.

Some philosophers have expressed concern that eliminativism is ultimately *self-defeating*. Eliminativists presumably *believe* in their theory, and present it in such a way as to encourage belief on our part. Were eliminativism true, however, no one would *believe* anything: beliefs are among the states of mind claimed by the theory to be nonexistent. Worse, perhaps, the theory, if true, is not one for which *evidence* could be offered, and certainly not one anyone could ever *reasonably accept*. The concepts of evidence and reasonable acceptance are closely associated with the concept of belief. If the latter goes, so do the former.

Considerations of this sort show that eliminativists are bound to find defending their thesis difficult without using a vocabulary they declare to be outmoded. Our current ways of talking essentially rely on propositional attitude concepts. It does not follow that the thesis is false. Consider a parallel case. It might be true of Wayne that everything he says is false. Were that true, of course, it would not be something Wayne could truly *formulate*. Indeed, if he announces, "Everything I say is false," his utterance seems paradoxical: if it is true, it is false! Eliminativists appear to be in the same boat. If their theories are correct, attempts to express them in everyday language are bound to have a paradoxical air. Perhaps this will change if advances in the neurosciences provide us with a new vocabulary. But even if this were not to happen, it would be hasty to conclude that eliminativism must be false because its formulation seems in certain respects paradoxical—just as it would be hasty to conclude that Wayne could not be a consistent liar because Wayne himself is in no position so to describe himself.

It does not follow, of course, that we ought to *accept* eliminativism. If you thought that folk psychology provided a reasonably satisfactory picture of our mental lives, you might doubt that this could be threatened by an advancing neuroscience. We understand everyday physical objects in our environment in terms of their solidity, color, and weight. These notions have no counterparts in basic physics. Objects we designate solid, for instance, in fact consist mostly of empty regions of space sparsely populated by tiny particles. We are not, however, inclined to deny that objects are solid on this account. Our "folk" depiction of objects coexists with our best physical theories. In fact, it is tempting to suppose that those theories *explain* what it is for objects to be solid, or colored, or weighty. Perhaps this is how we should regard the neuroscience envisaged by eliminativists. That science will tell us what it is for intelligent creatures to have beliefs, desires, and intentions.

■ CONSCIOUSNESS

Much of the philosophical community has been occupied with questions as to the nature of the propositional attitudes (beliefs, desires, intentions), but recently there has been a rebirth of interest in the nature of consciousness. Consciousness is a problem for anyone who aims at a materialistic account of the mind. The problem is that of seeing how consciousness *could* fit into a wholly material world. We encountered the difficulty earlier in discussing the identity theory. Since the 1950s and 1960s, when the identity theory was first promoted, much has been learned about the human brain. Ironically, the more we have learned, the more elusive consciousness has seemed. We now understand much about the brain's acquisition and processing of information that reaches it via the various senses. But nowhere in our investigations do we encounter consciousness per se.

You might get a very different impression if you read popular accounts of research in neuroscience. Researchers are fond of announcing that they have found consciousness in the brain or solved the problem of how a material process could underlie a conscious state. A closer look at the experimental literature, however, reveals a rather less encouraging picture. Researchers have discovered, for instance, that portions of the brain are active in particular ways when subjects are undergoing particular sorts of conscious experience. Connections among various parts of the brain and the sensory system are being carefully mapped and explored. The question how these neurological goings-on might be related to consciousness is as much of a mystery as ever.

In describing their work, researchers sometimes resort to weasel words. A certain area of the brain is described as the *seat* of consciousness, or the place where conscious *arises*, or the *source* of consciousness, or its neurological *basis*. This is fine so far as it goes, but it does not go far enough if we are puzzled over whether consciousness might have a material nature. If consciousness *arises from* a particular neurological process, this suggests that consciousness is something *distinct from* that process, something *produced* by it. Does consciousness, then, "float above" the brain? Is it present but invisible to outside observers?

Some philosophers have argued that this is as close as we can hope to get to consciousness. David Chalmers, for instance, argues that consciousness does indeed *arise from* neurological processes and that it is inaccessible to outside observers; only you have "access" to your own conscious states. On this view, consciousness is a by-product of neurological functioning. This by-product arises from material events, but has no material effects. The best model for this conception of consciousness is epiphenomenalism.

According to Chalmers, it is reasonable to think that consciousness "arises" in creatures once they achieve a certain level of internal complexity. What this level is, is anybody's guess. (Indeed, Chalmers allows that it is possible that *everything* is conscious to some degree: the ultimate particles have properties that, when collected together in appropriate arrangements, result in robust conscious experiences. This is **panpsychism**.) Panpsychism aside, Chalmers's idea is that the production of consciousness is governed by certain fundamental laws of nature. These laws ensure that consciousness will "arise" in systems with the right kind of material composition—just as the process of photosynthesis arises in systems possessing the right sorts of material structure. Because conscious experiences have no material effects, this is not something that need detain the physicists.

One remarkable consequence of Chalmers's view is the possibility of "zombies." Chalmers's zombies are not to be confused with the zombies of folklore and B-grade movies. Philosophers' zombies do not stagger about seeking out human blood. A zombie of the kind Chalmers imagines is identical to us in every physical respect, down to the last nerve cell in its brain. What zombies lack is consciousness. Zombies inhabit a world in which the laws of nature are precisely like ours, with one notable exception: there are no laws governing the production of conscious experiences. This is not something you would notice (remember: consciousness has no material effects) were you to visit the zombie world. In fact, the zombie world would be indistinguishable from our world to any outside observer. The zombie inhabitants would be functional replicas of human beings; they would laugh, argue about politics, write poetry, take drugs for depression, weep at weddings, complain of toothaches, and in general be indistinguishable from us by any behavioral or physiological standard. Zombies would, however, fail to be conscious: "all is dark inside."

To some, this consequence of Chalmers's view is enough to discredit it. Chalmers, however, has argued that it is simply the result of taking consciousness seriously as a phenomenon rooted in the material world. We can find a place for consciousness, but only by recognizing that it (as I have put it) "floats above" the material states and processes.

■ THE MIND'S PLACE IN NATURE

Perhaps Chalmers is right. Perhaps this is the best we can do. Perhaps we shall have to regard consciousness as a fundamental feature of our world that resists further explanation.

My own view is that this is to concede defeat. Perhaps, if we are resourceful, we can devise some alternative to Chalmers's mystifying picture. To do so, we shall need to look at some issues that lie in the background, but color our appreciation of the space of possibilities when we confront difficult issues in the philosophy of mind. In the following sections, I shall recount what I regard as a plausible conception of the mind's place in the world. The conception leans heavily on work by C. B. Martin. I shall not try to argue for Martin's view—there is insufficient space for that—but merely set it out as an option deserving consideration.

First, a warning: what follows is a compressed account of difficult material. An adequate spelling-out of this material would require far more space than is available here. Perhaps, though, I can say enough to whet the appetites of more adventurous readers.

■ Properties

The place to begin is not with a discussion of minds per se, but with an account of properties. Philosophical theories of mind are often presented as theories of mental properties. The mind–body problem is then conceived as a problem of the relation mental properties bear to material properties. But what are properties? Properties belong to objects: properties are *ways objects are*. The page you are looking at is white and rectangular. The page's being white and its being rectangular are ways the page is, properties of the page. In considering the page, you can consider it—the page—or a way the page is—its whiteness or its rectangularity. The page's whiteness and rectangularity are properties.

Objects *have* properties. An object may be made up of other objects (as the page certainly is). Properties are not *parts* of objects, objects are not *made up* of properties. The page *is* white and rectangular. The page is *made up of* molecules, which in turn are made up of atoms, which in turn are made up of electrons and quarks. Molecules and atoms are complex objects. What of electrons and quarks? Perhaps electrons and quarks are simple objects, or perhaps they, too, have parts. This is not a question a philosopher is in a position to answer.

Complex objects—those objects with which we are familiar: trees, stones, planets, human beings—are made up of simpler objects appropriately arranged. Properties exhibited by complex objects (ways those complex objects are) depend on properties of the parts and their arrangement. Properties of wholes are not something *in addition to* properties of the parts suitably organized: if you put the parts together in a particular way, you have the whole and its properties. (This is just to say that properties of wholes are not "emergent," they are not "over and above" properties of the parts in a particular arrangement.)

Imagine placing four matchsticks on a table so as to form a square. Each stick has a particular size and shape. By arranging the matchsticks in the right way, you produce a square. The squareness is not something in addition to the matchsticks so arranged. This is how it is for every complex object: its properties are nothing more than properties of its parts organized as they are.

What of properties themselves? Every property of a concrete object (concrete objects are to be distinguished from abstract entities such as numbers or sets) contributes in a distinctive way to the causal powers or *dispositionalities* of its possessors. In virtue of being round, the billiard ball rolls; in virtue of being red, it reflects light in a particular way. A property that made no difference to the dispositionalities of objects possessing it would be undetectable, so you might have trouble thinking of examples of such properties. I contend there are none. Objects behave as they do in interacting with other objects because of their properties and properties of objects with which they interact. The powers or dispositionalities of objects manifest themselves in concert with the powers or dispositionalities of objects they encounter. A single property can manifest itself differently with different *reciprocal disposition partners*. The ball, in virtue of its sphericity, would roll if placed on an inclined plane, reflect light in a particular way if illuminated (and so look spherical to you), make an impression of a particular kind if placed in damp sand: one disposition, many different manifestations with different reciprocal disposition partners.

Does a property's dispositionality exhaust its nature? No. In addition to making a distinctive contribution to the causal powers of its possessors, every property makes a distinctive contribution to its possessors' qualities: every property is *both* qualitative and dispositional. These are not "sides" or "aspects" of the property, they are the property itself differently described. A billiard ball's sphericity and its redness are qualities of the ball. But it is in virtue of being spherical that a billiard ball would behave in a particular way, and in virtue of being red that it would reflect light so as to look red to a human observer. Qualities and dispositionalities cannot be detached from one another. The quality is the power, the power is the quality: a surprising identity!

■ *Consciousness Redux*

What are the implications of such a conception of properties for our understanding of consciousness? First, human beings could be seen as made up of parts, the arrangement of which endows them with a host of complex dispositionalities and qualities. According to the functionalists, all there is to having a mind is the having of the right sorts of dispositional makeup. This apparently leaves out the qualitative side of our mental lives. Suppose, however, that every property were simultaneously dispositional and qualitative. Then sameness of dispositional makeup would bring with it qualitative sameness. You and a functionally identical twin must be qualitatively identical as well.

Functionalism obscures this point, because functionalists like to describe systems at a high level of abstraction. Are all toasters qualitatively identical? Of course not. A toaster is a device that takes untoasted slices of bread as inputs and yields toast as outputs. Described in this highly nonspecific way, many different kinds of entity could count as toasters: an ordinary electric pop-up toaster, an atomic-powered toaster, and a toaster consisting of you, a forked stick and a campfire. These systems are qualitatively diverse. But—and this is what functionalism makes it so difficult to appreciate—they are different dispositionally as well. You can say they are dispositionally on a par (hence, functionally equivalent) only so long as you rely on highly nonspecific characterizations. As it happens, devices that differ dispositionally (and so qualitatively) can count as toasters because they all satisfy the high-level, nonspecific description: takes-untoasted-slices-of-bread-as-inputs-and-yields-toast-as-outputs.

In the same way many different kinds of creature in many different kinds of state can satisfy the description "is in pain" because they are dispositionally (and so qualitatively) *similar*. Functionalists have erred in supposing that the dispositional and qualitative can come apart, and in supposing that, if very different creatures all fall under a description like "is in pain" they must share a single property. Because creatures satisfying this description differ in their material properties, functionalists have concluded that the shared property must be a "higher-level" property, something creatures possess in addition to their "lower-level" material properties. This "higher-level" property is said to be "realized in" creatures' "lower-level" makeup. This is to confuse higher-level *descriptions* with higher-level *properties*. The mistake, common in philosophy, is to imagine that corresponding to every true description is a distinct property.

Now we can appreciate both the appeal of functionalism and the point at which functionalism goes wrong. Functionalists regard the connection of causal powers (dispositionalities) and qualities as *contingent*: there is no necessity in the relation a system's qualities bear to its dispositional structure. This is what I am questioning. Every property makes a distinctive contribution to the dispositional-ities *and* qualities of its possessors. Creatures in pain possess similar (but not precisely similar) dispositionalities and are similar (but not precisely similar) qual-itatively. One consequence of a view of this kind is that Chalmers's zombies are flatly impossible. A creature dispositionally indistinguishable from a conscious agent must be qualitatively indistinguishable as well.

How could this be? When we look into the brain of someone undergoing a conscious experience, we see nothing that looks like a conscious experience. The worry is misplaced. Suppose you are having a conscious experience: you are looking at a red billiard ball on a green billiard table. This experience is a mutual manifestation of dispositions possessed by your visual system and the objects you are viewing (or, more accurately, the light radiation they structure). Now imagine a scientist observing your brain while you are undergoing this experi-ence. What should your experience look like? We have seen already that it is mistake to confuse properties of an experience of an object or event with prop-erties of the object or event. Your experience is of a red spherical object, but your experience is not red or spherical. Your experience has qualities, only not *these* qualities.

When a neuroscientist observers your experience, the neuroscientist has an experience that is the mutual manifestation of the neuroscientist's visual system and light structured by your brain. There is not the slightest reason to imagine that the neuroscientist's experience must resemble yours. This, incidentally, explains why *observing* (or experiencing) someone's experiencing red is nothing at all like *experiencing* red.

■ CONCLUSION

I have provided only the barest sketch of an account of the mind. The aim has not been to offer a knock-down defense of the view I favor, but only to stimulate you to think about the issues addressed in this chapter in new ways. By now you are well aware that there is much disagreement in philosophy. It would be a mistake to conclude from this that, in philosophy—as distinct from science—*nothing is ever settled*, or that, in philosophy—again, in contrast to science—*there is no progress*. At the cutting edge of science there are always more questions than answers. Moreover, the perception that science continually progresses is guaran-teed by the fact that we count as a scientific conclusion only what has in fact been settled. Philosophy, in contrast, suffers the opposite fate. Once an issue that excites philosophers is settled, it ceases to be counted a philosophical issue. What is clear is that our perspective on the mind has expanded manyfold since the time of Descartes. Puzzles remain, but our grasp of their parts—and of what makes them puzzles—has steadily matured.

Plato remarks that philosophy begins in wonder. Philosophers are those pos-sessing the capacity to find puzzling what others take for granted. If one day no questions about the mind remain, the philosophy of mind will have run its course. From where we now stand, however, that day is well beyond the horizon.

■ QUESTIONS

1. Descartes believed that nonhuman creatures—dogs, cats, gorillas—lack minds. When such creatures behave in ways that seem intelligent, this is due, he argued, to their being ingenious *machines*. The test for whether a creature possessed a mind was whether it could use language intelligently. What are the advantages and disadvantages of such a test? How would you distinguish creatures with minds from those who merely behave *as though* they had minds?

2. Materialism is sometimes accused of disregarding the subjective, qualitative aspect of mental states. An afterimage may seem to me greenish and blurry around the edges; a headache feels dull and throbbing. Nothing in my nervous system, however, appears to have these characteristics. Materialists argue that, in one sense, *nothing at all* has such characteristics. My *experience* of the afterimage or pain is identified with some state of my nervous system, but afterimages and pains, themselves, vanish from the picture. Explain the argument here, indicate how a materialist might answer the charge that he has ignored the qualitative aspects of mental states, and say how the maneuver is or is not plausible.

3. Could a machine think? feel pain? fall in love? How might a dualist answer this question? a functionalist? How do you think the question should be answered?

4. Many philosophers have seen the impossibility of mental-physical causation as a fundamental stumbling block to interactionism. Why is causation of this sort thought to present a problem? *Does* it? Explain.

5. Are you a zombie? Can you provide a compelling argument to the conclusion that you are not?

6. When a neuroscientist announces the discovery of the seat or ground of consciousness in the brain, should we take it as established that materialism is true? What might someone like Descartes say?

7. What are the chances that your mind will survive the death of your body? If your mind survived, would *you* survive? Explain your answer.

8. We tend to think of the material world as "causally closed." How does this belief pose problems for dualist accounts of the mind? How have dualists sought to respond to the difficulties? Are their responsses successful?

9. Eliminativists and epiphenomenalists agree that mental states play no causal role in the production of behavior. In what respects to they disagree? Which doctrine seems more correct?

10. Functionalism may be seen as a natural successor to philosophical behaviorism. Identify some alleged difficulties with behaviorism and explain how functionalism purports to overcome them. Is functionalism successful in this regard? Why or why not?

■ *FOR FURTHER READING*

Berkeley, George. A *Treatise Concerning the Principles of Human Knowledge*, originally published in 1710, available in various editions.

Chalmers, David. 1966. *The Conscious Mind: In Search of a Fundamental Theory*. New York: Oxford University Press.

Chappell, V. C. (ed.). 1962. *The Philosophy of Mind*. Englewood Cliffs, N. J.: Prentice-Hall.

Churchland, Paul. 1988. *Matter and Consciousness*, rev. ed. Cambridge, Mass.: Bradford Books/MIT Press.

Descartes, René. *Meditations on First Philosophy*, originally published in 1641, available in various editions and translations.

Fodor, J. A. 1968. *Psychological Explanation: An Introduction to the Philosophy of Psychology*. New York: Random House.

Heil, John. 1998. *Philosophy of Mind: A Contemporary Introduction*. London: Routledge.

Leibniz, G. W. V. *Discourse on Metaphysics*, written in 1686, available in various editions and translations.

Martin, C. B., and John Heil. 1999. "The Ontological Turn," *Midwest Studies in Philosophy* 23: 24–60.

Ryle, Gilbert. 1949. *The Concept of Mind*. London: Hutchinson.

Smith, Peter, and O. R. Jones. 1986. *The Philosophy of Mind: An Introduction*. Cambridge: Cambridge University Press.

Dualistic interactionism is advanced by Descartes in *Meditations on First Philosophy* (originally published in 1641 and now available in numerous translations). Leibniz's arguments for parallelism may be found in his *Discourse on Metaphysics* (written in 1686, but published posthumously, available in many translations). Berkeley advances a version of idealism in *A Treatise Concerning the Principles of Human Knowledge* (originally published in 1710, available in various editions). Epiphenomenalism is discussed in J. J. C. Smart's "Sensations and Brain Processes" (reprinted in V. C. Chappell (ed.), *The Philosophy of Mind*, Prentice-Hall, 1962). In that paper Smart defends the identity theory, as does U. T. Place in "Is Consciousness a Brain Process?" (also reprinted in the Chappel volume). Gilbert Ryle provides an elegant defense of behaviorism in *The Concept of Mind* (Hutchinson, 1949), and Jerry Fodor explicates functionalism in *Psychological Explanation: An Introduction to the Philosophy of Psychology* (Random House, 1968). Eliminative materialism is articulated by Paul Churchland in *Matter and Consciousness* (rev. edition, Bradford Books/MIT Press, 1988). The Churchland book provides an excellent general introduction to the philosophy of mind, as does *The Philosophy of Mind: An Introduction* by Peter Smith and O. R. Jones (Cambridge University Press, 1986). See also my *Philosophy of Mind: A Contemporary Introduction* (London: Routledge, 1998).

■ APPENDIX

Writing Philosophical Papers

LEEMON MCHENRY

■ *THE THESIS*

The art of philosophy is perhaps like the art of fencing, at least in one respect: you cannot learn it just from watching or reading books. Just as the novice fencer must take up the foil, épée or sabre; learn basic techniques of offense and defense; and then engage in a bout with an opponent, the student of philosophy must eventually take up the issues and problems, learn basic logical skills, and argue a thesis. In neither endeavor is there only one recipe for success. The progress is slow, but the more you practice, the more likely you are to get the swing of it.

One of the best ways to learn philosophy (though certainly not the only way— as Socrates clearly demonstrated) is to commit your ideas to writing. Here your imagined audience is your instructor, your classmates, and ultimately yourself because you are writing about what you believe to be the truth. Your task is to devise a convincing argument that shows you have done your work and know the material.

Philosophy papers are probably not very much like other papers you have written for English or history classes, even though basic writing skills such as spelling, grammar, and overall structure are just as important. What distinguishes a philosophy paper is its emphasis on critical analysis and argument of a thesis. In this respect, it is not a mere summary or paraphrase of an author's point of view. Nor is it a *collection* of quotations from several philosophers or commentators. Rather, a philosophy paper is the result of your taking up some problem, issue, or interpretation, subjecting it to careful analysis, and developing your own point of view. Thus, your *thesis* is the main *conclusion* of your paper that you support with *premises*. This gives your paper its essential logical structure such that the development of your essay is a process of articulating reasons for your main conclusion.

One point cannot be emphasized too much: *Your thesis is a proposition or statement that demands demonstration.* Therefore, the thesis should be less obvious than the reasons used to support it. An argument is a set of statements that support a conclusion, but if you begin to defend some point that is already well-established or uncontroversial, the paper is doomed from the start because there is no argument or any point that needs demonstration. A genuine thesis, on the other hand, should elicit the response from the reader: "Interesting, but let's see you prove it!"

■ *TWO TYPES OF PHILOSOPHY PAPERS*

There are two fundamental types of philosophy papers. The first is the topic or problem paper in which your aim is to take up some philosophical issue or problem (for example, "What is knowledge?" "Must morality be based on religion?" "Is capital punishment just?" or "What is an abstract object?") and attempt to argue for an answer. You develop your thesis by taking a stand on the issue and giving reasons to support what you believe. You may also want to criticize the views of those who hold the thesis that directly contradicts your view. In this way, you strengthen your thesis by refuting your opposition and, in the process, clarify for yourself the merits of the position you are defending.

The second type of philosophy paper is expository or interpretative. This type of paper requires the use of primary sources (original works) and secondary sources (commentaries on these works). In expository or interpretative papers, you concentrate on an original work or works written by some important philosopher(s) and attempt to uncover and explain the real point(s). For example, such a paper might discuss the definition of justice in Plato's *Republic*, Descartes's examination of the piece of wax in *The Meditations*, or the concept of duty in Kant and Ross. Here you defend some interpretation of these difficult-to-understand passages or works, answering such questions as "What do they mean?" and "What is the author really trying to say?" Your task is to illuminate and expose so that you make clear the key ideas, assumptions, implications, or meaning of terms. You may want to accomplish your exposition by referring your reader to other works or commentators to clarify the passages under analysis. This leads you to secondary sources that you may use either to support your interpretation or reject as inadequate to the proper understanding of the ideas, texts, and so on. Note especially that the expository paper still argues a thesis; it is your idea about how we should most properly understand and appreciate an idea or text.

In either kind of paper, you will typically have a beginning, middle and end, or:

1. a statement of your thesis or position—the view or conclusion for which you are going to argue;
2. an exposition and/or argument, with proper documentation of your sources; and
3. a conclusion—a final statement of the thesis, together with a brief summary of how you have reached it.

Because the thesis and defense are crucial parts of any philosophy paper, it is essential that you include a brief statement of your thesis at the very beginning of your paper. Doing so clarifies for your reader what you intend to accomplish in the paragraphs that follow. For the most part, the paper will be evaluated in terms of how successful you are in doing what you said you were going to do. You might clearly identify your thesis by saying: "In this paper, I will argue that. . . ." or "This essay will defend the view that. . . ." Now you can proceed to discuss the thesis and provide background information that explains its importance. Make certain that the reader is left with no doubt as to what you intend to accomplish. This sets up the main body of your paper, which contains the support for your particular thesis. To bring your paper to a close, you will need to summarize briefly what you have done and how you have done it.

■ SUGGESTIONS FOR GETTING STARTED

Getting started is often the most difficult obstacle to overcome. In many cases, a thesis will not be the first thing you think of, although it is often helpful to have some rough idea (and outline) before you plunge into the main body of the paper. You should regard your initial ideas as tentative and subject to revision as you explore the thicket of arguments for and against the view you hope to defend. Mozart once said that his musical compositions were committed to paper quickly because everything was already finished in his head before he picked up the quill. Most writers, however, rarely write papers in the fashion that Mozart wrote music. Leaving aside cases of extraordinary genius, for the most part philosophy papers grow out of successive revisions in which ideas clarify themselves as you engage in the process of writing.

The following suggestions should help you get started. First, find some topic with which you feel comfortable. If the problems of metaphysics and epistemology are too obscure and remote from your own personal concerns, then find a problem in ethics, aesthetics, or the philosophy of religion that excites your imagination or addresses some issue in your own life. In addition, do not try to cover too much territory. Narrow your topic, and do not try to defend a thesis that would require a book-length discussion. Find a topic suitable for the length requirement of the paper and pursue it in sufficient depth, showing that you have mastered some aspect of the problem or text. In many respects, your achievement will grow in proportion to what you decide to leave out.

Second, study the readings carefully, think about the material, and make notes.

Third, formulate a thesis about a problem and begin to explore what you think about the problem. In the most basic sense, your main task in writing a philosophy paper is to come up with some fairly original thesis or novel interpretation of the text. As we have noted already, this will probably be rather tentative at first.

Fourth, consider preparing an outline to help you formulate the logical structure of the paper.

Let us pretend that you are a Christian and want to defend the soul theory. You bring to this project certain assumptions that you have acquired from your background—home life, church, and personal experience. These may include a belief in an immortal soul or the resurrection of the body that survives death in an otherworldly paradise or in an otherworldly hell, depending on one's moral behavior and pious devotion in this earthly existence. You therefore begin to think about your beliefs within the context of the philosophical issue of personal identity and construct your thesis: "This essay will demonstrate the truth of the Christian view of the soul."

This is an ambitious project because you begin with the strong claim that you will demonstrate the "truth" of the Christian view of the soul, but it is a good starting place. Having read the various essays in this volume relevant to your thesis however,—"Personal Identity" (Chapter 11) and "Philosophy of Mind" (Chapter 12)—you are confronted with some serious objections to the very notion of a soul. Is there really such an entity in the first place? If so, what exactly is it?

You might be troubled by these problems but you remain confident that your original thesis can be defended against these objections if you modify it and proceed with careful analysis. Furthermore, you are advised by your instructor to read the relevant parts of Descartes's work that defend the soul theory, and now you revise your thesis to be slightly more modest: "This essay will attempt to demonstrate that there are souls distinct from our bodies that survive the death of our bodies." Notice that this thesis is narrower in scope because it does not commit you to all of the claims connected to the Christian view. For example, your thesis involves defending the independence of the soul from the body, but it does not commit you to arguing for the existence of heaven or hell.

This now gives you something on which to build an outline and begin writing the essay. At this point, your argument will involve addressing the objections to the notion of the soul and an attempt to overcome them with the help of Descartes. You will also need to show that your view holds up better than that of the opposition, for example, a purely materialistic interpretation that holds that persons do not survive the death of their bodies.

To sum up then, you have found a topic, constructed a tentative thesis, and modified the thesis in light of further reading and reflection. You can now get down to the business of writing and thinking through the problems.

This, of course, is the hard part. You must always guard against dogmatism. If, in the process of defending your thesis, you discover that your view really doesn't hold up against the opposition or that you have been assuming the truth of your position without critical examination, you must follow the argument where it leads you. Ultimately, your first and foremost obligation is to truth and honesty.

As you write and revise your paper, be aware of logical errors or fallacies that are commonly found in philosophical arguments. There are basically two types.

Formal fallacies are errors owing to the form or structure of the argument. Some of these mistakes are discussed by Takashi Yagisawa in Chapter Two. *Informal fallacies* are errors mainly owing to the content or context of the argument. For example, you are guilty of the straw man fallacy when you misrepresent the view of the opposition in the attempt to refute that view. Be careful, then, to ensure that you understand and fairly represent the view you set out to attack; otherwise, you are simply attacking your own misunderstanding. A thorough discussion of fallacies would take us well beyond the scope of this appendix. Two good sources on fallacies are listed in the logic books shown in For Further Reading.

In light of what you discover in thinking about your topic, you might have to abandon your original beliefs and begin to think afresh about your paper. If, in fact, this happens, in no way does it mean failure, for the whole point of writing the paper is to confront yourself with this very process of critical examination. What survives this process is worthy of defense; what does not survive and forces you to reconstruct your beliefs is an intellectual step forward.

Once your paper is finished, read it over to look for spelling and typographical errors, faulty grammar, logical errors, or incoherence in the flow of your argument. It is always a good idea to write your paper well in advance of the deadline so that you can lay it aside for a while and come back to it again with a fresh eye before you deliver it to your instructor. It is also helpful to have someone else look over the paper for you, but make sure that you choose someone whose judgment you can trust. After you have made corrections and incorporated suggestions, you are ready to prepare the final draft.

■ FOR FURTHER READING

Edwards, Anne Michaels. 2000. *Writing to Learn: An Introduction to Writing Philosophical Essays*. Boston: McGraw Hill.

Hurley, Partick J. 2000. *A Concise Introduction to Logic*. Belmont, Calif.: Wadsworth.

Kahane, Howard. 1995. *Logic and Contemporary Rhetoric*. Belmont, Calif.: Wadsworth.

Martinich, A. P. 1989. *Philosophical Writing*. Englewood Cliffs, N.J.: Prentice-Hall.

Strunk, William Jr., and E. B. White. 1979. *The Elements of Style*. New York: Macmillan Publishing.

GLOSSARY

Accidental property   In Aristotle's metaphysics, a **property** that may change and not affect the persistence of an individual **substance**. See also **essential property**.

Actuality   In metaphysics, what an individual **substance** *is*. See also **potentiality**.

Aesthetic experience   In aesthetics, a pleasurable experience typically resulting from contact with works of art or natural beauty.

Aesthetics   The theory of art. Philosophical investigation of the beautiful and **sublime**.

Agnosticism   In philosophy of religion, withholding belief regarding the existence or nonexistence of a god.

Analytic   A sentence is analytic just when it is true solely in virtue of its meaning. See also **synthetic**.

Analytic ontology   An approach to **ontology** that is restrictive and conservative. Philosophers concerned with this approach emphasize careful analysis of language to determine what is real. See also **speculative metaphysics**.

Analytical philosophy   A philosophical movement born in the twentieth century, based on logical rigor and devoted to clarity of thought and the determination to be objective in the pursuit of truth.

Androcentrism   In feminist ethics, the tendency to place men/masculinity at the center of analysis, and/or to portray a masculine point of view as objective and universal.

Antecedent   That part of a **conditional statement** that immediately follows the word *if*. See also **consequent**.

Anthropomorphism   The attribution of human characteristics to a nonhuman being or thing.

A posteriori   Latin term for "from what comes after." In epistemology, a claim that involves knowledge dependent on experience (see **empirical**). See also *a priori*.

A priori   Latin term for "from what is before." In epistemology, a claim that involves knowledge independent of experience. Anything known in this way cannot be refuted by experiment or observation. See also *a posteriori*.

Argument   A set of statements one of which is the conclusion and the others are the premises. The premises are intended to support the conclusion.

Argument from morality (or **objective value**)   In philosophy of religion, an argument that attempts to deduce God's existence from the alleged necessity of a divine source of objective morality or value. See also **cosmological argument, ontological argument, teleological argument**.

Atheism   The belief that there is no god. See also **theism**.

Atomism   In metaphysics, the theory that reality is composed of tiny, indivisible material particulars or atoms and the **void**.

Aural experience   In aesthetics, a sensory experience due to the sense of hearing.

Axiology   Value theory including ethics, aesthetics, and political philosophy.

Behaviorism, philosophical   In the philosophy of mind, the view that mental states and processes are identifiable with or reducible to behavior or **dispositions** to behave depending on how one is stimulated (see **identity theory, reduction**). See also **functionalism, psychological behaviorism**.

Behaviorism, psychological   In the philosophy of mind, a collection of methodological precepts and empirical theory. Because psychological behaviorists disagree about these and other matters, a precise characterization of the doctrine is not possible. See also **behaviorism, philosophical**.

Body theory   In the theory of personal identity, the view that person X = person Y if, and only if, X's body = Y's body. See also **brain theory, psychological continuity theory, soul theory**.

Brain theory   In the theory of personal identity, the view that person X = person Y if, and only if, X's brain = Y's brain. See also **body theory, psychological continuity theory, soul theory**.

Categorical imperative   In ethics, the fundamental principle of right conduct featured in Immanuel Kant's moral theory. It states that an action is right if, and only if, you can consistently will that everyone act on the general policy (that is, the maxim) of your action.

Circular definition   A definition is circular when it makes use of the expression to be defined (or any expression whose definition contains the expression to be defined).

Classical theism   In the philosophy of religion, the view promoted especially by the great medieval philosophers that there is a God who is both the God of biblical revelation and the perfect being of Greek philosophy. This God is the source of the universe and sustains it in being from moment to moment. See also **deism**.

Coherence   In epistemology, a relation between a belief (statement) and other beliefs (statements). Beliefs (statements) cohere to the degree that they mutually support each other's truth or likelihood of being true.

Coherentism   In epistemology, the view that the justification of a belief is a product of its coherence with other beliefs. See also **correspondence theory of truth**.

Common sense realism   In Aristotle's **metaphysics** the view that reality is revealed in sense experience and that our common mode of speech accurately represents what is real.

Compatibilism   The thesis in the free will debate that it is possible for there to be beings with free will in a deterministic universe, that is, free will is compatible with **determinism**. See also **incompatibilism**.

Concept   A mental construct that subsumes all of the objects or events classified together according to their common properties. Concepts are abstractions or general ideas.

Conditional statement   The type of statement the standard form of which is "If P, then Q." See also **antecedent, consequent**.

Conditional (or subsequent) necessity   In medieval philosophy, the sort of necessity that does not entail causal force or compulsion but that follows from the fact that some thing or state of affairs actually exists and/or is known to exist.

Consequent   That part of a conditional statement which immediately follows the word *then*. See also **antecedent**.

Consequentialism   In ethics, a type of moral theory according to which right action is to be understood entirely in terms of the value of the action's consequences. See also **deontology**.

Contingent being   A being that might possibly exist and might possibly not exist. Neither an impossible being nor a **necessary being**.

Contingent statement   A statement that is not a **necessary statement**.

Contradiction   A statement of the form "P and it is not the case that P." A contradiction is necessarily false. See also **tautology**.

Correspondence theory of truth   In epistemology, the view that a statement (belief) is true if it correctly describes reality. When reality corresponds to or agrees with its depiction, the depiction of reality is said to be true. See also **coherentism**.

Cosmological argument   In the philosophy of religion, an argument for the existence of God that attempts to deduce God's existence from the alleged necessity for a first cause or ultimate explanation of the universe. See also **argument from morality, ontological argument, teleological argument**.

Deductive argument   An **argument** that is purported to be **valid**. See also **inductive argument**.

Deism   In the philosophy of religion, the belief in a god that caused and designed the universe but does not sustain it in being and may not interact with it at all after the initial creation. See also **classical theism**.

Deontology   In ethics, a type of theory according to which the notion of intrinsic value is not more basic than the notion of right action, and so right action cannot be explained in terms of considerations of intrinsic value. See also **consequentialism**.

Determinism   The thesis in the free will debate that there is at any instant exactly one physically possible future.

Disposition   In the philosophy of mind, a propensity; a causal power; an intrinsic **state**, usually characterized by reference to its possible manifestations with suitable reciprocal dispositions.

Distributive justice   In political philosophy, justice in the distribution of benefits and burdens.

Divine command theory   In ethics and the philosophy of religion, the theory that it is the command of God alone that makes something right or good.

Dualism   In metaphysics and the philosophy of mind, the view that minds and bodies belong to distinct, nonoverlapping metaphysical domains. Minds are nonphysical entities, bodies are nonmental. See also **monism, pluralism**.

Dualistic idealism   In Plato's metaphysics, the view that reality comprises two types of entity—concrete **particulars** and abstract **Forms**.

Eliminativism   In the philosophy of mind, the view that, as science progresses, we shall have reason to doubt the existence of the entities, states, and processes referred to in **folk psychology**. Progress in the neurosciences will reveal that people have no beliefs, desires, or intentions. Eliminativism is distinguished from reductionism. (see **reduction**).

Empirical   Knowledge derived from sense experience—sight, sound, touch, smell, or taste. See *a posteriori*.

Empiricism   The theory that all knowledge of facts is derived from sense experience. This theory rejects the view that knowledge is innate or constructed by reasoning independent of experience. Also see **rationalism**.

Entailment   The premises of an argument entail the conclusion if, and only if, the argument is **valid**. If the premises entail the conclusion, the conclusion is said to *follow from* the premises.

Epiphenomenalism   In the philosophy of mind, the view that physical **events** can have mental effects, but mental events are causally impotent. An occurrence in the brain may produce a certain feeling, for instance, but that feeling has no effects whatever, mental or physical. What appear to be the effects of mental occurrences are in reality caused by the physical events responsible for those mental occurrences.

Epistemology   The theory of knowledge. Philosophical investigation of the nature and conditions of knowledge.

Essential property   In Aristotle's metaphysics, a **property** without which an individual **substance** could not exist. See also **accidental property**.

Eternity   In **classical theism**, the condition of being outside of time.

Ethics   The philosophical study that inquires into the nature of morality.

Euthyphro dilemma   In philosophy of religion, the question: Does God love what is good because it is good, or is something good because God loves it?

Event   A nonrepeatable, dated occurrence, typically involving a change.

Evidence   In epistemology, a natural relation between things or events such that one carries information about the other.

Externalism   In epistemology, the view that knowledge may depend on factors beyond one's grasp, awareness, or control.

Fallacy   In logic, an error in reasoning. A fallacy is always absurd or illogical, though not always obviously so; it is not to be confused with the purely factual error of reasoning on the basis of false information. See also **invalid argument**.

Feminism   A diverse social and political movement devoted to understanding, criticizing, and ending the oppression of women. See also **oppression**.

Folk psychology   The psychological theory we learn as we grow up naturally. Folk psychology explains behavior by reference to postulated beliefs, desires, and intentions (see **propositional attitude**) which are taken to be the hidden causes of that behavior.

Form   (1) In Plato's metaphysics, Form is an immaterial and independently existing entity that determines the nature of particular things in the material world. (2) In Aristotle's metaphysics, a form is the essential characteristic of an individual **substance** but does not exist independently of the substance. Also see **universal**.

Foundationalism   In epistemology, the view that for some belief to be known or justified there must be basic beliefs that do not depend on other beliefs to be known or justified.

Four-dimensionalism   In the philosophy of religion, the view of the nature of time that holds that all of time—past, present, and future—exists all at once.

Free will defense   In the philosophy of religion, the attempt to reconcile the existence of God with the fact of moral evil by arguing that moral evil is the result of free will, which is, in itself, a very good thing.

Functionalism   In the philosophy of mind, the view that states of mind are functional states of creatures possessing them. A functional state is a state characterizable in terms of its causal propensities. See also **behaviorism**.

Golden rule   In ethics, the principle that an act is right if, and only if, in performing it, the agent treats others as he or she would want others to treat him or her.

Hedonic value   In ethics, the net **intrinsic value** of an act, that is, its overall value considering both its positive intrinsic value and its negative intrinsic value.

Hedonism   In ethics, the view that only states of pleasure are intrinsically good and only states of pain are intrinsically bad. See **intrinsic value**.

Hedonistic utilitarianism   In ethics, a version of **utilitarianism** according to which an action is right if, and only if, its consequences would have at least as much **hedonic value** as would the consequences of any alternative action.

Higher-order psychological states   In the philosophy of mind and the theory of personal identity, psychological states that are *about* psychological states, for example, a belief about a belief.

Historical functionalism   In aesthetics, an item is an artwork at a time t, where t is a time no earlier than the time the item is made, if, and only if (a) either it is in one of the central art forms at t and it is made with the intention of fulfilling a function art has at t, or (b) it is an artifact that achieves excellence in fulfilling such a function whether or not it is in a central art form and whether or not it is intended to fulfill such a function.

Idealism   In metaphysics and the philosophy of mind, the theory that ultimate reality is composed of mind or spirit. There are no material (or physical) substances, states, or events. See also **materialism**.

Identity   A relation of selfsameness holding between any item and itself. If A is identical with B (A = B), then A and B are one and the same.

Identity theory In the philosophy of mind, the view that mental phenomena are identical with physical phenomena (see **identity**). *Type-identity* theories hold that mental properties are identical with certain physical properties (perhaps complex neural properties) of conscious agents. *Token-identity* theories hold that every mental particular is identical with some physical particular.

Incompatibilism The thesis in the free will debate that it is not possible for there to be beings with free will in a deterministic universe, that is, free will is incompatible with **determinism**. See also **compatibilism**.

Indeterminism The thesis in the free will debate that **determinism** is false.

Inductive argument An **argument** that is purported to be **strong** rather than **valid**. See also **deductive argument**.

Inference The process of reasoning expressed by an **argument**.

Innate Knowledge that is inborn. This contrasts with the idea that knowledge is acquired with experience.

Institutional theory In aesthetics, the view that an object is a work of art if, and only if, it acquires a special status in a social institution known as the art world.

Instrumentalism In philosophy of science, the view that scientific theories neither provide nor purport to provide true or false descriptions of the world. Instrumentalists are distinguished from realists, who take scientific claims to provide descriptions, true or false, of reality. See also **realism**.

Intentional-historical definition In aesthetics, an artwork is a thing that has been seriously intended for regard in any way preexisting artworks are or were correctly regarded.

Interactionism In the philosophy of mind, the view that, despite fundamental differences, minds and bodies causally interact. Mental events produce changes in bodies, and physical occurrences have mental effects. See also **dualism**.

Invalid argument An argument that is not **valid**. See also **fallacy**.

Libertarianism The thesis in the free will debate that combines **incompatibilism** and the thesis that at least some human beings have free will.

Logic Systematic investigation of the general principles of **deductive** or **inductive argument**.

Logical positivism Philosophical movement of the Vienna Circle in the twentieth century. A variety of empiricism that stresses the **verifiability criterion of meaning**.

Matter In Aristotle's metaphysics, the indeterminate stuff that receives determination by being imbued with a **form**. In modern thought, matter is the base of physical reality subject to quantitative analysis and is usually contrasted with mind. Also see **materialism, substance**.

Materialism   The theory that reality is fundamentally composed of **matter**. In the philosophy of mind, the view that every **substance, state,** or **event** is a material substance, state, or event, where "material" is equivalent to "physical." Physical items are those describable and explainable in the natural sciences. See also **idealism**.

Metaphysics   Systematic investigation into the most general principles of reality.

Misogyny   The hatred of women and female characteristics.

Modified platonism   In metaphysics, a version of Plato's theory of **Forms** that recognizes the reality of both **universals** and **particulars**.

Monism   In metaphysics, the theory that there is only one **substance**, or that all of the constituents of the universe are of one kind, usually, either mental or spiritual (see **idealism**) or material (see **materialism**). See also **dualism, pluralism**.

Moral evil   In philosophy of religion, morally wrong choices (sin) and the pain and suffering that they cause. See also **natural evil**.

Moral monism   The view that there is some single basic underlying feature of actions in virtue of which they are right or wrong. (One can also be a monist about value.) See also **moral pluralism**.

Moral philosophy   See **ethics**.

Moral pluralism   The view that there is a plurality of basic underlying features of action in virtue of which they are right or wrong. (One can also be a pluralist about value.) See also **moral monism**.

Natural evil   In philosophy of religion, the pain and suffering caused, not by morally wrong choices, but by natural phenomena. See also **moral evil**.

Naturalism   The belief that all the phenomena of the universe can be accounted for without reference to the supernatural.

Necessary being   In philosophy of religion, a being of which the nonexistence is impossible. Neither an impossible being nor a contingent being. See also **contingent being**.

Necessary condition   P is a necessary condition for Q if, and only if, if it is not the case that P, then it is not the case that Q. See also **sufficient condition**.

Necessary and sufficient condition   P is a necessary and sufficient condition for Q if, and only if, P is a **necessary condition** for Q and is a **sufficient condition** for Q. If P is a necessary and sufficient condition for Q, then P and Q are equivalent.

Necessary statement   A statement that is either necessarily true or necessarily false. A necessarily true statement is one that cannot be denied without **contra-**

diction or logical inconsistency. A necessarily false statement is one that cannot be affirmed without **contradiction** or logical inconsistency. See also **contingent statement**.

Nominalism   In metaphysics, the view that denies the real existence of **universals** conceived as the supposed referents of general terms. Nominalism thus repudiates any theory of abstract entities such as Plato's Forms.

Occam's razor   The principle of theoretical economy or parsimony named after William Occam (1285–1347). Occam expressed the principle in several ways, but the most common is "Do not multiply entities beyond necessity." Also see **nominalism**.

Occasionalism   In philosophy of religion, the view that all things and events are immediately caused by God alone, and not by any causal powers possessed by created things. See also **secondary causation**.

Omnipotence   In **classical theism**, God's power that enabled Him to do anything possible consistent with His perfect nature.

Omniscience   In **classical theism**, knowledge of God encompassing everything knowable, including all that is past, present, and future.

Ontology   The branch of **metaphysics** that attempts to determine what exists. The study of being or existence.

Ontological argument   In the philosophy of religion, an argument for the existence of God from the concept of God and a metaphysical principle involving comparison of modes of existence. See also **argument from morality, cosmological argument, teleological argument**.

Open concept view   In aesthetics, the view that there are no necessary and sufficient conditions for an object to qualify as a work of art.

Oppression   A system of interrelated forces and barriers that subordinate one group of people to another, keeping the subordinated group relatively powerless and often in a condition of service to the dominant group.

Paradox   Two or more statements that are plausible when considered separately but that seem (and perhaps are) self-contradictory or otherwise illogical when considered jointly (see **contradiction**).

Panpsychism   In metaphysics and philosophy of mind, the view that mind (or consciousness) is all pervasive; everything, and every part of everything, exhibits consciousness to some degree.

Parallelism   In the philosophy of mind, the view that minds and bodies do not interact causally, but function in parallel. Mental occurrences may be correlated with changes in bodies, and physical events may coincide with mental happenings, but the relations are not causal.

Participation   In Plato's metaphysics, the relation whereby concrete **particular** entities depend on the **Forms** or **universals**.

Particular   In metaphysics, a concrete individual entity. Also see **universal**.

Pascal's wager   In philosophy of religion, the attempt to show that if reason cannot decide between theism and atheism, one ought to commit to belief in God because one will gain happiness, in this life and possibly in an afterlife, and one will lose nothing. Named after Blaise Pascal (1623–1662).

Personal identity   In the theory of personal identity, the relation that holds between person X and person Y if, and only if, X is one and the same person as Y. Personal identity is numerical identity: if person X is identical to person Y, then there is just one person: if they are not identical, there are two individuals. See **identity**.

Philosophy of mind   Distinguishable from psychology, though not sharply. Psychology concentrates on empirical aspects of mind. The philosophy of mind, in contrast, focuses on conceptual matters.

Physicalism   See **materialism**.

Pluralism   In metaphysics, the view that the world comprises many distinct substances or many different kinds of substances. See also **monism, dualism**.

Political philosophy   The study of whether the state is justified, of what the purpose of a justified state would be, of what obligations citizens have to their state, and of what the state should do for its citizens.

Possible world   In metaphysics, any real or imagined, but logically consistent, maximal state of affairs.

Potentiality   In metaphysics, what an individual **substance** can become. See also **actuality**.

Pragmatism   American philosophical movement that rejects absolute metaphysical foundations or principles in favor of theories or beliefs that are useful and result in effective modes of adaptation.

Prima facie   Latin term for "at first appearance." In ethics, a *prima facie* duty is an action that, because it possesses some feature (e.g., is an act of beneficence), one has some, but not necessarily overriding, moral reason to perform.

Principle of utility   In ethics, the fundamental principle of right conduct featured in **utilitarianism** according to which an action is right if, and only if, its consequences would have as much overall **utility** (**intrinsic value**) as would the consequences of any available alternative action.

Property   In metaphysics, the repeatable characteristics of an individual **substance** or **event**.

Proposition See **statement**.

Propositional attitude A state of mind characterizable by reference to two factors, a particular **proposition** and a particular attitude toward that proposition. See also **folk psychology**.

Psychological continuity theory In the theory of personal identity, the theory that attempts to explain personal identity partly or wholly in terms of psychological continuity. See also **body theory, brain theory, soul theory**.

Qualia Plural of *quale*. In philosophy of mind, a quality of conscious experience; often equated with the "what-it's-like-ness" of a conscious experience.

Quality See **property**.

Rationalism The theory that all knowledge is gained through intuition and reason independently of experience. This theory rejects the view that knowledge is gained by experience. See **empiricism**.

Realism In the philosophy of science, the view that scientific claims provide descriptions, true or false, of reality. See also **instrumentalism**.

Reduction Applies to concepts or entities, and sometimes distinguished from *elimination* (see **eliminativism**). X's are reduced to Y's when it is shown that X's are nothing but Y's.

Reliabilism In epistemology, the theory that identifies knowing that something is true with having a true belief that is based on evidence that would not exist unless what it is evidence for were the case (See **evidence**).

Reliable argument A **strong argument** whose premises are all true.

Rights In ethics and political philosophy, just claims or entitlements.

Scepticism In epistemology, the view that knowledge or rationally justified belief, as we usually conceive of it, is unobtainable.

Secondary causation In **classical theism**, the power created objects have to produce effects, though they and all their properties are sustained in being by God, the primary cause.

Solipsism In the philosophy of mind, the view that all that exists is myself and my own thoughts.

Soul (*psyche*, Greek; *anima*, Latin) (1) principle of life; (2) a person's inner life, self or personality; (3) subject of conscious experience.

Soul theory In the theory of personal identity, the view that person X = person Y if, and only if, X's soul = Y's soul. The soul theory is held by a number of religions and is thought by many people to be the only theory of personal identity that allows for an afterlife. See also **body theory, brain theory, psychological continuity theory**.

Sound argument   A **valid argument** that has all true premises.

Speculative metaphysics   An approach to **ontology** that is expansive and broadly based. All manner of entities are included, provided that they serve some important function in the general theory. See also **analytic ontology**.

State   A nonrepeatable, datable condition. Distinguished from an **event** by the absence of change.

Statement   The content expressed by a complete declarative sentence. Statements are the primary bearers of **truth values**.

Strong argument   An **argument** such that it is improbable for the premises to be true and the conclusion false. In a strong argument, it is likely that if the premises are all true, then the conclusion is true. Since likelihood is a matter of degree, strength is a matter of degree.

Substance   In metaphysics, the essential reality of a thing that is fundamental and exists independently; that which has or underlies properties. See **property**.

Sufficient condition   P is a sufficient condition for Q if, and only if, if it is the case that P, then it is the case that Q. See also **necessary condition**.

Syllogism   An **argument** consisting of two premises and a conclusion.

Synthetic   A sentence that is not **analytic**.

Tautology   A statement that is necessarily true in virtue of its logical form. See also **contradiction**.

Teleological argument   In philosophy of religion, an argument for the existence of God from the alleged fact that nonrational things act for purposes and engage in orderly behavior and from the apparent unity and harmony of the universe. See also **argument from morality, cosmological argument, ontological argument**.

Teleology   A branch of metaphysics concerned with purposes and goals in nature.

Theism   Belief that there is a god. See also **atheism**.

Truth value   There are exactly two truth values in standard logic: Truth and Falsity. When something is true, it is said to have the truth value Truth, and when something is false, it is said to have the truth value Falsity.

Universal   In metaphysics, abstract entities that are the referents of general terms such as "white," "table," or "horse" and understood as entities distinct from any **particular**. Also see **Form**.

Utilitarianism   In ethics and political philosophy, the view that the morally best dispositions, actions, and social institutions are a matter in some direct or indirect way of what would reasonably be expected to produce the greatest overall well-being.

Utility   In ethics and political philosophy, the good, or well-being, of individuals.

Valid argument   An **argument** such that it is impossible for the premises to be true and the conclusion false. In a valid argument, it is a matter of necessity that if the premises are all true, then the conclusion is true.

Veridical   Truthful. A veridical perception is distinguished from an illusory or hallucinatory perception.

Verification, verifiability, verificationist   A sentence is verified if it is shown to be true. A verifiable sentence is one capable of being shown to be true. A verificationist is one who thinks that unverifiable sentences lack meaning. See also **verifiability criterion of meaning**.

Verifiability criterion of meaning   The fundamental principle of **logical positivism**: a sentence is meaningful if, and only if, it is verifiable.

Virtue   In ethics, a desirable or admirable character trait.

Void   Empty space or the receptacle for atoms.

Wisdom   A knowledge that involves theoretical as well as practical understanding. Thought by some philosophers to be the goal of philosophical reflection.

World view   A general and coherent way of understanding the world; from the German *Weltanschauung*, one's view of the big picture.

CONTRIBUTORS

Frederick Adams is professor of cognitive science and philosophy and chairman of philosophy at University of Delaware. He has previously taught at Central Michigan University, Lawrence University, University of Wisconsin, and Augustana College. He publishes in epistemology and in cognitive science.

Gary Fuller is associate professor of philosophy at Central Michigan University. He has previously taught at the University of Oxford and the University of Florida. He publishes in the philosophy of mind, philosophy of the human sciences, and personal identity.

John Heil is professor of philosophy at Monash University and Paul B. Freeland Professor of Philosophy at Davidson College. He publishes in metaphysics and the philosophy of mind.

Brad Hooker is professor of philosophy at University of Reading. He has previously taught at Virginia Commonwealth University and the University of Oxford. He publishes in social and political philosophy and in ethics.

Leemon McHenry, coeditor, is lecturer in philosophy at California State University, Northridge, and Loyola Marymount University. He has previously taught at the University of Edinburgh, Old Dominion University, Davidson College, and Central Michigan University. He publishes in metaphysics, American philosophy, and the philosophy of science.

Alfred R. Mele is the William H. and Lucyle T. Werkmeister Professor of Philosophy at Florida State University. He has previously taught at Davidson College. He publishes in action theory, philosophy of mind, metaphysics, and ancient Greek philosophy.

Katherin A. Rogers is associate professor of philosophy at University of Delaware. She publishes in philosophy of religion and in medieval philosophy.

Robert Stecker is professor of philosophy at Central Michigan. He has previously taught at the Massachusetts Institute of Technology, University of Houston, and the National University of Singapore. He publishes in aesthetics, ethics, and the history of modern philosophy.

Mark Timmons is professor of philosophy at University of Memphis. He has previously taught at Illinios State University. He publishes in ethics and in epistemology.

Rebecca Whisnant is assistant professor of philosophy at University of Southern Indiana. She has previously taught at University of North Carolina at Chapel Hill.

Takashi Yagisawa, coeditor, is professor of philosophy at California State University, Northridge. He has previously taught at Case Western Reserve University, University of Minnesota, Twin Cities, New York University, and the University of North Carolina at Chapel Hill. He publishes in the philosophy of language, philosophy of mind, and metaphysics.

Index